D0938400

Theraplay

*A New Treatment
Using Structured Play
for Problem Children
and Their Families*

ANN M. JERNBERG

Theraplay

A New Treatment Using Structured Play for Problem Children and Their Families

Jossey-Bass Publishers

San Francisco • Washington • London • 1983

THERAPLAY
A New Treatment Using Structured Play for Problem Children and Their Families
by Ann M. Jernberg

Copyright © 1979 by: Jossey-Bass Inc., Publishers
433 California Street
San Francisco, California 94104
&
Jossey-Bass Limited
28 Banner Street
London EC1Y 8QE

Library of Congress Cataloging in Publication Data

Jernberg, Ann Marshak, 1928-
   Theraplay.

   (The Jossey-Bass social and behavioral science series)
   Bibliography: p. 445
   Includes index.
   1. Play therapy. 2. Family psychotherapy.
I. Title
RJ505.P6J47   618.9′28′9165   79-88769
ISBN 0-87589-432-1

Manufactured in the United States of America

JACKET DESIGN BY WILLI BAUM

FIRST EDITION
      First printing: December 1979
      Second printing: July 1980
      Third printing: September 1983

Code 7934

The Jossey-Bass
Social and Behavioral Science Series

Preface

Scene: It is a spring day with an overcast and threatening sky. In the living room of the country house, the hostess looks on as the visiting family members (Clarissa, age three, and her mother and father) prepare for a morning walk. Clarissa, excited at the prospect, looks up at her parents and asks, "Should I wear my boots?"

Mother: I don't know, darling. That's up to you.

Clarissa: (impatient) But should I wear my boots?

Mother: Sweetheart, I can't help you. You'll have to decide those issues for yourself.

Clarissa: (turning in despair to father) Daddy, should I put my boots on?

Father: Clarissa, I don't have the answers. You must learn to make up your own mind.

Clarissa: (on the verge of tears) Yes. But should I wear my boots?

Mother: I have no idea. Besides, you know Daddy and I feel that in this world people must take responsibility for their own actions, dear.

At this point Clarissa begins to cry, and the hostess, no longer finding it possible to remain the polite bystander, interrupts. "It's going to rain, Clarissa. Put your boots on." The little girl looks at her with surprise and obvious gratitude and begins to dress for her walk.

An isolated incident? A uniquely pathological family? A rare case of parental abdication of responsibility? Unfortunately not. Nursery school teachers and pediatricians will recognize this scene only too well, for it is a truism that this same small drama is played out again and again in the examining room and in the preschool locker room as well as in the home. Teachers and physicians might ask themselves, "What is missing in this relationship? Where is the fun? The frivolity? The intimacy?" Doubtless there are even those who feel tempted to provide these qualities.

Disquieting as the interchange with Clarissa and her parents may be, the scene is nonetheless a normal one. The family is visiting in the country for a day. They are not patients in a mental health center, nor is Clarissa an enrollee in a special school. The child has not yet been so frustrated that she no longer expects good caretaking or fails to trust that others will make her comfortable.

There are those who would not have handled this situation the way the worried hostess did. Some would feel that Clarissa's parents are enhancing her creativity and helping her to develop autonomy; others would admire the adult way she is being treated. Possibly, "It's going to rain, Clarissa. Put your boots on" will strike some as a little intrusive, a bit too arrogant; as an attempt to invade the child's "space" and impose adult values and judgments; perhaps as not properly "democratic."

Scene: Ignoring Billy's screams ("Leave me alone! I hate you!"), his therapist, looking down intently at the flailing four-year-old in his arms, says firmly, "I've got you, Billy, and I'm going to take good care of you." Authoritarian? Disrespectful? Presumptuous? To what extent is it appropriate to make decisions and take actions designed to benefit others? If we were to take the position that it is necessarily presumptuous to take responsibility for another individual's action, then, carried to its extreme, we would have to ask, "Is it presumptuous to take the sleeping pills from an adult bent on suicide?"

Professionals working with troubled children will recognize the dilemma and the internal dialogue: "To intrude or not to intrude? To take charge and do what I know needs doing or to respect the client/patient's dignity?" Too often the clinician looks for permission to take charge and, finding no precedent, backs off and allows the child to call the shots. "Taking charge" is just one aspect of Theraplay's more general aim, which is to replicate the healthy parent/infant relationship. Child therapists (including psychiatrists, psychologists, and social workers), pediatric nurses, child care workers, special educators, and speech and physical therapists will find Theraplay a challenging, gratifying, and often enjoyable method for treating troubled children. Those in the field of primary prevention will find it a useful philosophy for reducing mental illness—particularly those in Education for Parenthood programs.

Although many have benefited from Theraplay, little has been written about it—perhaps in part because, whereas reading and writing are verbal and cognitive, Theraplay is nonverbal and active. Through examples, case histories, and dialogues from film scripts, this book describes how Theraplay is done and with whom, and it examines why it works. Additionally, it cautions that there are situations when Theraplay is not appropriate. There are some readers for whom doing Theraplay is not appropriate either, and one chapter instructs those individuals to monitor their own "insides." This is a book written not only for those who directly provide service but also for administrators of mental health or special education programs and agencies. The sections on wide-scale applications of Theraplay are directed to those who have these latter responsibilities.

The justification for proposing yet another psychotherapy will become apparent in the pages ahead. With its roots in psychoanalysis, developmental psychology, and nursery school practice, it is not so much a break with tradition as it is a gleaning from a number of fields. It is in its practical application and in its insistence on quick, visible results that it is probably most different from its forebears. Theraplay is a compound of empathy and acknowledgment of the adult's authority role. Theraplay is Structuring, Challenging, Intruding, and Nurturing (SCIN); Theraplay is like mothers and fathers interacting with babies. And Theraplay applies all the foregoing to children—and sometimes adults—who are referred for help because they show behavioral or emotional problems.

Chapter One shows how Theraplay differs from other child therapies and how it is alike and different from the work of Austin Des Lauriers. It then traces Theraplay principles to the mother-infant nursery day—particularly those intimate, empathic, playful parts of the day that evoke competence, trusting, and joy. The chapter goes on to discuss client determinants, specifically developmental level and pathological type, as client characteristics that determine therapeutic style. Indications and contraindications for Theraplay are considered, and alternative therapy techniques are suggested for those instances wherein Theraplay does not apply.

Chapter Two discusses Theraplay in view of the ways sessions evolve over time and in view of the evolution that takes place within any given session. A section on Do's and Don't's and another entitled "What If . . . ?" complete this chapter.

Chapter Three illustrates the most frequent use of Theraplay—for the individual child—and Chapter Four shows the application of Theraplay to children in groups. Chapter Five then illustrates family Theraplay by means of sample cases from the point of intake, through diagnosis (the Marschak Interaction Method), to treatment and later checkup.

Chapter Six surveys the variety of settings and locations in which Theraplay is being used. The greatest number of children seen in Theraplay have been treated right in their schools or classrooms (including those of Head Start, special education classes, and centers for training the handicapped). The most obvious Theraplay localities have been outpatient treatment settings (including mental health centers, hot lines, and speech clinics), and the least traditional has been the child's own home.

Always mindful that there are, of course, children whom Theraplay cannot hope to help, the next three chapters consider the kinds of children who *can* benefit from such treatment. In-depth examples are given of Theraplay with underactive and overactive children in Chapter Seven and with handicapped children (including "learning disabled," deaf, blind, and cerebral-palsied children) in Chapter Eight. The autistic child, being the most profoundly Theraplay-starved of all, is dealt with in Chapter Nine.

Given a well-trained and self-aware therapist, Theraplay with adolescents can be a challenging, exciting and highly effective enterprise. Chapter Ten shows the application to, including the necessary modifications for, Theraplay with adolescents. Neurotic, schizophrenic, aggressive, autistic, and acting out teenagers are all considered, and each is illustrated with a relevant case. Chapter Eleven briefly discusses Theraplay for troubled adults in individual and group sessions.

Of value to all mental health practitioners, but indispensible for individuals practicing Theraplay, is awareness of "What goes on in the therapist's head?" Chapter Twelve covers recommendations for screening, selecting, and training therapists so as to forestall and combat the occupational hazards that generally arise from unresolved countertransference.

Chapter Thirteen looks at the potential of Theraplay with the very, very young and the very, very old and concludes with the hope that this treatment method may one day render future case study books and treatment manuals unnecessary.

Although there are many practitioners of psychotherapy who will take issue with some parts of the Theraplay theory and practice; although there are some who will be shocked at its authoritative stance; and although there are others who will be put off by its insistence that the therapist neither engage in verbal discussions nor attend to what he or she defines as inappropriate behavior, there are probably few indeed who will quarrel with the jollity and fun that underlie the Theraplay intention.

Acknowledgments

This book is the culmination of the dedicated efforts of many valued friends and colleagues. First and foremost among the people without whose courage the Theraplay "experiment" could never have been launched ten years ago is Lillian Tauber, director of Children and Youth Services for the Department of Human Relations of the city of Chicago. In allowing us to undertake what was at that time a revolutionary concept, and in her confidence that Theraplay would benefit her program, she made it possible for us to modify and to rethink, to retain and to discard, and so to develop the principles and techniques we have used with thousands of "her" children.

I also thank Ernestine Thomas, whose exuberant spirit and intuitive wisdom, together with her concern for excellence, have led all of us to pursue the search for Theraplay perfection; Charles West, whose vibrant enthusiasm, compassion, and eagerness have guided us, his co-workers, as much as they have helped the children he has treated; and particularly Phyllis Booth, who from the beginning helped me understand *why* what we were doing was working so well, who helped me formulate new hypotheses, and who generously shared others' insights as she uncovered them in the literature. I am most grateful for my association with Terrence Koller, whose contributions to Theraplay, going far beyond our most imaginative expectations, must surely be the happy consequence of his humor, his perspective, his flexibility, and his keen empathy. Were it not for Martha Fowler, there would have been no book to tell the story; she has been my alter ego at all stages of the writing and has led me from inception to assembling to copy editing. Her patience, her gentle persuasiveness, her clear foresight, and her experience in the publishing world have been invaluable.

My warmest gratitude goes to the one person who encouraged yet challenged; lent his strength, yet never intruded; the one person who gave of himself, his time, his knowledge, and his resources at every step of the way, from first seeking a treatment solution for Head Start children, through producing the three films about it, to the launching of the Theraplay Institute, and, finally, through the writing of this book. For all this I am deeply grateful to Theodore Hurst, president of Worthington, Hurst, and Associates and executive director of the Theraplay Institute.

And finally, my special and warmest thanks go to the many children and families who have been my friends and my teachers during the past ten years.

Chicago, Illinois　　　　　　　　　　　　　　　Ann M. Jernberg
October 1979

Contents

The Author

Ann M. Jernberg is clinical director of the Theraplay Institute in Chicago, a position she has held since the institute's inception in 1969.

Jernberg was born in Germany in 1928; she was awarded both the Ph.B. degree in liberal arts (1948) and the Ph.D. degree in human development (1960) from the University of Chicago. Following teaching at the University of Chicago's kindergarten (1948) and its nursery school (1949, 1950), she began her clinical work in the Department of Psychiatry there (1955-1960) and was research associate in the School of Social Service Administration for a special project to study emotionally disturbed preschoolers and their parents (1959-1960). From 1960 to 1967 she was senior staff psychologist at Michael Reese Hospital in Chicago. From 1967 to the present she has been developing and supervising psychological services to the Chicago Head Start, Title XX Day Care, and Parent-Child Center programs encompassing some 5,000 children annually. Since 1970 Jernberg has also been chief psychologist at the LaPorte County Comprehensive Mental Health Center in Indiana. In the summers of 1968 and 1969 she was director of psychological services for the Head Start program in the Virgin Islands.

Jernberg has been a member of the extension faculties of Goddard College in Vermont, Northeastern Illinois University in Chicago, and Elmhurst College in Elmhurst, Illinois. She has conducted Theraplay training in Massachusetts, Arkansas, New York, Michigan, and Indiana, as well as in various cities in Illinois.

Jernberg has published and presented to professional societies numerous articles and papers on a variety of topics, including parent-child relationships, psychosomatic medicine, anorexia nervosa, the psychologist as consultant, adoption, the role of the paraprofessional, and Theraplay techniques. She has directed three films: *It Can Be Done, There He Goes,* and the award-winning *Here I Am.* In addition, she has put together training videotapes in three series: Theraplay techniques, parent-child interactions, and autism.

Jernberg's other professional interests and activities include a private practice in psychotherapy, psychoanalysis, family therapy, and supervision; and the training of personnel at, and consultation to, other agencies. Her professional memberships include American Psychological Association, Illinois Psychological Association, Indiana Psychological Association, American Orthopsychiatric Association, National Society for Autistic Children, National Association for the Education of Young Children, and Psychologists Interested in the Study of Psychoanalysis.

She is currently working on another book, *Enjoyable Parenting,* based on her conviction that parents and children need to interact more *and* at an earlier stage of their relationship.

> *To my late father, Jacob Marschak, who was my model for creative scientific leadership, generosity and humility.*
>
> *To my mother, Marianne, who is my model for patience and perseverance and who has that rare combination of poetry and scholarship.*
>
> *To my daughters, Julie and Emily, who have been the willing and responsive crucibles in which so many of my ideas have been tested.*
>
> *Julie, whose vigorous optimism and tender caring have stimulated me and cheered me.*
>
> *Emily, whose sensitive analyses and warm compassion have helped me and inspired me.*
>
> *To my late husband, Pete, whose courage and laughter in the face of pain and tragedy helped to still my own fears.*

Theraplay

*A New Treatment
Using Structured Play
for Problem Children
and Their Families*

1

Theraplay: History and Method

History

Many of the techniques and theoretical positions on which the Theraplay method is fashioned were developed by Austin Des Lauriers (1962). Working with schizophrenic and autistic children, Des Lauriers developed a therapeutic style not often reported in earlier literature. The mode of child psychotherapy prevalent in the 1930s was exemplified by Rudolph Ekstein (1966, pp. 8-9), a proponent of dynamic (psychoanalytic) "talking" therapy, in which the therapist interprets to the child his underlying wishes, fears, and impulses—often in terms of the past.[1] Dynamic child psychotherapy was to be followed by Vir-

1

ginia Axline's ([1947] 1969) client-centered play therapy—in
which the therapist reflected feelings but made no interpretations. Rarely, in previous therapies, was there physical contact,
an intrusive approach, or a focus on the concrete or the here-
and-now. Des Lauriers did all of this. Whereas a psychotic child
could easily "tune out" the traditional child psychotherapist, it
was virtually impossible for him to tune out Austin Des Lauriers. If he looked away, Des Lauriers turned his head toward
him or jumped into his line of vision. If he attempted not to
hear, Des Lauriers spoke louder. If he tried to leave the room,
Des Lauriers laid down on the floor to block his passage. The
basic objective of Des Lauriers' work was to force the psychotic
child to take account of the therapist's human presence.

    Whereas Des Lauriers' work has been primarily with autis-
tic and schizophrenic children, work at the Theraplay Institute
has focused on children with lesser degrees of pathology in addition to psychotic children. Even though differing in some respects from Des Lauriers' original work, Theraplay, as it has
evolved at the Theraplay Institute, has assimilated most of Des
Lauriers' principles. With regard to vigor; intrusiveness; body
and eye contact; focus on intimacy between child and therapist
(particularly with regard to individuation; that is, helping the
child to see himself as unique, different, and separate from others); emphasis on the here-and-now; and ignoring the bizarre,
the past, and fantasy, Theraplay is the direct application of Des
Lauriers' approach. Theraplay differs from Des Lauriers' original format if not in kind then in the degree to which the therapist initiates, structures, and takes charge of the session, and,
perhaps as a result of this heightened degree of Intrusiveness,
the Theraplay therapist may encounter more resistance and
must be more prepared for temper tantrums.

    We owe other differences in part to the work of Viola
Brody. Even before she became a coworker of Des Lauriers,
Brody (1963) introduced active physical contact, physical control, and singing into her therapy sessions. She applied her Theraplay-like treatment (which she calls *Developmental Play
Therapy*—Brody, 1978) to children in groups. Like Theraplay,
her method also deliberately sets out to treat the child at his or

her current developmental, not chronological, level. She has demonstrated the effectiveness of Developmental Play Therapy in her work with small groups of psychotic children and with school-based groups of children who have problems in learning. It is to Ernestine Thomas, field supervisor of the Theraplay Institute and a past student of Viola Brody's, that Theraplay owes one of its most important variations: an explicit emphasis on the child's health, potential, and strength. Even though it often seems to work through defensive denial, Thomas' optimistic message does communicate to the child that there is hope, that even for his brief weekly (or twice or three times weekly) session he can feel "normal," and that no matter how sick, how unattractive, how ill behaved, or how rejected by everyone else, there are certainly some things about him that are nonetheless lovable. This goal of having him view himself as lovable has been conceptualized by Phyllis Booth, coordinator of the institute staff, as follows: He must come to see, reflected in the therapist's eyes, the image of himself both as lovable and as fun to be with.

Theraplay, as practiced at the institute, thus resembles the therapies of Des Lauriers and Brody far more than it differs from them. Yet it does differ—in intensity, vigor, and perseverance, and in its regressive dimension: Nurturing. It differs also in that, while retaining spontaneity and fun, Theraplay sessions are carefully preplanned and structured. With the exception of the administering of the Marschak Interaction Method (MIM), a parent-child diagnostic interaction (Marschak, 1960, 1979), the Theraplay therapist does not "wait to see what the child will do" and, except in rare cases, does not allow the child to lead the way. Where it seems appropriate, the Theraplay therapist encourages, indeed even insists on, the child's nursing from a bottle, smearing finger paint or chocolate pudding, or participating in the new and unpredictable. It is in this area of firm (although never punitive) insistence in the face of a child's active protest, that Theraplay most markedly differs from the therapies of Brody and Des Lauriers.

In addition to these variations within sessions, the application of Theraplay to situations other than that of the imme-

diately referred child patient is also new. The treatment arena is
broadened to include family Theraplay and adult Theraplay (including Theraplay for parents). Beyond the individual con-
sumer, there is Theraplay for groups, and beyond the immediate
therapy room, telephone (crisis) and home-based Theraplay.

In 1970, while we were searching for a name for a treatment method that is both playful and therapeutic yet that is
totally unlike Axline's client-centered play therapy, Charles
Lyman, the filmmaker of *Here I Am* (1969), suggested the
name "Theraplay." Theraplay was first taught in 1971 and was
written into an HEW proposal in March 1972. Soon Theraplay
sessions were conducted not only in Head Start classrooms
(Jernberg, 1976) but in the especially constructed Theraplay
treatment room in Chicago as well. Thereafter it became apparent that a few individuals around the country, having heard
something of Theraplay, were treating children in ways we
found questionable and were calling these treatment methods
Theraplay. It was for this reason that in 1976 we registered
Theraplay as a service mark.

Underlying Principles

The Parent-Infant Relationship

The best way to understand the principles underlying the
Theraplay method is to rediscover the basics of the mother-
infant relationship: What are the typical daily pleasurable interactions in the nursery? What does a normal mother do to and
for her baby? How does the healthy baby respond? What characterizes the cycle they thus set in motion between them? And
what are the specific effects of their reciprocal behavior on each
of the partners involved?[2]

Daily, the mother in the nursery with her baby nuzzles
his neck, blows on his tummy, sings in his ear, hides his eyes (or
hides her face) when playing "peek-a-boo," and nibbles his toes.
She picks him up, twirls him, spins him, rocks him, bounces
him, flips him, and jiggles him. She holds him close and nurses
him. She powders him, lotions him, combs him, washes him,

pats him dry, and rubs him. She whispers, coos, giggles, hums, chatters, and makes nonsense sounds. She peeks at him, pops out at him, peers from upside down at him, winks at him, blinks at him, looks wide-eyed with surprise, and beams at him. In addition, she holds him, confines him, binds him, restrains him, protects him, defines his life space, his property, his relationships, his use of time, his degree of deviation from safety (and soon, what is morally appropriate and not appropriate for him to do and be). And finally, by gently teasing, chasing, and eluding (and returning), she remains one step ahead of him, thus encouraging him both to learn the art of mastery and to enjoy the challenge.

Her baby, in turn, coos at his mother, smiles at her, reaches for her, strokes her, worships her, imitates her and enjoys being mirrored by her; he gurgles with her, and, finally, he names her. Although her child may sometimes protest them, he responds to his mother's definitions, limits, and structures, and he rises to her challenges. But above all he stares at her and gazes deeply into her eyes.

Eventually the baby welcomes the clarity, security, and predictability; the easy warmth and tender softness; the happy excitement, surprise, and stimulation; and the opportunity to strive a little. Most of all, of course, he welcomes the certainty, implied throughout, that there is reliability, empathy, and caring.[3]

The cycle thus set into motion is a reciprocal one, a "mutual admiration society" (Maria Piers, personal communication). "Once we consider the dyad, we must at once conclude that *both* actors actively and significantly influence each other" (Lewis and Lee-Painter, 1974, p. 46). Each is eager to please, protect, and cherish the other, and each one responds by showing pleasure and concern in turn. The gratitude at having been given so much pleasure leads to greater and greater efforts to please, protect, and cherish.

The effect on each of the partners is, of course, to enhance and clarify the view of self each holds and to portray the world as a fun, caring, and loving place. As parents find increasing pleasure in being with their new baby, he in turn becomes more pleasurable to be with. The baby comes to see himself as clearly differentiated, attractive, safe, enjoyable to be with, lovable, and capable of making an impact. In addition, his mother acquaints him with his body parts (as when she "counts" his fingers or plays "this little piggy" with his toes), and helps him distinguish himself from the reality of the world at large (as when he plants the soles of his feet against her cheeks and pushes, or when she puts her big hands up against his little ones, or, later, when she tells him she wants him to wear galoshes in the rain). She teaches him about physical realities such as gravity, time, and motion (as when she tosses him up high in the air and waits to lower him to the ground); or, later, about moral and social realities such as "Do unto others. . ." or "It hurts when you pinch me, and I can't let you do that." In the process, the mother comes to see herself as lovable, giving, and feminine, yet at the same time resourceful, strong, and competent. She finds in her new motherhood the confirmation of many qualities in herself that she may have doubted—including a capacity for intimacy and a firm sense of self. She also finds in it the opportunity to experience vicariously the idyllic togetherness she had or would have liked to have had with her own mother.

Ideal as these Structuring, Challenging, Intruding, and Nurturing interactions obviously are, and meaningful as they are for both the mother and her infant, they are, unfortunately, not always possible. Perhaps the environment precludes the establishing of a close bond. Reality pressures may hinder them—a rental lease that forbids children, in-laws who harass, financial worries, or a husband who resents the baby. There may be competing demands from the house, a job, or other members of the family. Or there may be outsiders or books pressuring, "Don't spoil him" or advocating, "Let him do what he wants." If there is much external stress and strain, mother and baby may not find the time and freedom to enjoy each other's company. (Or it may be too difficult for the mother to reconcile opposing views.) Indeed, as she buckles to reality demands she may find herself increasingly inclined to prop the bottle, to turn on the television set, and to attend only to his physical needs. Frivolity, fun, surprise, teasing, and warm moments become fewer as she tends to the necessary, the routine, and the serious problems of family survival. Lorene Stringer (1971, p. 130) reminds us of the consequences: "I think we shall find that the adults who are incapable of forming lasting love relationships, in which they both enjoy and feel enjoyed, had been babies whose parents never played with them in loving and enjoying ways." Prescott (1976) blames similar childhood deficiencies for later violence as well as for drug and alcohol abuse.

Other than the environment, what else may cause there to be no joy, or peek-a-boo, no soft singing or playful teasing, and no jolly tosses up in the air? Indeed, there may be factors making their relationship "disengaged" that have nothing to do with outer reality, with the environment—factors that explain why the baby, deprived of Structuring, Challenging, Intruding, and Nurturing, lies in his crib alone while his mother, feeling deeply dissatisfied, occupies herself elsewhere. What could be these nonenvironmental factors? If there is no externally tense or manipulative environment, what else could be the matter? If the difficulty comes not from factors external to the mother-infant relationship, then the relationship itself may indeed be responsible. Why, in the "disengagement" scene just described, have mother and baby so tuned each other out? Let us ask how well are the mother and her baby matched? Or, to quote Chess and Thomas (1972, p. 39), how good is the "fit"? Is there perhaps a "mismatch" between them so pronounced from the outset that an early and mutual turnoff has been the result? A vigorous, aggressive, demanding, unpredictable, physically robust infant, for example, may have been boisterously catapulted into the soft, artistic, gentle routine of his frail, dreamy mother; or, conversely, a driving, energetic mother may find herself with a limp, lethargic child. ("During the process of the mother's attachment to her infant, it is necessary that the infant respond to the mother by some signal such as body or eye movements. . . . 'You can't love a dishrag' ") (Klaus and Kennel, 1976, p. 14). Even granted the best of all external circumstances, such matches can easily lead to conflict if one or the other partner fails to adapt—or is hindered in the adaptation process.

But it may be that, in some cases, neither their joint contribution nor the external realities of their lives interferes with a good relationship; perhaps, as implied earlier, the mother's or the child's contribution alone causes the interference. For, whereas every baby requires empathy and sensitivity, some babies are not only deprived of the experience of reciprocal interaction, but are expected from early on to meet their mothers' needs—for example, by smiling just to please her (Bennett, 1971). Should these needs of hers go unmet, "from her own feelings of rejection by the child, she can be led, in turn, to reject the child" (Sameroff, 1975, p. 290).

Although every baby requires Nurturing—cuddling, catering, pampering, and holding (Massie, 1978)—some mothers cannot give these. Every baby needs to be Intruded on, stimulated, excited, aroused, and delighted. And every baby needs to be gazed at intensely. But some mothers cannot do this. Not every mother can Structure—and thus help him to understand—his own confines and the boundaries of the world around him. And every baby needs the Challenging that some mothers cannot give. What gets in their way? Her personal reality may make appropriate mothering difficult for one mother; a second may have physical difficulties; and a third, psychological ones. Work schedules, finances, or other real demands, particularly when compounded by a lifetime of poor coping (Evans, Reinhart, and Succop, 1972), may make appropriate mothering impossible, as may illness, anemia, fatigue, or pain. Maternal nonresponsiveness for even a brief period (see experiments by Tronick and others, 1978, p. 8) produces reactions of increasing despair in their infants: "Finally he completely withdraws." Mothering becomes difficult and burdensome when demands from her baby conflict with a mother's own hurting, tired, run-down body, or with her depressed, anxious, or confused state of mind. Her cathexis toward her baby may be diminished or impoverished by the illness of her husband (Robertson, 1965) or the death of a parent (Evans, Reinhart and Succop, 1972; Walsh, 1978) or even of a parent-in-law (Walsh, 1978). Robertson describes the reactions in two babies—possibly with long-term effects—when their mothers suffered acute emotional distress.

Furthermore, even though the minds of some mothers function adequately with respect to their daily lives, they may resist, consciously or unconsciously, the idea of self-as-mother (Benedek, 1970) or the idea of baby-as-he-is (Broussard and Hartner, 1970). They may even, in their efforts to demonstrate their truly maternal qualities, unconsciously perceive biological similarity where none, in fact, exists. In an earlier study (Jernberg, 1958), adoptive mothers reported their own psychosomatic predisposition as being identical to those of their adopted infants.

As we have said, every baby requires Structuring, Challenging, Intruding, and Nurturing. And not every mother can Structure, Challenge, Intrude, and Nurture. Some mothers can perform some of these functions but fail at others. Why? Why is it hard for some mothers to Nurture their babies? Perhaps, for example, they have always heroically denied their own regressive longings, only to have to come face-to-face with them when confronted with their own hungry, dependent, helpless infants. Why is it hard for other mothers to Intrude, arouse, excite, or stimulate their babies? Perhaps intimacy is frightening, excitement feels too stimulating, and arousing the baby seems like the intrusion a negative version of which they fear themselves. Why might Challenging be something some mothers find it easiest to do without? Perhaps they feel more comfortable with a perpetually helpless, clinging infant than with a child who has the potential for autonomy and separateness. And why is Structuring, defining, and setting limits for their babies difficult for other mothers? Perhaps they fear that taking charge is being assertive, and for them assertiveness means aggression. Perhaps they fear that alienation will be the end result. Perhaps, as one further example, they have simply viewed themselves all their lives as incapable of making an impact. Many of the emotional difficulties in mothering may have had their origins in the mother's own infancy, in her own early experiences of being mothered (Spitz, 1970).

We have said that perhaps a "mismatch" is responsible for the mother-infant breakdown, and we have suggested that perhaps it is the mother's makeup that is "to blame." Let us return once again to the other side of the equation, the side having to do with infant effectiveness (Ainsworth and Bell, 1974). Perhaps, in other words, it is, after all, the infant who is at the outset "to blame." Ethologists and others attribute human [maternal] responsiveness to the physical construction of the human infant; that is, thick head, prominent forehead, large eyes, rounded body form, soft surface texture, round "chubby" cheeks, small features, small chin, general shape of head, and so on (Wickler, 1972; Brooks and Hochberg, 1960; Gardner and Wallach, 1965). Sameroff (1975, p. 277) suggests that "Constitutional variability in children strongly affects the parents' attitudes and caretaking styles"; others suggest that particular postures (Harlow, Harlow, and Hansen, 1963), movements (Clarke-Stewart, 1973), and behaviors (Lewis and Lee-Painter, 1974) so affect the parents. Many neonatal specialists (for example, Brazelton, 1969; Bergman and Escalona, 1949; Fries, 1944) have postulated, and many mothers can attest to the likelihood that, quite apart from maternal impact on infants, different babies are born with different personalities—different thresholds to incoming stimuli and different capacities for responding.

As a matter of fact, during the first weeks of life even the most normal of babies reacts in negative ways. Up to the age of three months, the newborns studied by Charlotte Buehler (1960) responded adversely (for example, by freezing or withdrawing) to bright lights and quick movements. Continuing this theme of differentiated "infant temperament" (Thomas, Chess, and Birch, 1970), Margaret Fries (1944) describes babies as displaying high- or low-activity patterns. The highly active child is responsive and alert, while the baby at the other extreme is calm and passive. Middlemore (1941), dividing babies into three types, observed that nursing mothers handled roughly the group labeled "irritably inert." (The babies, in turn, reacted to this handling by grimacing, withdrawing, and with "stiff immobility.")

Brazelton (1969) characterizes babies as active, quiet, and average, and Bergman and Escalona (1949) postulate a protective barrier against stimulation (the *Reizschutz* first described by Freud, 1922) the permeability of which varies from infant to infant. Thus some infants react to a minimum in stimulation, while others require an intense dose before they can perceive that a stimulus is impinging on them at all. "These children start life with a high degree of sensitivity against which they eventually succeed in building some defenses. . . . Some of these defenses start early; in fact, . . . ego functions set in prematurely, apparently in connection with this defensive purpose. It seems therefore justified to us to tentatively regard the unusual sensitivities as not essentially related to qualities of the ego, but rather to something more primitive, constitutional. . . . The following graphic representation shows [that] degrees of excitability would . . . be identical with 'protective barriers' of different thickness" (Bergman and Escalona, 1949, p. 345).

The overexcitable organism, "thin protective barrier"

The normal organism, "normal protective barrier"

The underexcitable organism, "thick protective barrier"

Hypothetically, even the infant for whom a "thin" *Reizschutz* (or barrier) is postulated could "create" a thicker (or pseudo-) barrier if the incoming stimuli were too painful, threatening, or strong; some highly sound-sensitive infants are observed to stick their fingers in their ears in reaction to a buzzer or vacuum cleaner (Anthony, 1958).[3] Most noteworthy with regard to barriers that deny an infant sensory stimulation, of course, is blindness, about which Selma Fraiberg writes "It is reasonable to presume that whether a child is deprived of experience through central impairment of the systems for registering and integrating stimuli or through extreme deprivation of the stimulus nutriments for sensorimotor organization, the result may be the same—a child who does not know 'me' and 'other,' 'I' or 'you' " (Fraiberg, 1977, p. 9).

In terms of postinfancy behavior, the child who "rejects" all stimuli—or, as Rimland (1964, p. 79) puts it, apprehends but does not comprehend them—and who has come to live exclusively in a self-fashioned world is classified "autistic." He interacts with no one, looks at no one, talks with no one, gives in to no one. He alone determines his life-style, and he makes certain there are no surprises in it. His *Reizschutz,* whether built or inborn, appears impenetrable. The extreme of the child who "permits" all incoming stimuli is the highly sensitive, motorically and/or emotionally hyperreactive child whose response to even low-level stimulation is total-body irritability or total-feeling expression. Mothers of babies like this (sometimes included in the catchall description "colicky") come to realize that unless their children are provided a highly structured "cotton wool" environment, they will greatly interfere with the everyday lives of those around them. Their high level of excitement and ready reactivity to stimuli (for example, bright lights, loud music, and late hours) require everyone about them to walk on tiptoes. These, then, are the two extremes—the underreactive and the hyperreactive. Underlying both modes may well be a biological basis—postulated for the underaware (autistic) by Des Lauriers (1962), Ritvo and others (1976), Rimland (1964), and by others and postulated for the hyperreactive by a great many more, probably (including Bax and MacKeith, 1963, and Cantwell, 1975), than the number who see it as having primarily behavioral origins. Sontag (1966) and Ward (1969) date some babies' susceptibility to later emotional disturbance back to the stress placed on them in utero. Rosen (1978) finds that after thirty weeks the fetal brain can be seen to respond to stimuli from the mother as well as to her emotions. If the mother is excited or upset, the fetal heart may beat faster, just as hers does.

Let us assume then that the newborn does arrive with a predetermined *Reizschutz.* Let us assume further that this *Reizschutz* in normally healthy babies serves—in relation to the outside world—to protect them from being flooded by excitement on the one hand, while, on the other, keeping them alert to variations. The stimuli thus admitted to the normal child's recognition include many sounds, sights, and changes. The stimuli thus admitted also include the most important of all, the communications (in the form of language, both verbal and non-verbal) that, from the earliest moment on, make him or her a participant in a social system (Schaffer, 1971; Richards, 1974).

Bergman and Escalona (1949, p. 347) hypothesize that "the infant who is not sufficiently protected from stimuli either because of a 'thin protective barrier' or because of the failure of maternal protection may have to resort for such protection to premature formation of an ego. When this premature ego breaks down, possibly as a consequence of a trauma, the psychotic manifestations are thought to set in."

Given this concept of the *Reizschutz,* could the average mother, were she faced with a baby whose inborn permeability is at one or the other extreme, help him make that *Reizschutz* more permeable or less so? That is, could she "decrease" the permeability of a hyperreactive baby or "increase" it in one showing autistic tendencies?

If the processing of stimuli is what differentiates the two extremes—the autistic rejecting, the overreactive indiscriminately admitting—then conceivably a mother could manipulate the amount and kind of stimulation that impinges on her child. Conceivably she could ensure that the child who, by virtue of his own screening process, receives too little stimulation, is given a lot and that the child who receives too much stimulation has the amount reduced. Conceivably the mother could regulate the dosage if she could be aware that she needed to do so for, "From the very moment of birth . . . differences become apparent and begin to determine the tone of parents' reactions. . . . [Differences] can be infinitely rewarding to the mother and father who recognize the strengths of the individual with whom they have been presented" (Brazelton, 1969, p. xvii). If her child could only tell her that, while just right for any normal baby born with a normal *Reizschutz,* what she does is simply not enough or is too much for him, then, being the empathic mother she is, she would "perceive and respond to his disturbed psychological balance"; she would know just how to come on stronger or modulate her input (Kohut, 1977, p. 85). Having alerted her to the condition of his *Reizschutz,* her baby could

warn her that he needs her help to avert unhealthy consequences. He could let her know, for example, that because of
his too-thin permeability he may otherwise become either
hyperreactive and irritable or may construct his own too-thick
barrier and withdraw. Above all, in the area of emotional survival, he would inform her that her anxiety, if she reacts with
anxiety, is making him more anxious yet. If she does not come
on strongly enough to penetrate an otherwise impermeable barrier, it will be as though he cannot fully see, hear, feel, touch, or
understand her, and he will have to stimulate (for example,
rock, twirl, head bang, masturbate) himself. His experience
may, in other words, be compared to that of the subjects in the
sensory deprivation experiments. In the absence of visual, tactile, and auditory cues from outside, these subjects develop
their own internal, frightening, fragmented, and boundaryless
worlds. In the area of emotional survival, moreover, if his
mother is unaware of, and unsoothing to, his heightened anxiety, he will never learn to master those feelings himself (Kohut,
1977, p. 89).

If, rather than resort to self-stimulation, he could only
tell her, "Hey, Mom, what you're doing may be OK for most
kids, but not me; I need more. Could you just swing me higher,
blow on my tummy harder, chatter to me louder?" Then she
could do just that, because, being a normal mother, she enjoys
pleasing him, and the pattern of pleasurable interaction will
have begun. If he is a baby who perceives even normal-level incoming stimuli as too exciting, he could tell her, "That song
you're singing hurts my ears, Ma. Please could you tone it down
a bit?" And for this baby, too, a pleasurable mother-infant give-
and-take could then be established between them.

Unfortunately, most babies cannot indicate that they
have such extreme needs, and so what may have begun as totally the baby's side of the "responsibility" equation soon
becomes "responsibility" on both sides: baby for having such
unusual needs, mother for not understanding what they are.
From here on, there may be tragic repercussions: Mother picks
up her baby and sings, for example (or rocks, or caresses, or
kisses). Her baby responds, if he is hyperreactive, by screaming

or backing away from her. His mother, feeling rejected and as though she has hurt him, drops him quickly back into his crib. A second mother, with an underreactive baby, looks at her baby's face, softly coos to him, and lifts him up to fondle him. Except to turn his eyes away and stiffen, or make some irrelevant sounds, he reacts hardly at all. For the most part, he behaves as though he were all alone. This mother also, bewildered and feeling she has made no impact, eventually feels the negative feelings any normal person has on being rejected. As her baby fails her more and more (by not returning her smile, not answering her gurgling, not lifting up his other foot for tickling, not reaching up his arms for hugging), she naturally approaches him less and less. (Besides, she notices that he really seems more content playing or just "being" hour after hour, all by himself in his crib.) Understandable as are the reactions of both mothers to their overreactive and underreactive babies, the outcomes nevertheless are unfortunate and unnecessary, for in both cases the baby's overt behavior, rather than the mother's taking charge, has ultimately determined their common fate. Taking the baby's *Reizschutz* condition into account, the mother ideally should convey, "I'm in charge. I know what's best for you, and I can provide you what you need." Then, unresponsive or protesting as her baby may be, she would persist in stimulating him at the level he covertly needs: the nonreactive child at a high level, the overreactive one at a low level. In neither case would she give up just because he resists or cries or fails to respond. She would be gently soothing, low-keyed, and reassuring yet firmly structuring with the overreactive child. She would make her presence felt and would encourage him to respond to her. With the underreactor, however, she would be vigorous, intrusive, insistent, and full of surprises. She would urge him to an ever-increasing display of variety, never allowing him to "leave the scene" nor to retreat into the predictable world of his own making. Robertson (1965, p. 117) described the following effort to help an understimulating mother become more stimulating: "John had not responded, and . . . the mother's activity had dropped to the level that was no more than sufficient to meet his lessened demands. I therefore suggested to the mother that she should stimulate John beyond the extent called for by his meager demands, that she should play and handle him more than she was doing. . . . I was surprised by the success of her efforts after only one week."

Sometimes, of course, the two kinds of behavior coexist in the same child. Screaming in response to body contact may characterize a child who is diagnosed autistic as well as one who is hyperreactive. It will be a matter for his mother's wise intuition to determine the origins of his behavior and the genuineness and extent of his pain. It will be up to her to set the course she should consequently follow. In this regard, although the foregoing descriptions of what babies need and what mothers should provide may appear to refer only to variations in stimulus input, it cannot be too strongly stated that emotional "in-tune-ness" of a mother with her baby is the highest priority of all. "The mother's responsiveness to the child's needs prevents traumatic delays before the narcissistic equilibrium is reestablished after it has been disturbed, and if the shortcomings of the mother's responses are of tolerable proportions, the infant will gradually modify the original boundlessness and blind confidence of his expectation of absolute perfection. . . . If, however, the mother's responses are grossly unempathic and unreliable, then the gradual withdrawal of cathexis from the image of archaic unconditional perfection is disturbed. . . . The behavioral manifestations in general . . . consist in a hypersensitivity to disturbances in the narcissistic equilibrium with a tendency to react to sources of narcissistic disturbance by mixtures of wholesale withdrawal and unforgiving rage" (Kohut, 1971, pp. 64-65). The truly empathic mother will know intuitively at what level of impact to aim the stimulation for her particular baby. Barring later obstacles (as, for example, a mother who, although in tune with her child as an infant, is nonempathic with him once he becomes self-assertive), furthermore, these "understood" infants, in contrast to those who missed out on early empathic understanding, should be less likely to manifest profound psychological damage later.

There are films that clearly portray the misfit between some mothers and their children. Condon's (1974) slowed-down movie showing a mother in interaction with her adolescent twins, one healthy and one schizophrenic, and Stern's (1976) microanalysis of a mother interacting differently with twin infants, one healthy and one less healthy, attest to the importance of being emotionally "in sync." Marschak's (1967) film comparisons of disturbed and normal preschool children in structured interactions with their mothers and Minuchin's (1978) films of children with anorexia nervosa in lunchtime interaction with their parents all bear stark testimony to behaviors that are and are not empathic. And, finally, the Theraplay Institute has produced videotapes of mothers learning to "mirror" their autistic children (Jernberg, 1979).

Some children (for reasons we are hard put to understand, much less explain) respond less in motoric ways than in ideational ways—that is, at a thinking level. Whereas some attain their own stimulatory input through twirling, finger twiddling, head banging, and so on, or ward it off through jumpiness and screaming, others think, imagine, daydream, reason, infer, deduce, or hallucinate. (Again, "normal" children, of course, respond with a combination of the motoric and ideational—both in moderate degrees.) Children who are predominantly ideational, like those who are predominantly motoric, can be viewed on a continuum. Predominantly ideational, like predominantly motoric children, vary also from "hyper" to "hypo"—from too much to too little. Certain thinking styles characterize the two extremes. At one end are children diagnosed intellectually as slow, depressed, "retarded," not because of limited capacity, but because of their apparent dull-wittedness, curtailed effort, hampered understanding, intellectual unresponsiveness, concrete thinking, or lack of curiosity. At the other end are the children whose ideas, imagination, reasoning, and symbolic vigilance work overtime, rather than being slow. They make quick, albeit often inaccurate, connections, indiscriminately combine cause and effect, attribute false properties and false motives to other people, and formulate false conclusions. They are hyperreactive in a thinking sense, one symbol touching off a host of thoughts and fears. At the extreme, they are labeled confused or schizophrenic. Yet neither kind needs to be seen as hopeless, and both can be assumed to have the potential for responding to intervention.

The Therapist-Child Relationship

Just as "Overt demonstration of affection has been empirically related to enhanced infant development, involvement with the *mother,* social and play initiative, and ability to cope with stress" (Clarke-Stewart, 1973, p. 2), so also the Theraplay *therapist* must find appropriate means for intervening if he is to enhance his or her patient's development, involvement, social and play initiative, and ability to cope with stress. Intrusion, Stimulation, and Arousal are as inappropriate for the confused-to-schizophrenic child (except for purposes of making initial contact) as they are for the motorically hyperreactive. The schizophrenic child, living in his bizarre nightmare fantasy, would benefit far more from a predictable, trustworthy, structured reality than from being either *charged up* or tickled, surprised, swung, spun, or having his face painted with clown designs.

Yet Intrusion, Stimulation, and Arousal may be most appropriate and helpful for the child who appears unresponsive and slow, the child labeled "functionally retarded." Lack of structure or reality testing are not his problem; ideational liveliness, engagement, excitement, courage, tolerance for stimulation, and adaptability to change are what he lacks. Surprises, fun, and the introduction to delighting stimuli should be offered in place of his ideational lethargy.

The issue of prescription and follow-through is not a "democratic" one. It is not a matter of limiting what is done to and for the child only to what and as much as he "wants" done. Both the decision and the execution rest with the adult. Even though the child may protest his loss of autonomy, the adult does the child no favor to sit passively by, watching him elaborate his hallucinations or sink further into his ideational emptiness. "Inconsistency in parental discipline and *abdication of the parents' leadership role is harmful.* . . . The parent should insist on respect for his position. The parent has the physical, financial, and intellectual power, and he should use it to impose his will in his own particular style" (emphasis added, Robertiello, 1975, p. 73).

Just as Brazelton (1969, p. 36) has advocated that parents of children with different temperaments treat the children differently, so also the Theraplay therapist is advised to use different Theraplay techniques with one child from those he uses with another. One child may require soft cuddling, rocking, and lullabies; another may require vigorous wrestling and pillow fights. Yet, extreme as these two approaches seem, they probably share more similarities than differences. This is particularly striking, of course, when Theraplay is compared to other techniques of child psychotherapy. A Theraplay session for a withdrawn child has more in common with a Theraplay session for an overactive child than it has, for example, with psychoanalytic therapy (Klein, 1932), client-centered (Axline, [1947] 1969) or behavior modification (Bandura, 1969) sessions. This is not to say Theraplay does not share some properties of each: It shares with both client-centered and behavior modification the attention paid to the child's present level of functioning, and it shares with all three a focus on his need for change. It shares with psychoanalytic child therapy the deliberate (rather than accidental) utilization of the authority role, and it shares with psychoanalysis the psychodynamic formulation of each child's problem. It shares with classical behavior modification the deliberate giving of rewards (albeit interpersonal rewards, rather than tokens, and rewards for nonspecific "relating," rather than for performing). The Theraplay therapist shares with John Rosen (1953, p. 9) the principle that "he must be the idealized mother who now has the responsibility of bringing the patient up all over again . . . providing the proper instinctual response which the benevolent mother must make to (his) unconscious needs." However, he does not share with him the use of incisive verbal interpretations of the patient's implied meanings.

Incredible as it may seem, the Theraplay therapist even shares some properties in common with Tanzanian shamans, as noted in this review of Rappaport and Dent (1979): "The shaman, not the client, defines the problem. The shaman does not cajole . . . or explore the client's views . . . with little discussion, the shaman summarizes the problem and tells the client how to cure it. . . . The shaman's charisma is central to therapy. He attributes success to his ability to project a sense of his omnipotence to arouse the client's positive expectations" ("Charisma, Friendliness Helpful. . . ," 1979, p. 1).

Theraplay shares with Gestalt therapies (Perls, Hefferlein, and Goodman, 1958) attention to physical, concrete, here-and-now experiencing rather than to the process of insight and "talking." Unlike Gestalt approaches, however, Theraplay is deliberately structured. It is not directed to reenacting old conflicts (although it certainly is directed to filling old needs), nor is the patient himself required to formulate goals. Unlike Adlerian therapy (Dreikurs, 1950), there are no concerns with the taking of responsibility for one's own actions, although a parent of a child in Theraplay may be asked to decide, "If you say you want your son to become more law abiding, is it or isn't it worth it to change your behavior with him?" Yet, in spite of its having something in common with so many therapies, Theraplay probably has the fewest elements in common with client-centered therapy. Of all the mental health professionals who have been enrolled in training programs at the Theraplay Institute, it is always those from client-centered backgrounds who report that the diversity between their approach and Theraplay is too great to bridge. The Theraplay therapist sees himself as having not only every "right," but indeed the obligation to intrude into the patient's pathology. And in this sense Theraplay perhaps resembles most of all the problem-solving therapy of Jay Haley (1976, p. 171): "the responsibility for change belongs to the therapist. He is expected to plan a strategy of change to bring about what the patient is paying money to achieve." He bases this contention on his description of Milton Erickson's hypnosis model, as follows: "Out of hypnotic training comes skill in observing people and the complex ways they communicate, skill in motivating people to follow directives, and skill in using one's own words, intonations, and body movements to influence other people. Also out of hypnosis come a conception of people as changeable, an appreciation of the malleability of space and time, and specific ideas about how to direct another person to become more autonomous" (Haley, 1973, p. 19).

In this connection, the Theraplay therapist's agenda of custom-tailored, relationship-oriented tasks-to-be-done resembles the agenda of the "structural" therapist Salvador Minuchin (1978). Structural therapists, particularly in their work with families, certainly do manipulate the ways in which family members behave with respect to one another. Yet, in spite of the similarity, two elements are missing that Theraplay provides: (1) the element of "fun," spontaneity, and frivolity and (2) the focus on body contact, whether it be vigorous, playful, and competitive or tender, soothing, and Nurturing. One further major difference in the two therapeutic approaches, of course, is the virtual absence in structural family therapy of the application of this method to individuals, particularly to children.

An Overview of the Clients

Age as Determinant of Theraplay Style

Although it may seem that Theraplay, like school or entertainment, should be specifically age graded, this is in fact generally not necessary (with the exception of Theraplay for adolescents and adults—see Chapters Ten and Eleven). There is altogether more overlap in activities from one developmental level to another than there is distinct difference. Children from two to twelve enjoy the Nurturing of being given watermelon chunks to eat or having their feet washed, happily engage in the Challenge of wrestling matches and spitting contests, and like the Structure of measuring, weighing, as well as of games such as hopscotch, Mother, May I? and Simon Says. Of course, some variations on these themes are more appropriate for some levels than for others. In hiding M&M's, for example, it is not redundant for a therapist to say to a preschool child, "Hide them on me so I won't find them," whereas these same directions obviously must be varied for an older child ("Hide them on yourself . . ."). Yet variations in many cases are determined more by level of intelligence, restlessness, fearfulness, and difference or similarity in the language spoken by the two participants, than by chronology or developmental stage. There is one exception: The introduction of the baby bottle, if its use is indicated, will need greater tact and diplomacy, the older the child. A two-year-old can be directly held and fed; a latency-age child will need some time to play give-and-take games with the bottle (for example, dripping drops on the therapist's tongue, closing his eyes and guessing the taste).

Pathology as Determinant of Theraplay Style

So far only autism and other pronounced psychopathological conditions of childhood have been described, together with corresponding methods of intervention. There are other conditions, of course, calling for similar types, but perhaps not so extreme a degree, of intervention, and other conditions yet that require altogether different types of help. The following presentations of other disorders and their most appropriate treatments are deliberately oversimplified.

Among the somewhat less serious disturbances of childhood, two in the motoric realm and two in the ideational will be selected for discussion. At one end of this scale is the over-active, aggressive child who darts or struts about, swings at his classmates, utters profanities, and kicks his teacher. At the other end is the underactive child who rarely participates in classroom activities, seldom interacts with his classmates, is quiet, unmoving, shy—if not altogether nonverbal—and neither initiates nor defies. The first child exudes the image of "tough guy"; the second, "helpless baby." From the initial battery of maternal behaviors (Structuring, Challenging, Intruding, and Nurturing) each troubled child requires a selection of specific and very different kinds and combinations of intervention. Again, the adult takes full responsibility for deciding which modes of intervention are to be used and how they are to be carried out.

The "tough-guy" child who is overactive and aggressive often seems to be harboring a frightened, hungry baby. With regard to the question of appropriate Theraplay emphases, his need is certainly not for Intrusion—stimulation and excitement (except, of course, as these may be necessary initially for purposes of establishing rapport; for example, avoiding the endless no's with which he is all too familiar, releasing tension, or keeping up with him in order to "capture" him in play). Since he appears to be already so far out of his depths, Challenging, too, would seem to be contraindicated.

His greatest needs are two: The first is for Structure—limits, quieting down, and firm organization. He needs to know that his world is well defined and that there are bounds beyond which he may not venture. The second is for regressive, indulgent Nurturing. His tough-guy swagger and his provocative talk are often found to conceal the longings of a needy infant. Not only is Nurturing the appropriate treatment for the little boy who has a "macho," tough-guy swagger, but cuddling, lullabies, and the giving of a baby bottle are also the activities of choice for the little girl who gives ready, adultlike kisses and has a too-seductive wiggle. For these children, it is not enough to intervene with limits and organization. Eventually they must be encouraged to accept the very cuddling, babying, and feeding they so vehemently denounce. The intervention message to these children must be "It's all right to be an infant; it's OK (and safe) to want to nurse." The shy, withdrawn, and passive child, however, has his own too-firmly defined internal boundaries, his own strict rules for what he allows and does not allow himself to do. In the process, he has sealed out the world—not to the same degree as has the autistic child, but enough to ward off a good deal of stimulation, nonetheless. Intervention with him should be Intrusive, invigorating, and exciting—all within the most appealing context possible—even though he may attempt at first to ward off such experiences. This prescription for Intrusion means bouncing him and spinning him, surprising him and teasing him. It means never allowing him to lie or sit when he can hop or jump, never "allowing" him to frown when he can smile. Yet, for the withdrawn, passive child, intervention in the form of Intrusion, excitement, and stimulation is not enough. For him, too, there must be an added dimension, and

for him, as for the overactive aggressive child, this must be in
the dimension of age-appropriate expectation. Whereas for the
overactive, aggressive child, babying is the direction to be taken,
for the withdrawn child Theraplay is more often planned to
take the direction of Challenge. The added dimension should be
not regressive but progressive. He should not be assured that it
is all right to be an infant but rather that he can do better, act
bigger, shout louder, and require more of himself—not in the
sense of achievement (for example, toilet training, reading, and
writing), but in being stronger and bolder, and more aggressive,
and in taking more risks.

Just as the mother teases the infant with peek-a-boo,
thereby requiring him to do a little coping, so also the adult
working with the withdrawn child should require him to
"reach" a bit as well. (It goes without saying, of course, that
some profoundly depressed, deeply deprived withdrawn children are in need of immense amounts of Nurturing—even in
place of Challenging—and some, like Tammy (see Chapter Two),
require it every now and then.) These two kinds of children,
then, the overactive aggressive and the underactive withdrawn,
in general require two different kinds of interventions: The first
requires Structuring and Nurturing; the second requires Intruding and Challenging.

Among neurotic children, obsessive-compulsive and
hysterical ones, even though generally less obviously disturbed
than those just described, require yet other combinations of
maternal caretaking. The obsessive-compulsive, grown-up-
appearing child, fully and tightly in control of himself and his
world, giving the appearance of a miniature adult, needs neither
Structure—order and predictability—nor Challenge. He is striving too hard as it is, and he values organization too much already. Adams (1973, p. 220) asserts, regarding play and nonverbal therapy, "Nothing is more practical for the obsessive
child than to be taught to let go and play. Play requires considerable drive and zest, and that shortage is what makes the obsessive child so unplayful and so lacking in the spirit of commitment one sees in a playing child." The obsessive-compulsive
child needs the spontaneity of surprise and delighted Intrusion
to supplant the order, together with regressive cuddling and

Nurturing to supplant the striving to be grown up. Adams (1973, pp. 23, 88) also observes, "Obsessive children are preoccupied with power relations more profoundly than other children. . . . The obsessive child goes to great lengths to be one-up." Above all else, this child, with his chronic need for power, more than many other children needs the experience of being not in charge. Declares Adams (1973, p. 220), "The therapist, without making himself into a ridiculous clown, can not only show some lightheartedness and good spirits generally, but can actually serve as a model for the obsessive child to imitate. If the therapist enjoys physical play, all the better. . . . Chess and checkers should not be in sight in the psychiatrist's playroom when he has an obsessive patient among his patient group, for these are games that play into the child's obsessive ways."

The hysterical child, in contrast, generally being as in a dream (Ferenczi, 1926) or on a stage, often clinging and babylike, living for the moment and denying frustrating reality, requires quite the opposite. Shapiro (1965) describes the hysteric's subjective world as "a colorful, exciting one, but it is often lacking in a sense of substance and fact" (p. 119). "It is their diffuse impressionistic experience of the world—the general absence of a sharp look at, and a clear sense of, plain hard fact—that makes possible the avoidance of . . . serious questions" (p. 123). Infantilizing and carefree spontaneity will not help him, whereas planful Structure and Challenge will—perhaps in line with the traditional aim of "making the symptoms ego-dystonic" (Laybourne and Churchill, 1972).

For every one of the conditions described, it is important for the adult to remain "in charge." The following sections on Theraplay technique present the rationale for these recommendations, the means by which to carry them out, and further discussion of the kinds of problem children requiring the various kinds of interventions.

Indications and Contraindications

Indications

Theraplay is a useful form of treatment for many emotional, social, and developmental problems. Its usefulness is very likely a function of its supplying the very kinds of attachment-fostering and autonomy-enhancing experiences that children referred for help have so often missed.

Theraplay is indicated for children who, probably as a result of these early deprivations, have low confidence in themselves and little trust in their worlds. The term *Theraplay* describes the form of treatment that is insistently intimate, physical, personal, focused, and fun—a form of treatment that replicates the Structuring, Challenging, Intruding, and Nurturing inherent in the mother-infant relationship. It describes an adult-child interaction in which the adult is "in charge." Whether he or she is in charge for purposes of Structuring (guiding and defining), for purposes of Challenging, for purposes of Intruding (arousing and exciting), or for purposes of Nurturing (feeding, cuddling, and caring), the sessions are playful and recreate healthy parenting. Even though he will ultimately come to enjoy Structure, Challenge, Intrusion, and Nurture, and even though it would seem all of these should appeal to any child, there may be many struggles before a particular child referred for help is able to give up his resistance against them. The child for whom Theraplay is recommended is one who behaves in ways that keep distance between himself and the kind of relationship his therapist, as parent surrogate, knows he needs.

Contraindications

Theraplay, in its purest form, is not indicated for *every* child, however. Children who feel *no* self-confidence whatsoever, for example, who feel themselves incapable of making any impact, warrant a form of treatment that is only partly Theraplay (the play or fun part, together with some opportunity for "taking charge"). Those who have suffered a recent trauma should be treated only with Nurturing or should not be treated with Theraplay at all (at least until the trauma has been worked through, using more conventional supportive or insight techniques).

The Sociopathic Child

Theraplay has been found to be effective with only a very few sociopaths and then only if two conditions are met: (1) if the child is preadolescent and (2) if the parents are willing and able to give up passive acquiescence toward (if not outright encouragement of) their child's behavior. A dramatic shift may have to be made in their own dynamics, in their marriage, and in the kinds of satisfaction they obtain from their roles as parents. It goes without saying that this degree of willingness is not often found in parents of delinquent children. The prospects are dim for the adolescent whose parents only give lip service to their wish for change. He may come to enjoy the attention, spontaneity, and limit setting of the sessions, but a change in real-world behavior is unlikely.

The Traumatized Child

Also, Theraplay is not the treatment of choice for children whose presenting problem has been the experience of a recent trauma. A child who has recently lost a parent, been molested, or suffered surgery is not appropriately treated by most of the components of the Theraplay method. Neither fun nor insistent intimacy is indicated for the traumatized child. His is not a problem of fleeing the proffered Structure, Challenge, Intrusion, or Nurturing. His behavior is probably neither motorically nor ideationally inappropriate. A child who has suffered a recent trauma has the following therapeutic needs: (1) the need to understand fully and factually just exactly what happened to him; (2) the need to express the feelings the trauma has aroused in him; (3) the need for reassurance that, even given his prior, or coincidental, unacceptable wishes, he did not bring about the episode; (4) the need to become convinced that, whatever happened to the victim (if this was someone other than himself), it is not of necessity going to happen to him; and, finally (5) the need to know that he is not going to be punished for what happened. The following messages, thus, must be conveyed to him or her:

1. "Even though you may have wished it, you weren't the cause of it."
2. "You're not going to be next. You're different (for example, very healthy, very young, or very strong)."
3. "There will always be someone to take care of you."

4. (And, finally) "Life will go on. You have the capacity to find again the joy you felt before."

Traditional child psychotherapy (with or without dolls or puppets for purposes of helping the child to reenact the trauma), not Theraplay, is the appropriate treatment for the traumatized child. Anthony Vitiello, of the community mental health center in Michigan City, Indiana, encourages the child to describe what happened through drawings with crayons, thus helping him or her to relive the trauma.

In the absence of trauma, children are rarely so delicate and easily hurt as to require significant amelioration of the therapist's behavior. As demonstrated in Chapter Eight, even children with severe physical handicaps can often be—and usually should be—treated with a good deal more vigor and forcefulness, always in the spirit of having a good time, than most of us can believe at first.

The "Fragile" Child

In the initial stages of therapy with some children, however, certain of the Theraplay techniques must be modified or perhaps not used at all. For those few children who are particularly fragile emotionally—those who respond to even gentle approaches with panic or terror—the more vigorous and intrusive approaches may be inappropriate until a firm relationship has been established between child and therapist. Some initial cues can serve to identify these particularly tender children.

These children genuinely feel they can make no impact and thus have never even tried. They make no attempt to "take charge." They do not even do the whimpering or soft crying that causes other people in their worlds to rectify their ways. They respond to the approaches of others with terror, and they panic when they are recognized as special or unique. Only through a vivid fantasy life do these kinds of children free themselves from environmental constraints. Overtly, they appear most comfortable when they are indistinguishable from the woodwork. Although the vigorous part of Theraplay—including the therapist's "taking charge"—is not the appropriate way to improve their mental health, the fun part in itself is quite appropriate. In these cases, initiative must be taken by the child, instead of by the therapist. Thus there will be gaiety, eye contact, laughter, and wiggling toes, but wherever possible the child's ideas are followed, rather than the therapist's. These kinds of children need to learn that they are safe and that they can effectively make an impact on others.

It should be noted once again that relatively few children require this degree of caution. More often than not, over-concern with regard to intrusion or taking charge reflects problems in the therapist rather than in the child, as seen in Chapter Twelve.

The Abused Child

Increasingly, as the public awakens to the rights of groups heretofore considered of low status, the individual is offered protection from all manner of abuses. Children are among those of the lowest status and are the most commonly abused. Whereas previously parental rights always guaranteed parental freedom in parenting, nowadays the rights of children, not of parents, have priority. As a result of the laws that enforce protection, many more cases of child abuse are brought to light in schools, hospitals, social service agencies, mental health centers, and Theraplay.

The possible "causes" of child abuse, in addition to the oft-cited tensions of poverty and crowding, are many. Often the parent was abused as a child, and his or her parents in turn were abused when they themselves were children. Often, too, marital conflict or parental "hunger" finds its release in abuse of one of the children. Or the parental personality—particularly lack of self-esteem and low frustration tolerance—is to blame. The child's genetic composition of or a parent-child mismatch such as those previously described also may contribute and must be considered in the treatment planning.

Abused children need therapy that primarily provides crisis intervention—the kind of therapy that would be appropriate for a child who has suffered any other kind of recent trauma—for example, parent loss—together with Nurturing

Theraplay. Through the use of words or dolls or drawings, and in the hope that an understanding of what happened in the recent past would make for decreased feelings of vulnerability in the immediate future, traditional child therapy allows the child expression of his fear and anger. In conjunction with this emphasis on affects, relationships, and realities, Nurturing Theraplay is appropriate. The bruises are gently washed, and the scratches are kissed, blown on, and bandaged. The child who has been abused before now becomes gently cared for. He is cradled, rocked, and sung to. His generally low self-image is raised. Rather than being made to feel deserving of ultimate rejection, he is made to feel lovable instead.

In ideal instances, love-evoking behavior supplants rejection-evoking behavior. The vicious pattern of some abuse evoking yet more abuse is broken. Self-love evokes love from others. Although occasionally we have seen complete recovery (particularly when the abuse is of recent onset rather than being of chronic standing), more therapeutic effort is generally required. First and foremost, the "guilty" parent(s) must become involved, in not only marital but also family counseling. Family Theraplay (Chapter Five) is often effective in helping parents actively to see their child as lovable and themselves as loving parents.

This latter therapeutic effort, having as its goal more than immediate coping with a recent trauma, involves Theraplay strategems beyond Nurturing. Often the child, like the parent, has poor control of impulses. Often his own outbursts follow a period of frustration and uneasy "testing," just as the parent's outbursts follow the same period of dreary "nagging." Neither parent nor child hears the other, and neither one knows how to set ongoing limits. Family Theraplay for abuser and abused (in addition to providing the ever-present fun) adds the element of Structure.

We will illustrate with Vladimir, one of Phyllis Rubin's cases referred for child abuse in the special education district in which she works. Vladimir was seven before it was learned that his hyperactive behavior and his high state of anxiety were both cause and result of his mother's injurious beatings. He was seen alone at first, in therapy that combined his expression of rage and terror with soothing, Nurturing Theraplay. His therapist applied creamy lotions and soft powders to his bruises, conveyed in coos and lullabies how much she cared for him, and always made it clear that she felt he was so special she wanted to make sure nothing bad would ever happen to him. Although he at first struggled to reject his baby bottle of orange juice, he at last sucked eagerly. Yet, in spite of his generally more relaxed condition, he still was testing his mother, who still could provide him no consistent limits. Mrs. Rubin planned a series of Structuring sessions, and describes a part of the first one, as follows.

"Vladimir is refusing to have his shoes put back on today. Every time one shoe is on, he takes off the other. Every time the other is put back on, he waits for a free moment to remove the first." Finally Mrs. Rubin sat on one completed foot and worked on the second. She picked him up quickly and walked him to the gym for the joint session with his mother. Stopping briefly to rearrange the gym mats, she found that he was getting ready to remove his shoe once more. With his mother watching (later she was directed to do it herself), Mrs. Rubin made a firm statement: "Vladimir, I'm going to have to help you. Here is my hand. Hold on." She reached for his hand as she said it. She adjusted his shoe, and they moved on. According to her report, this first Structuring session consisted of one shoe-replacing struggle after another. Each time, his therapist anticipated his maneuver, and each time she persisted in sticking to her limits.

Only weeks later did Vladimir and his mother work out together a pattern of alert anticipation and clear Structuring—a far cry from the uneasy, undefined, and unengaged situation in which he tested, she ignored, he tested some more, she nagged until at last his "badgering" led her to "explode" and beat him —the resulting guilt then having to be assuaged through promises of toys and money.

Children now in foster homes and in adoptive placement who were abused in earlier family settings make up a large proportion of children coming in for treatment. If the abuse happened years earlier and in different environments, Theraplay alone may be sufficient. Rather than directing them to "work through" the traumas from their distant pasts, it may be important to (1) help the children to find themselves more lovable, (2) help the new parents evolve that image with them—often by way of creating what should have been a normal infancy, and (3) help the children abandon abuse-evoking behaviors, such as teasing, testing, and provocative mannerisms. Theraplay training for foster and adoptive families is discussed in more detail in Chapter Six.

Since abusing parents generally are under stress, were never properly parented, are friendless and isolated, and are depressed, dependent, deprived, and need care as much as their children do, Theraplay for them is often indicated. Jasper's mother was one such. Herself deprived and childlike, she whipped her children daily and locked them in their barren bedroom. On her visits to their schoolrooms, she devoured their breakfasts and played with their Play-Doh. She eagerly agreed to the offer of twice weekly Theraplay for herself. In the sessions, her arms were lotioned, her hair was restyled, orange slices were fed to her, and she was presented with aluminum foil impressions of her toes and fingers, as take-home souvenirs of the session. In time, as the therapists had hoped she would, she began to feel cared for herself and become less abusing and neglectful of her children.

In summary, based as it is on the healthy mother-infant relationship, Theraplay is Structuring, Challenging, Intruding, and Nurturing, all in the context of empathy, authority, and fun. These basic techniques of Theraplay, separately and in combination, underlie the treatment program for most of the children referred for help. The child's particular problem, representing his particular needs, determines which aspects of Theraplay will be the most likely to succeed.

Notes

1. For simplicity and consistency, *he* is used for the child or patient. See note 2.

2. For purposes of easier reading, the words *mother* and *she* are used instead of *parent* and *he or she*. Even by modern-day standards, references to pregnancy, childbirth, nursing, and

the earliest skin-contact experiences are more appropriately described as *hers* than as *his or hers,* recent authors on father-child relationships notwithstanding (for example, Greenberg and Morris, 1974, on father-newborn "engrossment"; Parke, 1974, on father-infant attachment; and Lamb, 1976, on the father's role in child development). Also, in keeping with the format of other recent authors (for example, Kaplan, 1978), *he* is used for baby, instead of *he or she.* To be consistent and to avoid these same awkward constructions, the generic *he* will be used for the child or patient when the sex is indeterminate. For the same reasons, and also in the hope that this might entice more male workers into the childcare field, therapists are *he* unless the context makes it clear that the therapist is female.

3. For purposes of discussion, the particular relationship between mother and infant that will provide the answers to these questions is that found in our immediate culture only. The differences between one culture and another with respect to mother-infant relationships is enlightening indeed. For purposes of future comparison, these differences are often best portrayed by means of films. One filmed example is found in LeBoyer's footage of an East Indian mother and her infant. Although neither looking at nor speaking to her baby, she is unquestionably relating to him through her tireless massage—a vigorous, regular, slowly moving involvement in his entire body, followed by an intense, powerful concentration on each tiny body part (*Calcutta,* 1978). Daniel Freedman's scenes in his footage (1978) of the somber togetherness of a Navaho mother and her baby are in sharp contrast to the typical scene of a white, middle-class urban American mother cheerfully chattering to her young child. Margaret Mead, in her film *Four Families* (1959), compares individual caretaking scenes (feeding, bathing, and so on) in Japan, France, Canada, and the United States; and Marschak, in her film (*Two Climates of Israel,* 1975), compares kibbutz- and family-reared Israeli children in structured interaction with their parents. Brazelton (1978) and Condon (1974) in their films break into discrete seconds of time the interactions of mothers and babies.

4. *Delighting* is Ernestine Thomas' word for her particular brand of Intrusive Theraplay.

2

Theraplay Sessions and Instructions for the Therapist

What to Expect as the Treatment Evolves

A course of Theraplay typically unfolds in a quite predictable pattern. Theraplay has a high degree of predictability, primarily because the therapist is, as compared to many other therapies, continuously "in charge" of the way the session runs. This is not to suggest that "predictability" of a therapeutic course is necessarily a virtue but rather that it is more true of Theraplay than of most therapies that the direction and course of the treatment is controlled more by the therapist than by the vagaries of the patient. There are only a finite number of reactions a child can make to an insistent, intrusive, interested, and intimacy-seeking adult. To illustrate: When a friendly adult "comes on strong," a child cannot ignore him, continue to "do his own thing," or disassociate himself from the situation. He may accept him, he may reject him, or he may try to flee the situation, but any of these behaviors is a response to the adult's insistence and is not simply child determined. The predictability in Theraplay, in addition, naturally results because individual sessions are tailored to the needs of each child and thus explicitly planned, although not so overplanned that they exclude spontaneity.

Theraplay differs from traditional play therapy (both insight-dynamic and client centered) in the degree to which the therapist assumes responsibility for the activities carried out within each session and for the progression of activities from one session to the next. Thus the child does not enter a playroom stocked with available dolls, dollhouses, chess and checker games, water, clay, sand, crayons, paper, soldiers, and miniature dishes or guns. He is not told that he may use the session as he wishes. Rather, the room is virtually bare. There are gym mats (or other protective covering) on the floor and a mirror on the wall. While Theraplay equipment may include large floor pillows, soft toss pillows, a bathroom scale, and measuring tape, most "props" remain out of sight, to be used only in conjunction with a particular planned activity. Throughout, the therapist uses himself and the child as primary objects for play. Only for backup and variety does he resort to pillows, bubbles, popcorn, tinfoil, or baby powder. If food is used at all, it is used for spitting; decorating fingers, ears or toes; smearing; throwing; mutual feeding; tickling; feeling, and finding, hidden, on someone else's body. Never is food set out in a dish with the invitation to "Help yourself whenever you feel the need for it." Never is it used as a reward for a task well done. Throughout, it is the therapist who directs the activity; for example, he says "I want to see how tall you are," "I'm going to let you stand on my bucking bronco back today," "Come over here," "Sit right there," "Let's spit these orange seeds onto my big toe," "Here, let's see who can win at a leg wrestle," or "Today we're going to make some prints of your feet." He never asks permission, never checks for accordance or approval. He never, therefore, introduces his suggestions with "Shall we . . . ?" or "Would you like to . . . ?" or "How about . . . ?" nor ends them with "OK?" His implicit message throughout is "I recognize that you hurt. Come here, I can fix it so you feel better."

Theraplay may be understood as having six phases, which may be modified somewhat according to age and pathology while maintaining essentially the same flavor.

1. Introduction
2. Exploration
3. Tentative acceptance
4. Negative reaction
5. Growing and trusting
6. Termination
    a. Preparation
    b. Announcement
    c. Parting

Introduction Phase

Although they are never spelled out as such, the ground rules are clearly set in the introduction phase:

· The Theraplay sessions will be fun.
· The Theraplay sessions will be clearly directed by the therapist.
· The Theraplay sessions will be action oriented, rather than talk and insight oriented.[1]
· The Theraplay sessions will be clearly delineated as to time, space, and therapist and patient roles.

In the introduction phase, the therapist first approaches the child. Saying "Hi, Joey," the therapist moves toward the child in a way that tells him, "I know you're basically a strong, fun loving, and fun-to-be-with person, and I'm going to present you right off with the most appealing picture of the world I can conjure up." After announcing, "I'm Chuck," the therapist may say, "Come on, jump aboard; I have a ride for you" or "I've just been waiting so long for you to hop down this hall with me" or "See, I can make this special 'chair' for you to ride on. Put your arm around my shoulder, and you can sit on it." Thus "hooked" together, therapist and child leave the waiting area and head for the therapy room. The action is swift, the level of excitement high. There is little opportunity for the child to dwell on his doubts or to verbalize his reservations. Of course, such an abrupt greeting or joyful departure may not always be possible. The physical facilities may not allow it, nor may the parents, nurses, teachers, or school principal. Some few children may not "allow" it either. We are not referring here to a child's being resistant or surprised but rather to his being genuinely frightened. In the very few cases where this form of introduction may simply not be possible, the therapist of course modifies the introduction.

Exploration Phase

In the exploration phase, child and therapist actively get to know each other. They get to know who has the largest hands, the curliest hair, the longest toenails, and the strongest muscles. In the process, the child comes to view himself in a new light. He may not have known, heretofore, that the hairs on his arms stand up when the therapist blows on them, that he can jump gracefully into the air off a table, reach to touch the ceiling, or that he has—teasingly—twenty-one knucklebones. Using methods of paradoxical intention (Frankl, 1963, p. 196), even his negativistic behaviors are turned around to show a more lovable side of him. He may never have been told what a skillful "rag doll" he is when he defiantly goes limp. He may never have been asked to "Be sure not ever to look at me" when he turns his head to avoid eye contact. The chin that stiffens when his mouth closes tight may respond with jolly wobbling to a tickle; the piercing "no" may change to a musical "no—oh—oh—" when the therapist plucks his (the child's) upper and lower lips. But, most important, he may not have known before that he is lovable even at his most resistant, because he has big brown eyes, a soft voice, a special way his legs bend, or a contagious belly laugh. His being lovable is not conditional on his behaving politely, on not tracking dirt through the house, or on not hurting his sister; nor on building a straight tower of blocks, talking, or spelling his name correctly.

At the end of the exploratory session, the child has become aware of the therapist's person, his facial features, his voice, his physical strength. Indeed, the Theraplay session can only be considered a success if he has come to perceive his therapist as clearly differentiated from himself, omnipresent, and fun. In his training, the Theraplay therapist learns that he must make every effort to ensure that when the child lies in bed at night after each Theraplay session he will be able to clearly call to mind the image of his therapist. "The therapist must establish himself as the most important intruding factor in the life of the patient. . . . It is the matter of a forceful, insistent, intrusive, inescapable presence of the therapist" (Des Lauriers, 1962, p. 63). If the child only has a vague impression of a shadowy figure that he remembers in some amorphous way, the session and the therapist were failures. (It goes without saying, of course, that the failure would be greater yet if the image were clear but the recalled quality cruel.)

About five minutes before the end of the exploratory session, as will be true of those that succeed it, the Theraplay therapist alerts the child: "We only have a few more minutes. Let's get your shoes. Here, I'm going to put them on you" followed by, "I'll be back to play with you again on Tuesday." Then, leading him back to his classroom or to the waiting area, the therapist says, "Goodbye, Joey," and adds, "Don't forget to bring those tickles with you again next time" (or some equally cheerful message relating this session to the next one).

Tentative Acceptance Phase

During the tentative acceptance phase, the child pretends or may actually attempt to "play the game." It is often pseudo-involvement only, however. Tentativeness, even apprehension, is the underlying tone.

During this period, the therapist continues to be intrusive and insistent, indulging or challenging, surprising, appealing, and fun. The child may appear bewildered, excited, reserved, or interested. Even when he reacts with enthusiasm and apparent intimacy, however, this reaction is often too premature to be evidence of a genuine relaxed engagement. It may be, rather, a defensive, apprehensive maneuver whose purpose is to keep the intruding therapist at bay.

Negative Reaction Phase

In the negative reaction phase, the child becomes clearly resistant to any further efforts at intimacy. This kind of behavior, which follows the phase of apparent involvement, can confirm how only "apparent" the involvement heretofore really was. In this subsequent phase, the child who had previously appeared so willing and accepting—if not outright cooperative, enthusiastic, and participating—may suddenly become negativistic, resistant, limp, or mute. The therapist's implicit response continues to be insistent and matter-of-fact, conveying to the child that what they are about to do together would be fun for any normal child. He is not put off by weeping, tantrums, or refusals to join in. The resistance may continue over a few more sessions in the same or varied form. In the face of the therapist's firm perseverance (Robertiello, 1975, p. 12) and implied hopefulness, however, it will diminish in intensity and eventually disappear. The first clues to its reduction often come in the form of surreptitious eye contact, unintended calm behavior, or even a fleeting smile that appears as though it had broken through in spite of itself.

Growing and Trusting Phase

During the growing and trusting phase, the child first experiences the pleasure of interacting with another human being in a "normal," reciprocally satisfying way.

With the help of the warm but firm and omnipresent therapist, the child has mastered the "negative phase" and is now ready to move into growing and trusting. He is ready to begin to develop confidence in himself and trust in the world. During this period, which constitutes the bulk of the therapeutic effort, child and therapist increasingly become partners in a plan to try out new variations on old themes (including mutual teasing and playful shifts in initiative taking),[2] to enjoy longer and more intense periods of intimacy, and, of course, ultimately to genuinely enjoy each other's company. At first, the moments of closeness are fleeting, and the laughter will come primarily from the therapist. As progress is made, there is reciprocal laughter, mutual peek-a-boo, and a harmonious sitting close, looking into each other's eyes while softly singing rounds or playing patty-cake. Once both therapist and child have found this high degree of pleasure with each other, it is time to introduce other members of the child's community into the sessions. A playmate or a parent may be invited to participate. The therapist may accompany the child on tours of the school in which they stop to visit librarians, cooks, janitors, or other members of the school staff (for example, saying, "Mrs. Jones, Pat and I just came by to see whether you have any of that good chocolate milk today"—Ernestine Thomas, personal communication). Eventually therapy may take place in the classroom itself. An effort is made to heighten the child's self-esteem through increasing his status in the eyes of his classmates (for example, "Susie, you hold Jennifer's fingers still. John, you hold onto this nail polish bottle. Beth, you hold Jenny's arm. And Chris, you get to polish her nails really pretty.").Or the therapist, poking her two fingers through the holes in taunted, dirt-caked Cindy's tattered dress, says, "OK, you all. I know Cindy's dress has holes, but I bet you don't know how neat those holes really are. Look at what those holes can do" (Ernestine Thomas, personal communication). And the therapist's fingers begin to do a little dance, while she sings.[3] (In no time, all the girls are begging for holes in their dresses.)

Termination

The phase leading up to, and including, the termination of the Theraplay treatment course, although encompassing a short span of time relative to other therapies, consists of three distinct phases: (1) Preparation, (2) Announcement, and (3) Parting.

Preparation. Teachers' and parents' reports of decrease or disappearance of symptoms, as well as the child's increasingly harmonious and enjoying behavior with respect to himself and his world, have led to the introduction into his Theraplay sessions of the other "therapeutic" agents described earlier (such as classmates, cooks, and janitors). Gradually these others narrow down to two or three "close friends." Following evidence that these particular expansions of his emotional universe have been appropriate and enjoyable, he is considered ready for termination. Although the relationship with his therapist has become meaningful and intimate and although the sessions themselves have become important in his everyday life, the termination period need not be ushered in with gloom, nostalgia, long-term preparation, or tentative misgiving.

Announcement. If possible, the Theraplay therapist announces the termination plans within the context of gains the child has made. For example, "Jimmy, the way those eyes sparkle when you smile these days, you won't be needing me to help you make friends any more." Or "You're getting to be such fun to play with and John and Danny enjoy playing with you so much that you won't be needing me to come here and play with you much longer." Then, after a pause to make sure Jimmy has understood, his therapist may set the date. "We'll have our two sessions this week and next week, and then the week after that on Thursday we'll have our last session."

For the next few sessions, the emphasis is on "tricks" the child has learned in his Theraplay, if possible in the company of the one or two children who will participate in the remaining and final sessions. The object is to redirect his cathexis away from the therapist and onto the people who will comprise his posttherapy environment ("[The] behavior of patients reflects more and more feeling of independence, need to belong to a family, their pleasure at being themselves in their interests and their actions" [Des Lauriers, 1962, p. 155]). After each of these termination phase sessions, the child is reminded of how many more "times together" remain. He is not encouraged to explore his hidden reactions to separation. If he shows clear evidence of anger, sadness, impotence, or bewilderment, these feelings are "labeled" for him and acknowledged, just as his body parts or his feelings were labeled and acknowledged earlier (for example, "I know you feel angry that we won't be together any more"). If—although this seldom happens—the anger were to be acted out destructively, he is reminded, "You can tell me how you feel about it, but I can't let you hurt me."

During the course of the next-to-last session, the therapist will remind the child, "Remember, Tom, Thursday will be our last time together." During this next-to-last session, whether in the presence of one or two friends or of his family, the child may like to replay some activities he has enjoyed during his previous sessions. During the quiet time near the session's closing, there may be planning for the final party. At the end, he is again reminded that the next session will be his last one.

Parting. By the time of the termination party, an alliance has been established between the child and the real-world contacts that have been brought into the Theraplay scene (the selected one or two friends, his teacher, or his parents). The therapist by now has backed off into the position of friendly participant. The theme of the party is a future-oriented reaffirmation of the child's strengths and identity. Guests, child, and therapist all wear party hats, share party treats, and sing songs about the child's unique attributes. Discussion may include the birthday to come, the school year ahead, and so on. Souvenirs, in the form of foot- or handprint pictures, for example, may be distributed, or a special song taught to everyone. The child himself is presented with a Certificate of Personal Excellence or a tee-shirt with the slogan "I'm One of a Kind."

At the end of this final session, the therapist acts as anyone would at the close of a meaningful relationship. He may give the child a big hug, tell him how much he has enjoyed playing with such a special person, and tell him he knows from now on he (the child) will be having fun with his own friends. The therapist then turns him over to his parents or returns him to the classroom, always making sure that he is immediately incorporated into some favorite group and fun activity.

Planning the Session

Stephen Bennett (1971, p. 322) has observed that "maternal ebullience and skill in handling can lead to extraordinarily complex combinations of arousal and calming," that "experienced mothers and baby nurses [know] that . . . by rocking, tickling, singing to, and stroking the infant's face they can produce a state of aroused vigilance evidenced by an intensely animated expression," and that this can result in "a striking involvement between mother and infant." Since these attitudes and behaviors are indeed the goals of Theraplay, the methods by which they are brought about at the earliest developmental levels are the methods that each Theraplay session attempts to replicate.

Sequence

Just as in the course of a good nursery school day, so also in the course of each Theraplay session, activities vary in a predetermined way. Between the opening and the closing of each Theraplay session, large-muscle, boisterous experiences alternate with low-keyed, soft, quiet ones. Competition alternates with cooperation, individuation with merging. Of course, any one session need not follow this suggested format unvaryingly. Sometimes, for example, a child may appear for his session in such an agitated condition that it is best to begin, following the greeting, with activities that "settle" him (such as Nurturing activities). Sometimes his life has been such a series of confrontations and conflicts that he requires only order and predictability (such as Structuring activities). Both greeting and closing, however, are necessary elements of any Theraplay session. Children who require Theraplay often lack spatial and temporal demarcations in their lives. Bedtime and mealtimes, for example, may occur anywhere and virtually at random.[4] The opening and closing of treatment sessions, as well as their physical location, therefore, should be clearly articulated. A child who is permitted to float in at the beginning and drift out at the end of his sessions—sessions that themselves are haphazard or "on the run"—may feel even more confused as to his identity and may have an increased sense of diffuseness about the world.

The Opening

1. *Greeting activities.* The object of greeting activities is to allow the child to experience unrestrained pleasure at being discovered. The initial greeting ordinarily takes place at the location where therapist and child first meet.

In voice, facial expression, and choice of words, the therapist communicates his unambivalent excitement and delight at being reunited with an old friend. The model for the manifestation of this pleasure is, once again, found in the parent-infant interaction. On entering the nursery in the morning, a mother may greet her baby with an eager, "Susie!" and, seizing her foot, may tease, "Let me see those great big eyes this morning. Oh! They're lovely polka dots, aren't they? Just like yesterday!" And, "Let me see how big you are today!" or "I'm coming to get you . . . I'm coming to get you! Here I come! Whee!" (spinning her around in the air). The Theraplay therapist may do the same. Depending primarily on the needs of the child and his previous relationship with his therapist, and only minimally depending on his age, the following are samples of appropriate and joyfully stated greetings with which to usher the child into the Theraplay session: "Oh! If it isn't my friend Bobby, with that nice curly hair!" "Well, Jim, all day I've been waiting to see you!" "You brought that beautiful smile with you again!" "What! Even more of those gorgeous freckles today?" "I know your game! Right under this arm, you're hiding one great, big, bubbly tickle," "Those lovely lashes. Wait! Let me count them!" As is clear, the greeting should be intense, cheerful, and extremely personal. The child should come to feel that a particular part of himself has been singled out as special and lovable. Although it may not always be appropriate for children with a too-rich fantasy life, most children welcome a gleeful "Oh, I just know there's something inside those socks!" or "Let me taste that ear. Umm . . . yum yum . . . good sugar!" Again, this parallels the mother's cooing to her infant: "You're so sweet I could just eat you up!" The message is clear: "I love everything about you: the way you look to me when I look at you, the way you feel when I touch you, and the way you taste when I nibble you" (Hedda Bolgar, personal communication—commenting on scenes in the Theraplay film *There He Goes,* Jernberg and others, 1975).

The initial greeting, as between mother and baby, is never formal, symbolic, or perfunctory. It does not include "We're going to play for a little while," "Follow me to my office," "Hello, how are you today?" or even "Did you have a hard trip down?" If, as they separate for the child's Theraplay session, either the parent or the child looks anxious, the parent may be told, "We'll be back to see you in a little while, Mom. You wait right there until we get back." In this way, separations are usually easily accomplished. If they are not, the parent may be invited into the Theraplay room for a brief, "Let's show Mom what a great balancer you are before she goes back out to wait for you." Mother looks, is helped to applaud, and then is ushered out. All of this, of course, refers to the situation in which she is deemed by the therapist, or feels herself to be, not quite ready to join in the session (as described later). Once again, occasions necessitating such concessions are few indeed. (They are known to have occurred less than half a dozen times in all the more than 3,000 Theraplay cases conducted through the Theraplay Institute to date.) Thus excessive use of this concession is a reflection of the therapist's discomfort rather than the child's genuine need (see Chapter Twelve).

2. *Checkup activities.* The purpose of checkup activities is threefold: (1) an opportunity for therapist and child to become reacquainted with each other, (2) an opportunity to give the child a sense of consistency of self, and (3) the opportunity to convey to the child that he is capable of growth and growing.[5] The checkup typically takes place directly on the entry of the therapist and child into the treatment situation. As part of the checkup, the therapist may cheerfully measure and compare the child's height today against a mark on the wall indicating his previous height. He may weigh and compare with a previous weight. He may check out this week's muscle size, number of teeth, breadth of smile, length of hair, and height of kick, jump,

or throw. Measurements should be chosen for elements that can be guaranteed to show growth.

The Session Proper

The Theraplay session proper consists of a choice of any one activity or a combination of two or more kinds of activities. Although these are carefully selected according to the patient's present needs, their determination may in fact be made "on the spur of the moment."

1. *Structuring activities.* The purpose of Structuring activities is to clearly delineate time and space and to teach mastery through the internalization of rules. Structuring activities include building a tower of five pillows; walking with hats balanced on head; "Wait till I count to three, then jump"; "Mother, May I"; "Walk only on the blue squares"; and drawing around hands or bodies.

2. *Challenging activities.*[6] The purposes of Challenging activities are two: to provide the frustration that makes it possible for the child to experience himself as separate and to teach him that combat, competition, and confrontation can release and focus pent-up tension and anger in a safe, direct, controlled, and playful way. Challenging activities may include peek-a-boo, hide-and-seek, wrestling (leg, arm, or thumb), tug of war, pillow fights, or water pistol duels. They may include "I'll bet you can't jump into that yellow square" or "I'll bet you can't spit that bean into my arms." The therapist may introduce a Challenging activity this way: "Let's see if this week *I* can beat *you* at leg wrestling," adding mischievously, "You'd better watch out—I've been practicing." It goes without saying that any one activity may be classified in more than one Theraplay dimension. For purposes of descriptive clarity, however, it helps to ask, "Which is the primary goal to be accomplished?" Thus, peek-a-boo, for example, may serve both to Intrude and to Challenge. The purpose for which it is being undertaken and the manner in which it is carried out determine whether this particular game of it is Intruding or Challenging.

3. *Intruding activities.* The purpose of Intruding activities is to teach the child where he leaves off and the rest of the

world begins, to enhance his experience of himself as a separate individual. With a spontaneity and freedom seldom equaled in the rest of her everyday life, the talented mother creates games out of her baby's every movement. Lying on his back, for example, he lifts his feet toward her. She grabs his feet and unexpectedly peeks at him through his open legs. The talented Theraplay therapist may find himself spontaneously making just this move (Norma Resnik, personal communication).

4. *Nurturing activities.* The purpose of Nurturing activities is to communicate to the child that he can get what he needs without always having to work for it, deny the existence of the need for it, or be rejected for expressing the need. Nurturing activities may include tummy rubbing, eyelid blowing, lullaby singing, cuddling, rocking, applying lotion or powder, and bottle feeding.

In spite of their variety and their intrusiveness, all these are at the same time alliance-fostering activities and as such serve to (1) offset the child's chronic experience of mistrust, loneliness, and isolation; (2) enlist the child's cooperation against the time when child and therapist together must ward off health-retarding tendencies (the "negative phase"); (3) negate the child's "bad," worthless, alienating, or impotent self-image; (4) allow the child to view himself as a contributing team member. Particularly enhancing of the therapist's alliance are activities that include singing rounds such as "Row-Row-Row Your Boat," child walking on therapist's feet, Wheelbarrow, mutual hand or foot painting, combing each other's hair, and feeding each other.

The Closing

1. *Parting.* The object of parting is to provide closure to the session without closing off the relationship and to encourage carryover to the child's everyday life. While putting shoes back on or feeding bites of food or candy to one another, therapist and child discuss what was fun about this session and what is planned for the week ahead (for example, "Boy, Tim, I really liked the way you did that tip-toe trick today. I want you to try that trick out on some of your friends this week").

2. *Transition.* Following the parting, the therapist "straightens" the child's hair and clothing in preparation for his entering "the outside world." He reminds him, "I'll see you on Wednesday," and then, just as he collected him from his care-taker at the outset, he now delivers him directly to this same adult. The therapist tries not to leave the child alone in a wait-ing room or allow him to negotiate his own way down a long corridor to his classroom. Instead, he takes his hand and con-nects him directly with whoever is next responsible. Every time, as he does so, he voices aloud a message to that individual to provide continuity between the two situations (for example, "Mrs. Jones, be sure you let Cindy show you that special little curl in the back of her hair" or "Mom, don't you think Bobby looks great when he flexes those muscles? And he's got some other neat tricks he's going to show you, too").

Do's and Don't's

The following Do's and Don't's (not exhaustive by any means) provide some of the guidelines for Theraplay. They are, it should be noted, guidelines only. The Theraplay therapist:

1. Is confident and has leadership qualities
2. Is appealing and delightful
3. Is responsive and empathic
4. Is in charge of the session at all times (Robertiello, 1975, p. 12)
5. Uses every opportunity for making physical contact with the child
6. Insists unwaveringly on eye contact
7. Places intensive and exclusive focus on the child
8. Initiates, rather than reacts to, the child's behaviors, antici-pating the child's resistant maneuvers and acting before, not after, they are set into motion
9. Is responsive to cues given to him by the child
10. Uses every opportunity to differentiate himself from the child[7]
11. Uses every opportunity to help the child see himself as unique, special, separate, and outstanding[8]

12. Uses the child's moods and feelings to help the child differentiate himself and label his feelings
13. Keeps his sessions spontaneous, flexible, and full of happy surprises[9]
14. Uses himself as the primary playroom object[10]
15. Structures the session so that times, places, and persons are clearly defined
16. Attempts to keep the session cheerful, optimistic, positive, and health-oriented[11]
17. Focuses on the present, the future, and the here
18. Focuses on the child as he is
19. Sees to it that within each session there are many different segments, each one having a beginning, a middle, and an end
20. Offers some minimal frustration, challenge, discomfort[12]
21. Uses paradoxical methods when appropriate
22. Makes his insistent presence felt throughout the duration of a child's temper tantrum[13]
23. Conducts his sessions without regard to whether the child "likes" him
24. Curtails and prevents excessive anxiety[14] or motoric hyperactivity
25. Attends to physical hurts
26. When at a loss for ideas, incorporates the child's body movements into his repertoire

   1. The therapist is confident and has leadership qualities.

   Do: The good therapist, like the good parent, has a positive self-image and conveys the ability to guide and protect.
   Don't: The therapist is not anxious, uncertain, or meek.

   2. The therapist is appealing and delightful.

   Do: The therapist offers such jolly temptation and such joie de vivre that any normal child will find himself inexorably drawn to join in.
   Don't: The therapist is not aloof, worried, or even subtly rejecting. He never gives messages which say "stay away from me" or "what I'm doing you wouldn't want to do."

3. The therapist is responsive and empathic.

Do: The good therapist, like the good parent, knows when to listen and when to soothe. He is able both to perceive underlying needs and to respond to them.

Don't: The therapist does not "use" the child for his own ends, does not "tune him out," nor respond to him only partially or in terms of his (the therapist's) own unmet needs.

4. The therapist is in charge of the session at all times.

Do: Just as the healthy parent feels no need to make apologies to the one-year-old for organizing the day's activities, so also the Theraplay therapist "calls the shots." The therapist, typically without saying it, conveys the message, "We are doing this activity this particular way because I know eventually you'll enjoy it." He makes the statements and carries out the actions with full awareness of the consequences. He is fully in control from the moment the child appears in the therapy room until his departure at the end of each session.

Don't: The therapist does not ask permission, wait for approval, or apologize for taking action. He does not allow the child to "call the shots." Nor do question marks belong in Theraplay. Queries such as "Would you like to jump today?" or "OK?" or "May I take off your socks?" communicate to the child that the control of the session is a joint endeavor and thus invite a "no." Once stated, his "no" calls for a face-saving retreat by the therapist (even though the session may have been planned otherwise), and a power struggle ensues. As for apologies, if a child has been accidentally hurt as a result of a Theraplay maneuver, of course the therapist apologizes, as any respectful human being would apologize for such an occurrence. This is different, however, from an apology that "takes back"—a move initiated by the therapist to which the child can respond implicitly or explicitly with "Stop, I don't wish to participate in that." Asking "Do you like this?" is a borderline case. To the extent that it resembles the chattering of a mother (who has no intention of changing her activity) during the caretaking of her infant (for example, while diapering), asking "Do you like this?" may be all right. To the extent that it invites a vote from the client child, however, it is not. The questions, "How do you feel today?" "Can you tell me what made you do that?" and "What are your thoughts about our terminating?" all may be unanswerable, particularly within the generally noncognitive, noninterpretive, and preverbal focus of Theraplay.

5. The therapist uses every opportunity for making physical contact with his patient.

Do: Just as healthy parenting activities involve many kinds of physical contact between child and parent, so also the Theraplay therapist structures each session so that it affords a hundred different opportunities for body contact. It matters little whether these take place through large or small muscles, through pushing, pulling, stroking, tickling, blowing, or bathing. Nor does it matter, at this point in our discussion, whether the object is to demonstrate height, beauty, silkiness, or muscles.

Don't: The therapist does not discuss, interview, dispute, reflect, or interpret. He may chatter in the manner of a mother with her small baby, but even this chattering is in the context of other (physical) activities.

6. The therapist's insistence on eye contact never wavers.

Do: The therapist pursues the child's eyes with his own no matter how apparently painful this is or how evasive the child becomes in his efforts to avoid it. Even if he has to stand on his head, initiate unplanned peek-a-boo's, recruit a second therapist, or focus heavily on games that involve the area around the eyes, the Theraplay therapist lets nothing deter him from giving eye contact the highest priority. Nevertheless, the pursuit of eye contact is done in an enjoyable, gamelike context.

Don't: The therapist does not forgo or permit himself to be subtly "talked out of" any opportunity for eye contact, no matter how frivolous it may seem. The therapist, however, never allows "eye contact" to become a task-oriented, serious matter between him and the child. Thus, there is no room in Theraplay for rewarding a child's eye contact as though it were a job well performed (as in "That's *good* looking, Jane").

7. *The Theraplay therapist's focus on the child is intensive, exclusive, and often intrusive.*

Do: The therapist must have only one awareness during their short session together: the child and his potential for health. He must direct all his physical energy and his emotional investment into his charge with such intensity that this one half-hour is crammed full of therapeutic experiences.

Don't: The therapist's focus on the child is neither fleeting nor diluted by other thoughts or messages. If he finds himself daydreaming or even formulating hypotheses, the therapist is not fulfilling the high-intensity part of his job commitment.

8. *The Theraplay therapist initiates, rather than reacts to, the child's behaviors. He anticipates the child's resistant maneuvers and acts before, not after, they are set into motion.*

Do: The therapist is aware that, in trying to avoid intimacy, the child will maneuver, mechanize, conform, defy, and so on. Knowing that, the therapist will make every effort to initiate before the resistant action is set into motion.

Don't: If the therapist finds himself saying "No, don't do that" or is constantly redirecting activity the child has already embarked on, he should be aware that he has delayed too long and initiated too little.

9. *The Theraplay therapist is responsive to cues given to him by the child.*

Do: The therapist is alert to signals given by the child that indicate interest in, without intent to direct, meaningful kinds of activities. The therapist selects the signals to which he attends, and it is he, not the child, who determines the form and variations.

Don't: The therapist is not wholly guided by the child's cues. Whereas the child's suggestion, "Today let's play cowboys" does not determine the makeup of the session, his coming in with boots or a cowboy shirt might.

10. The Theraplay therapist uses every opportunity to differentiate himself from the child.

Do: The therapist calls frequent attention to his (the therapist's) own unique features, special strengths, clothing, likes and dislikes, and, particularly with autistic children, along with touching and looking at, also encourages the child to smell (Meltzer, 1975, p. 15) and taste him (the therapist).

Don't: The therapist minimizes references to ways in which he and the child are alike or identical.

11. The Theraplay therapist uses every opportunity to help the child see himself as positive, unique, special, separate, and outstanding.

Do: The therapist delineates the body image of the child and calls attention to special characteristics of the child, all in a positive context.

Don't: Except in rare cases, the therapist does not provide merger experiences for the child; he does not engage, for example, in the kinds of symbiotic rocking that makes them into Siamese twins. Under no circumstances are differentiations to be "put-downs" (for example, "I have a beard and you . . . why . . . you have nothing but skin there!").

Note that the one outstanding exception to the rule about avoiding merger experiences lies in the intense mirroring of expressions, tone of voice, and inferred feelings, which Theraplay therapists find so beneficial in working with autistic children, such mirroring serving more as Intrusion than as merging for these particular kinds of children.

*12. The Theraplay therapist uses the child's moods and
feelings to help the child differentiate himself from others
and label his feelings.*

Do: Just as the therapist conveys "You have two long
legs," or "That nice curl is *yours*," or even "All that nice saliva
you just spit in this bowl comes from *your* mouth," so the therapist helps the child to appropriately identify his own moods.
Thus the therapist may translate, "You're crying because you're
unhappy" or "You want to hit me because you're mad about
what I just did."

Don't: The Theraplay therapist does not infer unconscious processes or "deeper" causes. He would not tell a child,
"You're hurting me because you're mad at Mommy."

*13. The therapist keeps the sessions spontaneous, flexible,
and full of happy surprises.*

Do: From the child's perspective, the therapy session itself is unpredictable, fun, "unpreparable for." Although they
are carefully tailored to the child's particular level of development and his developmental needs of the moment, the activities
within a session flow naturally from one to another.

Don't: The session is neither diffuse nor confusing. Yet it
is not so rigidly planned as to be mechanical nor is any one activity so repetitiously carried out as to be predictable.

14. The therapist uses himself as the primary playroom object.

Do: The therapist himself—his actions, movements,
words, and noises—constitute the major and indispensable
"props" of Theraplay. The therapist moves and acts vigorously,
quickly, alertly, and often humorously. From the child's point
of view, the therapist must come across with such clarity and
with such impact that the night after a session—and for the next
several days—the child has no difficulty recalling his therapist's
face or what they did together.[15]

Don't: There is no place in Theraplay for extensive props. Books, dolls, puzzles, and checkerboards do not belong in the Therapy room. As a rule, though, candy, milk, or other food may be used sparingly for particular nurturing or playful purposes, as may baby powder and lotion.

15. The therapist structures the session so that times, places, and persons are clearly defined.

Do: The therapist defines the boundaries within which the session will take place and conveys clear rules and expectations. The sessions are scheduled at a certain time each day or week and are scheduled to last a certain number of minutes. The Theraplay space is limited to the Theraplay room, to the Theraplay mat in the center of the room, and so on. The Theraplay therapist is the one person who predictably shows up there each session.

Don't: The Theraplay sessions do not take place whenever one or the other participant feels like it. Unless specifically planned, they do not take place in the grocery store nor spill out into the corridor. Although Theraplay can be very useful in activities with teachers or classmates or a grandmother, these cannot be ad hoc casual substitutes for a formally promised Theraplay session.

16. The therapist attempts to keep the session cheerful, optimistic, positive, and health oriented.

Do: Barring traumatic happenings or hurts, the healthy parent for the most part remains cheerful, optimistic, and health oriented. The therapist, likewise, communicates to the child (1) that the world is an appealing, happy, fun-filled place and (2) that he, the child, being basically strong, has the potential to enjoy it.

Don't: The therapist does not focus on the gloomy, the discouraging, the sick, or the frustrating. He does not present himself as one more bitter figure, nor does he convey that the sadness and obstacles in the world are just too much for anyone to overcome.

17. The Theraplay therapist focuses on the present, the future, and the here.

Do: The therapist gives the message that the present matters now (for example, "We're together now" or "My, you look pretty today"), that the future is good and imminent ("Tomorrow you're going to be tall up to here" or "Soon you'll be *so* strong"), and that what matters to both of them is in this very space they are sharing ("I knew I'd find you *right* here with me").

Don't: The therapist does not concern himself with, ask about, or respond to the past nor to the vagaries of the child's fantasy life.[16] He does not ask about what went on before they met (for example, "When did your mother have your little sister?" or "What age were you when your grandma died?") nor does he attend to space outside the immediate Theraplay situation (for example, "Does your house have a yard?" or "Does your uncle live near you?"). If a child's attention is directed elsewhere (such as to the schoolyard, the moon, or his home), the therapist responds with efforts to return to the Theraplay scene (for example, "Your Mommy's at home? I'll bet she is at home. And I'll bet she's thinking about her little boy with these gorgeous dimples, and these curly eyelashes, and these ten cute toes" or "The moon? (singing "I see the moon,/ The moon sees me./ The moon sees somebody/ I want to see./ I like you and you like me,/ And together we both are happy as can be"). The Theraplay therapist does not play contrived, "Let's pretend you and I are somebody or something else" games—those serve only to provide to both therapist and child an escape from the here-and-now.

18. The Theraplay therapist focuses on the child as he is.

Do: The therapist attends to what the child is, how he looks, how strong his muscles are, how beautiful his hair is, how well he can jump or bounce or fall.

Don't: The therapist's love is not conditional. He does not praise the child for tasks performed, for meeting the therapist's expectations, or for being "good."[17] The child receives the therapist's attention because he is Johnny or she is Susie, not because he did not wet the bed last night or because she is doing such "good sitting," "good smiling," or "good looking" (a behavior modification phrase we often find is used with autistic children).

19. The therapist sees to it that within each session there are many different segments, each one having a beginning, a middle and an ending.

Do: Whenever possible, each segment of each Theraplay session should be a little playlet in itself. Each of the many segments within each session should evolve from a beginning to a middle to a conclusion. Thus, for example, (1) therapist blows on child's ear → child squeaks → (2) therapist says, "Make that squeak again and let's see if you can blow me over this time" → (3) child squeaks → (4) therapist falls over.

Don't: The therapist does not allow session to be either (1) one diffuse, undifferentiated plateau (for example, long, drawn-out rocking) or (2) a collection of sporadic, choppy, undeveloped segments (for example, bursts of irrelevant tickling).

20. The Theraplay session contains some minimal frustration, challenge, and discomfort.

Do: The Theraplay therapist urges the child to accept a healthier view of himself and the world and to perform in a healthier manner than is typical for him. The optimism implied by the therapist's expectation that the child can reach, stretch, and grow is ego enhancing.

Don't: To the degree that apparent "comfort" means continuing pathological ways, the Theraplay therapist is not concerned with making the child "comfortable." Thus vacant rocking, finger gazing, or contact fleeing may be behaviors with which the child appears to feel familiar. The Theraplay therapist is not so concerned with protecting the child's equilibrium as he

is with coaxing him to try alternatives—even though the child
may at first react to this as though it causes pain.

21. The Theraplay therapist uses paradoxical methods when it is appropriate to do so.

Do: When it is appropriate to do so, the therapist, laugh-
ing but with mock seriousness,[18] tells the child "do (something
he should not)" or "don't (something he should)." Ernestine
Thomas tells the resistant Pat, in the film *Here I Am* (Jernberg,
Hurst, and Lyman, 1969—see Chapter Three), for example,
"Close your eyes, Pat, and put your thumb in your mouth."
Pat's amusement attests to the appropriateness of the directive.
If not overdone, this technique is particularly helpful in work-
ing with highly resistant children who use "face saving" in an
oppositional manner.

Don't: (1) The therapist does not overdo paradoxical
methods. Used too frequently, this approach loses both its
effectiveness and its potential for humor. (2) Don't omit the
communication that this is nothing more serious than just another "wrestling match." (To do so is to invite unwitting "los-
ing" on the part of the therapist and with it a subsequent potential for therapist sadism in the form of taunting, allowing the
build-up of anxiety in the child or prolonging an activity to the
point where it becomes painful.)

22. The Theraplay therapist makes his insistent presence felt throughout the duration of a child's temper tantrum.[19]

Do: The Theraplay therapist helps the child to gain mastery over a temper outburst. He stays right there, in physical
contact with him, verbalizing his confidence in the child's ability to regain control. He may have to hold the hitting fist, con-
strain the kicking foot, clap his hand over the biting mouth, or
restrict spitting by redirecting the child's entire position. He
may have to sit on him.[20] It is quite appropriate to label the
child's anger, but labeling anger in tantrums is not in itself considered therapeutic. Throughout, however, the therapist tells

the child, with confident reassurance, "I can't let you hurt me" and "I'll have to hold your hand until you're ready. You let me know when you're ready." And, finally, after releasing the child's hand gradually, "Yes, I can see you are ready."[21]

Don't: The therapist should not lecture to the child, encourage him to "verbalize his feelings," or banish him to a "time-out" room.

> *23. The Theraplay therapist conducts his sessions without regard to whether the child "likes" him.*

Do: The Theraplay therapist does his work and attempts to convey to the child that there is something about him (the child) which is likable, regardless of whether or not the child views him (the therapist) in the same way.

Don't: The Theraplay therapist does not "seduce" the child by lowering demands, obliterating conflicts, or withdrawing challenge in order to gain his admiration, fondness, or love (Robertiello, 1975, p. 12).

> *24. The Theraplay therapist curtails and prevents excessive anxiety or motoric hyperactivity.*

Do: The Theraplay therapist maintains a careful watch and firm control so that the child will not experience excessive anxiety or find himself too "wound up."

Don't: If the therapist feels the child is too bewildering or makes him uncomfortable or if the therapist finds the session boring or moving too slowly, he must neither prod nor "wind up" the child nor pass along his own anxiety. Rather, he must attempt to convey extra reassurance and calm leadership.

> *25. The Theraplay therapist attends to physical hurts.*

Do: However minor the bumps or cuts, the therapist nurses them tenderly.

Don't: The therapist is not concerned with unconscious causes underlying the hurt. Nor does he concern himself with whether attention will reward self-destructive behavior or with whether regressive caring of this kind may preclude later autonomy.

26. The Theraplay therapist, when at a loss for ideas, incorporates the child's body movements into his repertoire.

Do: The therapist uses the child's slightest movement as a foundation on which he builds a Theraplay maneuver (Ernestine Thomas, personal communication). Thus even mute, immobile, stone-faced children provide programs for Theraplay when they blush, look down, keep their faces expressionless, or plant their feet to the flooring. "Oh, you hold your face *so* still! Here. Let me see how you *do* that" (peering at child). "You keep such a straight, stiff back! I wonder if I can do mine that way. Is that right? Is this? What a *neat* trick you have!" For children who resist overtly, the program is easier yet: "You have the quickest scoot when you scoot away like that. *Do* it again! Oh, you really are a super scooter. Oh! There! You scooted away some more . . . and some more. I'm going to scoot too. You show me how you do that. Is this the way?" All of this is done lightly, warmly, interestedly—neither threateningly nor demeaningly. "Oh! There you did it just right! You swung around and turned your back! You're a mighty good back swinger. Let me see you do that again!" "What you got there on the insides of your fists? Let me look! Oh, you got a palm there! Wow! And another one *there*? Let me see if you got one in your other hand too . . ." (Regina Roth, personal communication). "You pull your arms away so strong . . . Look! *Both* arms! Now *that* is *one* neat trick!"

Don't: In the presence of the child, the skilled Theraplay therapist is never at a loss for ideas. He never remains preoccupied and silent, never searches to fill his repertoire.

Custom Tailoring

As has been stated earlier, children are referred for Theraplay for a number of problems, complaints, behaviors, and maladjustments. Symptoms range from aggressive acting out and

Running Commentary of Theraplay Session
Therapist (Susan Riley) and Autistic Six-Year-Old

(Therapist's Statements)

"Where's Sherry gone? Where's Sherry gone?"

"*You're* a wiggly one."

"Where's Susan? Oh (laughs). Here's Susan."

"Where's Sherry. *There* she is!"

"No crying now. Push. Push *hard!*"

"Ooh! You pushed me over! *Right* over! You're *strong!* *Do* it again!"

hyperactivity on the one hand to psychosomatic illnesses, learning disabilities, and withdrawal on the other. The severity of problems ranges from autism and schizophrenia to neurosis or classroom misbehavior. The overriding therapeutic goal for all referrals, of course, is to help the child replace inappropriate solutions or behavior with healthy, creative, and age-appropriate ones.

The Theraplay technique as it has been broadly defined is equally applicable to virtually all children referred for help. However, some Theraplay approaches are appropriate to one kind of child, while other Theraplay approaches are appropriate to others.

Using the normal mother-infant unit as the model, the following are the classifications of maternal behavior that are being considered for their attachment-promoting and autonomy-enhancing qualities: (1) Structuring behavior, (2) Challenging behavior, (3) Intruding behavior, and (4) Nurturing behavior. Some examples follow:

1. *Structuring.* The mother limits, defines, forbids, outlines, reassures, speaks firmly,[22] labels, names, clarifies, confines, holds, and restrains her baby.
2. *Challenging.* The mother teases, dares, encourages, varies, chases, and plays peek-a-boo with her baby. She offers her cheeks for grabbing, makes noises for imitating, and wiggles her fingers for catching.
3. *Intruding.* The mother tickles, bounces, swings, surprises, giggles, hops at, and pounces on her baby.
4. *Nurturing.* The mother rocks, nurses, holds, nuzzles, feeds, cuddles, envelops, caresses, lies next to, and hugs her baby.

Perhaps because, as infants, some children had too little of some kinds and some children had too little of other kinds of attachment-fostering and autonomy-enhancing experiences or had a particular ratio of affection to direction (Marschak, 1979) at a time when another ratio would have been more appropriate (or had an inappropriate quality thereof), different children with different problems require different kinds of remediation.

Again, simplistically stated, and divided for purposes of easier prescription into motoric and ideational, their differing behaviors classify them as acting with or through their bodies or acting "in their heads." Motoric behaviors describe those activities that can be clearly observed in the classroom or on the playground to differentiate one child from his peer group. At one extreme of severity of motoric deviance is autistic twiddling, twirling, rocking, or catatonic posturing. At the other is hyperactivity or withdrawn lethargy, aggressive acting out or passive clinging. Ideational behaviors take place in the realm of ideas, or thought, or fantasies. Often the presence of ideational pathology becomes apparent only through an analysis of talking or drawing or after a close scrutiny of facial expressions. The overt movements may appear age appropriate, while the covert communications are not. At one extreme of severity, thought pathology is schizophrenic; at the other, it is obsessive or phobic.

Although children's behaviors differ widely and one autistic child, for example, may look quite different from the next, it is possible to arrive at some suggestions for custom-tailored Theraplay. It may be counterproductive to engage a child who requires Nurturing in an activity that is primarily Challenging. It may be unnecessarily rigid to limit a child who needs both Challenging and Intruding to only one and not the other.

If a program is not custom tailored, its course may be a hodge-podge of trial-and-error encounters. When there is no purpose and no direction, the benefits of one session or one gambit may be canceled by the blunders of the next.

Children with different problems, different life experiences, different coping styles, and different everyday behavior patterns require different kinds and degrees of Theraplay, but certain specified behaviors within the therapy situation itself also may preclude, or at least call for greatly modified, Theraplay. These styles, histories, and so on can be assessed according to two different sets of criteria: (1) the children's lives outside of the Theraplay room and (2) their behavior during the session. The assessment of both is necessary if we are to do Theraplay that is responsive to the special needs of each individual child.

Outside influences are assessed through the intake interview in clinics and mental health centers and through teacher and social worker reports (if parent interviews are not possible) in schools. The intake interview is described in detail in Chapter Five. The conscientious therapist carefully monitors the child's behavior during the Theraplay session for signs of a possible need to revise the treatment plan. The following illustrate such behaviors.

1. *Physical discomfort.* The child responds to physical contact with genuine distress (not for the purposes of manipulation, which will be described later). Such a reaction may not rule out the eventual use of the touching aspects of Theraplay. For the moment, however, other applications of the technique are recommended, such as peek-a-boo, singing, therapist "tricks," and clowning.

2. *Fear.* The child appears genuinely frightened. (Again, this is not the display of fearfulness that is designed to discourage intimacy, also to be described later.) Theraplay must be introduced more gradually than is generally indicated.

3. *Overexcitement.* Some of the Theraplay activities appear to overexcite the child. A modified technique must be used.

4. *Eroticized perception.* The child responds to the Theraplay activities by becoming sexually stimulated. This happens in rare cases (usually where a child's home experience has made him sexually responsive to all physical contact). A modified technique must be used.

5. *Request for enlightenment.* The child asks for information, not as a means of controlling the session (to be discussed later), but because he has a genuine need for information. Theraplay techniques are held in abeyance until the therapist has met the need.

6. *Sharing an unhappy experience.* The child tells an unhappy story, not so that the session shall proceed according to his own rather than the therapist's plans, but because he has a genuine need to express his unhappy feelings. The therapist puts aside his program until after the child has told his story.

7. *Genuine expression of anger.* The child shows angry

behavior other than that which is designed to keep the therapist at bay. The therapist acknowledges the child's angry feelings (saying, for example, "I know you don't like it when I do that," "You look awful mad at me," or "I can see you're feeling angry") and if necessary holds the child rather than permits attacks on himself (for example, saying, "I can see you're angry, but I can't let you hit me"). To spin or flip or tickle a child who is experiencing genuine anger is to mislabel his feelings. To mislabel his feelings is akin to mislabeling his body parts (although deliberate mislabeling of body parts in the spirit of fun is appropriate at other times).

8. *Ethnic and cultural differences.* The consideration of each client's ethnic and cultural origins is crucial to his diagnosis (Moses, 1978) and to the planning of his or her particular program of Theraplay. Not only do the quantity, location, or time of the sessions vary according to cultural milieu, but also the emphasis, methods, and treatment goals most certainly must be taken into account. A shy little girl in a Chinatown kindergarten may require no treatment at all. A withdrawn Italian adolescent may be quite another story. Involving a Puerto Rican or Egyptian mother in family Theraplay may be easy. Involving a Puerto Rican or Egyptian father may be impossible. Body contact may be acceptable to a family from one milieu, taboo for a family from another.

9. *Socioeconomic differences.* When mapping out a particular Theraplay strategy for use with a particular child, not only must the child's pathology be taken into account, but, especially in working with his family, socioeconomic circumstances, in addition to the aforementioned cultural ones, must be considered also. In families that arbitrarily structure and strictly and punitively enforce, the children's needs and wishes are often of only secondary importance. In families where their needs and wishes are paramount, however, structure, rules, and clear authority may be virtually absent. Although there are a good many exceptions, these two approaches can generally be said to have two broad socioeconomic correlates. Working-class and poor parents of necessity often deal with their children in a practical, short, authoritarian, and arbitrary way. "Family

democracy"; lengthy, all-family discussions; and intensive attention to the psyches of their individual children are luxuries the poor can ill afford. Permissive attitudes and permissive behavior on the part of parents toward their children require patience, and patience requires time. Families laboring under the real strains of everyday living often do not have the time for patient attention to any one family member—least of all to those members not yet capable of contributing financially. There are exceptions, but it can be safely stated that a child born into a blue-collar or deprived rural or urban family is less likely to be patiently listened to than is the child whose parents are middle class. In poor families, often not even husband and wife communicate extensively. The dinner table, which in middle-class homes is frequently the forum for discussion of family issues and individual ideas and experiences, is often in lower-class families the scene of virtually silent, task-performance eating. As for playfulness or fun, one welfare mother explained the role of "fun" in her family this way: "How can I have fun with my children? The world they're going into isn't fun. Isn't nothing out there except work and hunger and a lot of danger." Middle-class parents, however, are often (although not always) overly concerned with "understanding" and with encouraging open expression of feelings—often, in the process, giving in to their child's every mood, need, and inner wish. They fear, they say, that they may squelch his creativity, alienate his affections, interfere with his social comfort, or frustrate him in some other way. They lean over backward to avoid being authoritarian. It is for this latter population, no doubt, that Robertiello (1975) wrote his book *Hold Them Very Close, Then Let Them Go.*

The difference between the two groups is nowhere more apparent than in parent group discussions, in the way the two groups perform the MIM, or in discussion sessions during family Theraplay. The working-class parents ask, "What do you mean, 'Let him play'? Life is hard. It wouldn't be right to let him think he could play. He may think he can play forever."

The middle-class parents say, "Who are we, his parents, to think we have the right to make decisions for him or tell him what to do?" The results of the two approaches, of course, are quite different. The freedom offered the middle-class child often makes him anxious (Kris, 1950). The strictures on the lower-class child may make him feel impotent. Thus, whereas the middle-class child often needs limits, not laissez faire, the lower-class child needs stimulation and the freedom to explore.

To the extent that Theraplay remedies early deficiencies, the particular Theraplay emphasis may vary with the particular social class. Theraplay for children of middle-class parents may include more Structuring; Theraplay for poor children may include Intruding. Children in both classes who have been too early Challenged (to be toilet trained, for example, or to read), may need Nurturing. Because a child referred for treatment often has been reared unempathically, his Theraplay therapist must remain especially "in tune."

Particularly for therapists doing family Theraplay, it is often helpful to keep social class differences in mind. Nothing emphasizes so clearly the danger of following hard and fast rules as the fact that a set of Theraplay principles quite appropriate for a family of one social class may be totally inappropriate for a family of another. Thus, although Theraplay therapists may work to help middle-class parents do less listening, discussing, or reasoning with their children, they may advise lower-class parents to do just that. In both cases, the interpreting therapist guides the parents through demonstration, participation, discussion, and the giving of active family homework assignments. Observing behind the one-way mirror while their child is engaged in a Theraplay session, the interpreting therapist may ask middle-class parents, "You see how Jimmy keeps trying to engage them in a discussion of why he can't do this and that? Notice what they do each time he does that?" The parent may answer with some surprise, "Why, yes. They seem to be ignoring him. They just go on about the game they're playing with him. Why do they do that?" And the interpreting therapist explains, "If they respond to the topics he brings up, the session will go exactly as he decrees it should. Then it will be quite predictable from his point of view, and he will have learned nothing. He does too much running of the show that way already. The therapists want to demonstrate to him that it's safe to let someone else be in charge once in a while. They want to show him that it can even be fun to be surprised." Observing their child in Theraplay, the parents of a lower-class child, however, may be asked, "Notice how Kevin is being encouraged to ask questions and to tell how he feels about what's happening?" The parents may be puzzled. "Why do they want to know that?" they may ask. The interpreting therapist, whose role of translator to the parents as they observe their child's session is detailed in Chapter Five, explains, "They want to help him see that what he says and what he wishes and what he feels are important. They want him to understand that because he is so special he can make an impact on his world." Homework assignments given to both kinds of families include the directive to carry out between sessions the kinds of behavior and attitudes toward their children that they (the parents) have observed behind the one-way vision screen.

10. *Differences in family styles.* Just as families differ according to who constitutes "the family" (for example, grandparents, foster children, infants, and next-door neighbors), and what their social class is, so they differ also according to their history (that is, legends of their forebears and experience with one another), their tradition, their behavior codes (for example, morality or life-style—including noisy or quiet [see Hess and Handel, 1959]), their living space (open farm land, cramped apartment, indoor versus outdoor climate), and so on. All of this, of course, will be understood through careful interview, skilled inference, and alert observation. And all of this, in turn, determines Theraplay strategy.

"What If . . . ?"

The following discussion of "What if . . . ?" pertains primarily to the question, "What if a child for whom Theraplay is indicated behaves in a certain peculiar manner?" Additionally, it pertains to the question, "What if the therapist begins to feel inadequate?"

Most of the difficulties confronting the beginning therapist arise from (1) the child's resistance to the therapist's efforts to Nurture him; (2) the child's resistance to the therapist's efforts to limit, organize, or Structure; (3) the child's resistance to the therapist's efforts to Intrude on him; and (4) the child's resistance to the therapist's efforts to Challenge him. Above all else, almost all children seen in Theraplay, to a greater or lesser degree, resist acknowledging that the therapist is in charge.

The avoidance of intimacy on the child's part may take any number of forms. He may escape Structuring, Challenging, Intruding, or Nurturing (SCIN) efforts by withdrawing, running away, rocking, reading, or "discussing." Possibly the greater his underlying need for closeness, the greater is his determination to avoid it and the more intense will be his efforts to "escape." With the rationale, "He's too uncomfortable when I come close," the beginning Theraplay therapist may feel inclined to "cool" the relationship. The experienced therapist addresses himself directly to the intensity of the need (which, he has come to assume, underlies an equally intense drive to pull away), whether this underlying need be for Structure and limit setting, for Challenge, for Intrusion, or for comfort, cuddling, and Nurturing. Many children, in addition, need someone to take control of their lives at last.

Given the importance of setting straight the child's earlier deficits, it becomes the job of the Theraplay therapist (1) to be aware of the frustrated needs, (2) to remain therapeutic in spite of determined resistance, and (3) to be certain that in meeting the child's needs the therapist is not motivated to satisfy some unfulfilled desires in himself. Some of the issues that arise when the therapist attempts to maintain the approach and attitude dictated by these first two points will be discussed in this section. The third point will be taken up in the section on countertransference (Chapter Twelve).

"What if He Will Not even Let Me Relate to Him?"

Let us begin by considering those children referred for Theraplay who clearly try to escape relating to their therapists. They may do this through refusal to participate, appealing to others, attempting to attack the therapist, or trying to run away. They may attempt to hurt themselves, become hyperactive or bizarre, go limp, cry, or masturbate. These behaviors, if left unchecked, interfere with, or altogether preclude, an intimate relationship between therapist and child, at least in the immediate future. (Traditional forms of child psychotherapy may indeed advocate the therapist's acknowledging the child's uneasy state of mind, but in general, except for reflecting his feelings or interpreting his underlying wishes, fears, and impulses, they encourage him to move at his own pace.) Theraplay may acknowledge how the child is feeling but seldom allows him to move at his own pace. The Theraplay therapist, on the contrary, rather than "permitting" the child to remain in his private world, insistently tries to extricate him from it. The Theraplay therapist, rather than acting as though he were another (albeit healthy) part of the child's inner self, persists in making his unique, differentiated presence felt. Like the autonomy-enhancing parent, the Theraplay therapist puts a stop to "unhealthy" behavior. The therapist in the Theraplay session actively prevents the child from being hyperactive, from running away, from hurting himself or his therapist, from angrily withdrawing, and from behaving peculiarly. The Theraplay therapist always repositions the child so that there can be good eye contact and so that the activity can be redirected toward self-esteem and fun.

"What if He Particularly Resists My Nurturing and Indulging Overtures?"

Behaviors of children denying their need for nurturance are included in the list of clearly recognizable escape maneuvers. Particularly characteristic of these children is the intensity of their drive. Unhindered, they either hit hard, curse loud, withdraw angrily, and run fast, or they ceaselessly reason, argue, and debate. The Theraplay therapist, always in the spirit of fun, must often be as loud, as hard, as fast, or as immune to legalisms as they are legalistic. Because "saving face" is so especially important to these children, nurturing activities should be offered both imaginatively and playfully. Baby bottles, for example, could be used first for squirting the milk from a distance in the manner of a competitive sport.

More often than not, Nurturing is a most effective form of Theraplay, not only for little boys who make experienced sexual overtures or verbalize obscenities far beyond their years but also for flirtatious little girls with precocious come-ons; for both, baby food feeding, soft blowing, rocking, and nursing bottles are appropriate activities.

"What if He Particularly Denies My Efforts to Structure?"

Behaviors of children denying their need for structure tend to be more subtle, more adept, more beguiling. Before the therapist has had a chance to recognize how it happened, for example, the child has rearranged the rules. Since the value of Theraplay for a child who does this lies in his being the recipient of someone else's rules and structure, the Theraplay therapist must be constantly in control and vigilant of the child's efforts to defeat him. Children who deny their need for Structure may do so by (1) attempting to take the initiative, (2) defying the therapist, or (3) "engaging" him. Initiating may include telling the therapist what to do or deciding what he himself will do. Defying the therapist includes countering the therapist's suggestion with one of his own or, in response to a therapist-initiated activity, pleading pain, incompetence, boredom, or obedience ("My mother won't let me"). "Engagement" includes "cute" behavior, scintillating discussion, insightful observations, scholarly questions, and bringing toys, books, or food from home. Any experienced child therapist will quickly recognize how difficult it is to resist and divert these maneuvers. Indeed, traditional child therapy may capitalize on them. Seen by traditional therapists as expressions of the child's real inner life, these behaviors are often utilized as the key to further exploration of fantasy, wish, dream, and memory. The Theraplay therapist, however, views these maneuvers as tactics employed by the child who, fearful of giving himself over to someone else's lead, uses these ways to maintain his familiar position of vigilant control over himself and his world. The therapist, having recognized the maneuver, must insist on staying in charge. Even at the risk of invoking a temper tantrum, he must "stick to his guns." Although he must not do this cruelly or arbitrarily or inappropriately with regard to the child's capacities, he must try his best to be firm and consistent, yet patient and kind.

1. *Initiative.* In the event that the child initiates what the therapist was about to do anyway, the therapist must quickly change his own plan or at least be prepared to modify it.

2. *Defiance.* If the child defies the therapist by resisting or challenging the initial therapeutic overtures, the therapist must nonetheless persist. He should get caught up neither in arguing nor in defending his position. "This is what we're going to do today," he says, "so let's get started." The temper tantrum results when the child is confronted with demands obviously at odds with what he wants at that moment. The therapist must stay with the child through the tantrum and not allow it to dissuade him from his plan for the therapy. While flexibility, spontaneity, and alertness to cues coming from the child are important ingredients of the Theraplay therapist's behavior, these should not be used as crutches to avoid unpleasant confrontations with the child. There is no need for discussion, apology, or backing off, nor does Theraplay subscribe to sending the child off to a room to reflect on his behavior. Rather, the issue stands, the tantrum having persuaded no one. The therapist assures the child that he is right there with him (thereby letting him know that he is "safe" and that this behavior does not make him "bad"). He communicates that he will hold him firmly if he is in danger of hurting the therapist or himself, and in the meantime he acknowledges that this state of things has its painful aspects for which he (the therapist) can provide relief.

3. *"Engagement."* The word "engagement" has been placed in quotes because it represents resistance rather than genuine engagement. Its motives are not to *enjoy* the company of the other, but to make him a slave. "Engagement" consists of flattery, of offering interesting discussions, humorous anecdotes, news items, fantasy or dream revelations, and questions. The "engaging" child is irresistible—every child therapist's

model patient. It is far easier for the therapist to respond to the proffered goodies than to persist with his original intent by ignoring, changing the subject, deflecting the theme, and so on. The skilled Theraplay therapist expects the "engagement" play from particular kinds of patients and thus is prepared, gently but firmly, to regain the structuring position.

"What if He Will Not Allow Me to Intrude on Him?"

Among the ways children in Theraplay resist Intrusion are crying, feigning illness, becoming limp, arching their backs, and protesting verbally. The Theraplay therapist must be very sure to assess the situation exactly—both the child's actual underlying need and his own motivation (see Chapter Twelve). Given that the aims for both are exclusively health promoting, the Theraplay therapist must be consistent but not rigid, intent on intruding but not without fun. He must be willing to back off momentarily to allow the child to "save face," but he must not be conned into changing his overall strategy.

"What if He Resists My Challenging?"

The child who clings to infantile symbiosis responds to the therapist's challenges with further regression. Asked to stand, he lies; required to ask for something, he points. The skillful therapist determines how quickly he can be expected to progress without sacrificing the pleasure of being challenged. Therapist Brenda Winslow describes her work with an infantile, clinging child as follows: "I went to put Tammy down, and she would not straighten her legs out. I said, 'Hey, let me see those strong legs of yours.' She then straightened her legs, and we walked out of the room. I told her what a big girl she was and tried to guess how old she was. I started at 'seven' and worked down. We did some bouncing, jumping and flips. I took the flip in stages, first putting her up on my waist, then letting her touch the floor backward. Next I put her on my shoulders and gave her a flip. Yet through her helplessness and nonparticipation she still tried to 'control' what we did. When it was time to go, she began to act like a baby. I told her again that it was time to go and that I would be back. She still wouldn't come out of the baby behavior. So I had her act like a soldier. I said, 'Let me see how tall you can stand. Look how tall you are. Look at this big girl. Come on, let's go.' I had her jump down the steps. And we walked like soldiers back to her classroom." Challenges may also be presented in paradoxical form (Frankl, 1963, p. 196); for example, "I'll bet you can't tell me where you go to hang your coat"; "I want you to stay curled up there ; now put your thumb in your mouth"; or, pointing to his red shirt, "That's a pretty green shirt you have."

"What if He Cries?"

Before he can appropriately respond to a child's crying, the therapist must determine the reason for it. Crying in Theraplay may be a genuine, direct response to internally or externally generated pain or may be the end result of the child's conscious (or unconscious) manipulation. Thus, before taking action, it is important for the therapist to decide whether the crying is in response to physical sickness, genuine sadness, anger, or fear or whether it is an attempt to keep the therapist away—by evoking his pity, shame, guilt, or anxiety. If it is manipulation, the course of action will be reasonably clear, as outlined earlier in this chapter, in the section on resistance. If the therapist concludes that the crying is a function of illness, sadness, anger, or fear, however, his alternatives become more complex and demand further evaluation.

If illness is causing the crying, the therapist must determine its severity. Minor discomfort calls for slowed-down activity and an increase in vigilance. Major discomfort calls for discontinuation of the session altogether and for placing the child in the hands of a responsible caretaker. Yet it should be noted that therapists conducting home-based Theraplay (see Chapter Six) can see an ill child at the bedside. Plenty of Theraplay activities can be conducted with both therapist and child closely confined and relatively quiet. Cool cloths, peek-a-boo, and "messages" written or pictures drawn on tummies in baby powder, for example, can all serve to make a child feel the continued and joyful intimacy with his therapist, an intimacy sometimes all the more necessary during times of illness and concomitant isolation and worry.

If sadness is causing the crying, the therapist must be in tune with the sadness. Both verbally and nonverbally, he must communicate to the child that he understands that the child is feeling very sad. He must not attempt to cheer him, distract him, or tell him he "will be feeling better soon."

If anger underlies the crying, the therapist must acknowledge the anger, permitting expression of it if appropriate. Extending the palms of the therapist's hands for hitting, for example, provides the child a harmless outlet and the knowledge that his feelings are legitimate yet still within the adult's control. Ernestine Thomas, in the film *Here I Am* (Jernberg, Hurst, and Lyman, 1969) tells Pat "I can see you're angry . . ." then, extending the palms of her hands for hitting, directs her, "*harder* than *that, harder* than *that. Bigger* than *that!*" Extending a human hand conveys more understanding of the angry feelings than does the directive to "punch Bobo" or to throw darts at a dartboard. The palms of the hands allow the therapist to receive the blows without discomfort or ambivalence. No other body part serves this purpose so well. Giving the command to hit, rather than being a passive recipient only, conveys adult control and responsibility and thus ensures that the angry activity will not go out of bounds.

If fear is the reason for the crying, the therapist's alternatives become more complicated yet and thus necessitate further evaluation. It must be determined whether the child's fear is a function of the situation's novelty, the separation from teacher or parent, the intrusion of the therapist, or the fear of being in a bodily off-balance position, possibly stemming from a vestibular defect. If novelty of the situation (for example, the new adult or the strange room) is causing the child to cry, the therapist may acknowledge this briefly ("You never met me before, so you're frightened") but then moves on quickly ("But we've got such *fun* things to do together, like *this* trick . . ."). Or, if the child shows only mild apprehension, the therapist may ignore the crying altogether. If separation from mother or teacher is the problem, the therapist will briefly reassure the crying child (for example, "Mommy's waiting for you right outside" or "You'll go back to see your teacher just as soon as I check to see what you brought to school today inside these nice striped socks . . . ooh, you brought some yummy toes. Here, let me see . . . And now I want to . . ."). If the child's crying seems to stem from fear of the therapist's intrusions and if this crying is not in fact an effort to ward intrusions off, then the therapist will have to reevaluate the appropriateness of his actions. Sometimes a momentary retreat may indeed be called for—but momentary backing off is generally all that is needed. Thus the therapist may want to voice aloud, "I can see I frightened you. I don't want to frighten you. We won't do that any more. Tell you what I'm going to do instead . . ." (Ernestine Thomas, personal communication). This possibility for the therapist to "back off" emphasizes once again that, while Theraplay is authoritarian, it is not sadistic or tyrannical.

The fear of being in an off-balance position is found more often in autistic children than in any others. The parents report that from early on these children protested bitterly to being held at an angle or in a horizontal position, or to being raised up high. Now, in Theraplay, the protest continues. Each time the therapist moves the child from the vertical, the pained moans or the screaming begins. The biological, possibly vestibular, origin of this kinesthetic nightmare cannot be ruled out. Nor can biological origins be ruled out as underlying the apparent physical discomfort and resulting panic that some autistic children seem to experience when, for example, the soles of their feet make contact with a foreign body (such as slippers, skates, or finger paint). In our experience, there are only two possible alternatives for dealing with these terrors: (1) the therapist can agree that these are areas of experience too dangerous for the child to undertake and therefore not worth venturing out to meet (even if such restrictions do make for a seriously curtailed life-style), or (2) the therapist can help the child look beyond the immediate misery and urge him to explore and learn to tolerate these painful stimuli (just as he learns to tolerate new tastes, new sounds, new sensations, and new relationships) all in the effort to broaden his horizons and thus his self-confidence and his trust in the world as a safe and manageable place. The degree to which these new sensations are pushed on the child, and the intensity with which he is expected to experience them, are entirely a function of the Theraplay therapist's sensitivity and skill.

> *Permeating All Other Beginning Therapists' "What If"*
> *Questions Are "What If I Run Out of Ideas?" and*
> *"What If Another Adult Criticizes Me?"*

1. *What if I run out of ideas?* The very best antidote to running out of ideas is periodic, volunteer, playful interaction with (or observation of a parent with) a normal six-, ten-, or fifteen-month-old, followed by the same with a normal pre-school child. Not only will this feel refreshing, but it will generate new approaches and new variations on old themes. Another antidote, of course, is observation of a fellow Theraplay therapist.

Of more immediate help, if the therapist runs out of ideas within the session, is to use as a "takeoff base" the child's own (unwitting) contribution. Thus, a leg that pulls away, a face that looks away, or an inadvertent or objecting sound all can provide the foundation on which the particular activity of the moment is built. An averted face can lead the therapist to exclaim "Oh, you turn your head so good! Here, let me see how you did that!" or "Pull it away! Pull your arm away! That's it. You're tricky, you know that? The way you pull that arm away?" Thus, when all else fails, the therapist at a loss for new activities can turn to the child's own reactions as a ready-made pool of innovative ideas.

2. *What if another adult criticizes me?* Criticism by another adult is to be expected in most settings that traditionally look with suspicion on, for example, crying and regressive, boisterous, intimate, physical, and joyful interactions between child and adult. Schoolteachers or principals, nurses, and some parents require extra attention if they are to be prevented from

sabotaging therapeutic progress. The Theraplay therapist learns to make it part of his work to explain his technique to adults without hampering his interaction with children. With confidence, he tells the worried bystander, "Josie is going to be all right"; communicates, "I know very well what I'm doing"; and adds, "I'd love to talk to you about it later on if you have a moment." Given a response like this one, few adults will continue their concern.

Two final comments regarding "What if's": (1) The beginning Theraplay therapist should remember that he is not alone in having these concerns, and (2) the more experienced he becomes, the less the "What if's" will haunt him.

Notes

1. "Like the mother, the therapist has to become the entire world of [the patient] during the therapy session. The goal of the therapist is definitely not to bring the patient to learn how to perceive himself and how to relate to others. More basically, the effort is to foster a maturational process in [the patient] by repeatedly involving his affective-interest-cathexis in various parts of himself and in totality of himself as responding to the therapist's presence" (Des Lauriers, 1962, p. 64). While Des Lauriers in this book discusses only schizophrenic children, we have found that many of his observations are pertinent to a wide range of children in Theraplay.

2. "Interaction occurs more and more at the initiative of the patient" (Des Lauriers, 1962, p. 152).

3. John Rosen (1953, p. 10) observes, "From the point of view of the patient, perhaps this very slovenliness is unconsciously created to make his withdrawal easier [in that] because of dirtiness he will alienate [others]. The benevolent mother will bypass the conscious disgust and . . . will respond with healing libido."

4. Although chaos may characterize the external world of autistic children, these children institute their own rigid, predictable, ritualized routines. In order that they not incorporate the Theraplay session as yet one more predictable routine, they

require in Theraplay a more varied, open, and open-ended approach than do other children (see Chapter Nine).

5. Klaus and others (1970, pp. 187-192) describe typical postdelivery behavior of the parent toward the newborn as follows: "There is a predictable and orderly progression in inspection and contact—from fingertip touching on the extremities to massaging, encompassing, and palm contact on the trunk."

6. Robertiello (1975, p. 3), writing of young adult failure cases, says the following: "What happened? How did their upbringing fail them? It seems that it failed them in that they were presented with a situation optimal for furthering their emotional growth, but one that was essentially devoid of hardships, deprivations, and challenges that they would have had to fight to overcome. Because of this, they never developed the particular kind of strength necessary for meeting such challenges. That strength is what is essential to the achievement of success in any area."

7. "Skin sensations, touch, pressure, warm, and cold are most important . . . to help bring the child's attention to his own physical boundaries and to his distinction and separation from his therapist" (Des Lauriers, 1962, p. 73).

8. "The more you tell your child he is beautiful, adorable, lovable, the more he will be apt to grow up that way. Whereas being 'permissive' and vacillating about discipline and being overprotective can be very destructive to a child, being adoring can be very helpful" (Robertiello, 1975, p. 85).

9. Des Lauriers (1962, p. 142): "With the awareness of his (the patient's) permanence and stability, the patient has a point of reference from which he can recognize what is not permanent, what is not stable, what passes in a transient sort of way. The therapist reinforces this experience by changing routines."

10. "Like the mother, the therapist has to become the entire world of the patient during the therapy session" (Des Lauriers, 1962, p. 64). "The therapist constantly makes sure that the patient recognizes him always as an intruding reality in his life" (Des Lauriers, 1962, p. 141).

11. "We believe that some teachers are more positive in

their attitude toward children and are, perhaps, better teachers. If children are fortunate enough to begin their schooling with an optimistic teacher who expects them to do well . . . they are likely to perform better than those exposed to a teacher who conveys a discouraging, self-defeating outlook" (Pederson, Faucher, and Eaton, 1978, p. 23). "It was said of Miss A's teaching that 'it did not matter what background or abilities the beginning pupil had; there was no way that the pupil was not going to read by the end of grade one' " (Pederson, Faucher, and Eaton, 1978, p. 22).

12. "If, from the very beginning, the mother were so 'good' that she would instantly provide the complete satisfaction of every need of her child, there would be, as Fenichel (1937) pointed out, no ego formation, no experience of, or relationship to, reality" (Des Lauriers, 1962, p. 102). "If the object were so totally attractive as to have no negative values of painful or frustrating quality, it could be expected that it would become lost in the subject, or that the subject would lose himself in it" (Des Lauriers, 1962, p. 35).

13. Rosen (1953, pp. 16-17): "The patient's aggression must be brought under control. . . . We explain it this way: The idealized mother must protect her child, and sometimes this protection involves controlling his uncontrollable behavior. . . . If you protect him from his aggression, he will neither be punished according to the Mosaic law nor will he be called upon to suffer the unbearable guilt feelings that accompany rage and destruction directed against a love object. The patient learns that his aggression is nowhere near the world-shaking catastrophe that he envisioned. Furthermore, he takes another look at you with a new kind of interest, seeing you as a person who can protect him in the real world."

14. "The therapist cannot allow the patient to be overwhelmed by anxiety or any other wild, uncontrolled feeling any more than he can allow him to be carried away by wild, uncontrolled actions that would destroy any possibility of ego development or reality structure" (Des Lauriers, 1962, p. 86).

15. In this connection, Pederson, Faucher, and Eaton (1978) in the field of education have recently produced a relevant study. When Teacher A's pupils were followed into adulthood, they were found to be markedly higher in status than

were pupils of Teachers B, C, and so on: "She invariably stayed after hours to help children. Not only did her pupils remember her, but she apparently could remember each former pupil by name even after an interval of twenty years. She adjusted to new math and reading methods, but her secret for success was summarized by a former colleague this way: 'How did she teach? With a lot of love!' One would add, with a lot of confidence in children and hard work" (p. 20). "Despite the general difficulty of remembering every teacher, not a single subject who had been in Miss A's class failed to recall that fact correctly. Of those who had *not* been Miss A's pupils in first grade, 31 percent had no recollection of who their teacher had been, fewer than half identified their first-grade teacher correctly, and four subjects incorrectly named Miss A as their teacher" (p. 19).

16. "The therapist cannot allow delusional or autistic behavior to be carried on in his presence" (Des Lauriers, 1962, p. 86). "He must be directly helped to control the ideational" (p. 77).

17. "The child may reflect on whether the parental rewards received are solely contingent on performance (exchange) or whether they are signals of parental love and esteem (signification)" (Jones and Berglas, 1978, p. 204).

18. To quote Allport (1956, p. 92), "The neurotic who learns to laugh at himself may be on the way to self-management, perhaps to cure."

19. "The therapist must give reality structure to her (the patient's) experience. By staying with her and continuing to intrude on her, he demonstrates, in fact, that her hatred has no devastating proportions, that he is with her in her fears and anxieties, and that he also cares very much for her" (Des Lauriers, 1962, p. 86). See also Rosen (1953, pp. 16-17).

20. Jay Haley describes how one mother has learned how to handle a tyrannical child: "His mother . . . smiled at him, seized him, threw him quickly to the floor on his stomach, and sat . . . upon him. . . . The boy struggled furiously against the odds of his mother's weight, strength, and watchful dexterity. He yelled, screamed, shouted profanities and obscenities [and] sobbed. . . . With the [episode] finally finished, the mother got

up and so did [the boy]. . . . At bedtime [the boy] went to bed voluntarily" (Haley, 1973, pp. 214-216).

21. First observed by the author in use by Mona Podore in her Hyde Park Unitarian Cooperative Nursery School, Chicago.

22. "A significant difference was found between mothers of disturbed and mothers of normal control children in the assertiveness of voice quality associated with the verbal expression of approval and disapproval. Mothers of normal control children demonstrated more assertive voice quality when expressing verbal approval and disapproval than when making neutral statements. In a direct pattern, the mothers of disturbed children used less assertive voice qualities when expressing verbal approval or disapproval than when making neutral statements" (Bugental and Love, 1975, p. 3).

3

Individual
Theraplay
for Children

Treatment

The Theraplay that is carried on in individual sessions with children provides the prototype for all other Theraplay endeavors. Group Theraplay, crisis intervention Theraplay, individual Theraplay with adults, and diagnostic Theraplay, for example, are variations on this one original theme. Therefore, a case of individual Theraplay with a child will be shown in detail; other examples of Theraplay will be sketched.

Individual Theraplay can take place at any of several locations. Generally, it tends to be home based, school based, or clinic based.

Pat, the little girl to be presented in this chapter on individual Theraplay, receives her treatment at school. School-based
Theraplay, as mentioned before, is usually carried out on referral by the school's (or a consulting) psychologist.

Pat's sessions were filmed (Jernberg, Hurst, and Lyman,
1969), and the film's narrator describes the treatment course
and process as follows:

Here I Am

[Scene opens with Pat, in the midst of a group of active children, lying alone curled up in a corner of her preschool classroom.]

*Narrator: Pat desperately needs a Theraplay therapist.
She is withdrawn, unnaturally quiet, and considered strange by
other children. While they play cheerful games, she curls up in a
corner and will not answer when spoken to. She has been this
way since the beginning of Head Start, three months ago.*

*When Pat was referred for help, her teacher said of her,
"She does not communicate with other children at all. She iso-
lates herself. She doesn't talk to them. She never speaks of her
own accord. She is considered odd by her classmates."*

*Pat is withdrawn. She will try to ignore her therapist and
act oblivious of the camera crew.*

[Pat and her therapist, Ernestine Thomas, wearing coats, arrive
in the basement room, across the street from Pat's school, for
their first Theraplay session.]

Session 1

Therapist: Take off your coat. I'm going to put my coat right
              over here, and yours . . . I'll put yours . . . right
              on top.

*As a first step in therapy, Mrs. Thomas will insist that Pat
be aware of her every moment the two are together. She will
demand that Pat speak to her and touch her. She wants Pat to
meet her eyes.*

Therapist: Patty-cake, patty-cake, baker's man,/ Bake me a cake as fast as you can;/ roll it, and roll it, and toss it up high (raising Pat's arms),/ and get it in the tummy . . . (pokes Pat's tummy) get it in the tummy for you and I. Now you do it. Come on, that was a good game! Do it again. This way!

Pat: Uh-uh.

Therapist: . . . then I'll do it this way! Patty-cake, patty-cake, baker's man;/ bake me a . . .

Pat: Uh-um. (attempts to hit therapist's hand)

Therapist: Uh-um?

Pat: (hits therapist's extended palm)

Therapist: Do it again.

Pat: (hits again)

Therapist: Oh, harder.

Pat: (hits)

Therapist: Can you do it harder?

Pat: (hits)

Therapist: Do it harder! Harder!

Pat: (hits)

Therapist: Come on. Bigger than that.

Pat: (hits violently)

Therapist: Bigger than that.

Pat: (hits yet more violently)

Therapist: Good! Do it again!

Pat: Uh-uh.

Therapist: Do it again. Do it again. Are you getting angry? Huh? Are you angry now?

Pat reacts to these demands with anger. At the same time, she has become sharply aware of Mrs. Thomas.

Therapist: Now I know what's in your mouth. Can I have a thumb? Give me one of these good fingers . . .

Pat: Uh-uh.

Therapist: This one?

Pat: Uh-uh.

Therapist: This one?

Pat: Uh-uh.

Therapist: Uh-uh? Well, can I have this one then?
Pat: No.

Pat has just uttered her first word to her therapist—a very
important word, no.

Therapist: No?
Pat: (whimpering) No.
Therapist: Oh . . . (emphatically) Why not? Why not?
Pat: 'Cause you're evil (begins to cry).
Therapist: I'm evil? I'm not evil. I like you very much.

This is the beginning of the inevitable negative phase—a
phase essential to the child's ultimate mental health.

Therapist: Hm? Can I have some? (refers to Pat's finger) Um
              yum . . . I want some right there (reaches for her
              finger). OK. I want mine there.
Pat: (retracts her finger)
Therapist: OK, I'll take it here.
Pat: Uh-uh.
Therapist: Oh, that's good sugar. That's good sugar . . . um,
              um. That's good sugar . . . Oh, did I mess up your
              bangs? Hm?
Pat: (withdraws hand)
Therapist: Well . . . I want some fingers, too. Give me some
              fingers.
Pat: No . . . not you. (indistinguishable words, deep
              sobbing)
Therapist: Hm? Oh, I don't want you to cry. (with compas-
              sion) Don't cry . . .
Pat: (restrained sobbing)
Therapist: Don't cry. Oh? Huh?

Pat has rejected all approaches and retreated to tears.

Therapist: (sounding sorry) Oh! Don't cry.
Pat: (sobs)
Therapist: Huh?

But in spite of herself Pat has become aware of a new
friend with whom she can cuddle for comfort.

Therapist: Oh . . . don't cry. I don't want you to cry.

Session 6

[Pat and therapist enter and sit down on mat.]

Therapist: OK. I'm going to take my shoes off. You take
             yours off, hm? (takes off own and Pat's shoes)
Pat: (hides her eyes)
Therapist: You know something? I can't see you. Bend over.
             Let me see your thumb. Let me see you.
Pat: (sniffles)
Therapist: Do you need a Kleenex? Huh? Well, I've got some.
             I've got some right here. (getting Kleenex from
             purse) Let me see. (wipes Pat's eyes) Let me see if
             you look better.
Pat: (looks sullen and on the verge of tears throughout)
Therapist: Ah yes. You look better. You look better but
             you've got something stuck in your mouth. Let me
             see what that is. Let me see. Is that a lollypop? Let
             Mrs. Thomas see.
                 Ah! It's not a lollypop! It's a good thumb.
             It's a good thumb. Hey, let me see. What's this on
             your ears? (moves closer to them) There! (blowing)
             I blew it away! I blew it away!
                 What you got in your shoe? (reaches for
             Pat's shoe) You got something in your shoe? Let
             me take a look. Let me take a look. Oh, that's
             a nice shoe. Those are those new shoes. Let's
             see what's in your shoe. (removes shoe from
             Pat's foot) There's a sock! Hm! Look what I
             found!

    *Mrs. Thomas tries to make her share the intimacy and fun
of bare feet.*

Therapist: Some toes! Some toes I found!
Pat: (cries)
Therapist: Can you tell me about it, Pat? Is there something
             you want to tell me about? Hm?
Pat: (looks away, sobbing)

Pat rejects her. But today Pat is more willing to share openly all of her feelings.

Therapist:	I'm going to rock you and help you feel better, huh?
Pat:	(sobs)
Therapist:	Huh? Does that make you feel better? Hm? Here, let me show you something.
Pat:	(sobs deeply)
Therapist:	Here. Here's a Kleenex.
Pat:	(gasps; reaches for sock)
Therapist:	Oh, you're going to put your socks back on? Huh? You're going to put your stocking back on. Put your sock back on?
Pat:	(gasps loudly and sobs)
Therapist:	You need help with your sock.
Pat:	(sobs)
Therapist:	OK. (picking Pat up and straightening her dress) First of all, I'll tell you what. Come here. First of all, let's not cry. Let's not cry. Here, let's not cry.
Pat:	(sobs)
Therapist:	So . . . wipe your eyes. Wipe your eyes. Now . . .

Children like Pat often cry in the early stages of effective Theraplay. Indeed, Pat sobs uncontrollably for a full fifteen minutes. Gradually she becomes more relaxed and calm.

Therapist:	(places her hand inside Pat's shoe and moves it closer; finally "tickles" Pat's chest with it) Tickle you there (musically).

Then Mrs. Thomas again begins to press Pat in an attempt to force her to respond.

Therapist:	Tickle you there. That's what you told me to do. (lifting her) Up you go . . . and down . . . down again . . . You like being down. Huh? Let's do it again. Let's see if you can jump up high. One, two, three . . . whee! Do it again.
Pat:	(weeping) No.

Therapist: Let me wear your shoe. Here. (places Pat's shoe on top of her own) You can wear mine. You can wear mine. You can wear mine. (places Pat's foot with shoe inside her own shoe) Let's see . . . ah! See that! You got a big shoe, Pat. Is your foot that big? Huh?

Pat: (reaches to remove it)

Therapist: Take it off! Now . . . can I wear your shoe? Can I wear your shoe? (not waiting for Pat's reply) Thank you! Unbuckle it here? (continues, again not waiting for Pat's response) Huh? Should I unbuckle it? Let me see . . . let me see. How do you get it off? How do you get it off? Do you take it off right here? Like this? Just like that? Huh? Now . . . I can wear it on my hands? (puts shoe on her hand) See? I can walk on my hands . . . and I can tickle you (singing) with your very own shoe. See? I can tickle you.

Pat: (reaches for shoe)

Therapist: Do you wear shoes on your hands? Huh? Hey! You're going to give those shoes to me, aren't you?

Pat: (reluctant) No.

Therapist: Yeh. I can wear it on my head. How do I look? There. How do I look with this shoe on my head? Hm? I bet you can't find it. I bet you can't find your shoe.

Pat: (begins to cry; reaches for shoe)

Therapist: Don't cry. You can't find your shoe like that. Find it. Go on and find it, and put it on.

For the first time, we see Pat take purposeful action. She uncurls, reaches up, and takes her shoe from on top of Mrs. Thomas' head.

Therapist: You found it! You found it!

Pat: (cries)

Therapist: Now I'll have to help you . . . now I'll have to help you put it on.

Then Pat again retreats to tears.

Therapist:	Sit up. Sit up. Sit up. Here now, put it on. Come on.
Pat:	(whimpers)
Therapist:	Oh, hush the fuss and put your shoe on, girl! Come on! Put your shoe on! (helps her)

Session 11

[Mrs. Thomas and Pat enter, Pat on Mrs. Thomas' shoulders.]

Therapist:	In you go! (carries her and sets her down on table) In you go!
Pat:	(hides her eyes with her arm)
Therapist:	Look on the table . . . look on the table.

By this time, Mrs. Thomas is a familiar figure in Pat's life. Pat is still resistant. She still reverts to her old gesture of hiding her face. But today she is increasingly willing to approach Mrs. Thomas, to look at her, even to touch her deliberately.

Pat:	(stands on table, leans forward . . .)
Therapist:	Huh? You'd better watch what you're doing so you don't fall . . .
Pat:	(picks paper hat off table top)
Therapist:	Ah! Look what you've found! Put your hat on . . . come on. Can you put a hat on for me too? (does not wait for Pat's response) Huh? I need a hat. Maybe there's a surprise under my hat too. (laughs)
Pat:	(picks other paper hat off table top)
Therapist:	Oh, my goodness! Look at that! Look at that! Oh! Good job! Good job! Woops! My hat's coming off . . . my hat's coming off. (fixes it) There. Let's see how you look with these (has a beaded neck-lace) on, huh? Hold your head up. You got to move your thumb . . .
Pat:	(does so)
Therapist:	Hey! Do you remember what a horse says? Huh? Stand up. Come on, stand up. Stand up. You got

	to stand up! That a girl! You remember what a horse says? OK, let me see if you know. I'll give you a ride.
Pat:	Giddy up.
Therapist:	Whee, whee-eee. Oh-oh, he's out of gas . . .
Pat:	Giddy up.
Therapist:	You have to look up. You have to look over there at the camera crew and say "giddy up" real loud.
Pat:	Giddy up!
Therapist:	Giddy up who?
Pat:	You!
Therapist:	OK . . . whee, whee, whee. There! There! Oh-oh! I lost my fun hat. Can you get it for me?
Pat:	(retrieves fallen hat)
Therapist:	Put it on me?
Pat:	(puts hat on Mrs. Thomas; then slouches)

Pat has begun to have fun. But the moment Mrs. Thomas lets her go she returns to her familiar, withdrawn stance.

Therapist:	That's good. You can't have fun without a fun hat.

Mrs. Thomas does not permit her [Pat] to leave the scene. Slowly she cajoles her back into focus.

Therapist:	I can catch you . . . I bet I can catch you. (chasing her around table) I bet I can catch you. I bet I can catch you. I bet I can catch you . . . (catching her) and tickle your fat tummy . . . (catches her, tickles her, hugs her) I bet I can catch you.
Pat:	(hangs her head, closes her eyes, and puts her thumb in her mouth as Mrs. Thomas hugs her)
Therapist:	Oh, Pat! Keep your eyes closed now. Cover your eyes . . . cover your eyes. Put your thumb in your mouth! Stick your thumb in your mouth . . . that a girl. (laughs)
Pat:	(giggles)
Therapist:	Give me one. Give me one. You got two. I need one . . . I need one. Hey! You know what I told you I was going to bring for that thumb? Hm? Let

me see . . . let me see. A tickle under here. (produces large lollypop from inside paper bag . . . unwraps lollypop) Would you rather have a thumb or a lollypop? Hm? Hm? Take a look. Hm? Would you rather have this? Should I eat it? (does so)

Pat: (shakes head no)

Therapist: Should you eat it?

Pat: (reaches for lollypop)

Therapist: Oh, well, here . . . take it. Here.

Pat: (arm covers her eyes)

Therapist: But you have to take your hand down.

Pat: (removes arm from eyes)

Therapist: That's a girl. That's a girl. You going to give me some? Hm?

Pat: (extends lollypop to Mrs. Thomas)

Therapist: Ummm, mm-m-m-m-m. That's real good. You going to eat some? Hm?

Pat: (takes lollypop into mouth)

Therapist: You going to eat it all? You can have all . . . oh boy! Can I have a bite? Can I have a bite? Can I have a bite?

Pat: (hands her the lollypop)

Therapist: Uh hm-m-m-m. (piece falls to floor) Oh! (laughs) That's all to that lollypop. (puts broken pieces back into bag)

Pat: (runs away quickly around behind table and crouches out of sight with only the peak of her "fun hat" showing)

Therapist: I don't see you, Pat. Where are you? Anybody seen Pat? Where is she? (searching) There you are. (viewing tip of fun hat moving along behind table) Here I come. (laughs) Here I come.

Pat: (scoots around to other side of table)

Therapist: Hey! How'd you get way over there? (laughs) You're too quick for me. You're too quick for me. (catching her, hugging her) I can get you here, though. (laughs, tickles her) You can't catch me. (takes off and runs away around table)

Pat:	(pursues Mrs. Thomas)
Therapist:	No, oh no! Oh no! You can't. (suddenly turns around and grabs Pat) I got you. Now I got you, see? See, I got you . . . (catches Pat, lifts her, swings her around and places her, standing, upon table) One . . . two . . . three . . . jump! (holds out her arms for Pat to jump into them)
Pat:	(jumps into her therapist's arms)
Therapist:	Good for you! Do it again. Climb up! Real fast!
Pat:	(climbs back up onto table)
Therapist:	Boy, you're a good climber! You're a real good climber. Come on! Jump to me!
Pat:	(jumps into therapist's arms)
Therapist:	Wheee! (catches her) See, I caught you right in the air. Yeah! Let me see you do it! Hey! What a fancy trick! What a fancy trick!
Pat:	(thumb in mouth)
Therapist:	What happened? Thumb get stuck? Hey! You can't put that in your mouth after you ate the lollypop. (laughs) You ate up the lollypop, so don't put your thumb in your mouth. (laughs)
Pat:	(removes thumb)
Therapist:	There's something else in the bag. What's in the bag? Come over here, let's see what's in the bag. Come on, over here, let's take a look at what's in the bag. Come on. Over here.
Pat:	(comes over to look)
Therapist:	Oh! Hey! Let's open it up . . . let's open this up. (opens bag of potato chips and pours some into hand) Come on. I'll give you some. Shall I give you some? Huh? Huh? Huh? You know how you get things, don't you? You have to ask for them. You have to ask for them. Sit down. You ready?
Pat:	(sits on floor facing therapist but with arm over face)
Therapist:	Oh, OK, I thought you were. Uncover your eyes and open your mouth, and I'll give you some. Here. (extends a potato chip to her)

Pat: (removes arm from face, but leaves thumb in
                mouth)
Therapist: You got to take your thumb out, though. You
                can't get anything in there with your thumb in
                your mouth.
Pat: (removes thumb from mouth)
Therapist: Here you are. Open up!
Pat: (opens mouth for therapist to feed her)
Therapist: Ahh ... (opens own mouth while feeding Pat)
                There you go! There you go! Here you go, there
                you go ... Can you give me some? Give me some?
Pat: (feeds her therapist)
Therapist: Um-um-um. Give me some, too ... ahh.
Pat: (hands several potato chips to her therapist)
Therapist: No! I don't want them in my hand. I want you to
                feed them to me.
Pat: (feeds her)
Therapist: Um-um-um-um.

   *Pat now has a friend she can share with. Then, unexpect-
edly, Pat widens her world to include the camera crew.*

Therapist: Does anyone else want potato chips? (looks
                around) Who? Who wants potato chips? Hm?
Cameraman 1:   Um-hm.
Therapist: Charley wants some.
Pat: (turns to Cameraman 2 instead and extends
                potato chips to him)
Therapist: Tony first? Tony's your friend, huh? Give
                Tony some first! That a girl. That's right! (ex-
                tends hand with chips to Pat) Here's some for
                you, too. We like you. (feeds her)
Cameraman 1:   Hey, Pat! Hey, Pat! Is there one more potato
                chip? Could I have one more? Please?
Pat: (Peers into potato chip bag. Grinning, she ex-
                tends it to therapist to demonstrate there are
                none left.)
Therapist: (laughs) Show him, show him that they're all
                gone. Show it to him.

Cameraman 1:	(disappointed) Ahh! They're all gone? Ohhh!
Therapist:	Show him where they went. Where did they go?
Pat:	(big smile on face as she points to her stomach)
Therapist:	(laughs)

Session 17 (final session)

Today is a party for Pat's final session and for her class-mate, Kevin [who has also been in Theraplay]. The camera crew joins in the festivities. To begin with, everyone exchanges hats.

Pat:	(puts her own hat on her therapist)
Therapist:	Woops! Let's see what's the matter with that hat? (wiggles own head) Can I move my head now?
Pat:	Yeah.
Therapist:	What'll happen?
Pat:	It'll stay on!
Therapist:	Let's see. (wiggles head) You're right!

Until now, Pat's therapy has been with Mrs. Thomas exclusively. She is now ready to relate to other children.

| Therapist: | Huh? Go get Tony's hat. |

Mrs. Thomas has brought a surprise for Pat.

Therapist:	You know what? You know what I have today, Pat? Huh? In this box, I've got a very special hat . . . and you know what I'm going to do? I'm going to put this hat on you because it's a real special hat! Close your eyes. Now don't open them until I tell you to, OK? Wait till I tell you. Wait till I tell you. (removing bridal veil from box) Oh! You're going to look so pretty, Pat. (places veil on Pat's head) Now! Go look in the mirror. Go look in the mirror and see what you look like.
Pat:	(stands entranced in front of mirror)
Therapist:	You look like a bride! A bride. Aren't you pretty? (laughs) Turn around so Tony can see you! Wait;

let's show Tony. Look, Tony! Turn around so
Tony can see you! Turn around. Show Charley
too!

Pat: (turns to face cameramen; she is beaming with
                pride; her head is cocked coyly to one side)
Therapist: See how pretty she looks!

Pat reacts as any little girl would.

Therapist: See the bride! Hm . . . How d'you like that hat,
                Pat? Hmm? Am I as pretty as you? Huh?

*In the meanwhile, Kevin . . . has slyly removed the hat-
box from the table top, sat back down on the floor, and placed
the box over his head.*

Therapist: Where's Kevin? (laughs) There he is. There he is.
                Kevin was hiding from you, Pat. Can you find
                him?
Pat: (walks over to Kevin and removes the box that
                conceals his face)
Therapist: Ha! There he is. (laughing) Ho, ho, ho. What a
                funny hat, Kevin.
Kevin: (hides head inside box again)
Therapist: Where's Kevin? Anybody seen Kevin? (laughs)
                There he is! I'm going to hide Kevin. (hides him
                in box) Pat, you can't find Kevin! (laughs)
Pat: (smiles as she uncovers him)
Kevin: (laughs)
Therapist: (laughs) You're a funny fellow, Kevin. (hugging
                him) You're a funny fellow.
Pat: (runs around table)
Therapist: I bet you can't find Pat, Kevin. Where's Pat?
                Let's see if we can find Pat. Let's see if we can find
                Pat. You can't catch her.
Kevin: (gives chase)
Therapist: You got to catch her first. First you got to catch
                her . . . I got her, I got her (laughs), I got her.
                (catches her, envelops her, hugs her) Ummm, I
                got her. We'll put her in the box (covers Pat's

	head with box) and wrap her up for Christmas (musically), wrap her up for Christmas. There she is! (laughs)
Pat and Kevin:	(both laugh)
Therapist:	(reaching for bottle of grape soda) Hey! Let's have some soda pop, huh? Let's have some pop, huh? OK? Where's the can opener?

[Pat and Kevin search for the can opener.]

Therapist:	Anybody seen the can opener? Where's that little mouse? Huh? Where did it go?
Pat and Kevin:	(still searching)
Therapist:	Come on, Kevin, come over here. (pulling him close)
Pat:	(works on opening bottle)
Therapist:	Ohh (groans) boy! Look at that! Is it hard? Here, let me help you. (groans) (helps her, her hand over Pat's) Oh . . . almost. Oh, still needs some more. Come on, help me some more. You help me too, Kevin. Come on. I need lots of help.
Kevin:	(places his hand over Pat's, which is on top of therapist's)
Therapist:	Oh . . . whew! We did it! You like orange pop? You like orange pop, Pat?
Pat:	(grins)
Therapist:	Did you say something?

[Scene changes to classroom. Enter Pat and Kevin.]

The party over, Kevin and Pat return to the classroom. Now they will be asked to introduce Mrs. Thomas and the camera crew to their classmates. It is hoped that Kevin and Pat can make it from here on their own. Even though their therapists will be available if needed, their formal sessions are over.

[Pat and Kevin walk into group and join classmates on floor.]

| Teacher: | (hands musical instruments to Pat and Kevin) |

	You look like you were at a party. Did you go to a party?
Pat:	Yep.
Teacher:	What did you have?
Pat:	Pop.
Teacher:	You had some pop? What kind?
Pat:	Grape.
Teacher:	Grape pop? Did you eat anything else?
Pat:	Potato chips.
Teacher:	Was anyone else at the party?
Pat:	(nods)
Teacher:	Who was there?
Pat:	(with her musical instrument, points to one participant)
Teacher:	He was there?
Pat:	(points to another, and another)
Teacher:	And he was there? He was there?

[Holding their instruments, the children march around the room to the music of the piano. The film ends with group scenes of teacher asking, "Where is everybody?" and the children, including an enthusiastic Pat, jumping up and loudly shouting, "Here I am."]

Epilogue I (five months later)

Of Pat, the teacher says, "She is much more loving. I'm amazed at the change in her. When she comes in, she hugs me. She talks a lot more. She has still a long way to go, but she is more outgoing now and never nods her head or cringes like she used to."

[Camera shows Pat blowing bubbles and running to catch them, then shifts to Pat up in teacher's arms, hugging her.]

Epilogue II (three years later)

Three years later, Pat is revisited. . . . Still in Chicago, Pat is now eight years old. Her mother was interviewed while Pat jumped rope outside her house. During these years, Pat has done well at school and is described by her mother as being "Just a very happy little girl."

[Film shows Pat in middle of group, jumping rope and chanting along with her friends, "M-I, crooked-letter, crooked-letter, I, crooked-letter, crooked-letter, I, P-P-I."]

Questions typically asked by audiences at the conclusion of this film include the following:

1. "What is Pat's social history?"

Pat is the seventh of nine children. Neighbors have observed her looking unhappily burdened, lugging around a baby with a bottle in its mouth. Both parents are at home.

2. "What is Pat's medical history?"

Pat is reported to be "in perfect health." The only comment in her welfare clinic records notes that she may be allergic to penicillin.

3. "Has Pat been on medication?"

Pat has never been on psychotropic medication. In cases where children are taking behavior-altering medicine (usually for "hyperactivity"), Theraplay therapists require that the pa tient's physician discontinue the medication for the duration of the treatment. Reinstatement has hardly ever been necessary, and in only two or three cases has it seemed warranted to do Theraplay with a child who, for family "peace of mind," is medicated at home. This policy does not, of course, refer to Dilantin for epilepsy or medicine for "medical," not "behavioral," disorders.

4. "Was the family treated too?"

No. It was reported of Pat's mother at the onset of treatment that she was so painfully fearful of contact that communications with the school were conducted in writing only and slipped under her door for signatures. Although therapists prefer to involve family members in the treatment sessions, this is not always possible. It is a principle of Theraplay that no child shall be refused treatment because of the unavailability of family members.

5. "Without family cooperation, how do you account for Pat's marked improvement?"

As stated by Theodore Hurst, producer of the film *Here I Am* (Jernberg, Hurst, and Lyman, 1969), in cases where parents cannot participate, the aim of Theraplay becomes one both of insulating the child to protect him from what may well be a damaging environment and of providing him with the skills and the personality to evoke positive responses from others (Hurst, 1974). The insulation itself can vary in "thickness" and in effectiveness. The "thicker" it is required to be, the greater the necessary compensatory talent that must be developed, if it is to be effective in ensuring continued mental health. Thus, according to this theory, a child whose home life is genuinely threatening to his survival will have to learn extensive techniques for evoking loving attention elsewhere and will have to construct such "thick" protection as to render him impervious to most experiences at home. Given the best of all possible solutions to these unhappy situations, the child copes as follows: "Bad" input is screened out; "good" input is called out from others through the skills learned in the Theraplay experience and with the resulting "new" personality. It is this "new" personality that probably accounts for Pat's continued improvement. As her father confided in his interview three years after termination, "I used to never even notice Pat. She was my least liked one. Then she got to be so bubbly and bright, now she's my favorite of them all!" Morris Stein has suggested that Pat's improvement is a function of her being presented with tasks that call for ever-increasing ego mastery.[1]

6. "Was any systematic before-and-after evaluation carried out?"

Pat was given a standard psychological battery, complete with projectives and intelligence tests, by an outside tester (Laima Vanderstoep), before and after Theraplay. Although she did not show change in all areas, the following excerpts and the summary do point to those changes that did occur:

Report of Follow-Up Testing

Two months later, Pat was less draining and more fun to be with. She showed more independence, more direct control, and more opposition in our interaction. She expressed her need to go to the bathroom, let me know she could take care of herself, initiated contact, controlled the amount of physical contact, and sought a more active role in the testing, spontaneously putting away materials and turning cards. Her self-absorption and self-sufficiency had a less defensive quality and seemed indicative of a shift toward autonomy and separation.

Pat was more interested and more involved with me, initiating contact early in our time together. On the previous testing, there was no initiation on her part. This time she was playful and teasing with me, at first gingerly, through eye contact and smiling, then through initiating games of peek-a-boo and hiding. She was less interested in the objects and toys with which we were working. Her involvement with them was more focused and had a new contact-oriented aspect. She put the little family dolls away after a few minutes and turned instead to the doll she had brought from the classroom. She used the doll both to engage me in more direct interaction with her and to express some of her ambivalent and angry feelings toward me.

She is more open to interpersonal experience, and there is an increased push toward communication, but not through the free use of language as yet.

While there is some quantitative change in Pat's intellectual functioning (from IQ 99 to 105), the qualitative shifts in her performance and approach are more important. Pat is generally more alert and more aware perceptually. She is better able to retain and execute sequential directions, passing the complicated three-commission sequence. Her approach to problems is more focused. She shows an increased ability to differentiate essentials from nonessentials. There is less fumbling with objects and less false starts and false moves. Perceptual motor coordination is better and more controlled. On the initial testing, she could not articulate the corners on the square. On retesting, she could articulate the angles and produced one marginally scorable square, working at this with marked persistence.

Pat's performance on the language parts of the Binet shows less shift than in the area of spatial skills and general problem-solving approach. Her ability to deal with perceptual relationships has increased markedly. She has acquired more labels and is able to express more vocabulary. There is a shift in her awareness of what is going on around her, and she is beginning to clarify and express these everyday relationships.

Parallel to a loosening up of her behavior is a tightening up in her fantasy and associations. In general, anxieties and feelings are more defined, and she seems to have better control over them.

In all of her behavior and fantasy, one senses a more active Pat. She is making more impact on her world. There is increased feeling contact with her environment. Her feelings are less explosive, less egocentric, and more related to life around her.

Pat is more aware of her own role in interactions. She is more involved with others and is more active in having her needs met.

Summary: There has been some change and growth in Pat during this very short therapeutic intervention. There is some gain in intellectual functioning beyond that expected on the basis of maturation, learning, and familiarity with tests and tester. The shifts occurred primarily in the area of a more focused awareness and organization and increased ability to perceive relationships. These are changes that derive from increased self-awareness and receptiveness to experience and better organization of these experiences. The gains on the intelligence test hold despite her new oppositional behavior. In general, Pat is more aware and open to experience and more active. She has begun to develop better ways of dealing with her world and her feelings and has learned new techniques for engaging adults in more gratifying interactions with her.

7. "Has there been any further follow-up?"

Epilogue III (Seven years later; not filmed)

Mrs. Thomas is shopping in a grocery shop in Pat's neighborhood. Pat, now a tall, handsome teenager, appears, studies Mrs. Thomas for a moment, then asks:

Pat: Ain't you Mrs. Thomas?
Therapist: Yes?

Pat: (beckoning and yelling to a group of adolescent girls in the back of the store) Hey, y'all, come here. I told you that was Ernestine!

In spite of the stress of adolescence, Pat's emotional growth is continuing. As it does, she attracts others to her, and their investment in her nourishes her further.

Diagnosis

Psychological Evaluation Using Theraplay Methods

For children who are emotionally disturbed or simply very frightened of examinations, the traditional pediatric, neurological, or psychological procedures used are occasionally premature, impossible, or sometimes not even necessary. For these children, diagnostic Theraplay has been found to be a useful technique. Children referred for diagnostic Theraplay have most often been generally untestable for any one of a number of reasons, including distractability, fearfulness, and oppositional reaction. Sometimes children are referred because their diffuse and confusing behavior makes it difficult to ascertain just which specialist should be consulted. Occasionally children are referred for diagnostic Theraplay in the hope that, thus "settling down," they will no longer act as though they suffer minimal brain damage, aphasia, hearing loss, poor vision, psychosomatic disorders, and so on. And, all too often, children whose names are on long waiting lists of crowded metropolitan facilities are referred for diagnostic Theraplay as a stopgap measure—as much for the peace of mind of their parents and teachers as for the happiness of the children themselves.

Although a further medical or psychological workup is still often recommended following short-term diagnostic Theraplay, the special objective of such a workup is often more clearly delineated following a few diagnostic Theraplay sessions when a child's behavior has become more focused.

In conjunction with the later medical or psychological

workup, diagnostic Theraplay is directed to answering one or
more of the following questions:

1. What is the degree of emotional overlay? (That is, how much
   do emotional problems cloud the underlying organic ones?)
2. What is the optimum level of intellectual and physical functioning of which the child is capable?
3. What, if any, are the most effective methods for instituting
   growth?
4. What precautions, if any, should be taken in further diagnostic or treatment procedures?

It is readily apparent that these questions boil down to
the testing of hypotheses based on an understanding of the
child that is far more personal than is usually possible in outpatient clinics or large-scale evaluation screening procedures.
Thus diagnostic Theraplay, in its peeling away of a child's resistance to being prodded, poked, and questioned by strangers,
is more equivalent to an examination by a family physician who
is a lifelong family friend. In the process, the specific problems
become highlighted, thus often rendering sweeping investiga-
tions unnecessary.

One boy, Harry, for example, was brought to the Theraplay Institute because his intense screaming and violent thrashing about made it impossible to examine him medically. He, of
course, reacted to the therapists' approaches in the same manner. In spite of his efforts to "drive them off," however, the
Theraplay therapists persevered in their playful activities. Eventually he calmed down, became more trusting, and began to
enjoy their company. There was then no evidence of the ear-
ache that was thought to underlie his screaming.

Once the emotional overlay is reduced through Theraplay, however, some children referred for emotional problems
do show unsuspected visual, auditory, or cognitive defects.

Generally children with severe hyperactive or extremely
fearful and withdrawn behavior are the most difficult to diag-
nose. Diagnostic Theraplay is most useful in these instances.
Further, it is most often children suspected of "minimal brain

damage" or "learning disability" whose problems clear up most dramatically through Theraplay, negating the need for a subsequent traditional diagnostic workup.

It has been found that even a few Theraplay sessions often serve to remove those barriers to optimal functioning that have worked against an accurate assessment of the individual's true potential. Thus, diagnostic Theraplay serves a purpose sometimes before traditional screening techniques are applied and sometimes in lieu of them. When operating at its best, true differential diagnosis now is possible or sometimes even becomes unnecessary in cases where the symptoms have disappeared.

Diagnostic Theraplay is designed to elicit the broadest conceivable range of responses within the context of an optimally comfortable therapist-child relationship. The "comfortable relationship" having been accomplished through play, empathy, and skillful perseverance, the therapist "tests" a variety of responses to the playful interaction. Thus joyful hopping, balancing, nose touching, throwing, hand squeezing, and wrestling, for example, give clues to body tonus and large muscle coordination. "I bet you can't jump on the square (or push me to the red tile, or go under—or over—the table)" give some indication of concept formation (such as *on, to, under,* and *over*). The activity initiated by "Let's feed each other M&M's" assesses fine motor coordination; "Remember what I told you my phone number is?" assesses memory functions; ball throwing, hand preference, and games of eye and ear performance assess possible vision or hearing deficits. None of these "tests" is presented as a serious task having pass-fail potential. None is carried out under the eye of an authoritarian master. None is in a setting with school placement or medical hospitalization as an implicit consequence. Nor is any in its own right sufficient as a basis for medical judgment, of course.

In addition, evaluations of emotional health, designed among other things to help determine psychosexual development, interpersonal approach, tolerance for anxiety, and capacity for coping, can all be made within the context of the Theraplay relationship. It already tells something, for example, when a child persists in withdrawing from a relationship that is seen by normal children to be fun, persists in being obstinate when the activities call for flexibility, is fearful when offered clay to play with, or rejects offered food or candy. Each of these behaviors suggests hypotheses about the child. And each hypothesis can be investigated further. Although by no means standardized, the technique of diagnostic Theraplay can be seen very nicely to lead the way to further exploration. The following summary statements about children represent some uses of the diagnostic Theraplay method:

Child 1. Ten-year-old boy referred for further understanding of his behavioral problems. During the seven or eight half-hour Theraplay sessions, there was evidence that, even when he was his most integrated, he was unaware of the consequences of his acts. He was described as "fading away" when he played with the therapist and was referred for further diagnosis, including neurological exam.

Child 2. Head Start child described as "very immature, oppositional, has no language." Referred for diagnostic Theraplay because his constant screaming had made it difficult to evaluate him. During short course of diagnostic Theraplay, he turned out to be a bright child, highly responsive to his therapist. When finally ready for testing by the school psychologist, he was found to be of normal intelligence.

Child 3. Kindergarten child referred for diagnostic Theraplay in an effort to better understand his "soft autisms," "strange behavior," and failure to use "useful language." In a few sessions, the Theraplay therapist was able to determine that this child suffered from an organically based communication problem. As his "strange" behavior disappeared, it became evident that he knew some isolated facts (colors, letters, numbers) but was unable to express them or put them together even though he clearly longed to do so. He was referred for further screening.

Child 4. First-grader referred for acting "odd." When Theraplay therapist spun him around in first diagnostic session, his eyes went "out of focus." Even when the spinning stopped, his eyes seemed to go round and round as if the spin had been too fast. In the diagnostic sessions, he appeared to focus less easily on the nearby and obvious than on little details far away. There was a question of confusion in his visual field, particularly since, unless he really concentrated, his eyes tended to diverge. He was referred for a complete medical workup.

Child 5. Five-year-old child who was sweet and cooperative in classroom was referred because of bizarre postures and jerky movements. In Theraplay, he alternated exceedingly strong, violent, and overreactive movements with total limpness. He made sounds: "eh eh." It was hard to know if he was hearing his therapist. He seemed to "go off into different worlds" and made incoherent verbalizations when he did talk. He was referred for further workup.

Child 6. Staff felt the primary problem of this four-year-old girl was her bad speech. In the second diagnostic Theraplay session, after child seemed calmer, it was possible to observe her more closely. By the third session, bizarre, autisticlike hand movements were becoming apparent. The iciness of her hands was now evident when she was being held. Referral was made for extensive medical evaluation.

Child 7. Preschool boy referred for diagnostic Theraplay because of pronounced submissiveness and combination of reading ability, on the one hand, and obliviousness to instructions, on the other. He improved considerably as a result of Theraplay, and now that he was happier and more responsive to others his possibly neurologically based behavior became clearly apparent. He was referred for further evaluation.

Child 8. Referred for diagnostic Theraplay after nine months in Head Start by medical team for suspected organicity. Although he had previously been referred for neurological evaluation, the neurologist reported he was unable to perform exam because patient screamed so much. After eight weeks of Theraplay, every evidence of neurological involvement had disappeared.

Child 9. Kindergarten-age child referred for diagnostic Theraplay because of very delayed speech and poor motor control. Neurological problems were suspected. Referral for further evaluation was considered premature, since child screamed when anyone came close. The Theraplay therapist persisted, despite screaming, and after some sessions there was enough improvement for child to be referred to a diagnostic evaluation center for a speech workup and other workups.

Child 10. Head Start child assigned for developmental evaluation[2] because he was nonverbal, nonparticipating, emotionally unresponsive, and motorically tense. The following report, an example of the Theraplay-like developmental evaluation, was written by Regina Roth:

> Willie is an attractive little boy, tall for his age, with elongated brown eyes, close-cropped curly hair, and pronounced ears. He is referred for evaluation because of his fearfulness, nonparticipation, and nonspeaking.
>
> As I started the diagnostics, he was still unsure of me. Unlike most other children, he let me find no smiles when I "bounced" him. He began to warm up, however, as I proceeded to give him a "horsey ride," counted his "five little piggies," played "patty-cake," counted his teeth, and made his cheeks make funny noises. He enjoyed pointing in the direction in which I was to swing him.
>
> His human drawing, while not having traditional integration of parts, does have an integration of its own and conveys tension and confusion. While he had some trouble copying the triangle and square (as do a majority of Head Start children), he followed well the clear directions to copy circle, lines, and cross. His handling of scissors was awkward, yet he was able to cut paper adequately.
>
> He repeated the first three digits accurately but said "fif 2" for 652 twice, and "mm mm mm" for 777. He repeated "Peter Piper" but his articulation was slow and strained. He was quite aware of sounds in the environment, touched me, pointed, and asked "Who that?"
>
> Although Willie at first appears somewhat slow and ponderous, he is probably of at least average intelligence. Emotionally, however, possibly because of his early hospitalizations, Willie is a small baby who needs to learn that the world can be a safe and giving place.
>
> I definitely recommend Theraplay for the pleasur-

able, trusting relationship it will afford Willie. His therapist should start with games like peek-a-boo and hide-and-seek to help him overcome some of the leftover anxiety over separation. In addition, he should be helped to differentiate different aspects of his body parts ([for example, by placing] finger paint on his toe, powder on his nose, plaster of paris on his feet, and "crazy foam" on his hands) and to differentiate himself from the world at large. Pushing and pulling as in "tug of war" would be recommended for this purpose. Games like hopping, skipping, jumping, and throwing would benefit his gross motor coordination; swinging, bounces, and being surprised (Intruding) would help Willie learn to expand his world and his expectations of self and others. A great deal of Nurturing is, of course, recommended. As he begins to make appropriate sounds, his therapist should encourage but never drill him in communicating, and when he babbles his therapist should imitate his babbling (much as the mother of an infant would). Throughout all this, Willie's therapist should be careful *not* to make him talk—*not* to require anything of him. His speech will improve as he finds he has more and more to communicate. Instructions to him, on the other hand, should be clear-cut and spelled out step by step.

Diagnostic Theraplay does not need to be the province of the Theraplay therapist alone. Speech therapists, audiologists, ophthalmologists, and other medical practitioners, when dealing with small and not-so-small children, often would do well to incorporate Theraplay principles into medical procedures—whether diagnostic or treatment.

Speech Evaluation Using Theraplay Methods

Some diagnostic procedures so typical of good speech evaluations, such as "Bet you can't spit in this jar," "Blow me over with a 'P'-'P'-'P'-'P,'" "Touch your nose with your tongue," accompanied by loud noises, gleeful laughs, and the therapist's jolly thumping to the ground when well blown-over, fit right in with the playfulness of Theraplay. Bligh, Kupperman, and others at the Elmhurst College Speech Clinic have worked out many other elaborate, Theraplay-like methods for assessing speech competence in children referred with speech and language disorders.

Medical Evaluation Using Theraplay Methods

The following illustration of Theraplay principles, although applied to minor surgery performed on a small child, could apply equally well to operating room diagnosis. Since surgery of any kind constitutes a trauma for a small child, setting of limits, letting the child know "Who's in charge," and so on have no place in the operating room.[3] Raising self-esteem and increasing trust in others, however, do have a place here.

Julie, age three, was to have a myringotomy (the cutting of a small opening in the eardrum for purposes of draining accumulated fluid). Calm and cheerful throughout the pokings and proddings with fingers and instruments, she had entertained an audience of operating room personnel with her spunk, even during the frightening blood tests. Now she was being undressed and prepared for surgery. During the process, Anesthesiologist 1 arrived. "Why isn't she ready yet?" he demanded of the nurses. And then, turning to Julie, "Get her out of that undershirt." Beginning to protest that that was her undershirt, she insisted, "I keep it on." The anesthesiologist became annoyed and began to argue with the little girl. She became frightened, and, tightly clutching the one piece of familiar clothing, she began to cry. By now in a rage, the physician approached her and attempted to yank the undershirt from her body. The scene was painful for all concerned. Her mother, with the surgeon's approval, was on the phone, contacting another anesthesiologist, a family friend.

Anesthesiologist 2 entered, saying, "Why, Julie, how nice to see you! And what a gorgeous undershirt you have there! That white just matches your pearly teeth. In fact, you know what? You look so pretty it makes me feel just like picking you up and dancing with you." He swooped Julie up in his arms and, waltzing to his own cheerful singing, he gently placed the anesthesia mask over her smiling face.

Parent-Child Relationship Evaluation

For purposes of making determinations as to how to proceed with Theraplay with respect to therapist-child interaction, the Marschak Interaction Method, or MIM (Marschak, 1960, 1979), is an ideal tool. In its focus on the relationship that presumably contributed to the child's problem in the first place and in its inclusion of Theraplay-like tasks, the MIM allows the observer to formulate a clear therapeutic program. A child who cries in the presence of a withholding mother, tyrannizes a shrinking father, or joins a meticulous parent in squeamishness is writing his own blueprint for Theraplay. The tasks of the MIM point to difficulties in a variety of areas of relating, conflict, activity type, and coping and suggest the developmental level at which child and parents currently operate. In addition to assessing the relationship between parent and child, the relationship between therapist and patient, teacher and pupil, foster parent and foster child, or prospective adoptive parent and adoptive child all can be usefully evaluated by means of the MIM. The MIM, furthermore, can be useful for purposes of psychotherapy supervision and for initially matching a particular therapist with a particular child.

The use of Theraplay for diagnosis, in conclusion, differs from its uses as treatment described throughout this book. In diagnostic Theraplay, Theraplay has a purpose that is neither direct cure nor direct treatment. Its purpose, instead, is to make possible either a further diagnostic procedure or a further clarification of a suspected diagnosis. Rather than being an end in itself, diagnostic Theraplay is a method for determining the most appropriate next course of action.

Suggested Theraplay Activities

Therapists beginning to do Theraplay often find themselves at a loss for ideas. The following illustrations provide only the basics of a Theraplay repertoire. They are intended not as thorough cookbooks but as examples of the kinds of activities therapists can best begin to generate themselves. The activities are illustrated rather than just verbally described to communicate some of the sensations which both therapist and child experience.

Sample Theraplay Activities

Nurturing

Pudding

Materials: Small jar of baby pudding

Procedure: Maximizing the opportunity for eye contact, therapist feeds child's pudding-dipped toes and fingers to him.

Lullaby

Materials: None

Procedure: Therapist cradles child in arms in such a way that eye contact is fully maintained. Therapist sings lullaby to child, inserting, wherever possible, child's name and descriptions of his or her features.

Nibbles

Materials: M&M's, grapes, cherries, cheese curds, and so on
Procedure: While maintaining eye contact, the therapist feeds nibbles to the child one at a time, commenting on the food and how glad the therapist is that the child is enjoying it.

M&M Hunt

Materials: Half a dozen M&M's
Procedure: Child lies down and closes eyes. Therapist "hides" M&M's on child (behind his ears, inside his shirt, under his hair). Child opens eyes, and therapist begins to try to find "hidden" candy, feeding each piece to child as he does so.

Dusting

Materials: One small can of baby powder
Procedure: Therapist kneels straddling, or alongside child. Gently powders chest, tummy, neck, arms, and so on. Note: Eye contact must be maintained throughout.

Ice Cream Man

Materials: One ice cream pop-sicle

Procedure: Therapist cradles child, maximizing eye contact, and allows him to suck popsicle slowly.

Nursing

Materials: One baby bottle filled with milk, juice, water, or soft drink (for children beyond in-fancy, hole in nipple may need to be enlarged)

Procedure: Therapist holds child in a position that allows maxi-mum eye contact and physical closeness. Singing is effective if done softly; jostling is generally not.

Beauty Parlor

Materials: Cold cream, hair brush, ribbons, and so on, and mirror

Procedure: Child sits on chair facing mirror. Therapist stands behind or to one side, main-taining eye contact through mir-ror. Therapist makes child "beautiful," being sure to keep up a steady commentary regard-ing the child's natural assets.

Structuring

Floppy Doll

Materials: None
Procedure: Therapist and child
work slowly and carefully to
help one limb after another to
become limp and stiff, limp and
stiff. It is important to do this in
cheerful, optimistic setting.

*Count the Freckles (or Teeth or
Ears)*

Materials: None
Procedure: Therapist straddles
or kneels alongside child. Then,
very slowly and deliberately, he
counts (and comments on) the
child's freckles, teeth, ears, and
so on.

Mother, May I?

Materials: Floor marked with a few large grids

Procedure: Therapist gives directions ("Hop on your left foot to the yellow square"). If child misses, he is guided gently but firmly to repeat it until he gets it just right. Spirit must be optimistic and cheerful.

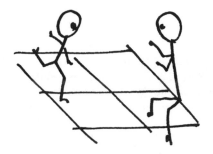

The Yardstick

Materials: Ruler or tape measure, graph paper, and pencil (paper should be attached to wall if possible)

Procedure: Therapist measures child in discrete units (for example, wrist to elbow, tongue, knee to shoulder, and ear to nose). After each measure is complete, it is "recorded" on graph sheet or on outline of child's body.

Hand Prints

Materials: Finger paint and finger paint paper

Procedure: Therapist covers child's palm and fingers with paint and then presses child's hand firmly to paper (making certain every knuckle has made an imprint). Note: Paint applied in multicolored layers produces multicolored handprints. All four hands make interesting paintings and good souvenirs of terminating session. Feet make good footprint paintings. Child's name can be added to picture—therapist guides a finger paint-dipped toe or finger for the inscription process.

The Wall Walk

Materials: Baby powder or finger paint

Procedure: Therapist carries child, supporting him in such a way that child's powder- or finger paint-covered soles can make walking prints on paper mounted to the wall, or on mirror or blackboard. Feet can be made to walk up the wall and then back down again.

Life-Size Portrait

Materials: Large size newsprint or shelf paper, crayons

Procedure: Child lies on back—arms and legs outstretched—on paper that has been secured to floor. Therapist, kneeling alongside, traces outline of child's body with crayons. When it is all finished, child and therapist take drawing to mirror, and, studying child and picture, they fill in facial features, buttons, cuffs, belts, collars, buckles, shoes and socks, and so on. Note: Timing of this activity is important. Except with children who are being helped to learn delay, this activity should take no longer than is absolutely necessary.

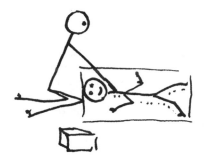

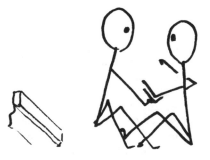

Elbow Trophies

Materials: One roll of aluminum foil

Procedure: Therapist and child sit facing one another. Therapist wraps sheets of double-thickness foil around child's elbow and molds it carefully to fit snugly around elbow. Then he removes it cautiously and compares wrinkles and indentations in "impression" with wrinkles and protrusions in child's elbow.

Intruding

Peek-A-Toes

Materials: None
Procedure: Child lies on back, legs extended. Therapist kneels at child's feet. Therapist opens and closes child's legs, peeking out from between them as he does so.

Noses

Materials: None (or pretzels)
Procedure: Maintaining eye contact, therapist and child touch noses, share a pretzel (with hands behind backs), or exchange eye winks.

Hello-Goodbye

Materials: None
Procedure: As they face one another, both standing, child straddles therapist's waist with legs. Therapist holds child firmly and gradually lowers him until child's head gently contacts floor, at which time therapist swoops child back up, making eye contact. Caution: Child's head must be protected at all times.

Peek

Materials: Book, towel, or cardboard
Procedure: Therapist and child sit facing each other. Unexpectedly, therapist "peeks" out at child from behind his "shield." (Standing mirror or folding screen can be used.)

Hello Up There

Materials: None
Procedure: Therapist lies on back on floor. Child sits astride him. Therapist raises child up into air so that there is eye contact with child looking down. Then therapist surprises child by lifting him on over his (the therapist's) head and then back down again. Caution: Therapist must be absolutely certain as to location of child's head when not in view.

Greetings

Materials: None
Procedure: Therapist simultaneously shakes child's foot and
hand. Caution: Tickling while
carrying out this activity should
be limited to children already
having a certain degree of self-
confidence. All others should be
given firm support.

Lollypops

Materials: None
Procedure: Therapist removes
child's shoe. As he begins to remove sock, he muses aloud,
"Hm . . . I wonder what I'll find
in here . . . Ah! I do believe it's
lemon drops . . . or, wait a minute . . . potato chips?" Then,
slowly removing sock, "I *knew*
it!! A lollypop-toe!"

Finger Count

Materials: None
Procedure: Child lies on back.
Therapist "counts" child's fingers (or toes) as follows:
"1-2-3-4-5. There are five on this
one. Now let's check this other
one: 10-9-8-7-6. OK, six on that
one. Now let's see: five on the
first one and six on the second;
five plus six makes eleven. You
got *eleven* fingers (or toes)?!"

Challenging

Balancing Act

Materials: One (or two) medium-sized textbooks
Procedure: Therapist helps child to walk with book carefully balanced on his (child's) head. With increasing skill, the load of books becomes more complex. (Note: This activity is also Structuring.) Eventually child is challenged to try his balancing act while at the same time being tickled.

Leg Wrestling

Materials: None
Procedure: Therapist and child lie on floor, heads in opposite directions, legs are touching and raised off floor, hooked to one another. On count of "three," therapist and child proceed to try to roll each other off balance.

Doughnut Dare

Materials: One classic doughnut
Procedure: Child and therapist sit on floor close together. Child (or adult)'s finger is put through doughnut hole. Therapist and child take bites in turn.
Object: To keep from taking the bite that will knock the doughnut off.

Pillow Push

Materials: Two pillows approximately 24" × 24"
Procedure: On the count of "three," child and therapist push hard against each other, trying to push each other off "base."

Wheelbarrow

Materials: None
Procedure: Therapist places child's hands on floor and then picks up child's feet and "walks" child around room upside down.
Caution: Floor must be cleared of thumbtacks, and so on.

Water Fight

Materials: Two plastic squirt containers (such as ketchup bottles), two waterproof coveralls (such as large plastic garbage can liners with holes made in them for head and arms)

Procedure: Therapist and child have water "duel."

Object: To leave a larger number of water drops on the other than each has put on him- or herself.

Caution: Room should be well-heated, and puddles should be dried up before next activity.

Pillow Bump

Materials: Six pillows (24" × 24")

Procedure: Depending on the size of the child, three to six pillows are stacked one on top of the other. Child and therapist stand back to back with the pillows between them. At the count of "three" (or "two" or "twenty-six"), both participants rush to claim the largest area of pillow space. Then both stand up, remove top pillow, and the contest begins again. The next pillow is removed after that, and so on, all the way down, until only the floor remains.

Notes

1. To the degree that Theraplay sessions with Pat (1) enhance her body awareness, (2) provide her with stimulus complexity, (3) establish feelings of trust, and (4) build feelings of competence, Theraplay with Pat effectively strengthens her ego. Paraphrased from comments made by Morris Stein, presenting *Here I Am* on Sunrise Semester, New York University television, July 1976.

2. This particular developmental evaluation technique has been applied to approximately 1,000 children in the Chicago Board of Education's Head Start program and was developed in 1974 by Phyllis Booth.

3. "His questions and his fears and his attempts to protect his integrity should be respected" (Brazelton, 1970, p. 16).

4

Group Theraplay
for Children

Group Theraplay is appropriate for children who have difficulty relating to peers. If the difficulties stem from inability to share with others, reluctance to initiate relationships, or discomfort with intimacy, for example, then group Theraplay is an appropriate treatment form. If, however, the peer-relating difficulties are secondary to a more thoroughgoing developmental defect, then, appropriate as it may seem to be, the group experience must be postponed until the underlying developmental problems have been individually attended to.

Group Theraplay is based on the same assumptions and follows many of the same principles as individual Theraplay (see Chapter Three). The goals of both individual and group Theraplay are to enhance self-esteem and to increase trust in others through concrete, personal, positive experiences. The basic assumption is that if the therapist can be aware of the under-

126

lying needs (for Structure, Challenge, Intrusion, or Nurture) and can begin to attend to these needs then the child's overt behavior will change in the direction of greater appropriateness. The accurate understanding of the underlying need depends not only on the clarity of the tension message sent by the child but also on the therapist's skill in reading it. Thus, simplistically stated, a child who announces to the group that his father has built the world's tallest building could be communicating his need for status as could a child who introduces himself by distributing coins or candies. A child who rambles diffusely or runs about wildly could be in need of Structure; one who is too tightly organized and organizing, in need of Intrusion and flexibility; and the child who is too quick to give up, too dramatically passive, or too "artificially" infantile, in need of Challenge. It is the job of the therapist to render unnecessary these substitute maneuvers by (1) beginning to fill the need that generated them in the first place and (2) by teaching the child skills for more satisfying social interactions. Thus, with respect to filling the need, the therapist may set about to increase the braggart's self-esteem. He may infer the child's neediness from his boast about his father's potency and may know from this that he in fact feels impotent. The therapist may ask the group both to feed him and to call attention to his powerful muscles, his ability to throw, or his strength in lifting a fellow group member. By the same token, a therapist may also infer that, underlying candy or coin-distributing behavior, there may be a pervasive wish to be loved and nurtured. Moving in the direction of satisfying that wish, while yet of course recognizing that the wish itself can never be fully met, the therapist may organize the group members to give other kinds of attention (for example, caring for bumps and scratches, soothing with lotion, fanning to "cool off," feeding popcorn, saying "ten nice things," singing a song in the child's honor, and carrying him in a blanket). Viola Brody (1971a) describes maturation in a group level of functioning over time as corresponding to the psychosocial development of the small child.

The teaching of social skills comes later in the treatment —long after the members' underlying needs have been attended to—and is conducted around specific issues, just as the meeting of needs is directed to specific deprivations. The social issues chosen may apply to more than one child and should be carried out in such a way that all children in the group will benefit. The teaching of social skills is conducted by means of role playing. During a quiet time, the therapist may address the members of the group as follows: "OK. Now we'd like each of you to tell us three good and three bad things that happened to you this past week." Out of the three "bad things" particular themes will emerge, often having to do with troubles or with disappointments involving adults, peers, or siblings. Troubles with peers will usually center around themes of awkwardness, rejection, misunderstandings, frustration, anger, and failure. These themes can then be acted out with the participation of the other members in a group role-playing situation. "I tried to get 'Josh' at school to shoot baskets with me when he was playing, and he wouldn't," Don may volunteer. "OK," the therapist may say, "Bill, you be 'Josh'; Ted, you tell us what 'Josh' is thinking; and, Richard, you tell us what Don is thinking. Ted and Richard, go and stand right behind Don and 'Josh' and say out loud what you think their secret thoughts are. Don, you tell them where to stand and what to do."

The ensuing scenario may go something like this:

Richard (Don's secret thoughts)	Don	'Josh'	Ted (Josh's secret thoughts)
"Boy, do I wish I could join in with him."	"Give me the ball."	(dribbling basketball across court)	"I'm really having a good time all by myself out here."
		(continues dribbling)	
			"What's he want from me?"

Richard (Don's secret thoughts)	Don	'Josh'	Ted (Josh's secret thoughts)
"If he's not going to give it to me, I guess I'll have to take it."	(grabbing for ball)		
	"I want it."	"Hey! Cut that out!"	
			"He's scaring me."
"There! Now he's made me mad!"			
		"Get outa here." (grabbing ball back)	"I better grab a'hold quick. Else what's he going to do next?"
"Can't he see that all I want to do is play with him?"	(gets ready to kick Josh but falls down instead)		
			"I'm glad he's down, I sure don't want *him* in my game!"

Needless to say, the therapists keep a tight control, interrupting if the action goes out of control or interrupting for discussion if one person's speech is inaudible. The particular scene just described may be reenacted several times, and participants or audience may be asked, "What is it that Don really wants?" "How would 'Josh' like to be approached?" "Does Don's way of doing it get him what he wants?" "What would make 'Josh' cooperate with Don?" and so on.

Group Theraplay, thus, is directed, first, to meeting underlying needs and, second, to teaching socially satisfying skills. Each session follows a format that will allow both. Beyond that, the organization of a session, like that of a day in a well-functioning nursery school, alternates active and quiet,

task-oriented and playful, adult- and child-focused activities.

A word of caution to readers who ask, "Why not start
right in with training in relationship skills?" It is only in combination with experiences that directly meet the child's needs,
and in the context of raising his self-esteem or increasing his
trust in others, that the training in relationship skills has any
lasting value. Only when learning takes place in the presence of
peers and adults to whom he has already formed some emotional attachment will a child readily give up one set of behaviors for another. Only after he has been "hooked," so to speak,
can we expect him to endure the pain of growing up. (We do
not maintain, it should be said, that growth is, or necessarily
need be, painful. However, it is almost a truism that disturbed
or deeply unhappy children are afraid to move forward, reluctant to increase their developmental repertoire.)

A Theraplay group should consist of anywhere from four
to eight children. Members should belong to the same general
chronological or grade level, and each participant should share
in common with at least one other child his particular problem
in relating (for example, pseudoconfidence, quarrelsomeness,
excessive shyness, or overcompetitiveness).

Unlike individual Theraplay, a group Theraplay program
typically is conducted by two therapists, not one. One therapist
alone would generally find it too difficult to observe, manage,
interact, initiate, and still remain cheerful throughout an entire
session of Theraplay with half a dozen exuberant schoolboys. In
addition, two therapists allow the use of one to talk *for* the
child and the other *to* him. Two therapists also simulate a two-
parent family. The first session begins with the therapists casually introducing themselves and then introducing the children to
one another. Guidelines are outlined, including times of sessions, appropriate clothing, and vacation schedules. One of the
primary benefits of group Theraplay, as is true of family Theraplay (see Chapter Five), is the newly acquired insight into, and
perception of, their children afforded the parents who observe
the sessions together with the interpreting therapist (see the
section on interpreting therapist, in the chapter on family Ther-

aplay). The introductory phase of child group Theraplay would not be complete without mention of the observing parents— together with a tour of the observation room for those children who may not be familiar with who and what is in there.

Following this brief introduction, the action begins. There is no heavy discussion of "problem areas" or of "what brought each of us in here." There are no questions of "personal goals," no forming of "contracts." Without further ado, the therapist may announce, "Let's make a tunnel. I'll be at the front, Chuck, you go to the back. OK, Jim, you're next; now Bert . . . Here we are, here's our tunnel ready to go. Bill, you're first to climb through. Ah! terrific, what a great tunnel! Joe, you're next. Come on, everybody! Build it up again!" And there is joyous laughing as the tunnel collapses and the members —and leaders—struggle through.

Meetings subsequent to the initial one, following the format of Viola Brody (1966, 1978), typically begin with a gathering of the group members in a small circle for the purpose of renewing friendships from the previous meeting and as an opportunity for each member to be reminded that he truly is important to the others. Thus, for example, there may be songs to welcome each participant—by name and with a personal commentary—for example, to the tune of "We Wish You a Merry Christmas": "We welcome our old friend, Bobby,/ We welcome our old friend, Bobby,/ We welcome our old friend, Bobby" and then, introducing the personal note, "And just look at that smile!" With so much enthusiasm even the most thoroughgoing depressive could not help but feel the impact.

Following the opening, the group may move into more lively activities—perhaps the forming of a human bridge for everyone to scramble over, or a game of leapfrog, or follow the leader. Perhaps a somewhat less strenuous activity will come next (for example, a tower of hands made by all the children in a sitting position, piling their hands on top of each other's. With increasing momentum, the underneath hands are pulled out from beneath and added to the top of the tower, everyone soon rising, standing, and finally stretching up on tiptoe to reach the very top. The lotioning of each other's hands before the game begins makes them especially slippery and adds to the excitement. When sitting activities are called for, this game may be done with feet instead of hands. "Pass It On" is another circle activity. Nudges, strokes, tickles, blows, whispers, and so on can all be "passed along." Or, more quiet yet, with closed eyes, each child must tell the eye color of his neighbor. Following these more subdued activities, there may be oppositional team ones (such as wheelbarrow races, tug of war, or pillow pushing) or all-group cooperative constructions (such as a group painting of "something fun we did last time"—or would like to do next time—using each other's toes as paintbrushes or such as a group "sculpture" comprised of all the bodies in the group). Then there may be a focus on the individual child, perhaps with these directions, "Jim and Ross, you make a statue of Jim's very favorite activity, and we'll guess what it is"; or through the use of stilts, with all group members aiding one child in maintaining his balance; or through all group members using dress-up clothes, combs, and makeup to turn one child into "the most handsome member of the group"; and so on.

The session ends with a reconvening in a circle on the floor for quiet singing, eating, and discussion. As he eats his treat and drinks his juice (or milk), each member may be encouraged to ask one personal question of one other member, or each member may be asked to describe his most recent birthday, or to tell what he likes the best about his fellow members, or what he looks forward to the most in the week ahead. At the end of the "snack and chat" time, each person puts a shoe on another participant's foot, and, last, there is the singing of a familiar song, each child's name being inserted in a strategic spot. There are goodbyes all around and the expression of enthusiasm over the upcoming session.

Effective group Theraplay follows these guidelines:

1. Each child is made to feel important.
2. The group is never out of the control of the therapist(s).
3. Activities are always within the abilities of every child.
4. Each session focuses on a particular problem. (For example, in the effort to lengthen their concentration, children

with short attention spans may be given, at the beginning of the session, an assignment to be carried out at the end. At the reunion that opens the session, each child is told five favorite hobbies by his neighbor, for example. At the ending of the session, during the quiet discussion time, he is to recite them back.)

5. The therapist(s), not the group, decide(s) the program.
6. Parents watch—from an observation room—whenever possible with the help of an interpreting therapist.
7. No member is allowed, physically or emotionally, to "leave the scene," nor is he ever permitted to be rejected, demeaned, or scapegoated by the others.
8. An unruly individual is kept in physical contact with the therapist and helped "until he can manage."
9. Unruly groups are helped to overcome their restlessness through the following sequence of steps:
   a. The activity is stopped. The therapist(s) may announce, "Stop! Jim is having trouble doing this one."
   b. The activity is repeated. The therapist(s) may say "Jim looks ready now. We'll start that one over again."
   c. If necessary, the activity is changed. "Well, it looks as though this isn't going to work today. We'll do *something else* instead."
10. The sessions can become increasingly age appropriate but should not begin with developmentally high levels of expectation.
11. Each session ends on a note of calm, optimism, and group harmony.

We have learned from years of teaching courses in Theraplay that there is no better way to convey the flavor of, as well as to provide concrete ideas for, group Theraplay than through stick figure drawings. The drawings in this section are not intended to be an all-inclusive listing of suggestions but rather an inspiration for choreographing as yet undiscovered activities.

Sample Theraplay Activities for Children's Groups

Magnets

Materials: None
Procedure: Group of children sit on floor at some distance from one another. Therapists sing "jazzy" song. When music stops, children gather together closer. Song resumes, then stops. Children gather until they have formed a small knot.

Queen (or King) for a Day

Materials: None
Procedure: As each child takes a turn to stand in front of the group, the others make up a song in which he or she stars.

Follow the Leader

Materials: Inner tubes, pillows, boxes, and other objects large enough to jump into, climb over, walk on, and so on.

Procedure: Therapist (or child who has been appointed leader) leads the way. Other children follow. When leader says "freeze!" all stop dead in their tracks.

Turtle

Materials: One lightweight blanket

Procedure: One of two therapists leaves room. Remaining therapist and group of children hide one child under blanket. First therapist returns and, knowing hidden child's identity, expresses longing for a child just like that one (for example, "I do so wish for a little girl with freckles and sparkly eyes and little ears on the sides of her head. Oh how I wish that I might find one just like that right inside this very blanket.") Therapist then "unwraps" the blanket. (This idea is thanks to Viola Brody.)

Bubbles

Materials: Large bowl, drinking straws, bubble liquid

Procedure: Children gather around bubble bowl, lying on their stomachs. Each child is provided one straw. All children blow bubbles. Finished bubbles are used to fashion fancy head gear for participants. Caution: Bubble liquid should be safe for eyes and stomach.

Statues

Materials: None

Procedure: Children in group "mold" one child into a statue of what they think "he or she would most like to be doing."

Leap Frog

Materials: None

Procedure: Children in group take turns "leaping" over crouched "frogs." As each child finishes leaping, he takes his place crouching at the front of the line of "frogs." The last child in the line becomes the new "leaper."

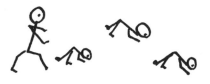

Rounds

Materials: None
Procedure: Children take different starting points for joining
the singing of a song.

Simon Says

Materials: None
Procedure: Each child takes a
turn to direct the group in what
actions they should do in what
sequence. Leader demonstrates;
others follow.

Hammock

Materials: One large, solidly constructed blanket
Procedure: One child at a time
takes a turn to lie in the center
of the blanket. Both therapists
and two or three children hold
corners of blanket, raise it gently
off the ground, and softly swing
it back and forth. Child lies
quietly inside it. Maintaining
maximum eye contact with him,
the group sings a little song
about the cradled child.

5

Family Theraplay

Although not precluding the value of individual Theraplay, the most effective Theraplay programs simultaneously treat a child and his parent(s). In addition to the positive impact on the child that stems from continued Theraplay between formal sessions, the parents should be enlisted as part of the Theraplay team because their unique relationship with the child can produce benefits that no other relationship can match. The greater the number of people trained to apply the Theraplay method during the hours intervening between formal sessions, the greater is the advantage for the troubled child. (In the most ideal case ever treated, mother, father, grandmother, teacher, principal, and classroom volunteer all came to the sessions.)

Family Theraplay is organized around an eleven-session core program as follows.

Diagnostic Session 1

The first session is essentially a traditional intake session. Parents are asked questions concerning the mother's pregnancy

138

and childbirth and about the child's infancy and later development, including, of course, reasons for his referral.

Since each question serves as the basis for the formulation and testing of a new hypothesis, it is a little difficult to prescribe exactly what the questions should be. The answers should provide useful information to the therapists (both to the therapist(s) who will be working directly with the child and to the interpreting therapist who will be explaining to the parents what is happening while they watch the treatment sessions from behind the one-way window).

In addition to familiarizing ourselves with the realities of their backgrounds, we must come to understand their corresponding attitudes and feelings toward their families of origin and their consequent expectations of their progeny. Further topics will include courtship and marriage, attitude toward the pregnancy, hoped-for sex of child, and reason for chosen name. It is hoped that this interview data will offer some clues about the child's biological strengths and weaknesses as well as about the family environment and parental expectations that greeted this newborn on his arrival.

In order to assess the kind of treatment he has been receiving at home, we will want to know his mother's degree of comfort with feeding and caretaking, and, because this is so often influenced by her relationship with her own mother, we will want to know about her view of that relationship. Thus we may come to predict of a mother who expresses disgust with the idea of breast feeding, for example, that in her own childhood her own mother was cold toward her and possibly even now is rejecting of her grandchild. In the area of the child's early development, questions include time and method of toilet training, expectations of cleanliness and conformity, and parental attitudes toward autonomy, exploring, and independence. The answers to these questions tell us the degree to which he has been allowed to "become his own person." Finally, in the area of genitality, questions asked will try to establish whether sexual exploration and pleasure is permitted, encouraged, or overstimulated. Questions about masturbation, sexual curiosity, family modesty or exhibitionism, and who sleeps

where are all-important. Again, it cannot be too strongly emphasized that no one format for interviewing will be appropriate
to all families. It is up to the individual interviewer to develop
the skill to formulate and test hypotheses as he or she goes
along, to be free to discard directions of inquiry that lead nowhere and to pursue those which suggest that "There is more
here than meets the eye." Only with much experience with
many parents, an openness to reliving one's own childhood, and
the freedom to call on one's related experiences as parent,
teacher, and babysitter, for example, can the good interviewer
truly supply the backdrop against which a particular family is
projected.

In order to give clues as to the marital interaction, wherever possible, the intake interview is directed to both parents
simultaneously. There are exceptions, of course, and these tend
to occur for one of the following three reasons: (1) Physiology
makes it appropriate to ask only one parent questions regarding,
for example, pregnancy, childbirth, or breast feeding; (2) a particular hypothesis may need to be tested with respect to a particular parent; and (3) one parent may be monopolizing the
interview to the exclusion of his or her partner.

Rather than presenting a three-way interchange (interviewer addressing both parents simultaneously), it may be well
at this point to show in-depth sections in which the interviewer
might address questions to each parent separately. The first,
regarding the presenting problem, particularly if the child is
male, is best directed to the father (if he is available for the
interview). Fathers tend to react to a son's problem both as
a blow to their self-esteem and as a cause for worry in itself. It
is the first of these two reactions, however, that makes it more
fruitful to address the father. A father, in his response to the
question "Why are you bringing your son in for help?" often
reveals not only the reasons for the boy's referral but also the
dynamic interplay between the two parents.

Sample Intake Interview

The following hypothetical interchanges between parent
and interviewer illustrate both parent-respondent and intake

worker's spoken and unspoken reactions. The first example, dealing with reasons for referral, comes at the outset of the interview. The second example, generally coming about one-third of the way into the interview, belongs in the section dealing with the child's birth and early infancy.

Example 1 is addressed to the father:

Interviewer		Father	
Unspoken	*Spoken*	*Spoken*	*Unspoken*
Let's see how accepting of, or threatened by, his son's problem this father is.	Mr. Jones, how do you feel about bringing Bruce in to see us?		
			Watch out! If I play this right, we'll have him out of this place in no time.
		Oh, he don't need to be coming here. That's what I say.	
			Besides, this is a place for crazy people, and places like that scare me.
OK, so coming here obviously wasn't his idea, and probably his son's pathology doesn't consciously			

	Interviewer		Father
Unspoken	*Spoken*	*Spoken*	*Unspoken*

bother him that much. It must have been his wife's doing, then.

If you feel *that* way, how come you brought him here?

I don't like this. I don't like admitting that I gave in to my wife, and I don't like thinking there's anything the matter with my son.

Well, we just thought we'd see what you folks have to offer . . .

There! That's put me back in the driver's seat. I was worried for a minute, but I'm OK now.

He really does need to save face. He must be feeling awfully vulnerable. I've got to be careful not to threaten him.

It sounds as

	Interviewer		Father	
	Unspoken	*Spoken*	*Spoken*	*Unspoken*
		though you're feeling pretty OK about that son of yours.		
			I am.	Whew! That feels much better.
		Tell me about him.		
				OK, this is safe. I'll just describe him.
			He's a real sweet kid, and he means well.	
	He's certainly involved with him. He needs support for that. He'll come around.	You like him.		
			I do.	You know, she's right!
	Keep supporting.	I can *see* that.		
			Yeh . . . that's why I wish he were a little more sure of himself.	Maybe she's not going to be against me. If I put it in terms of my boy, she won't have to see the weakness in me.
	He's still scared. He's understating the problem.			

Interviewer		Father	
Unspoken	*Spoken*	*Spoken*	*Unspoken*
Don't push.	He's not so sure?		
			She's OK.
		No . . . nothing as bad as my wife thinks, mind you . . .	
Should I pursue the conflict with his wife or stick with the boy? There is a conflict, but that can be explored later. Right now he must come to accept that he too sees that the boy has a problem.			
	Can you tell me a little about how you can tell he's not so sure?		
			That's an interesting question. It's safe, too, because I could still say, "Actually, he has no problem." But I won't. She's asking me as a kind of "professional."

Interviewer		Father	
Unspoken	*Spoken*	*Spoken*	*Unspoken*
			She respects my judgment. I like that.
		Well, you know, he's kind of a loner. No friends and all that.	
What degree of pathology is he talking about? But be careful. The best way to ask will be to get him to answer from inside the boy's skin, not from the point of view of the "tough guy" father.	Do you think he feels unhappy about being a loner?		Never thought what it must feel like for Bruce.
		Yeah, I bet he *is* unhappy.	
Good! He's got some capacity for change himself.	Very unhappy?		
		Yeah, I think so.	Poor Bruce! I

	Interviewer	Father	
Unspoken	*Spoken*	*Spoken*	*Unspoken*
			never real-ized.
	Then it's really good of you to bring him in for help at this time in his life.		
		I guess it is.	Hey! I'm getting credit!
Now, the marriage.	Bet that wasn't an easy thing for you to do, either.		
			She sure understands me. I might as well tell her more.
		It was really my wife's idea. She's always so worried about things.	
	"Things"?	Yeh.	
	More than you worry?	Yeh. She's always so tense about everything. Me, I like to just go out, have a good time.	
Their sex life may be in trouble too.	But not your wife.		
		No, she likes to stay home, do the same things.	

Interviewer		Father	
Unspoken	*Spoken*	*Spoken*	*Unspoken*
Sounds like Bruce! Do mother and son share some things in common? Does this exclude father? Is her involvement with Bruce perhaps even designed to supplant a more mature marital involvement? Test these hypotheses very slowly, moving the questions skillfully from one partner to the other . . .			

Example 2 is addressed to the mother:

Interviewer		Mother	
Unspoken	*Spoken*	*Spoken*	*Unspoken*
	Tell me about his beginnings in this world. How was he when he was still inside?		Watch out!
		He was fine! No problems! Perfect! Normal!	
That sounds			

| | Interviewer | | Mother |
Unspoken	Spoken	Spoken	Unspoken

Unspoken	Spoken	Spoken	Unspoken
like denial. Let's see if it is.			
	Sometimes pregnancy is a bit of a drag. How did *you* feel?		
		Generally all right.	
			There! That seems a safe enough thing to say.
"Generally all right" has a "keep a stiff upper lip" sound about it. Let's see what she is feeling so defensive about.			
	Generally all right?		
			OK, so she knows things weren't all that happy. Perhaps it's safe to tell her just a little bit.
		Well, sometimes I did feel a little untidy.	
"Untidy"? That's unusual wording. Is she saying the biological aspects of being pregnant repulsed her?	How do you		

Interviewer		Mother	
Unspoken	*Spoken*	*Spoken*	*Unspoken*
	mean "untidy"?		She sounds different from what my mother would say. She might even understand.
		You know, so fat and ugly.	
She's beginning to sound downright ashamed—but it's too soon to say that.	You mean you didn't like others to see you like that?		
			How did *she* know?
		That's right. I felt really ashamed.	
OK, if there's shame about sex and about pregnancy there's likely shame about other biological mothering functions too.	Ashamed of being pregnant?		
			She sounds as though I didn't need to have felt like that. But she also continues sounding like

Interviewer		Mother	
Unspoken	*Spoken*	*Spoken*	*Unspoken*
			she under-
	Yes.		stands.
Perhaps she was too ashamed of her breasts to breast feed? I'll ask her, but not in such a way as to make her feel guilty for using the bot-tle. The "why" part of the question will have to be built into the "how did you feed" part, rather than be added later as a separate question that she might hear as, "You did *not* breast feed? You bad girl, why not?"			
	After the baby was born, how did you feed him, and why?		
			She doesn't sound as though it mat-ters to her *which* I did, so I'll be open with her.
		I used the bottle. Why?	

| | Interviewer | | Mother |
| Unspoken | Spoken | Spoken | Unspoken |

Interviewer Unspoken	Interviewer Spoken	Mother Spoken	Mother Unspoken
		Because it was a cleaner, neater way to do it. Not so messy.	
"Messy" must be someone else's admonishment dating back to when she was little. Let's see.			
	Messy?		
			What? She doesn't think I'd be messy as a nursing mother? Hm. That's new.
		Yeah. I always thought nursing a baby was a disgusting thing to do.	
Who instilled that notion in her?			
	Disgusting? Who made you view it that way?		
			She sounds like she's on my side. Maybe I can begin to let her in on my difficulties.
		Well, my mother. She always said she couldn't bear to feed	

	Interviewer		Mother	
Unspoken	*Spoken*	*Spoken*	*Unspoken*

		her children that way and that she wouldn't come to visit me after my baby was born if I did.	
How about her own view? If she had been strong enough to break with her mother, would she have been freely nurturing with her baby?	Do you think if your mother hadn't made you feel that way you might have fed your baby differently?		
		Oh yes. I used to imagine what fun it might have been to nurse my baby.	Ah! Here's a lady who knows my true desires!
For that, she needs some reinforcement.	You know, a mother who		

	Interviewer		Mother
Unspoken	*Spoken*	*Spoken*	*Unspoken*

	feels she would have enjoyed breast feeding her baby, even if she didn't do it, surely must have been a most caring, loving mother.		
			That feels really good. I never even heard my own mother talk about me that way. If she had, I probably wouldn't have been so uncertain all those years.
I must keep in mind to find out later: How support- ive is mater- nal grand- mother these days? What was she like during moth- er's growing up with regard to "messing" and adoles- cence? and so on.			

The foregoing, of course, are only hypothetical examples.

Actual protocols will differ from these as widely as individuals differ from one another.

Diagnostic Sessions 2 and 3

Each of the two diagnostic visits, which are scheduled one week and two weeks after the initial intake session, consists of a parent-child interaction session between the child and first one and then the other of his parents. Initially designed to distinguish "affection-giving" from "direction-giving" parental patterns as determinants of imitation and identification in children (Marschak, 1960, 1979), the Marschak Interaction Method (MIM) is ideally suited as a basis for making a treatment plan. Depending on the nature of the parent-child interaction, the overall Theraplay plan aims to provide the kinds of experiences in which the family has been deficient. Thus it stresses Nurturing for a child whose parents have found it difficult to Nurture, Structuring for a child whose parents have failed to Structure. Emphases may change, of course, as family interactions change with treatment. The MIM sessions are conducted as follows. Child and parent sit at a table (if child is old enough; otherwise child lies in or near parent's arms) alone in a room, while other parent and staff therapists observe from the room adjoining. A stack of instruction cards lies face down on the table in front of the parent. (The seven to ten cards being used have been selected from a larger number of cards to answer specific questions about this parent and child unit, in line with the hypotheses formulated during and after the intake interview just described.) Next to the table is a suitcase containing large numbered envelopes, bags, boxes, and so on. With just a few exceptions, each instruction card assigns a task using the contents of one of the bags, envelopes, or boxes. The tasks are categorized according to the child's developmental level: neonate, infant, toddler, preschooler, latency child, or adolescent. Within each level, tasks vary on several dimensions, including the giving of Affection, giving of Direction (roughly equivalent to Nurturing and Structuring), Alertness to the environment (perhaps resembling Intruding), and Playfulness (which occasionally includes Challenging). Instruction cards consist of Intruding-type items such as "Parent plays peek-a-boo with child," Nurturing items such as "Feed each other M&M's" or "Parent powders child's back with baby powder," Structuring tasks such as "Parent teaches child something he doesn't know," and Challenging tasks such as "Adult engages child in three rounds of thumb wrestling."

A parent who refuses to powder a child's back with baby powder on the grounds that it would "spoil" him or who carries out the powdering but requires the child to spell the word *baby* tells us one thing about his or her giving and accepting of Nurturing; a parent who refuses even to consider the task that asks child to tell about "when he's a grown-up" or one who, in response to the request to "teach" the child something, puts him on his or her lap and sits staring off into space, shows us the degree to which he is comfortable with Structure/Challenge.

Instruction cards not only differentiate these clusters but, additionally, are divided between tasks that are carried out alone and those that are carried out jointly. Thus "Parent and child each get pad of paper and pencil and each 'draw something' " asks for behavior that is significantly violated if parent grabs child's hand with the pencil in it and begins to draw. By the same token, a parent responding to "Feed each other M&M's" by tossing the bag of candies across the table and saying to the child "Eat them," is not seen to be behaving in the called-for, mutually sharing way. Using this technique and keeping in mind these behavioral styles, the observer can determine the degree to which any set of parents tolerates, promotes, or squelches their child's infantile or ambitious behavior, the degree to which they operate apart from or in harmony or conflict with their child, the balance between the giving of affection and the giving of direction, and so on.

The foregoing, then, constitutes Diagnostic Sessions 2 and 3: the child and Parent 1 performing the MIM one week, child coming in for the MIM with Parent 2 the following week. Each session is observed by the other parent in the presence of the staff therapist(s). Each MIM is followed by a discussion with the participating parent. The MIM and follow-up discussion often lead to fresh insights on the parts of parents and a new willingness to deal with those of the child's behaviors that typically "turn them off." Questions raised with parents during the post-MIM discussion may include, for example, "Did you notice what you did each time your child moved over near you and tried to touch you?" "Yes, you frowned a little and moved away . . . I wonder what made you do that . . . " Or, "When it came to that item in which you were to ask him where on him you should put the Band-Aid, why did you insist he have a legitimate cut? Suppose you had just playfully put it where he wanted you to put it?" One-parent families of course have a total of two, not three, diagnostic sessions.

A sample MIM follows.

Marschak Interaction Method

Fourteen-year-old boy referred by school for:

- Truancy
- Drinking
- Theft
- Frequent running away from home

Father-Son MIM	*Mother-Son MIM*
Tasks:	*Tasks:*
1. Teach	1. Teach
2. Fortunes	2. Grown-up
3. Combing	3. Hats
	4. Moods

Father-Son MIM

1. Teach (Parent teaches child something he doesn't know)

Father: How many senators are there?
Child: 100.
Father: U.S. senators?
Child: Wait. One in each state.
Father: OK.

Child: Isn't there?
Father: How many justices?
Child: Nine?
Father: Nine.
Child: I was just kidding.
Father: I taught you something you didn't know. Now, re-
          member it. (laughs)
Child: I knew it.

Boy is unsure of self ("Wait," "Isn't there?" "Nine?"),
but covers this up with arrogant facade ("I was just kidding"; "I
knew it").

Father teaches through questioning. (Perhaps he is reluctant to assert himself?) When he finally does make an authoritarian statement, he demeans himself by turning it into a joke ("I
taught you something you didn't know. Now, remember it").

 2. *Fortunes (Parent and child tell each other's fortunes)*

Father: Now, this is very interesting.
Child: Yeah . . . tell what I'm thinking.
Father: I can't tell what you're thinking. Your hand's very
          similar to mine.
Child: What am I going to do in the future?

[They touch hands, push each other.]

Father: (studies scars on child's hands)
Child: That's from football.
Father: Careless?
Child: Just from football. (demonstrates, leaning back)
          What's wrong? Are you jealous?

Son manipulates father in a brazen way ("Yeah, tell what
I'm thinking"; "What am I going to do in the future?"; and,
finally, "What's wrong? Are you jealous?"[1]

Hard as he tries to do it ("Now, this is very interesting";
"Careless?"; "Your hand's very similar to mine"), father cannot
relate to his son ("I can't tell what you're thinking").

3. Combing (Parent and child comb each other's hair)

Child: Do I get to keep this (comb)? I'm just combing my own hair. You comb yours.

Father: (extends head for son to comb it)

Child: People could have lice. I'm very picky . . . like Mom.

Father: (looks at son, appealing)

Child: Comb your own hair. (keeps combing, smiling)

Father: Want to comb my hair?

Child: No.

Father: Why?

Child: *Because!* I told you I don't want to comb *nobody's* hair.

Son is hypercritical ("People could have lice"), is self-centered ("I'm just combing my own hair"), disrespectful and rejecting of father ("You comb yours," "Comb your own hair," "No," "Because! I told you I don't want to . . . "). He talks like a parent to an overly demanding child. He taunts father with his (son's) relationship with mother ("I'm very picky . . . like Mom.").

Father is tentative, pleading for son's attention. (He plays the role of the masochistic lover, the patient suitor.)

Mother-Son MIM

1. Teach (Parent teaches child something he doesn't know)

Mother: I was just reading that they're finding that the position of the baby . . . it's just as important when the baby's inside the mother . . . just as important . . .

Child: Mom, can I close the curtain? (referring to the curtain to the observation room)

The choice of obstetrics as subject matter appropriate to "teach" to a fourteen-year-old son is certainly an unusual one. He responds to mother's choice of subject matter by becoming suddenly self-conscious about being observed.

2. Grown-up (Parent asks child to tell about
when he's a grown-up)

Child: I don't know what I'm going to be.
Mother: It says tell about when you're grown up.
Child: I just want to be a good lover . . . a happy man.

She makes some effort to conform to the instructions. He continues the sexually provocative theme of the previous task.

3. Hats (Parent and child try dress-up hats on one another)

Mother: Oh God! This is embarrassing! Oh! My God! Look at this selection!
Child: That's just what I wanted! Give me the Spanish hat! (puts it on and dances) Hey! *Si! Si! ¿Como estás? Si amigo!*
Mother: I'm going to pick the worst one.
Child: Would you wear it?
Mother: No. I don't like the colors.
Child: (handling officer's cap) I wouldn't wear no pig's hat.
Mother: Why wouldn't you? Why?
Child: I would throw this hat into the military pig's face.
Mother: (trying small straw hat on self) How about this one? Like a little schoolgirl's hat . . . That's a pretty hat. I think *you* look best in this one, though.
Child: Yeah. I could go to a bar in this one (tries on hat she has selected for him).
Mother: Yeah. You would look much older.

Boy's behavior with mother is in sharp contrast to that with his father on a similar task (combing). Even in the absence of a male authority figure, his rebelliousness is apparent ("pig," "throw in his face," sneak "into a bar"). He is seductive and flamboyant.

Mother struggles with her own exhibitionism. She does not hesitate to flatter him and seems, if anything, to welcome his "macho" stance—including his defiance of authority.

4. Moods (Parent asks child to describe how the children on the pictures are feeling)

Mother: What would you say about this picture?
Child: Scared.
Mother: I don't see that . . . His mouth . . .
Child: Me. When I was a kid. Left out. Ugly. Sad.
Mother: (next picture) He looks left out, too . . . Looks bored . . .
Child: (taking next picture) Happy? Excited?
Mother: Yes. He looks very, very healthy.
Child: (taking next picture) Mad at her boyfriend.
Mother: That was a dumb one. I didn't like that one very much.
Child: We can sit here all day doing this.

Boy is still self-referent ("Me, when I was a kid"). Relates to her in comfortable manner ("We can sit here all day . . . "), with sexual overtones ("Mad at her boyfriend"), possibly reflecting a wish about the marital relationship between his parents.

Mother does not hesitate to contradict him ("I don't see that"), yet she is emotionally "with" him. She, too, is critical ("Looks bored" and "That was a dumb one"), and in that sense her son is identified with her, as was suggested in combing task ("I'm very picky . . . like Mom"). One can only speculate that it is father who is the object of their joint criticism.

Theraplay Sessions 1-4

In line with Jensen's (1963, p. 490) finding that when "what is going on in their child's treatment [is discussed with the parents], the whole procedure makes more sense to them and increases the possibilities of closing the case as a successful one," family Theraplay is strongly focused to include the parents. The following Theraplay sessions require a minimum staff of two. At the very least, there is one Theraplay therapist interacting directly with the child in the Theraplay room and an interpreting therapist seated in the observation room with the

parents. It is the interpreting therapist's job to carry out discussions of Theraplay principles, family dynamics, intrapsychic
conflicts, infant temperament, historical determinants, and so
on, as well as to encourage, redirect, educate, help in selecting
appropriate schools or summer camps, provide suggestions for
handling in-laws, make referrals to physicians or dieticians, and
so on. The interpreting therapist, in other words, must be a person of psychological sensitivity, thorough child-development
training, personal wisdom and maturity, sound judgment, and a
good deal of familiarity with the current world of childrearing
(for example, carpools, fad diets, park districts, and baby-
sitting).

The first four of the eight half-hour core family Theraplay sessions take place as follows: Parent or parents sit in the
observation room with the interpreting therapist watching the
child being played with by one or two therapists. (Although one
therapist is more economical than two, in intensity of impact—
particularly for vigorous tasks such as those of the Intruding
variety, and for insistent Structuring, particularly in the face of
some children's resistance to structure—and as a model for how
two parents can play with one child, the advantages of two therapists are often so great as to offset the additional expense. Two
therapists provide more than double the vigor and intensity and
more than twice the spirit of fun, surprise, and spontaneity.
Although two must be prepared to operate in synchrony and
thus make presession planning a necessity, two therapists are a
must for family Theraplay Sessions 5-8.) During the period of
observation, in addition to calling on the aforementioned other
areas of competence, the interpreting therapist engages the
parent(s) in an ongoing dialogue. (For example, "Watch closely
now . . . " "What do you see?" "Why do you suppose Johnny
keeps moving about—or talking, or going limp, or 'spacing out'
—like that?" "Why do you think the therapists are making up
Susie's face—or combing her hair, or rubbing noses with her?
That's right, it's to engage her in as much eye contact as they
possibly can." "This week at home did you do some fun eye-
contact things? You did? Tell me about them. Oh, that sounds
really great!")

Once again, there are almost as many examples of this

dialogue as there are kinds of problem children. The interpreting therapist must have the skill to balance the time allotted for explanation, listening, and discussion of past, present, and future, on the one hand, and time for quiet observation of the child and his treatment session, on the other. At the end of Session 4, parents are told, "Remember now, you're going to be joining in for the last half of Johnny's next four sessions. So dress comfortably."

The Theraplay session itself is planned with regard not only to the synchronous functioning of the therapists but also to the progression within the session. Thus, the session may begin with some checkup exercises (for example, "Let's see if he brought those great strong muscles he had here with him last week"); move into some spunky, lively, surprising (Intruding) activities; slow down for some soft, gentle, Nurturing ones; build up to a lively, perhaps competitive (Challenging) crescendo again; and end, possibly, with nourishment and a lullaby (Nurturing) in a quiet, integrated mood. Within this general format, specific issues (for example, the child's need to "run the show," his fear of new experiences, his avoidance of body contact, his discomfort with body disequilibrium, or his restlessness and hyperactivity) are dealt with through activities especially designed to help these problems (for example, by Structuring).

Theraplay Sessions 5-8

The first fifteen minutes of each remaining half-hour core family Theraplay session proceeds exactly as before, parents and interpreting therapist observing through the one-way vision mirror. For the last fifteen minutes, however, the parents are included in the Theraplay session. The introduction of his parents into the Theraplay room, where Johnny has been "playing," may follow one of any of a number of formats. His therapist(s) may, for example, say to Johnny, "You know, you are the world's best hider. Do you suppose if you and I hide behind this pile of pillows Mom and Dad could possibly find us? Come on, let's try . . . Build them up . . . Hand me another one . . . now another . . . OK, are we ready? Let's yell real loud . . .

Mom and Dad!! Come and find us!" Mother and father enter
the room at that point and make a big production of searching
everywhere—under the rugs, behind the curtains, in the closets.
"Where can he be? We've just looked everywhere!" "Oh-oh,
what's this funny lump over here. Come on, it looks like a good
place to rest. Let's sit down a minute and cool off after our big
search . . . whew! Oh-oh . . . you know what? I think I felt it
wiggle. Oh-oh, what's this? You know, I do think this is a foot
under here . . . " And so on. Of course, there are big squeals of
delight and much hugging at the reunion. Needless to say, parents have been well coached in advance of this entrance. They
have also been coached to be prepared for outspoken rejection,
which is always a possibility.

During the joint session, parents are worked with as intensely as was their child heretofore. Depending on their particular conflicts—as these have emerged during the initial intake,
MIM, and preceding four sessions of observation—the focus of
the family Theraplay sessions is carefully designed to confront
these conflicts. If, for example, father cannot tolerate passivity
in his son, he is asked to hold or powder him and is enthusiastically praised for the inventive, or strong, or cuddly way he does
this. If he or his son has difficulty competing, then water pistol
fights and father-and-son wrestling matches may be the activity
of choice—mother acting as cheerleader, umpire, or the mopper-
off of perspiring brows. If mother is unable to assert her authority with her child (or, in that case, probably also with anyone
else in her life), she is helped to develop assertiveness in a game
of "Mother, May I?" in which she is required, albeit in fun, to
brook no violation of the rules she establishes. If parent and
child merge too readily, they are encouraged to pillow fight,
wrestle, and play tug of war, physical and other differences between them being cheerfully emphasized by the therapists.
Sometimes there is a history of child abuse. In the family
sessions, therapists help parents see how lovable and attractive
their child really is. They participate in taking care of their
child's every tiny sore with lotions, warm water, and Band-Aids
and are helped to prevent every possibility for an accidental
hurt (for example, "Mom, when we hold his head this way he

could bump it. See, we have to hold it this way"; "Dad, that time he jumped too hard. He could scrape himself. Let's help him do it again carefully, so he'll be really safe this time"). Again, there are as many refinements to family Theraplay sessions as there are kinds of problem families.

During Session 6, the therapists announce that there will be just one more session before Session 8, at which there is to be the terminating party.

Session 8 may begin with familiar games and antics and may move on to more quiet reviews of "nice things that have been happening" and discussions of ways in which the child has grown. Next, each person may put a party hat on someone else, and, finally, each person feeds a treat to someone else. The session ends with a favorite song or lullaby—the child being rocked, perhaps, or held in the arms of one or both parents. There are fond embraces and goodbyes—with particular personal references wherever possible; for example, "Tony, you be sure to have fun with your new friend, Joe, at school" or "Beth, I want you to remember to show your grandmother how pretty you look in that new dress." And the session ends with a reminder about the date of the upcoming checkup visit.

The Checkup

Checkup visits are scheduled quarterly for the first year and annually thereafter. Checkup visits replicate Sessions 5-8 in format—parent(s) joining in for the last half of the session. At the outset, the therapists express their delight at seeing Johnny again and set about to find his familiar characteristics as well as those that have changed (for example, "Oh good! You brought those freckles with you . . . except, guess what? Here are some brand new ones. These must have come from those weekends at the beach." "Look at that, he brought his gorgeous smile along. And look! Two new teeth! Wow! What beauties!")

Children seem to love the checkup visits. Parents often report, "We don't know why we bring him. There really hasn't been anything wrong. But he does love to come back here . . . "

In the viewing room, during the first half of the checkup visit, parents bring the interpreting therapist up to date on recent developments and may ask, "We've been (having special baby times together, setting firm limits, or doing surprise activities, and so on) whenever he (gets tense and driven, or wordy and legalistic, or gets too disorganized, or becomes over methodical, and so on), just as we learned to do here. Is that still OK to do?"

Families return once a year over the next few years for their annual checkup visit. They are encouraged to phone the institute should problems arise in the interim. Most often these calls are handled in telephone consultation. Occasionally the whole family is signed up for an interim session or two.

Family Theraplay Example

The following is one more example of short-term family Theraplay.

Bonnie, three and a half years old, was referred for anger, fearfulness, bizarre actions toward other children, harming babysitters, and other behavior. The first child of two highly anxious parents, she reacted to the birth of her younger brother when she was two by lying face down on the floor, screaming, "No no no," needing diapers, and eventually demanding to be breast fed. Her parents, already strained by the demands of a sickly newborn, repeatedly attempted to find a babysitter for Bonnie. But her insistence on getting her way and her screaming when thwarted made these efforts fruitless. Her mother reported that if only she had had enough control over herself she would have told Bonnie quietly that she disapproves of her actions. As it was, the mother screamed and occasionally hit her and feared that one day she might actually hurt her. Particularly disturbing to her were Bonnie's poor judgment and infantile ways. "She's three years old," she said. "It's time she gave all that baby stuff up. She makes me so mad when she sucks on her sleeve. When she provokes me like that, I make her sit on a chair for an hour." She saw criminal potential in her having twisted the petals off the tulips the previous spring, although she had never told Bonnie not to do it. She said, she "should know better."

The diagnostic impression of Bonnie's parents made during the intake interview states: "Highly anxious family. Father very insulating of mother. Father diffused, intellectual, great difficulty focusing. Mother warm, competent, but overwhelmed, guilty, needy herself, and spread too thin. Tensions in marriage over husband's need to control her, to infantilize her, to be self-aggrandizing. Both very crisis-geared."

The following is a partial transcript of the interchanges between this rather difficult set of parents and the interpreting therapist, Terrence Koller, as they observed Bonnie's first two sessions of Theraplay from behind the one-way window:

Session 1

Father:	She seems to be a little bit bewildered.
Interpreting Therapist:	She's supposed to not have time to catch on enough to run things.
Father:	Seems like a lot of busy stuff. Doesn't look like much fun, to me, frankly. Looks like it's a couple of adults making like it's a lot of fun, but the kid doesn't really enjoy it much. That's how it looks to me. Babying. I'm not saying there's nothing in it, just that in a general sense it looks staged, to me.
Interpreting Therapist:	(to mother) What's your feeling? Do you have any questions?
Mother:	No, not yet. Just waiting to see.
Father:	There are some parts that she very obviously enjoys.
Interpreting Therapist:	She's got the nicest smile.
Father:	Yeah, when she smiles she means it. . . . (parents watch intently for a time) We're gonna play the game.

[At this point, Bonnie is becoming more and more upset with the therapists, crying, "I want my mommy!" and then screaming, "I *really* want my mommy!"]

Interpreting Therapist:	What usually happens to her when she

	says, "I want my mommy," or when she cries?
Father:	She doesn't do that very much.
Mother:	Oh, Jack, she *does!*
Father:	Well, not with me.
Mother:	She goes to nursery school and it happens, and at a friend's house the other day. . . .
Interpreting Therapist:	And what do you do?
Mother:	I *go* to her . . . She can't go outside or be outside for five minutes without wanting me.
Interpreting Therapist:	So, do you know what we're getting at?
Mother:	Well, yes, excepting that I feel really guilty about this . . . She's been put through too much already.
Father:	I don't feel particularly guilty about that. Right now, what I feel is quite resentful. What I'm resenting is the sense of manipulation, and Bonnie is not used to manipulation with me. Straight stuff. No bullshit. If anybody was playing with Bonnie, it would be in a spirit of "I like you, and you like me, and we're good, close friends, and we enjoy each other, and I'm not going to pull any stunts on you"; and I resent this, personally, because this kid is not used to being manipulated this way . . . I don't believe in manipulative bullshit, and I regard this as manipulative bullshit. . . . You asked for my reaction, and this is my reaction. I like straight stuff, and that's *all* I like.
Interpreting Therapist:	The point is to show her that even if she can't have you right at the mo-

	ment she asks . . . she can survive. She'll be all right. You'll be there when she really needs you.
Mother:	I see. OK . . . Because this is what she needs. (To husband) You don't really know it, but this is what I have to experience, this is what I have to live with. This is the torture that we've been talking about at night: that she can't go to bed without me.

[In the last two minutes of the session, mother describes further evidence of Bonnie's almost total inability to get along without the mother's actual physical presence at all times.]

Session 2

[Second session opens with Bonnie saying, "I'm tired! I'm *really* tired!" Therapist responds, "You look red and white, to me!" Almost immediately Bonnie begins to cry and holler for her mommy. This continues for almost the entire session, with only brief instances of quieting down, when she is surprised out of it, until, with only a few minutes of the session remaining, she becomes quite subdued and quiet.]

Interpreting Therapist:	The therapists have been getting a feeling for your difficulties at home from what it was like to be in there with her last week, and I've written down a couple of things they told me that we should be watching for.
Father:	Wait. I want to be watching this, if I can.
Interpreting Therapist:	Sure. Let me just prepare you for what to expect. We notice that when we get quiet, when we're not quick, she gets very uncomfortable. When we get babylike, she gets uncomfortable with that; when we talk to her, she gets uncomfortable with that; and if

	she has to repeat something she gets uncomfortable with that. So we're going to see what happens here. . . .
Father:	(later in the session) When I told her we were coming here this morning, she didn't like that. . . .
Mother:	Well . . . she ran to the door! . . .
Interpreting Therapist:	Does this remind you of your playground and school experiences?
Mother:	Somewhat. . . .
Interpreting Therapist:	(still later in the session) She'll learn that they're going to bring her back to you when they're finished.
Father:	How much time left?
Interpreting Therapist:	Let's see . . . twenty minutes.
Mother:	It looks to me like she's more screaming hysterically than just crying.
Interpreting Therapist:	What do you make of that?
Mother:	Well, I think she's more comfortable with this than she was last time. She was more scared and terrified last time.
Interpreting Therapist:	We seem to notice that when she is made to do things she loses control, and they'll be working on that.
Father:	When she loses control of the situation, that's very frightening for her. I don't see them permitting her to exercise even a smidgeon of control in this thing.
Interpreting Therapist:	Well, you see it's just *that* which she is trying to do with the crying and screaming. . . .
Mother:	Is to control. I see this, Jack. She tries to control situations this way.
Father:	I *know* that she does that, but I have a feeling that I have already expressed here, that I feel very strongly about.

There's a word that we haven't heard much in the last couple of years, and that I didn't use very much when it was stylish to use, because I thought that it was overdone, but I feel that the disregard, the bombardment by the adults of this child, that has the effect of, is equivalent to, ignoring what is going on within the child, in terms of the situation that is going on. I feel that it is an atrocity. As I told Dr. J., we're here to play the game, but I don't . . .

Interpreting Therapist: I don't understand. You see this as a "game"? It sounds like you're very worried about her, but this is a "game"?

Father: You know the expression. You're either *in* the game or you're *out* of the game. You're either in until the end of the game, or you're going to decide to quit. Now, we're here on the strength of the recommendation about Dr. J. And we are going along with her judgment despite my feeling that this is an atrocity. *I* think this is an atrocity!

Mother: I don't! Look how she's quieted down, Jack.

Father: Whether she's quieted down, or not, I think it is an atrocity! Listen . . . That's no kid who's being helped to learn how to be happy.

Mother: Well, Jack, she certainly hasn't been happy with a lot of the things that have been going on, and we, you and I both, don't know what to do about it.

Father: I agree with that, and that is why we sought Dr. R.'s recommendation, and

	that is why we are here. That's why we have gone along with it. That's what I mean: in the game. But I regard it as an atrocity. . . .
Interpreting Therapist:	I do admire your being able to hold on, to watch it.
Father:	I'm not holding on. I'm expressing it. And I'm maintaining my control, but my control also includes the option of walking in and taking my kid right out of there. I'm not giving my power away.
Interpreting Therapist:	I know. We wouldn't want that.
Father:	But I think you ought to know at least how *I* feel, and I think I ought to have an opportunity to express it. And have it listened to, as I feel she should, and I don't feel she is.
Mother:	Ok. But she's quieting down.

[At this point, the session over, a totally subdued Bonnie, accompanied by her two therapists, knocks on the door of the observation room.]

This marked not only the end of the session but, for the most part, the end of active opposition on Bonnie's part. At this point, the therapists began having fun with Bonnie. And it was also at this point that the father joined the mother in finding positive aspects in what was happening.

Two sessions later, both parents entered the Theraplay room for the last fifteen minutes of the remaining four sessions. As expected, the first of these joint sessions brought a revival of Bonnie's initial negativism and of her father's hesitancy to assume responsibility for her. The therapists' active engagement of both parents, however, soon led to the father's enjoying himself in spite of himself.

During Sessions 6 and 7, the father asked for hints on "tricks" to do with Bonnie, and during the final observation period he told the interpreting therapist stories of how he had been able to set limits during the period between sessions.

At the final (closing) interview, the father began by asking the interpreting therapist for staff observations concerning the changes in Bonnie. The interpreting therapist told him that Bonnie seemed much more at ease than she was at first; that he thought it was because, after that very unpleasant experience in the beginning, she began to realize she could relax and that the therapists were going to take the responsibility for making decisions. That seemed to make her feel more relaxed. The interpreting therapist said that, from the beginning, Bonnie's therapists tried to do things that were enjoyable, and, when she realized that she didn't have to call the shots, she relaxed and enjoyed the sessions. The interpreting therapist reminded them that Bonnie's therapists had to work through some resistance once again when her parents were introduced into the sessions halfway through the treatment program but that she'd soon relax and enjoy doing the same sorts of things with them. Bonnie's mother agreed.

The father indicated he believed that a lot of the activities worked because of the therapists' presence and said he doubted they could be successful without the therapists. The interpreting therapist reminded the parents of the many things they themselves had, in fact, done with Bonnie during the sessions and between sessions, telling them it was very important that Bonnie get the message that these activities would continue. The interpreting therapist told them that if Bonnie got the impression that the therapy office was the only place these things took place she would again become defensive and resistant, resorting to the behavior that had caused them to bring her in initially. The interpreting therapist talked about the need to assure her of the safety of activities, as well as of her parents' care and concern for her.

The interpreting therapist discussed the potential danger of the parents' expectations, which put pressure on Bonnie to act more "grown up" than was appropriate, and how to deal with her occasional controlling "I can do that. I don't want you to help." The interpreting therapist recommended saying, "I know you can do that, but I *want* to help you, this time." The interpreting therapist explained that the Theraplay has been designed to make *them* feel good, as well as Bonnie, and that their efforts to continue Theraplay after they leave should help the whole family feel better. This gave the father an opportunity to suggest that Theraplay hadn't really been the only factor in Bonnie's change, after all. There had been a positive change in the family situation as well, and this had caused Bonnie to be more relaxed and thus less of a headache. The mother said, with much more assurance, that she had learned techniques from the Theraplay experience that were helping her to deal successfully with Bonnie and her brother and that the effect had been a much better relationship.

The father spent quite a lot of time asking for specific activities (and demonstrations of how to do them), giving reasons why they wouldn't work (his bad back, Bonnie's reluctance, no time, and so on). The interpreting therapist was able to get him to promise to try and to remember always that he was in charge.

The mother wanted the interpreting therapist to recommend a school placement for Bonnie, based on her description of several schools they had looked at. The interpreting therapist asked her to tell which one she thought was best, based on what she had learned from Theraplay. She found this difficult to do, saying that it didn't matter what she did at home with Bonnie, that her efforts were going to be subverted anyway by the school experience. The interpreting therapist finally told her that it was *her* responsibility to make sure that Bonnie got enough at home to make her strong enough to deal successfully with the school situation. The interpreting therapist told her that often parents have too little control over the environment their children become exposed to but that he felt they could give their children the tools to deal successfully with that environment, whether good or less than good.

Follow-Up

Since the family subsequently moved from the area, Bonnie has not been seen again. Approximately three months later, a talk with the mother by phone revealed that Bonnie had been put into a school that both parents liked. She was in a carpool with other boys and girls and played with them a lot after school and without requiring the almost constant presence of her mother. The family members were communicating better, the mother reported. She said Bonnie wanted to go to school, although she was still not playing with all the children when she got there. There were still a few problems, some potentially difficult, but clearly she was not the same little girl who was seen at the beginning.

Treatment Summary

The following notes were made by Terrence Koller at the conclusion of Bonnie's treatment.

Beginning of Theraplay

Parents. They began Theraplay with much apprehension and doubt. They were worried that we were not concerned about their daughter's feelings (or theirs) and that we might do more harm than good. Although initially very concerned with Bonnie's behavior, they quickly forgot all that and acted as if she were OK except for the times we were with her. Her mother found it difficult to separate from her and was on the edge of her seat behind the mirror whenever she seemed the least bit upset. The father considered Theraplay an "outrage" and continually reminded us that they could quit whenever they wanted. He looked angry all the time and seemed not to listen to what we said. Despite all this, they never seemed to have enough time with us, continually found it difficult to end each session, and made frequent requests for extra time.

Child. Bonnie began each of the first two sessions in tears, always crying for her parents and accusing the therapists of abusing her. She wanted her own way and seemed on the verge of a tantrum when she would not get it. She tried to flee to the pillows or to the door all the time. She looked pathetic.

Treatment

We stuck with both Bonnie and her parents in the usual "We know what's best" manner. If the mother wanted to leave the observation room and rescue Bonnie, we explained to her that Bonnie needed to learn to be without her at times and reminded her that she would be with Bonnie after the sessions. We suggested that her school difficulties might be helped by a similar attitude. At times when the mother really couldn't stand it, we asked her to leave the room and get a drink of water. We consistently reinforced the father's statements that he would "play the game."

End of Theraplay

Parents. The mother came to relax considerably when playing with Bonnie. She was able to set limits in a warm, non-mechanical way. The father was surprised that Bonnie was like a lamb in the Theraplay room, and he really enjoyed both the attention he gave to her and the attention he himself received from the therapists. Despite previously complaining of a bad back, he asked to be taught new ways of physically playing with Bonnie. Although admitting that Bonnie had changed drastically for the better, he adamantly maintained that this was not due to Theraplay.

Child. Bonnie stopped screaming for her parents. She loved the activities—one time saying to her father after a session, "I liked playing those games in there" (pointing to the playroom). Bonnie struggled less and less and was able to listen to others. In striking contrast to their initial feelings, the therapists soon found her to be an attractive and enjoyable little girl.

Note

1. In fact, the boy was right. The father unconsciously did feel excluded from the relationship between mother and son.

6

Special Settings for Treatment

Theraplay in Schools

Theraplay conducted within the framework of a school system —as it is done in Michigan City, Indiana, for example—requires a particular format and presents particular problems quite unlike those found in doing Theraplay within a private clinic or a community mental health center. The differences, of course, arise from the differences in basic purpose of the two kinds of institutions: the former being designed for teaching, the latter for treating or curing. Thus, persons doing treatment within the confines of an agency set up for teaching are, in some sense, trespassers. This is true whether the school is a private school, a center for training the handicapped, a special education facility, or a Head Start site. They are trespassers, whether they work in a corridor, a teacher's lounge, a playground, or the classroom.

176

As such, Theraplay therapists must be prepared for conflict and criticism in addition to the cooperation, gratitude, and eagerness to share and learn that are often found. When faced with the problems that stem from being "on foreign turf," concession is the name of the game, although never at the sacrifice of a child's mental health.

In line with the need for concession is the need to provide early orientation, whether directed to teachers, principals, classroom aides, or parents. Orientation means familiarizing all individuals who will be involved with the intricacies of the Theraplay technique. Through films, descriptions, demonstration, and the opportunity for questions and discussion, school personnel can be helped to feel so comfortable with the prospect of Theraplay within their walls that conflicts can be held to a minimum. Although it may require extra time beyond the Theraplay itself, every effort must be made, once the treatment of children has begun, to keep the channels of communication open between the therapist and the school personnel. Thus time must be allowed for teacher feedback sessions, for parent conferences, and for staff in-service programs. Otherwise the unhappy consequence is too often sabotage and working at cross-purposes.

Four models by which Theraplay has been provided to four different educational facilities are described in this chapter.

Whenever possible, parent orientation and staff in-service sessions are scheduled early enough in the school year so that by the time the mental health consultant has made his first Theraplay referral all relevant persons are well informed. In public schools particularly, where conformity, order, quiet, and predictability are generally the rule, there is often little place for spontaneity, regression, giggling, insistent personal involvement, noisy fun, or physical contact. Even with adequate preparation of the teaching staff, a therapist could well be disturbed in his work by a principal who, responsive to his staff's complaints and apprehensions, interrupts a therapeutic encounter in which a child is attempting to "leave the scene" by crying. The skillful Theraplay therapist finds a way to communicate reassurance to the principal while yet continuing to work with the resistant child. Interruptions by school personnel are not limited to unhappy times. Many schools have implicit policies against children jumping off desks, removing their shoes and socks, playing with water, and against school-age (even preschool-age) children being treated like infants. In the best of all worlds, both the site staff and the child's parent(s) know what to expect, have given their consent, have offered to cooperate in the process, and look forward to the outcome with optimism. The Theraplay therapist arrives for the first session, introduces himself to the principal, teaching staff, parent, and child, and then sets off to begin the session in a place previously designated. Although the original session is generally one-to-one, later sessions may include the parent and/or teacher (or aide), classmates, and sometimes even the principal.

On their return to the classroom from each session, the therapist makes a special effort to provide the teacher some bridge between therapy session and classroom. Thus, the therapist may say, for example, "Miss Jones, Arthur has brought the most beautiful new tooth with him to school today . . . just look at this. Arthur, let's show your teacher what we found here." Trivial as they may seem, these carryover statements do bridge the gap for Arthur himself and do allow his teacher to feel included in, and thus more accepting of, the session. Sometimes the bridging may be physical. "Susie had such fun today, Mr. Conner. Will you take her hand so she can wave to me from the window as I drive off in my car?" Between sessions, teachers will be apprised of the child's progress and they and the parent(s) will be alerted to the onset of the negative phase (for example, "You should know, Miss Hunter, that Jeffrey looks as though he's about to go into that negative phase we talked about in the orientation meeting. Now you remember that means he may be difficult for a while—provoking, testing, demanding, resisting. Yet, just because he's oppositional doesn't mean that you need to give in. You'll be setting limits for him just as you would for any other disobedient child.")

As a child improves—improvement generally being defined by teacher and parent as well as by the mental health consultant—one or two other children often are gradually incorporated into the treatment session. ("Joanie, Jimmy, Sarah, and Craig, today we're going to braid Susie's hair *so* pretty: Here, Joanie, you hold these ribbons; Jimmy, you hold the mirror for Susie; and Sarah and Craig, I'm going to show you both how to make two pigtails.") Following this inclusion, the therapy may take place within the classroom itself and finally may consist of nothing more than the therapist's presence in the child's awareness as he (the child) goes about the normal class activities.

Theraplay in Head Start

Theraplay in Head Start has been a tradition in Chicago since 1968. Since then the Theraplay program has had the following general format: Psychological consultants to the Head Start centers identify children in need of special attention. (Approximately 10 percent of all Head Start children nationwide are considered to be in need.) Of those children so identified, about 20 percent are referred for other services, including neurological workups or more extensive psychological diagnosis. The remaining 80 percent are referred for Theraplay (diagnostic Theraplay or treatment: Diagnostic Theraplay has been discussed elsewhere; see Chapter Three).

Children referred for Theraplay are seen by therapists who make the rounds of referred children at their various schools in a particular area of the city. Each therapist has a caseload of up to fifteen or sixteen children. Each child receives treatment once, twice, or three times a week. Children are referred in about equal proportions for overactive aggressive and for withdrawn behavior. Immature, bizarre, and obsessive children make up the remainder. As mentioned earlier, children who have been traumatized are referred not for Theraplay but for traditional child therapy (see Chapter Two).

Often parents in Head Start are not available to play the part of cotherapist. In addition, it sometimes happens that a child's home environment is what could be described as malevolent. "In these cases," Theodore Hurst, executive director of the Theraplay Institute and producer of the Theraplay film *There*

He Goes (1970), advises, "Theraplay will have the additional purpose of insulating the child to protect him from further damage." Raymond, in the film, is a good example of necessary insulation. At the time of referral, Raymond lived with a mother so immature that when she came to visit his Head Start room she would play with his toys and eat his lunch. At home, she often fed Raymond no breakfast and on his return home at the end of the school day locked him into his bedroom with no stimulation whatsoever. Raymond was referred for behavior sufficiently disruptive to make him the only child in the city-wide Head Start program in serious danger of exclusion. At the time of follow-up three years later, although there appeared to be no significant change in his environment, Raymond had maintained the gains he made in Theraplay. The insulation-promoting effects of Theraplay would appear to be the only explanation. Theraplay may affect the absent, nonparticipating family as well as the child himself. Pat, star of the Theraplay film *Here I Am* (Jernberg, Hurst, and Lyman, 1969—Chapter Three), referred for being withdrawn, nonverbal, and "odd," was seen in her three-year follow-up to be even more active, engaged, and cheerful than she was at the point of termination of her therapy. In his follow-up interview, her father reported that, whereas of his nine children Pat had been of least interest to him previously, she came to develop such a "sparkling personality" with her Theraplay that for the last three years she had been his favorite. In a study by this author and Austin Des Lauriers (Jernberg and Des Lauriers, 1962) of changes in child-parent interactions over time, it was observed that children can behave in such a way as to engage parents who are otherwise disengaged.

Theraplay in Private Schools

Private schools tend to be more flexible, and thus somewhat more tolerant of the complexities inherent in Theraplay, than are public schools. Orientation presentations to parents and in-service programs for teachers are still important. Since private schools tend not to be bound by teachers' union regulations, there are fewer constraints on a teacher's availability and thus greater freedom for discussion between teacher and therapist. Private schools often allow a wider margin within which therapist and patient can carry out their sessions. Trips to secondhand shops to try on jewelry, use of the school's sewing room for making skirts, or permission for a short walk to the lakefront for wading or skipping stones—all usually forbidden in public schools—are generally freely available at private ones. A few private schools even make their audiovisual equipment available to therapist and child.

Theraplay in Centers for the Training of the Handicapped

Centers designed for the training of handicapped children depend on state education money. Thus their primary purpose, as in regular institutions of learning, is the education of their enrollees. This being the case, even those students whose problems make learning impossible are expected first and foremost to "learn." Thus, once again, although therapy may be the only experience to which these children are truly attentive, it is often seen as of only minor importance in comparison with their education. As such, the Theraplay therapist is once again a trespasser on foreign soil. The following two experiences may prove useful to therapists based in a special facility:

Center A, a large center for the training of the profoundly retarded, contracts for one year of biweekly Theraplay training and supervision of its staff. Although one or two of the key administrators are familiar with Theraplay, this is not true for either the director himself or for the majority of the staff members. No initial orientation of parents to Theraplay is possible, nor are there regular all-staff in-service sessions. Staff members feel, in fact, that an approach to children has been forced on them that they neither requested nor feel comfortable doing. Those who do attempt to do Theraplay—and some of them do so exceedingly well—are soon demoralized by the apathy and negativism of their coworkers. The lesson to be learned is obvious: Agency-wide Theraplay—particularly in agencies having another purpose (such as education)—requires agency-wide cooperation.

Center B is a small inner-city center for the training of

the handicapped. The population it serves is essentially the same as Center A's, and its funding comes from the same source. The contract for Theraplay services is carefully thought out, and its entire staff is eager to participate in ongoing staff development sessions at which teachers are trained in Theraplay. In the meantime, the center employs Nicole Vandervoort as senior and Brenda Broy as junior therapists on a regular twice-weekly basis, strictly for the purpose of conducting Theraplay. In addition, this center contracts for one half day per week of Theraplay supervision for the two therapists. So dedicated is the staff to this model that, where it makes sense to do so, teaching sometimes becomes secondary to helping a child in his emotional growth. (For example, a child may be allowed free socializing by his teacher during "seat time" if the forming of interpersonal relationships is seen as more important to him or her than is coloring, adding, or connecting lines.)

Theraplay in Special Education Facilities

In one publicly funded suburban facility for exceptional children, Susan Riley as senior Theraplay therapist and Phyllis Rubin as junior therapist are employed two half-days a week exclusively to do Theraplay. The school has a large population of autistic and severely retarded children, as well as children classified behaviorally disturbed (BD). The therapists conduct regular Theraplay-focused in-service meetings with the teaching staff, conduct group Theraplay sessions in the classrooms, and see individual children for Theraplay in the carpeted, pillow-stacked Theraplay room that the school provides. As for the therapists in this program, outside Theraplay supervision is also built into this contract.

In her paper, "Theraplay in the Public Schools: Opening the Door to Communication," Phyllis Rubin (1978) describes her work in a special education facility:

> For the past three years, I have seen children whose total needs have not been met by either formal speech and language therapy or the preschool classroom. These children can be described along two dimensions:

One dimension ranges from hyperactive at the severe end
to manipulative at the mild end. The second dimension
ranges from withdrawn at the severe end to shy at the
mild end. . . . Neither behavior modification in the classroom nor work on "attending" behaviors deals directly
with the needs of these children, and generalized behavior
changes are difficult to achieve. Although we may be able
to modify the child's behavior in school, he often still
assumes the role of the manipulative or shy child elsewhere. Before a child can begin to put energy into speech
and language development, he needs to have positive feelings about himself and must begin to leave behind the
manipulative or shy defenses that inhibit learning. Theraplay has been shown to be an effective technique for
achieving positive behavior changes and simultaneously
activating the development of speech and language. . . .
Theraplay is based on the philosophy that the child will
not get better while we wait for him to respond accept-
ably. In Theraplay, [children] receive immediate and unconditional attention. Aggressive behaviors are turned
into positive actions that could be used to have fun with
people. Although [aggressive children] gear [their] behavior to make [therapists] either leave them alone or hit
them back, [therapists] neither go away, hurt, or allow
[themselves] to [be hurt]. Instead [they] gradually
begin [taking] care . . . and [the children] begin to *let*
themselves be taken care of. . . . Theraplay techniques
differ with different types of children. Theraplay is being
used in the program presently with hyperactive as well as
[with] withdrawn children.

Rubin's preliminary results (see Chart I) "indicate that
for speech-delayed preschool children, Theraplay can achieve
positive behavior changes and, in so doing, can open the door to
communication. For children who need more structure to keep
them attending to the task, or need more confidence to activate
their desire to communicate, Theraplay provides an effective alternative to traditional speech and language therapy and can be an
important part of comprehensive special education program-
ming."
In order to set up this Theraplay program in the public

Chart I. Change in Test Scores Pre- and Post-Theraplay (Rubin)

Child	Test-Retest Period	Change in Score[a]
1	8 months	+ 7 months
2	6	+ 4
3	5	− 2
4	7	+ 7
5	5	+ 8
6	4	+ 11
7	4	+ 24
8	4	+ 8
9	3	+ 2

[a]Combined scores of the following tests: Peabody Picture Vocabulary Test (PPVT); Zimmerman-Pre-School Language Scale, Receptive and Expressive sections (PLS, Rec., Exp.); Illinois Test of Psycholinguistic Abilities (ITPA) (visual reception, auditory reception, auditory association); Vineland Social Maturity Scale; Developmental Sentence Analysis (syntax); Stanford Binet, Form L-M; Wechsler Pre-School and Primary Scale of Intelligence.

Source: Rubin, 1978, p. 56.

schools, it was essential for the Theraplay concept to have the professional support of the director of the special education district. Next, since the children were in special education classes in regular schools, a personal conference between therapist and each principal was necessary in order to prepare them for what Theraplay would be like and to warn them that it would be noisy. Each parent of every referred child then had to be contacted, Theraplay described, and explanations offered of why this treatment method would be appropriate for each particular child, including a statement of the goals of therapy for each. Finally, an in-service meeting was scheduled for teachers at which Theraplay was described and demonstrated. (As a result of increased interest, the special education district is now providing a ten-session in-service program for its staff, dealing with the theories and applications of Theraplay.)

Rubin concludes, "There remain areas that need further development in our public school Theraplay program. Parents need to participate regularly in the therapy sessions and also need to have the support of a parent group within which they can explore their own feelings and grow along with their chil-

dren. As teachers become trained in Theraplay, we need to develop ways in which they can incorporate the technique into
their classroom program and enable Theraplay to reach more
children."

Theraplay in Outpatient Treatment Settings

With their avowed purpose of helping individuals overcome emotional problems and their commitment to mentally
healthy life-styles, mental health clinics, child guidance agencies, and so on should be ideal spots for the addition of Theraplay to the package of existing treatment forms. But the concept that such centers should be the most obvious setting for
conducting Theraplay requires some discussion pro and con.

Certainly the theories underlying Theraplay are more
easily understood and the treatment principles more willingly
undertaken at mental health and child guidance facilities. Yet
the introduction and practice of Theraplay within an already
well-established center is not an easy matter. No matter how
flexible, courageous, eager for new ideas, or motivated for
growth, no agency finds it comfortable to add, to the known,
something that is unknown. Change prompts resistance in or-
ganizations just as it does in individuals, and even the introduction of one Theraplay therapist into a staff of twenty-five tradi-
tionalists is felt, and reacted to, as a threat to the system.
Knowing this, any mental health professional who aspires to
introduce Theraplay into his or her place of work should do so
with full awareness of the possible obstacles. Although differing
somewhat in the method by which it is carried out, preliminary
preparation is necessary before introducing Theraplay into mental health and child guidance installations, just as it is in schools.
Even the most ardent Theraplay practitioner should never believe his to be the only treatment method or, often, even the
best or most appropriate one. He thus wants guidelines for the
introduction of the Theraplay approach as one more treatment
modality into an ongoing therapeutic program. Since in the best
of circumstances Theraplay cannot be conducted in a vacuum,
the other persons working in the center—even if only by virtue

of their physical proximity to the treatment room—must be helped to understand the kinds of activities, interactions, and patient reactions to be anticipated in the course of any session. They must become familiar with the rationale for using this particular technique and when its use is and is not indicated. Although ideally the other staff members feel curiosity, excitement, and a willingness to keep an open mind, rivalries do exist—across staff and across disciplines—and often the best that can be hoped for is that Theraplay will not become an issue around which groups (or individuals) polarize. In agencies that can move beyond this stalemate, Theraplay in mental health and child guidance centers has some real advantages. First and foremost, the center, both because of its influence in the community and because of its frequent family-treatment bias, is a natural for family Theraplay. Second, Theraplay, with its short-term treatment style, and mental health and child guidance centers, with their short-term treatment goals, naturally belong together. In addition, a large and multitalented staff, as compared to one lone individual therapist practicing Theraplay either privately or on alien turf, can give one another the much-needed support, if not direct participation, particularly during difficult phases in treatment. Even the controversial treatment review procedure (in which publicly funded mental health workers must be accountable for their therapeutic strategy and for each patient's progress) has some benefits for Theraplay consumers. As previously mentioned, it is a part of the Theraplay procedure to plan each session beforehand and to evaluate its effectiveness regularly along the way. The treatment review adds structure to this dimension.

Five settings for outpatient Theraplay will be described: a traditional community mental health center, a college-based speech clinic, a child guidance clinic, a private-fee clinic, and a crisis hot line. They have been chosen because, in spite of the differences in staff, experience, clientele, and philosophy, they all carry out the Theraplay model of treatment effectively.

The Community Mental Health Center

As has been stated, the ubiquitous community mental health center is a natural place to carry out Theraplay. Its openness to referrals from the schools, courts, and local pediatricians makes it ideally suited for family Theraplay—in ongoing consultation with the child's teachers, physician, probation officer, welfare worker, and so on. No other setting is so geared to total community involvement in the progress of one child. Only mental health centers are staffed with community workers to bridge the gap to the home itself (including helping a mother to dress her child for the cold weather and/or driving nonmobile parents and children to the treatment site) or with nurses to attend to cuts and colds. All of this is, of course, very much in line with the recurring Theraplay message, "We'll take good care of you." When the presenting problem calls for it, Theraplay therapists at the La Porte County Comprehensive Mental Health Center in Indiana, under the supervision of Terrence Koller and Anthony Vitiello, treat children, adolescents, and an occasional adult.

One room in the new outpatient unit has been especially constructed and designated "The Theraplay Room." It has gym mats on the floor, carpeting on the walls, and, except for such specific Theraplay equipment as bolsters, mirrors, and dress-up hats, it has no toys, dolls, or traditional play therapy equipment. Along one wall is a one-way window allowing for students, other therapists and parents to watch from the supervisors' observation room.

Some therapists at the center see their patients for individual or group Theraplay on a regular basis as an established part of their caseload. The frequency with which they conduct Theraplay sessions depends on their own availability and the needs of their patients. Since there are sometimes as many as four or five therapists conducting this form of treatment, with as many as fifty children per week, frequent case conferences, reciprocal observation, discussion, and cross-fertilization of ideas are possible. As must be stated again and again, this degree of mutual support makes for the high degree of interest, good staff morale, and ongoing improvisation so necessary if outstanding Theraplay is to be carried on.

The College-Based Speech Clinic

Since a large component of speech problems in children is emotional (that is, developmental), it stands to reason that such problems would be particularly responsive to a therapy style that makes up for developmental deficits. Since speech and language have their roots in mother-infant interaction, furthermore, it would seem reasonable that the kind of therapy that replicates the healthy mother-infant model ought to be in large part effective for communication problems. This replicating feature of Theraplay accounts for its increasing use by speech therapists and for the increase in the number of Theraplay presentations at national speech and hearing conventions. In addition to the children with delayed speech that make up a large part of most speech therapists' caseloads, autistic children, because of their failure to communicate, are often referred to speech clinics before being sent anywhere else. Autistic children particularly are "naturals" for Theraplay (see Chapter Nine).

The Elmhurst College Speech Clinic in Elmhurst, Illinois, under the direction of Sally Bligh, conducts Theraplay on a large scale for children in the community needing help with developmental speech problems. Elmhurst College's speech department faculty is trained in Theraplay and, in conjunction with their teaching responsibilities, provides this service to many of the children applying for treatment. Two Theraplay rooms, each with an observation room, are set apart for treatment and training. Families observe, discuss, and participate in the treatment sessions. Inasmuch as the program involves a large number of student therapists, ample time is allowed for direct supervision and for the regular exchange of ideas and experiences. Again, given this degree of all-staff involvement, therapist morale is extremely high. It is in this setting, moreover, that Bligh and others (1979) have been able to conduct pioneering studies of developmental growth as a function of Theraplay.

The Child Guidance Clinic

At the State of Illinois Institute for Juvenile Research, Theraplay has been used in two different ways: (1) Together with other therapies, Theraplay has been offered to an outreach program for children referred by their schools for treatment within the school itself (rather on the order described in this chapter's section on Theraplay in schools), and (2) within the typical child guidance center model Theraplay is offered to the child brought to the center for treatment. Although Theraplay is by no means the predominant method of treatment in this agency, ongoing staff in-service sessions do make for a free exchange and provide an opportunity for support and for the sharing of new ideas for Theraplay.

The Private-Fee Clinic

The Theraplay Institute conducts Theraplay sessions for children and families. Referrals come from schools, pediatricians, neurologists, speech therapists, and from other mental health professionals, as well as from the friends, relatives, and neighbors of families already in treatment. The Theraplay room (15 square feet) is equipped with gym mats, floor cushions, sink, and video equipment and is surrounded by two observation rooms. It serves both treatment and training needs. Because of the large number of staff involved in each case, there is planning before each session and analysis of it afterward. These periods of planning and analysis, as well as the ongoing discussion of theory and technique, make for high group morale, frequent participation, and the excited sharing of insights and innovations.

The Crisis Hotline

Individuals who telephone hot lines or mental health center emergency lines generally do so in the middle of the night and in a state of mind ranging from mild anxiety to abject terror. The principal fear is of an imminent inability to cope. The urgency of the appeal for help depends on how imminent the threatened loss of control is felt to be. The content of the call can take any of a variety of forms, depending on the sufferer's history and the reality of his present life situation. Also, the nature of the overt appeal for help varies with the individual's characteristic attitudes toward help seeking. Thus if a person calls a mental health emergency service complaining of mild stomach pains and asks the therapist at the other end of the line whether it is therefore safe to drink hot tea, he may be crying for help as much as a person who directly describes an acute anxiety attack and directly appeals for comfort. A call after midnight asking for help in making a career decision may express the same amount of terror as a severely hypochondriacal call. Only skillful questioning can help the therapist determine which it is. Once the severity has been assessed and the real life situation determined, the immediate therapeutic task—providing symptom relief—begins. There are as many alternative courses of action as there are treatment modalities. The therapist can be soft-spoken, reflecting the patient's miserable feelings, and "understanding"; he can be exploring, encouraging the patient to expand on his fears and fantasies; he can prescribe medication; he can give advice on the handling of the "problem"; and so on. He can give short, direct, structuring responses or long, patient, permissive ones. In some circumstances, the kinds of help specifically called for are unvarying and immediate. Suicide is one such condition. Once suicidal intent has been determined, strict measures follow. There is no place for Theraplay either in a suicidal emergency or in a depressive episode. There are other emergencies, however, notably anxiety attacks and the schizophrenic's middle-of-the-night preoccupations, which often respond well to management by telephone Theraplay. Before the treatment strategy can be set into motion, the diagnostic determination is crucial. Skill is required not only in making the diagnostic judgment but also in gathering sufficient data on which to do so without frustrating the need for immediate relief of symptoms.

The following is the protocol of one real-life call taken on one emergency duty night by "on-call" therapist Terrence Koller:

Comments	Patient	Therapist	Comments
	(Hyperventilating) "This . . . the emergency?"		

Comments	Patient	Therapist	Comments
		Yes it is. My name is Mr. Koller.	Calm statement of fact.
	"Mr. . . . Koller?"		

Diagnostic Phase

Comments	Patient	Therapist	Comments
	My name's . . . Anna Hudson (seems to have stopped breathing momentarily)	Yes. What can I do for you?	Beginning of diagnostic phase.
She is virtually incoherent with anxiety.	"I'm all alone here . . . I don't know . . . (voice cracking anxiously) I don't know what to do."		
		What's happening right now?	Further effort to determine diagnosis.
	I can't sleep. I . . . just don't . . . know.		
Breathing effort seems to make speaking difficult.			
		Tell me. What are you doing?	Testing resourcefulness: Is she able to read or write? Is she totally incapacitated?

Comments	Patient	Therapist	Comments
Her crying is not of the sobbing, but rather of the panic-ridden kind.	I don't know what to do . . . (crying) I'm so upset.		
		Tell me exactly what you're doing now?	Suicide intention still remains to be ruled out.
	(agitated) Nothing. Just sitting here all alone.	What are you doing?	A certain diagnosis will require yet more information.
	Watching TV. I was watching TV.	How come you're watching TV at this hour?	
			Cause of sleeplessness needs to be determined.
	I want to go to bed but . . . I'm so upset . . . I just can't go to sleep.		
She begins to feel impatient because she is not feeling the expected immediate relief.	(more agitated) Do you know me? Maybe I should talk to someone else . . .		

Comments	Patient	Therapist	Comments
	How can you help me? Maybe I should just call somebody who knows me more.		
Her anger has been mobilized and with it some symptom reduction.		I don't know you yet. But I'm beginning to understand that you're upset and want to go to sleep.	The process of determining severity of symptoms can no longer be carried out without giving patient something in return. She needs to feel someone cares about her as a person.
		Tell me more about yourself.	Back to exploring the problem.
	I think I'm dying. I don't know what to do.		
			Ignores this expression of fantasy.
		Who lives there with you?	
			Determination of reality resources.
			External resources are limited. She will have to be integrated alone—entirely through this telephone call.
	Nobody. My husband's gone. I have no children. I'm all alone . . . and I'm awfully upset.		

Comments	Patient	Therapist	Comments
		What's happened in your life today?	Attempting to find precipitating event.
	Nothing . . . I don't do anything. I'm stuck here all alone. Nobody talks to me. Nobody visits.	Did something upsetting happen recently?	
She becomes more anxious as therapist explores the loneliness— probably because this rearouses her fear of dying and the related anxiety.	No. I told you. (Voice cracks. Breathing noise intensifies.) I'm alone. I told you. I have no friends.		Still searching for precipitating event.
			Increasingly, suicide appears less and less likely.
		How long have you been feeling this way?	
She is now more engaged with what she feels is a caring person.	All evening. Just before I called, it was getting worse. I started to scream. Then I remembered		

Comments	Patient	Therapist	Comments
	I read about this number. So I tried to call.		
		Has this happened before?	This question leads to the question designed to determine feelings of hopelessness and helplessness.
	Yes ... I get upset ... all alone here like this.		
		What have you done for yourself before that's helped?	
She does not say, "I've thought of killing myself" or ...	Nothing ever helps.		Suicide is ruled out with relative safety.
		What could you do now?	
... "sure, I could just take pills."			It is becoming apparent that the more her state of mind is explored the more anxious she becomes. The diagnostic phase completed, it is now time to begin the treatment.
She has no familiar way	I don't know.		If she were to come up with

Comments	*Patient*	*Therapist*	*Comments*
with which she sometimes overcomes her anxiety.			a solution that generally works for her, this would be incorporated into the treatment plan. A plan that originates from her own repertoire avoids the risk of a later "yes but . . . " (for example, "Yes, but it won't work.")
		Treatment Phase	*Note:* If each stage of exploration appears to escalate the panic, then tactics must be altered. If pursuing details causes escalation, this process should be stopped, or patient will hang up. (Hanging up in crisis calls is the telephone equivalent of "leaving the scene" in Theraplay.
		OK. Mrs. Hudson, it seems like I have a good picture of what's going on there. Sounds like you'd just like to relax and get things under control and feel better. But you'll have to listen to what I tell you to do.	

Comments	Patient	Therapist	Comments
			Both call for a reengagement.)
			The treatment begins. The therapist is clearly "in charge" and clearly has her best interest in mind.
Impatient as she communicates she is, she has heard him.	(sighing) (long-suffering, soft, moaning)		
		OK. Just hold it a moment.	"Hold it" are concrete words and seem to have a calming effect.
		Before we go any further, I'd like to know where you are in your house right now.	
She is suspicious, on guard.	What you need to know that for?		Her suspicion is understandable but to explain to her the theory underlying this method would be to defeat its effective-

Comments	Patient	Therapist	Comments
		Wait a minute! I need to know exactly where you are before we can go on.	ness (see section on Do's and Dont's of Theraplay, Chapter Two.)
The sigh indicates the anxiety is subsiding now.	OK. (sighs) OK.	OK. Tell me where you are.	This distracts her from her pain and conveys his intense interest in her.
	In the kitchen.		
		Where in the kitchen?	
	Standing right here by the phone.		
		Sit down.	The first of many directions for action. Having ascertained the diagnosis, the therapist is now free to convey an "I know what's best for you" attitude.
	I can't. I'm too upset.		
		You have to. It'll help.	
Further engagement in the treatment process. She begins to believe he can help her.	OK. I'm sitting.		
		Now I want you to describe to me exactly how you're sitting. Where your legs are, where your arms are, exactly how you're sitting.	The beginning of the attempt to strengthen some compulsive mechanisms. These will help her

Comments	Patient	Therapist	Comments
	OH! (exasperated) OK. My . . . arm . . . my arm is on the table. My left arm's on	Which arm?	to "bind" the free-floating anxiety. (Structuring)
She agrees to engage in some compulsive formulations.	the table. My elbow's on the table.		
		How about the phone? Which hand?	
	I'm holding the phone in my left hand.		
		And your feet?	
Caught up in the tasks of being exact and aware of her body's whereabouts, she is learning the process.	My feet, one is on the floor . . . the other is swinging in the air. And my right elbow's on my left leg, and I'm leaning against the phone. My left leg's on my right knee. My fingers . . . Both feet are on the ground now . . . What does all this have to do with my		

Comments	Patient	Therapist	Comments
	problem anyway?		
She is suddenly aware that she has been engaged (similarly, resistant children in Theraplay who unexpectedly find themselves smiling instantly retract their smiles).			
		Wait a minute! We're missing some parts. Where's your back?	Therapist ignores her efforts to "leave" and continues along his course.
	I'm sitting up straight. My back's not touching anything. I tell you I'm leaning against my left arm.		
		Does your chair have a back to it?	
	Of course.		
		Lean your back against the chair's back.	
Another momentary lapse.	Oh God! (She does so.) OK. It's back.		

Comments	Patient	Therapist	Comments
		That's good.	Now comes the hardest part. What does the therapist do now? The temptation is to say, "It sounds as though you're relaxing now." In 50 percent of the cases, the patient says yes, thus enabling the therapist to proceed rather quickly toward termination of the "session." In the other 50 percent, however, he or she says no, and the resistance and subsequent anxiety bounce back up. In this particular case, "Well, you sound much calmer now" would probably evoke a wound-back-up-again response. This patient would

Comments	*Patient*	*Therapist*	*Comments*
			ask, "What does all this have to do with my problem, anyway?" Before continuing, the therapist would have to say loudly and firmly, "Hold it!" and then would have to begin again the procedure of bringing her back to this point. It is for this reason that the therapist makes the decision to avoid emphasizing how relaxed she has become.
		OK. For the minute, things are going pretty well, but we need a plan for the rest of the night, and we need a plan for the morning: First of all, before we begin the	

Comments	Patient	Therapist	Comments
		plan, I'd like you to get up and go to the refrigerator and get a glass of milk.	
She is stunned.	(hesitates)		
		You have milk in your re- frigerator, don't you?	He ignores again what might other- wise become an escape maneuver on
	I . . . I'm not sure.		her part. He does not stop to justify his procedure to her.
		Take a look and come back and tell me.	
	I have milk.		
		OK. This is going to help. It always helps: I want you to warm up the milk. Do it while we're talking because I want you to drink the milk.	He takes charge and thereby allays her skepti- cism.
	Drink the milk? Now?		
		No. Not right now. But warm it up	

Comments	Patient	Therapist	Comments
		and get it ready to drink.	
	OK. It's warming.		
		OK. Now. While the milk is warming up, I want you to go to your room. Have you been in bed yet tonight?	
She threatens disengagement again.	No! Are you kidding me?		
		I want you to go to your room, turn on the light, turn back your covers, and come back to the phone. On your way back, I want you to check the milk.	He disregards the threat.

These are reality tasks that require ego responses. There can be little room for the concurrent experiencing of anxiety. |
	(leaves phone) (returning) I did that.		
	Yes.	OK. Is the milk warm? Take the pot off the stove; turn off the gas. Pour the milk into a cup.	
	OK (sounds very relaxed)		

Comments	*Patient*	*Therapist*	*Comments*
		Here's the plan: I want you to go to sleep now because it's late and you're going to have a lot of work to do tomorrow. Go and wash your face with warm water, not with cold water, until you feel all clean and relaxed. Then I want you to change into your night clothes, get into bed, pull the covers up, and then drink the milk. When you get through drinking the milk, I want you to turn off the lights.	
	Tomorrow?		
		Tomorrow. . . . I want you to talk to somebody about your life, tomorrow, to see if things	

Comments	Patient	Therapist	Comments
		couldn't be better. Call this number tomorrow morning. I want you to call before 10 o'clock. Do you have a pencil? OK. Here's the number:	The plan for Therapy is set into motion, while she is still moti- vated to seek it.
		———— .	
		And I want you to give them *your* name and number clearly so they can call you back. Here's who to ask for at that number:	
		———— .	
		Before you get off the phone, I want you to tell me what you're going to do.	
	(sounds tired) Drink milk and go to bed.		
		No. You've got to tell it to me in more detail.	
	Go to my room, go to		

Comments	Patient	Therapist	Comments
	bed, and drink the milk.		
		No, wait. You skipped a step.	The details are important
	What?		now to calm
		You forgot you're going to take that nice warm water, put it on your face, then go to bed, and pull the covers up. And then what?	the anxiety that may have been momentarily stirred up by the reference to her discomfort and the mention of her beginning treatment.
	Take the warm milk and drink it.		
		That's not all. You forgot a step.	Judiciously applied, a little humor is always therapeutic.
	Turn off the light and go to sleep (laughing).		

Calming individuals who are suffering anxiety attacks may often take this long and this intense an effort.

Surprisingly, it is often significantly easier and faster to quiet schizophrenic psychotics. An example follows—again from the telephone records of Terrence Koller. (It is 4:30 in the morning).

Comments	Patient	Therapist	Comments
	Hi! This Mr. Koller?		
		Yes.	
	This is Paul.		

Comment	Patient	Therapist	Comment
	You on call tonight?		
		Yes.	
	You know, I was just sitting here thinking, "I could be a dress designer." Do you think I could be a good designer? Do you know a good school where I could go?		Therapist ignores all these inappropriate outpourings. He tries to focus on the present reality.
		Paul. Wait a minute. What's going on?	
	I been drawing pictures all night, and I just seen I draw pretty good dresses.		
		Paul, why have you been drawing pictures at this time of night?	He points out the inappropriateness of his (Paul's) actions.
	John told me to.		
		Is John somebody that's not there?	Helps him test reality
	Yes, but I hear John.		
		OK, Paul, tell you what . . .	Taking charge—a real

Comment	Patient	Therapist	Comment
		I don't want you to.	person in place of the unreal "John"
He persists in his delusion.	Do you know a good school?		
		Wait!	Firmly, for purposes of curtailing bizarre behavior ("Stop!" is another good command.)
		I don't know why you're talking about dress designing now. Tell me where you are?	Reality testing
	In the den.		
		Sitting or standing?	
	Sitting.		
		Where are you sitting in the den?	
He fights the therapist. However, having located himself in time and space, he has already given up half his fantasy.	By the TV. Now tell me what school I should go to learn dress designing.		
		I want you to take some milk right now and go to sleep.	The "ignoring" strategy continues. (To attend to the fantasy would be to encourage it.

Comment	Patient	Therapist	Comment
			Bizarre elaboration would follow.)
		Good night, Paul.	
(Paul is all too willing to hang up the telephone and go to sleep.)	Good night, Mr. Koller.		

As can be seen from the foregoing, the Theraplay principles apply in telephone crisis intervention just as they do in the Theraplay room. The therapist always remains in charge, calls the shots, and focuses on health rather than on pathology. He always addresses himself to the coping task rather than to the undermining impotence. And he is always ready to switch to a new approach if a present one fails. In the effort to enlist hidden resources, he Structures, Challenges, Intrudes, and Nurtures. He makes heavy use of body awareness, and he focuses on the intimate "I" and "you" (for example, "*I* would like *you* to . . . ") even if the patient simultaneously attempts to flee this intimacy by talking about "the problem" or about "ten years ago." Like the warm, matter-of-fact mother preparing a somewhat overactive child for bedtime, the therapist simplifies the task and reduces the relationship to its most straightforward and calming aspects.

Home-Based Theraplay

Occasionally, for reasons of geography, finances, or other exigencies, a family is unable to bring a child into a center for regular treatment. School-based Theraplay may be out of the question because of school administration policy, inadequate space, and so on. Home-based Theraplay then provides the only remaining alternative. Conducting sessions within the child's home, on his own "turf," has many advantages: opportunities for naturalistic observation, total family manipulation, and a health-directed rearranging of the family's physical living style. But it also has problems. If the child and his family are rendered more available to the therapist's manipulations, the therapist himself is rendered more vulnerable as well. It is one thing, for example, for the therapist to appear at the classroom door, signal the teacher, and collect the child, willingly or otherwise, for their trip off to the treatment room. It is quite a different story when the therapist, arriving for the session at the child's own home, hears the door lock in response to his ringing the doorbell (not unusual if a resistant child has taken charge).

In order to best cope with the increased complexities of home-based Theraplay, the sessions must be particularly tightly planned, and the guidelines around the treatment situation itself must be firmly established with the parents.

For purposes of laying down time-and-place requirements, therefore, it is important that there be a preliminary orientation visit to the house. It is at this meeting, attended by the whole family, that the therapist states his goals, broadly outlines procedures, and clarifies the requirements that will be placed on each of the other family members. This is the time for discussion among all as to whether the den will or will not be free, how available the kitchen and bathroom will be, who will greet the therapist at the door, who will answer the telephone, and so on. Such discussion, of course, presupposes a family sufficiently intact to engage in planning. Plans for room distribution presuppose a house large enough so there are rooms to distribute. The degree to which a family is able to discuss, take responsibility, and arrive at workable solutions determines the degree to which the therapist can relinquish the authority role. A family where chaos and/or sabotage reigns needs a therapist who "comes on strong" with rules and regulations. This setting of ground rules may require the inclusion of alternative plans (for example, if Johnny is not able to stay out of Susie's room during the session, he will have to spend that time next door with neighbors). If the house has no convertible space, members may have to "emigrate" or temporarily stay in a garage, yard, or neighbor's house. In any case, since the site belongs to the child, not the therapist, the planning of each session must be so tight as to preclude even a momentary takeover by its occupant. As mentioned in Chapter Two, children referred for help often attempt to take charge, to run the show, and at all cost to avoid intimacy. A clever child has a far easier time doing this on his own home base than in alien treatment settings.

Topics for discussion during the orientation session include the following:

1. Time and duration of session
2. Room to be used
3. Areas that are out of bounds
4. Necessary equipment
5. What to do if
   a. The phone or doorbell rings
   b. Child needs to use the bathroom
   c. There is no one else at home
   d. Someone wants something from the therapy room, while the session is in process
   e. Someone from outside the family calls for the child
6. Plans for the child immediately following each session
7. Scheduling of next conference

Whereas in family Theraplay, the interpreting therapist counsels parents behind the one-way window while they are observing their child's session, in home-based Theraplay this is of course not possible.

Regularly scheduled family conferences, therefore, are all-important in home-based Theraplay. At these family conferences (attended by the child and his parents), the child's progress and the family's cooperation in the treatment are reviewed. Unless situations arise that call for greater frequency, family sessions are scheduled once a month.

The following description of the beginning sessions in Richard's treatment provides a useful illustration. Because of his poor school performance, low motivation, lack of peer relationships, and daytime wetting, Richard, eight and a half years old, was referred for Theraplay. The family lives in an affluent suburb that has child treatment facilities. However, Richard's parents could not avail themselves of these resources. They found it difficult enough to deliver him to school regularly each morning. They would find it just about impossible, they said, to arrange appointments for him that would mesh conveniently with their already too cluttered extracurricular commitments. Thus, although they themselves sought out nearby therapists, even a few miles distance made it impossible for them to keep scheduled appointments. They often cancelled these appointments, saying, "They are too far away," "Saturdays are too busy as it is," "After school is too late to be out," "That day and time would be all right sometimes but often we have other things going on then," and so on. Yet Richard badly needed help that he was not getting. It was decided that the best assurance of consistent help for Richard lay not in awaiting his parents' emotional maturity but in home-based Theraplay.

The Orientation Visit

Having already gathered the necessary intake information, Richard's therapist, Kenneth Searcy, met with Richard's family to set guidelines one evening when all were at home. First he described to them (in general terms) what he would be doing and what he required for his sessions in the way of space. He told them he and Richard needed an enclosed area as uncluttered and as isolated from the rest of the house as possible. Padded (carpeted) flooring and "safe" walls were necessary. He went on to say that it would be helpful if they could have access to water—perhaps a kitchen or bathroom. Fortunately, Richard's house offered all of these—with one exception: The room best suited for Theraplay was, unfortunately, the only one that had no door. The alternatives were discussed. Mr. Searcy asked who else would be in the house at the time arranged for the sessions. He was told that Richard's brothers would be. He requested that they occupy themselves in other rooms, and he stated that if this was not possible they would have to make arrangements to be elsewhere. Mr. Searcy next asked that the mother postpone her planned daily visits to her friends until after he had arrived so that she could be the one to greet him at the door. It was thus clearly understood that a responsible adult would be on hand before each session began, for it would not help the child if his therapist, coming on a scene of fighting siblings, first had to take time to resolve the fight. Nor would it help the child if he were free to lock the therapist out of the house altogether. Next it was decided that Richard's brothers, not he, would answer the phone and door-bell during the sessions and that, rather than interrupting him, they would take messages for Richard.

A tour of the house followed. Anticipating Richard's efforts to escape him, Mr. Searcy took special note of the bath-room locks. A mat was found for the floor of the den and a screen to replace the missing door. Mr. Searcy made certain that the telephone in the den had extension units elsewhere. On dis-covering that the kitchen was within view of the still-half-exposed den, he added a requirement that no one enter the kitchen while the session was in progress.

Lest Mr. Searcy's rules and regulations appear unneces-sarily arbitrary, it should be restated here that a Theraplay ses-sion cannot proceed effectively if it is accompanied by the giggling of two little boys playing cards or roughhousing in the kitchen.

The orientation session was completed, and Mr. Searcy arranged to see Richard on Tuesday at 4 o'clock.

Session 1

[As mother ushers Mr. Searcy into the house, Richard looks on excitedly. His greeting to his therapist is almost suspect in its eagerness.]

Richard: Hi, Ken.
Therapist: Hello, Richard. Here, let me take off my coat and put these things down.
Richard: Come, I'll show you my room.
Therapist: We're going to be using the den down here. Come on, let's get this plastic on the floor.
Richard: Oh, OK.

[Together, they lay down a plastic floor covering.]

Richard: I want to show you something upstairs.
Therapist: (ignoring his efforts to "take over") My, you have two long legs there. I didn't even notice those the other night. I brought my tape measure along. Let's see how long they are.
Richard: But upstairs I have some things . . .
Therapist: Here, you hold this end and I'll hold this.

[They measure one leg and then the other.]

Therapist: You know what? I'll bet your arms are just about that long too.
Richard: What I have upstairs is the car I made in school. I'll go and get . . .
Therapist: Oh, and you know what? I see a brand-new tooth coming in. Here, let me have a look.
Richard: (tries to struggle free) And *you* know *what*? I've got a *real* surprise up in my room.
Therapist: My, what a strong, pulling arm . . . let me see that arm. Oh! A muscle! I'll bet you can't wrestle *me* with that muscle. Because you know what? I am a super champion wrestler. Here, I'll betcha. Let's see.
Richard: (reluctantly accepts the challenge)

[They arm wrestle. Therapist wins; Richard wins; therapist wins. Richard wets. Recognizing that attention to the wetting and permitting him to change clothing now would give him permission to carry out the "escape" that Richard has been attempting all along, the therapist ignores the wet pants. He resolves, however, that in the future the mother should have a change of clothes handy in the den and should see that Richard urinates before the session. The phone rings.]

Richard: I'll get it.
Therapist: I'll get *you* instead. Here I come to get you! Watch out! (catches Richard and twirls him about in the air)

[For the rest of the session, in rapid succession, they carry out standard Theraplay activities. Five minutes before time is up, Mr. Searcy announces, "We have five more minutes," and enlists Richard's help in rolling up the plastic sheet and putting away the powder, lotion, and other Theraplay materials.]

Session 2

Richard:	(hiding under the table as Mr. Searcy enters the den)
Therapist:	(begins a mock hunt searching for the missing boy)
Richard:	(begins to giggle)
Therapist:	Oh! Look what *I* found! A little boy in a red plaid shirt with green pants ... and socks ... and ... look what is inside those socks! Toes! Five toes here, and one, two, three, four, five toes here, and they taste like ... yum, yum, yum, they taste just like bubble gum! Oh, boy! Am I glad I came to *this* house!

[During the remainder of this session, Richard is still intent on escaping—upstairs, to the bathroom, to the kitchen. Each time he tries to do so, Mr. Searcy foils his attempts and instead focuses on Richard.]

By Session 3, the efforts at leaving the scene had lessened. Richard, who had been the object of much pressure to act adult, settled comfortably into being nurtured. As Richard nestled in his lap, Mr. Searcy fed him apple slices. With unexpected smoothness, the family had settled into a routine around the twice-weekly Theraplay sessions of their son. As early as the third week of treatment, the mother reported he was more relaxed, less antagonistic, and doing better work in school. She prided herself in helping him now to get to class each morning.

By the fourth week, Mr. Searcy focused some of each session's activities on the wetting "problem." In one session, he brought bubbles for bubble blowing and straws for blowing water at a target. In another, he and Richard donned large plastic bags and had a water pistol duel—the winner scored the highest number of water spots on his opponent's face, and the counting itself provided a good way for evoking eye contact.

In the fifth week of Theraplay, Mr. Searcy brought along a supply of water-soluble crayons. Together they filled the bathtub and undressed Richard, and while he luxuriated in the bubble bath his therapist decorated beautifully colored designs all over his face and body. They admired their handiwork in the mirror, then Mr. Searcy rinsed him off again, dried him off like a small child and powdered and dressed him. Provided the family is casually prepared for it prior to the session, the opportunity to give a bath provides one of the real advantages of home-based Theraplay over all other kinds.

As can be seen, home-based Theraplay requires an inordinate degree of therapist competence and self-confidence. Already feeling defensive because home-based therapy implies helplessness, families like Richard's often begin treatment with mistrust and hostility. They seem plagued by an awareness that their kind of pathology allows no "ordinary" solution. Yet, when properly handled, home-based Theraplay eliminates many obstacles erected against treatment by such families and allows intense, consistent, and continuous sessions with children whose everyday lives are often devoid of predictability and order.

Theraplay in Children's Institutions

Children's institutions are designed to provide a homelike life for children who have spent their early years being shuttled "from pillar to post." Although residents of these institutions often appear self-sufficient, their underlying longings for dependency are all too readily apparent. Trust and self-esteem are at a minimum; raising both constitutes, in this population most crucially, the primary goal of Theraplay.

A staff psychologist, Janet Waxwonsky, and her coworkers provide Theraplay on a regular basis to children seen as good candidates for it at the Lutheran House in Topton, Pennsylvania. For most of their lives, these young residents have had numerous foster placements, minimal parent contacts, and no consistent adult interaction. Thus, they are ideal candidates for Theraplay, which they receive as part of their planned program.

Again it should be stressed, as it has been throughout this chapter, that Theraplay is only one treatment form for children with emotional problems. Because of the traumas they have often recently suffered, children in institutions often have problems calling for modified Theraplay. For a description of when Theraplay is and when it is not appropriate, see Chapter Two, the section on indications and contraindications for Theraplay.

At the House of the Good Shepherd in Utica, New York, Thomas Scott (1979) and his staff conduct Theraplay with children in their group of residents ranging in age from eight years through adolescence. The sessions are so designed that staff members observe one another, videotape their sessions, and join in as cotherapists when the child's age, size, or level of resistance calls for it. The children at the House of the Good Shepherd are primarily school exclusions and as such feel far from trusting of authority figures. Lessons in mutual staff support can be learned from this smoothly functioning program of close to 100 children, as well as lessons in flexible scheduling. As children require more Theraplay sessions per week, for example, staff members are allowed the freedom to provide them.

The physical space at this school is far from adequate, given the number of therapists and the number of scheduled sessions. Staff members have adapted to the limitations and conduct Theraplay in a variety of available settings, including the outdoors, the dining area, and a very small office with adjoining cramped observation room. Nonetheless, the children benefit from the playfulness, the firm limits, and the attention to their beauty, strength, talents, and so forth. The testing of limits seems to come a bit sooner than it does in outpatient settings and seems to have a determined intensity otherwise found primarily in autistic children. For this reason, staff members must be physically stronger and more on their toes than is true of most other programs. This observation is mentioned here as a word of caution only, for other residential programs for school-excluded children may well find themselves facing similar problems once they begin to institute Theraplay sessions for the residents. In view of this possibility, it would make sense to (1) thoroughly train the teachers and child care workers beforehand; (2) make certain that intrastaff team arrangements are clearly defined and working; (3) provide support for Theraplay therapists, particularly from staff members at the supervisory level; (4) arrange ongoing in-service meetings for purposes of joint discussion of problem cases and countertransference issues (see Chapter Twelve); and, if at all possible, (5) structure the physical space of the Theraplay sessions in such a way as to allow for maximum safety for both child and therapist, adequate viewing space, and the room to move about freely and creatively. Providing more than one such facility allows for the treatment of more than one child per unit of time, of course, and as such has been found to be highly useful by agencies that provide ongoing Theraplay. As further evidence of its dedication to intensive supervision, the House of the Good Shepherd is contracting for ongoing Theraplay supervision of its videotaped sessions by mail with the Theraplay Institute.

Theraplay in Social Agencies: Foster Care and Adoptions

More often than not, children placed by courts in the custody of social agencies have had a history of inconsistency at best, neglect and abuse at worst. By the time the courts assume responsibility for their welfare, the children are frightened, often symptomatic, and always lacking in self-esteem. The foster parents who are to become their temporary guardians, beyond providing for their physical needs, often are unprepared to deal with them. Yet these children, more than many others, require sound parenting. They require large doses of empathy, fun, and guidance. They require Structuring, Challenging, Intrusion, and Nurturing. Theraplay training for foster parents and Theraplay experiences for foster parent and child together, first at agency headquarters and then within the foster home, can act as a healthy antidote to a painful past. In its emphasis on drawing adult and child to one another, Theraplay builds the child's self-image and helps the adult feel capable of doing so.

Children adopted after infancy often have the kinds of histories just described. Charges of the courts for a period of time, with placements in one or more foster homes, they have been waiting around for the moment when their own parents agree to relinquish them forever. At the point where they become eligible for adoption, such agencies as the Illinois Children's Home and Aid Society in Chicago contact couples who are willing to adopt even an older child. Typically, the screening and matchmaking then begin. Couples are interviewed and observed in their homes, and letters of reference are gathered. In several agencies in Chicago, the MIM (see discussion of family Theraplay, Chapter Five) is administered to the final parent candidates in interaction with their prospective child. If the outcome is favorable but the child is so needy that, were he to be moved into it directly, he would disrupt or overwhelm his new adoptive home, then a period of preparatory Theraplay is begun. During this period, the child remains with his foster parents, and the adopting couple sees him once or twice weekly, only for Theraplay. Theraplay sessions can take place either at agency headquarters or within the foster home. They allow for a wholesome getting acquainted in a setting that encourages intimacy and self-esteem, yet they avoid the danger of resentment an older child can bring on himself when he suddenly crashes full time into a harmoniously functioning family. Gradually dissolving the potentials for future interpersonal conflict, preparatory Theraplay paves the way to a mutually enjoyable relationship. This is not to say that both the MIM and Theraplay might not be appropriate also for adoptive infants and their new families. Indeed, a few "practice sessions" can easily overcome a parent-infant mismatch.

7

Underactive and Overactive Children

Diagnoses of Theraplay consumers vary, as do the suitability of Theraplay and the custom tailoring of therapeutic strategy. Although by no means constituting all of the diagnostic categories represented, under- and overactive children seem to make up the largest proportion of Theraplay referrals. Because of the havoc he created in the classroom, the overactive child formerly was the one most readily referred for help. However, in recent years, teachers (in particular) have become as sensitive to the pain that withdrawn children suffer as to the nuisance restless ones create. Referrals, especially from preschools, are made as often for under- as for overactive children. These under- and

221

overactive children deserve a chapter for themselves; other kinds of children are discussed in other chapters.

The Underactive, Withdrawn Child

Withdrawn children require of Theraplay that, in addition to being vigorous, cheerful, and fun, and in addition to the therapist's remaining always in charge, the sessions be Intrusive and, to the degree that depression accompanies the withdrawal, Nurturing. Generally there is a place for Challenge even given the too demanding lives of many withdrawn children, but there is no room for Structure in lives that are already dreary with internal rules for what they may and may not do.

Theraplay with one withdrawn child has been so extensively described in Chapter Three that the present section serves more to broaden the picture of Theraplay with such children than to introduce new concepts or techniques. The reader will recall that Pat, who was withdrawn and gloomy, was treated in the film *Here I Am* (Jernberg, Hurst, and Lyman, 1969) primarily with cheerful surprise (Intruding), Challenging, and Nurturing. In spite of Pat's painful shyness and obvious resistance, Ernestine Thomas began her Theraplay without delay. There were no formal directions, no explanations, and no preparation of Pat for what was to happen. Joyfully but without waiting for her consent (thus Intruding), she was lifted up high and her ear blown on. Intrusively, she had her shoes removed, and was given horsey-back rides and games of tag. She was also fed (Nurtured), not only with potato chips and a giant lollypop but also by being engaged in infantile activities such as cuddling and patty-cake. Children who are more withdrawn than the little girl in the film may require yet more monologue on the part of the therapist and may respond best to silly games that the therapist virtually plays with him or herself using the patient only as a "straight man." The following example was developed by Regina Roth: "Now close your eyes while I hide these raisins on you. You got 'em closed? Keep 'em closed now . . . now don't move . . . " (hiding raisins under child's chin, behind his ears, between his toes, and so on). "Now, open your

eyes. Oh. I bet you I can find where they're hidden . . . Betcha
there's one under here . . . No? none under there? Oh! You're
tricky. I can see that. Well, right in here then . . . Wrong again?
Well, I just know there's one behind that handsome ear . . .
There! What'd I tell you? Here . . . I'll feed it to you . . . " Another form of the same silly dialogue, used with severely withdrawn children as an "ice breaker" and therefore of necessity
also a monologue is "I wonder what's underneath this hand?
Oh . . . I think I know . . . Do you know? Well let's just see . . .
(turning palm of hand over) Oh! It's just what I thought—looky
there! It's a *back* of a hand. You've got a *back* of the hand
there! Can you believe it?" Both of Roth's gambits, in children
who are severely withdrawn—not autistic, of course—soon elicit
a smile, even if only a feeble one. Other forms of the straight-
man act include: "Now you sit here on my lap perfectly still.
You hear me? I want you to sit *really* still." (Therapist then
jiggles lap.) "Now wait a minute. I said to sit still, didn't I?" (all
this with a mischievous tone, not ever punitive). Or (therapist,
jiggling child's chin), "You know what? Your chin keeps bobbling . . . why, that's the bobblingest chin I ever did see. Where
did you learn to do such good chin bobbling? Just show me
how you do that trick, will you?" Or, another version (therapist
turning child upside down), "How come you keep standing on
your head like that? Do you see other people all upside down?
You stand up . . . right side up, you hear me? oh . . . There you
go again, back upside down . . . " In addition to the therapist's
acting while the child is passive and to the therapist's activating
the child, the therapist can activate the child in such a way that
child appears to activate therapist (for example, child's toe is
directed to poke therapist's blown-up cheeks, which "pop" as
air rushes out of them). Light-hearted chatter and exclamations
of delight always accompany the therapist's maneuvers, in the
hope that the child will at least look at this adult as though to
say, "Now there's a silly adult if I ever saw one" and will at best
join in with the teasing and the fun.

　　Often all of these high-powered, Intrusive efforts at impact appear foolish, contrived, artificial, or manipulative to beginning therapists and parents. The interpreting therapist in

family Theraplay (see Chapter Five, Theraplay Sessions 1-4) may find himself repeatedly having to persuade parents "What's wrong with being manipulative? Just watch this video scene of you performing the MIM (Marschak Interaction Method) with her. Do you see? When you 'manipulate,' she comes alive, smiles, looks at, and responds to you. When you act what you call 'natural,' you lose her. She drifts away from you, withdraws; she's all alone again."

John (who at seven weeks old was "active and responsive . . . babbling and exchanging smiles") was described by Joyce Robertson (1965, pp. 111-127) at four and a half months old, following a family trauma, as follows: "His muscular development was not satisfactory. 'His back muscles were limp, his head not firmly held, and his limb movements few and poor." And his interaction with his mother was described thus, "I had no doubt that the level of interaction between them was too low." Robertson proceeded to try to institute a regime that can only be called Theraplay: "I therefore suggested to the mother that she should stimulate John beyond the extent called for by his meager demands, that she should play and handle him more than she was doing." Robertson's account of what subsequently happened in the mother typifies the pattern set up by many parents and beginning therapists. After one week, John "held his back and head more firmly, his movements were stronger, and he was generally more outgoing. He did not lie passively in his pram but cried until taken onto his mother's knee, where he watched the play of older children with lively interest. But a week later this improvement had disappeared. John was again passive, limp, and undemanding. I was puzzled but the mother had the answer—'I wouldn't go on doing it. It seemed so unnatural deliberately to upset his contentment by playing with him.' " Robertson later described the unfortunate decline of John, from the Theraplay point of view: "After the fifth month, John seemed unable to hold onto his livelier behavior. . . During the next month, his slowness became more and more apparent. At eight months, he was like a five- to six-month baby . . . and, finally, at twelve months when John sat, he slumped forward, with a rounded back. He was passive, un-demanding, and perhaps depressed; he babbled but did not appear to say syllables." Robertson ends her account of John as follows: "He was at least two months behind his peers and in some functions still more retarded. It is an open question whether more, or more skilfully applied, stimulation would have narrowed the gap still further." (Theraplay with with-drawn children is further described in Chapter Two in the sec-tion on custom-tailored Theraplay.)

The course of withdrawn children in Theraplay can be diagrammed as follows:

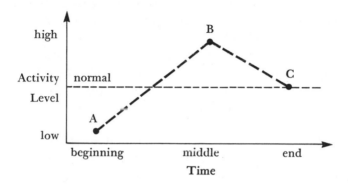

Point B represents a frequent occurrence part way (although not necessarily halfway) through the treatment period—a burst of outgoing, even sometimes rebellious behavior that occa-sionally leads parents and teachers to request, "Can't you make him back into what he used to be?" The termination point—a more participating child than characterized him at Point A, but a less explosive one than at Point B—is a happier solution.

The Overactive Child

In contrast to the underactive child, the course of treat-ment for overactive children can be depicted thus:

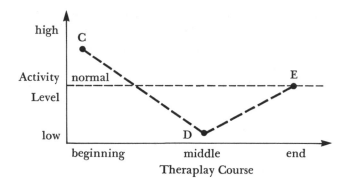

At Point C, the overactive child is at his most active, the point at which he is referred for Theraplay. The depression that often underlies this behavior surfaces at D. He becomes quiet, gloomy, and subdued. Treatment continues, and he bounces back up in his behavior, yet never so far back as to classify him "overactive." Although these diagrams represent purer patterns than are often obvious in real life, the contrast between the two courses of treatment often does apply.

Always seeking attention—often at the expense of others —always on the move, and always discharging rather than delaying tension, the overactive child is his own three-ring circus. Hyperactivity is made up of impulsiveness, distractability, and excitability (Cantwell, 1975). As the camera records one morning of Raymond's behavior in his Head Start classroom, in the Theraplay film *There He Goes* (Jernberg, Hurst, and Lyman, 1975), the following sequence is observed: Raymond snatches toy from child, fights with teacher's assistant for material he is not supposed to have, flings doll across room, runs out door, struggles with teacher, clobbers doll with toy teakettle, slides across floor, accidentally pokes child in eye with building block, runs out of room again, laughs wildly, dashes to far corner, and so on.

No teacher can teach, no parent can run a smoothly functioning home, as long as the setting contains even one overactive child. It is for this reason that such children constitute such a large proportion of the child population referred for help to child guidance clinics and community mental health centers.

Whether the origins of overactivity are inborn, the result of neurological damage, or learned could be an important area for future discussion. If a diagnosis that includes the word *neurological* precludes the idea of change, then the problems of a great many children who have benefited from Theraplay "must not have been organic." James S. Miller (1978, p. 217), basing his conclusions on nearly 2,500 children (of families representative of the U.S. census), states, "Hyperactivity is primarily an emotional problem" and goes on to quote Rutter and others (1970, pp. 11-12) as follows: "The view that hyperkinesis was always an indication of brain damage and that brain-damaged children were hyperkinetic was becoming widely accepted, although it bore no relationship to the relevant evidence. . . . The term 'brain damage' itself came to be regarded as a behavioral syndrome . . . (though) it runs counter to the available facts . . . it is of considerable interest as an example of how scientific myths can arise on the basis of equivocal findings and persist in the face of results which contradict them . . . the question had been put as to how it was possible for studies so nearly devoid of scientific merit to gain so influential and respected a place within scientific disciplines and to hold this place for so long."

Raymond is only one of hundreds of children for whom we made the discontinuing of methylphenidate (Ritalin) a prerequisite for Theraplay. Kent, described later on, is another. In all these cases, it is easy to say, after the fact, that the particular children treated and helped "obviously had no neurological involvement" in the first place. To quote Theodore Hurst, executive director of the Theraplay Institute and producer of *There He Goes* (Jernberg, Hurst, and Lyman, 1975), "It is a biological bias to say that if it is reversible it could not have been biological. It is even more of a bias if reversibility is permitted in one direction but not in the other; that is, if psychological tensions can lead to ulcers or heart disease but psychological help cannot remedy, for example, poor eye-hand coordination."

Traditional treatment—"talk" therapy or therapist relating to child through checkers games or doll play—may work occasionally with some overactive children, but for many this degree of delay is just too great. Their restlessness and inner tension make them take to their feet and run at just about the time the well-meaning therapist is formulating his impressions. It is for this reason, and because of the uncontrollable rage that often accompanies overactivity,[1] that this kind of child is often passed over—even in the distribution of treatment "cases" at the clinic case conference—in favor of a child who is verbal, has the capacity for insight, and is eager to form a relationship. Theraplay, which does not require these talents for the therapeutic endeavor, would seem to be an obvious treatment form. Its eventual activity-level goal—nearer-to-normal behavior—may be the same for the child who is overactive as for the one who is withdrawn. Its means for getting there, nonetheless, are often different.

Often, concealed behind the facade of swagger, brutality, and tough-guy talk of the aggressive type of overactive child is a depressed, frightened, lonely little baby longing to be fed.[2] The particular Theraplay strategy useful with those overactive children who are also aggressive is based on just this assumption.[3] Rather than Challenging these children to grow up, the Theraplay therapist—when they have calmed down sufficiently to do this—aims to Nurture, regress, and infantilize them. Rather than being surprised, Intruded on or having their routine varied, overactive children may require Structure, order, and predictability. The course of treatment with these children may begin at quite an unexpected point, however, and proceed somewhat as follows:

Intruding

In what appears to be an all-out effort at avoiding intimacy, at self-defense, and at mastery of all unknowns, the overactive child—the aggressive one in particular—is ever on the go, always hitting, throwing, pushing, and running. Before he can be coaxed into a therapeutic relationship with another person, he must somehow be "caught," calmed, and attended to. Although some therapists do this through a gradual and patient just-being-available, Theraplay therapists are different. The first obvious step is "catching" him. Then the Theraplay may take any one of a variety of forms. The therapist may turn into a positive some behavior of his heretofore always labeled negative (for example, "The way you throw those blocks—my gosh, you *are* a good thrower! Here's a 'nerf' ball. Bet you can't throw this one way over here at my hand!" or "What a good spitter you are! Can you spit real hard right at this Kleenex here?"). It goes without saying, of course, that unless the Theraplay therapist designates a particular spot, like the palms of his hands, he never permits or encourages behavior that is genuinely anti-social, like hitting ("No, I can't let you hit me"—or "him") or breaking or otherwise hurting either persons or property. The Theraplay therapist often presents his biggest surprise simply by being the first person in the child's world who does not label his actions as clumsy, inept, bad, messy, evil, or rude and who does not imply that the child himself is a failure.

Although not recommended with overactive children beyond the initial phase of Theraplay, the therapist may need to do some active Intruding or confronting as a means to remain in charge of, to keep up with, and to get through to the overactive child or sometimes simply to "wear him out" a bit. Thus, the therapist may find it useful to wrestle, run, or roughhouse with him, to tickle him or to spin, swing, or physically challenge him. Having thereby "gotten through to" him, gained his interest, and disarmed his suspicions, it is far easier to begin the more difficult job of Nurturing, for he will resist this next step with a vengeance.

Nurturing

Knowing that, for all his protest, Nurturing is exactly what the overactive (particularly the aggressive) child secretly desires, the therapist will insist on cuddling, holding, comforting, rocking, singing to, and feeding him. Ernestine Thomas' account of Tough Sam, a child seen by her in Theraplay, tells the story.

Sam was referred for help by his Head Start teacher, the most recent in a string of teachers exhausted by his never-ceasing movement and his outlaw actions. When he was not racing around the room alone, knocking over garbage cans, toppling tables, and scattering toys, he was hitting other children, kicking adults, and cursing wildly. Matters appeared to be even worse with the arrival of Mrs. Thomas. Aware that she had come to attend particularly to him, his hyperactivity went into full gear. She responded to his attempts to push down the fish tank by inserting herself between it and Sam. "You a motherfucker!" he screamed at her. "I am?" she asked. "How does a motherfucker walk? Does it walk like this? Or maybe like this?" "Naw!" he answered. "You dumb!" But, momentarily caught off guard, he had stopped in his tracks and was studying this strange lady who confronted action with action and was not frightened by his apparent power. A few sessions later, in his chronic wandering he swaggered around the room upending chairs and announcing "I the only one growed around here. I fifteen years old!" Mrs. Thomas intervened to make him right the chairs, and in the process she held him. He struggled to free himself, shouting obscenities as she half carried, half dragged him off to a chair in a secluded corner of the classroom. There she seated herself, placed the struggling Sammy in her lap, and began to rock and sing a lullaby. After a while, his cursings changed to tears, and then he was quiet, listening to her sing.[4] A few moments later, she had finished her song and stopped rocking. Sam raised himself from her lap, looked at her threateningly, and thundered, "Goddammit! You sing that again! You hear me? You better sing that song again!"

Only after the Nurturing stage (which may or may not include the presentation, while holding him, of milk or juice or cola from a baby bottle) has been well instituted has the relationship become meaningful enough to allow for progression, in the children who need it, to the next stage. Clem's protocol provides an example.

Eight-and-a-half-year-old Clem had been referred by his neurologist for hyperactivity (verbal and motoric). In line with Theraplay policy, it was requested that Clem's methylphenidate (Ritalin) be discontinued before treatment was begun.[5] The Dilantin to control his epilepsy, of course, was not altered.

Structuring

Clem resisted at first, then welcomed the several sessions of sucking grapefruit juice from a baby bottle. He was then ready for the Structuring phase of Theraplay, which, following as it does the Nurturing phase, is so helpful to these kinds of children. The therapist here, Charles West, is standing and holding Clem upside down (so that Clem's legs are draped around West's shoulders), swinging him gently and slowly around.

Therapist:	I'm going to turn you around just like this.
Clem:	(whimpers)
Therapist:	I've got you . . . and you're going to go down . . . I've got you just like this . . . You did it.
Clem:	I'm scared.
Therapist:	Everything's OK. I take good care of you.
Clem:	It's all over.
Therapist:	It's not all over. But I'm going to take good care of you. I'm going to lay you down just like that. I want you to make that mouth so lazy that it can't say a word.
Clem:	(laughs nervously)
Therapist:	Lazy mouths don't laugh, and they don't talk. Nice and soft (stroking mouth and cheeks) and this one (checking hand to make it floppy). Wait! That's a little tight. Make it loose.
Clem:	(talking)
Therapist:	Oops! That mouth is forgetting. You know what? When you laugh, it makes your whole body tight. I'll try not to tickle you. Wait! Your mouth is still wiggling. Your hair is soft, your mouth is soft, your cheeks are soft, your nose is soft. I think you're ready. I really think you are. Let me see. Let me see what you brought today. Your hair's getting longer.
Clem:	(squeaks)
Therapist:	Wait a minute! Your mouth is wiggling.

Clem:	(lies still)
Therapist:	OK. How many ears? Let me see. You brought all your fingers.
Clem:	(looks bland)
Therapist:	Are you with me? You're looking away again . . . and when you look away I don't know if you're listening . . . And your fingers (checks fingers) . . . and you brought your feet with your toes (checks them all).
Clem:	(tunes out)
Therapist:	Clem . . . *here* I am . . . You can stay right here with me. Let me see . . . your toes . . . one . . . two . . .
Clem:	(laughs a high-pitched laughter)
Therapist:	You can laugh later. We'll save the laughs for later. How about these toes? Seven, nine, three, five, six? Wait a minute! I know that's not right. Wait a minute. Slide down. I got a pillow right here for your head.
Clem:	(laughs)
Therapist:	Let me see. One, two, three, four, push! You did it! You came up. You did it right. We're going to see if we can pull each other up. All the way up on your feet. There we go. Slide up. You're going to pull me up.
Clem:	I can't.
Therapist:	Yes, you can.
Clem:	(jerks therapist up clumsily)
Therapist:	Wait a minute. That . . . was almost dangerous! You pulled too hard. You could have fallen. We'll do it one more time.
Clem:	(repeats action slowly, deliberately)
Therapist:	You did it just right that time. Good. Now, stand up real tall. Nice and straight. Put your feet like that. Make your arms real straight and make your elbows stiff. I'm going to pick you up just this high.
Clem:	No!

Therapist:	Make 'em real straight and stiff.
Clem:	Please don't.
Therapist:	Clem, you're all right. Clem, I'm going to take care of you. Make it hard as you can. You've got to make your elbows stiff. Here we go. Now the other one.
Clem:	(whimpers) I don't like to be picked up. (does it)
Therapist:	See? You're all right. I'm taking care of you. They're not stiff yet. *You* can do it. There you go. (lifts him up)
Clem:	(enjoys being up)
Therapist:	See? That was just right. We're going to go all the way around the mat on our tiptoes. Just like this. There we go. Now we're going to sit on the floor. Cross your feet like mine.
Clem:	My stomach hurts.
Therapist:	Come on and sit and you'll be all right. I think your stomach hurts because you got scared.
Clem:	Yeah.
Therapist:	Well, I'm going to take good care of you. Come on. Sit up straight. Lie back now. I can't see your eyes. Like this. I'm going to make this tummy feel better. I'm going to blow on it right here.
Clem:	It's so cool.
Therapist:	Does it feel good?
Clem:	Yeah.
Therapist:	You can tell me it feels good.
Clem:	It feels good.
Therapist:	*Rub* this tummy.
Clem:	Rub this tummy. (jittery singsong)
Therapist:	Oops-oops. (hand over Clem's mouth) There we go. Lazy mouth. Now up, up, up. All the way up. (pulls him up) Now down. You've got to keep your back straight all the way down.
Clem:	(laughs nervously)
Therapist:	One more time. You've got to stop laughing. All the way down.
Clem:	(still laughing)

Therapist: No laughing this time. You can stop. Come on, you
              can stand up straight. That's not straight, Clem.
              Keep still. I think we're going to try that one more
              time. Think it real hard to yourself, "I'm going to
              stand straight."
Clem: (laughs)
Therapist: Think it real carefully. No laughing. There you
              go . . . that's right. You're bending in the middle.
              Stand up. I want you to be straight. Hold onto me
              with both hands. Wait a minute. We bumped your
              head. That's because you didn't stay stiff. Hold on
              a minute, let me rub it. Right here.

Structured Theraplay was then expanded to include
Clem's father. (The father was selected for this session over the
mother because, although he had already had some sessions, he
was still passive and ambiguous in relating to Clem.)

Clem	*Father*	*Therapist*
		I'm going to call Dad in to let him
	(enters therapy room; helps Clem up from lying position by putting his toes to Clem's)	help us. Hey, Dad!
(begins to chatter)		
		Woop, woop, woop. (claps hand over Clem's mouth) There, we're going to put him right up on his feet, Dad. Look at that. He did it just right. One more time, Daddy.
(looks worried)		
		I'm right here. Make your body stiff. Good for you!

Clem	*Father*	*Therapist*
(distractedly look-ing away)		
		Clem is not listen-ing.
(chattering)		
		(hand over his mouth) That's bet-ter. Dad, I want you to tell us one thing to do, and we'll do it just right. Clem and I will stand over here.
	Clem, are you ready? I want you to skip one time.	
		Try again. Make it clearer yet.
	I want you to skip backward one time. Are you ready, son? Are you ready?	
Yeh. (skips)		
	I want you to skip twice.	
(skips three times)		
	Nope, nope, nope.	
		Nope, that wasn't two skips.
	I want you to do it nice.	
		I don't think "nice" means any-thing, Daddy.
	I want you to skip all the way to Daddy.	
Do it by myself.		
		You're not doing it by yourself. So I'll have to help you.

Clem	Father	Therapist
		OK. I want you to scoot right next to Daddy. We'll sing our song. Remember our song?
Yep.		
	(has hand on Clem's leg)	Twinkle, twinkle, little star. (has one arm around Clem, the other on father's shoulder) That wasn't clear enough. OK. Now let's see if we can do it over.
	(They repeat singing.)	
		That was very good. Now I'm going to pull the pillow out and put Clem down on it, like this. Now, Dad, can you make him all soft and floppy? And I'll put his shoes on. His toes are still wiggly . . . Ah, even his cheeks are floppy, now. That's good.
(chatters)		
		He might need your hand on his mouth to stop that chattering.
	(does so)	
		You can do it gently . . . there we go. He's hiding that lip . . . there we go.

Clem	Father	Therapist
		That's the best I've seen all day. That's perfect. There we go, just like that. That's fine, Daddy. That's fine.
(laughs)		Nope, nope . . . let's get him real quiet here. Tuck his shirt in.
(laughs)		We have to be careful about tickles.
(calm and quiet)		There we go. Dad, you take Clem's hand in yours and then go quietly down the hall together. Quietly . . . quietly . . . quietly . . .
(Holding hands, father and son tiptoe from Theraplay room.)		

"Handcuffing"

It goes without saying that Structuring is part of every session with the overactive child. From the very beginning, for example, the therapist keeps the overactive child so physically close that an observer may think the two were attached to one another with glue. When the therapist is not holding the child's hand or having an arm about his shoulder, he or she is ruffling his hair, patting his back, or encircling his waist. Only in rare circumstances is the child free to roam.

Predicting

The therapist's contact, rather than being a response to a behavior of the child's, is there right along—preventively, so to

speak. Anticipation of, not reaction to, what the child does is
the rule.

"One More Time"

Repeating activities, as is apparent in Clem's treatment, is
another valuable Structuring tactic for use with the overactive
child. Unlike to obsessive-compulsive children and to others
who decree what the people in their world are and are not
allowed to do, to overactive children "one more time" feels like
firm guidance.[6] Examples of "one more time" follow:

- "OK, Judy, now we'll do that jump one more time, to be sure
  we get it just right."
- "That wasn't a real 'sitting down.' That was more like 'slip-
  ping down,' Tony. I want you to do it one more time."
- "That tiptoeing was so nice and quiet. Now, do it one more
  time."

Maintaining a minimum of ongoing activities typical of
the first stages (Intruding, Nurturing, and Structuring) and certain that the overactive child is feeling better about himself and
is sufficiently "hooked" to his therapist, the Theraplay therapist can at last begin the more difficult activities of the problem-solving stage.

Problem-Solving Theraplay

It is a truism that the child referred for overactivity (and
the often-accompanying aggressive behavior) also has reality
conflicts he has not developed the skills to resolve. So inept and
inadequate has he felt himself to be, in fact, that he could not
earlier have admitted to these weaknesses.[7] Now, however, in
the context of his increasing self-confidence and an increased
trust in others, he is able to confess both his social and his intellectual deficiencies. Theraplay shifts to problem solving. Problem-solving Theraplay comes in two forms: (1) role playing,
which is a playing out, through the assigning of roles, of some
recent, interpersonal, real-life problems (the method does not

differ significantly from traditional role playing in the psycho-drama style) and (2) simulated "homework," a reformulating in concrete, body-related terms of the specific kinds of academic problems that are hampering school achievement.

Sample 1. Role Playing: Kent

Kent was referred from school to neurologist to Thera-play for his hyperactivity. He had difficulty with both his teach-ers and his peer group for all of his four years at grammar school.[8] He reportedly snatched others' playthings, hit if his overtures were rejected, provoked others on the school bus, and paid no attention to his teacher. He also had a short attention span and allowed his restless needs to spill onto the other chil-dren. This note from his teacher to his mother was typical: "Kent was bad at school again today. He kicked Kevin in the back and used foul language when I spoke to him. Please see that he is punished."

Kent was being seen in Theraplay by two therapists. They began with vigorous fun activities that, both physically and verbally, he tried his hardest to control (for example, "Come on, y'all do the same trick to me you did last week. OK?") Throughout these early sessions, he chattered nervously and without stopping. A few sessions later, a baby bottle was intro-duced. At first he ridiculed the therapists and of course refused the nipple. Two sessions later, however, he lay sprawled across their two laps, eyes closed, toes curling and uncurling like a small infant's, vigorously sucking the bottle. At the end of this and all subsequent sessions, he was relaxed and quiet. Structur-ing activities have since been instituted.

As the reports of asocial behavior at school continued, it was decided to begin role-playing Theraplay. The following description is of one typical role-playing session with Kent.

Either Kent or his mother (based on her observations or the teacher's accounts) presented a problem for each session. Specific problem areas for Kent included (1) appropriate outlets he could use for his restlessness in the classroom, (2) possible ways of managing during the long bus ride home, (3) ways in which Kent could deal with a bothersome classmate, (4) appeal-

ing approaches Kent could try for striking up an individual
friendship, and (5) methods Kent could draw on to get himself
included in a group activity he very much wanted to join.

Therapist 1	Kent	*Therapist 2*
Kent's mother says Kent had some trouble at school this week. Kent was asleep under a table, and Kevin hit him on the head and woke him up, and Kent handled that very well. He said, "I don't want you to do that, or else I'm going to tell the teacher."		
		Boy! That sounds terrific. Just like you showed us you'd do it in here last week, huh?
	Yeah.	
Kent, have you had any problems this week?		
	On the bus.	
		What?
	Bill.	
		OK. Now. Here we are on our way home from school. Here's the bus. (climbing into imaginary bus) There's the driver. What usually happens?
	(mumbles)	

Therapist 1	*Kent*	*Therapist 2*
Kent, I can't hear you when you're not looking at me. Now. *What* happens?		
		Kent, show us what happened with Bill on the bus.
	Bill kicks the seat.	
I'm Bill. How does he do that?		
	Kicks.	
OK. (kicking— mildly)		
		Now what do *you* do?
	Kick him.	
		You know that if you do that, though, you're going to get into trouble.
	(mumbles)	
		I can't see you, Kent. You're not looking at me again. What do you have with you on the bus? Books?
	No.	
		Anything in your pockets?
	No.	
		Here (hands him bean bag), this is a bean bag for your pocket.
	(swings bean bag)	

Therapist 1	*Kent*	*Therapist 2*
Teacher, teacher. He almost hit me with his bean bag.		
		Why did you do that?
	Because he's mean to me.	
		We'll have to find another way, Kent, for you to deal with that, and, remember, it's important for you to slow down when you get excited. Let's find something for Kent to do with his bean bag that isn't going to get him into trouble any more.
Now, Kent, pretend you're going home and here's your bean bag. Pretend you're getting nervous, Kent, as you sometimes do . . . but you don't want Kevin getting mad at you.		
		I'm Kevin. What you got there, Kent?
	A bean bag.	
		Where you get it?
	My Momma gave it to me.	
		Can I have it?

Therapist 1	*Kent*	*Therapist 2*
	Yeh. You can have it.	
		Now stop, Kent, we've got to talk. Kent, you didn't really want to give that bean bag to me, did you?
	Well . . . no. (fidgets)	
		Are you listening to me, Kent?
	No.	
		You didn't want to give that bean bag to me. Why did you do it? Why did you give it to me?
Did you want him to like you?		
	Yeah.	
		You know, Kent. It's fine for you to tell Bill you want to play with him sometimes. But you don't have to give your things away. Remember, your mother gave it to *you.* Let's try that one over again . . .
What you got there, Kent, a bean bag? You better not hit me with it.		
	I won't. You wanna play?	

Therapist 1	*Kent*	*Therapist 2*
		OK. That's fine, Kent.
	Last week I read *Pinocchio* on the way to school.	
		In the bus? You read *Pinocchio*? That's great, Kent. Show us how you did that. Here we are, going home . . .
	(demonstrates reading alone quietly)	
That's how you did it? Last week, huh? And you stayed quiet the whole time?		
	Yup.	
That was really good. It sounds like you did it really well.		

Sample 2. Simulated "Homework": Martin

Seven-year-old Martin's Theraplay had progressed through all the stages just described as characterizing the overactive child. Now, ready to admit his terrible struggle with arithmetic, Marty was ready to begin the simulated "homework" phase. Charles West had been his therapist right along. He now prepared Marty first for addition.

[They sit on floor facing each other.]

Therapist: Here, Marty, open your mouth wide. Here come three raisins.

Marty: (opens his mouth and permits therapist to feed the raisins to him)

Therapist:	Now the big question: If I add two more, how many will you have all together?
Marty:	Four?
Therapist:	Let's look at them. Here. Spit them into my hand.
Marty:	Oh-oh . . . there's five!
Therapist:	Right. Now let's try another mouthful . . .

[And then West prepares him for subtraction.]

Therapist:	Marty, let me have your arm. OK. Let's roll up this sleeve.
Marty:	(looks interested)
Therapist:	Now I'm going to make eight dabs of this nice, cool lotion right up your arm. (makes eight small pink dots) Count them . . .
Marty:	One, two, three, four, five, six, seven, eight.
Therapist:	Now, Marty, the big, stop-the-music question. If I . . . take . . . five of these away, how many will be left?
Marty:	There'll be four . . . three.
Therapist:	You're just guessing. Because I know arithmetic makes you nervous. So slow down and think. Think carefully. (holding Marty's hands)
Marty:	Three. It's three. I *know* it's three.
Therapist:	Let's see if that's the correct answer. ("erases" five of the dots by rubbing them softly into Marty's skin)
Marty:	Yeah! It's three! It's three! I told you it would be three!

[On this and every subsequent problem, Marty is so pleased with himself that he claps jubilantly and nearly jumps up off the mat.]

| Therapist: | OK, Marty. You see, you really do know how. You just have to remember to settle down and think each problem out. |

Once an individual child shows that the principles of shar-

ing, empathy, cooperation, and "legitimate"—not "illegitimate"
—appeal have been well established, it is possible to combine
several overactive children into one Theraplay group (see discussions of group Theraplay and Theraplay programs in Chapter
Four). Although it might appear at first glance that it would
make sense to start this kind of therapy right from the outset,
the use of groups and role playing any earlier would provide
superficial "training" only. If the therapeutic effects are to last,
therapists cannot overlook the underlying unfulfilled need that
hampered the child's age-appropriate socialization in the first
place. Otherwise, the resulting anger and low self-esteem will
always be there. As long as the hungry baby remains unsatisfied
and frustrated, his needs will always interfere. As long as he
feels genuinely unlovable, he will always act his anger out. It is
only when we provide these children some nurturing and some
experience in feeling lovable that they can begin the normal
process of moving on and growing up.

Notes

1. "Hyperkinesis is the outcome of excessive internal
anger" (Miller, 1978, p. 221).

2. Julius Segal of the National Institute of Mental Health
points out that children's symptoms of depression may often
appear as hyperactivity, restlessness, and antisocial behavior.
Reported in *Brain/Mind Bulletin,* 1979, *4* (13), 2.

3. To quote James S. Miller (1978, p. 221), "The hyperactive children in my practice have, I believe, problems with excessive internal anger, often self-directed, but intermittently
directed outward."

4. In describing a study by Ambrose, Bowlby (1969, pp.
293-294) states: "Preliminary studies show that in such circumstances [rocking the baby] every baby stops crying when it receives vestibular stimulation from the rocker. . . , at speeds of
sixty cycles a minute and above every baby stops crying and,
almost always, remains quiet. Furthermore, once that speed is
reached there is a sharp decline in heart rate . . . , breathing becomes more regular, and the baby becomes relaxed. . . . Rock-

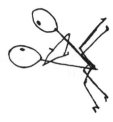

Running Commentary of Theraplay Session
Therapist (Susan Riley) and Hyperactive Seven-Year-Old

(Therapist's Statements)

Ricky, we're going to get *real* quiet . . . we're going to take off your shoes this way . . . Let's see how those toes are doing . . . How are those toes doing? Let's see . . . Hey! Look! There are more toes over here! Let's see . . . Do they match up?

Help him get his legs *real* quiet . . . Here's some powder . . . Powder helps him to get *real* quiet . . . and some nice cool air we'll fan on his tummy . . . Shhh . . . *No* talking . . . shhhh . . . (She strokes his cheeks as he lies quiet, unmoving). *Real* quiet . . . Did you see that? How gentle? How quiet? . . . And how relaxed he is?

Now come up with me so-o-o-o . . . slowly . . . And just resting on my lap . . . so quiet. And now a quiet, soft blow . . . not a spit . . . Oh, that was a nice, gentle blow. Isn't he so nice and quiet . . . and relaxed?

ing is a stimulus to which a baby appears never to habituate."

5. Except in rare circumstances, Ritalin seems to be counterproductive to effective Theraplay, because (1) it tends to render children less available to the therapy experience, (2) it allows parents to abdicate their roles of responsible and involved participants in their children's progress, and (3) it clouds the therapist's picture of the child's reactions. In particular circumstances, such as where an entire family cannot sleep at night unless the hyperactive member is subdued with Ritalin, the Theraplay therapist may have to make an exception.

6. To those children with power needs, as also to obsessive-compulsive children (see Chapter One), "one more time" often turns out to be the battleground on which their desperate need to remain in control is finally tested. For these children, one acquiescence can sometimes be easily enough rationalized without loss of face. "It happened," they perhaps say to themselves, "but nobody really noticed." A second acquiescence, however—a therapist's insistence that they repeat the activity "one more time"—brings to an issue the question of "who is in charge." It is at this point that genuine resistance often first appears.

7. To quote Malmquist (1971, p. 955), "Therapeutic work dealing with the personality structure beneath the external aggressive display sees a denigrated self-concept."

8. As described by Sundby and Kreyberg (1969) in their book, play relationships correlate directly with adjustment in the school-age child.

8

Handicapped Children

The terms "learning disabled" (LD) or "minimally brain damaged," while occasionally referring to an organic, albeit not clearly demonstrable, condition, more often are labels pigeon-holing children who cannot use what the educational system has to offer. As more and more children are considered to be LD and as more and more teachers are trained in this specialty, the term becomes increasingly vague. This development could be depressing were it not for one important redeeming feature: The heterogeneity of the children classified LD and the challenge of getting through to a child who cannot learn have at least led to an emerging cadre of new teachers who are inspired, imaginative, and motivated to see each child as unique and special.

Before discussing the application of Theraplay to children classified LD, it is important to distinguish between children

249

whom Theraplay can help and those it cannot. Some children's learning difficulties really are organic in origin. And there are, of course, children whose emotional disturbance is a consequence of the profound sense of impotence, incompetence, and the resulting peer rejection that understandably accompanies genuine—if not always detectable—brain damage. Indeed, these children cannot master normal classroom tasks even if they are helped to overcome their feelings of inadequacy. Children thus described, furthermore, do need special help if they are to develop the compensatory techniques and mechanisms that will make it possible for them to learn. Among the many children referred for help as "learning disabled," it is likely that only a very small proportion suffer from true brain dysfunction. As pointed out by James S. Miller (1978, p. 220), referring to his review of the literature, and Kalverboer (1975), "There is no scientific evidence linking behavioral disorders [for example, hyperkinesis, commonly associated with learning disability] and independent signs of neurological dysfunction." The remainder are labeled "learning disabled" for any of a number of reasons, one being that parents find the concept reassuring, because, by implicating genetics or biochemistry, it takes off their shoulders the felt responsibility for cause and for treatment. As Jackson (1962, p. 78) explains, "All of us are only too eager to deny our effect on our children and others around us—just as we have little hesitation in *blaming* the *other* guy. It is small wonder that parents are more intrigued by hereditary and chemical explanations of their child's emotional problems, and it thus becomes an unpleasant but necessary part of the psychiatrist's job to assess responsibility without laying blame." Schools, specialists, and equipment for the learning disabled abound, and, once labeled "learning disabled," disruptive children can be justifiably disposed of. It goes without saying, of course, that a child who, although well liked by his peers, generally confident and happy, and performing adequately in his everyday life, has difficulty in reading, writing, counting, or communicating, may well be said to be "learning disabled." The following is one example of how learning disability is described in one catalogue (Rogan, n.d., p. 1) of a school for learning-disabled children. "One child in seven suffers to some degree from a learning disability. The problem itself is an invisible one. The child has normal intelligence, but is unable to receive and process information in the same way as his classmates. For reasons which are still unknown, a child with learning disabilities may be unable to learn how to read, write legibly, or calculate numbers." It may even be that a child who reacts with inappropriate behavior to specifically frustrating task assignments may be suffering "an emotional overlay to organic deficiency." But to automatically label as "learning disabled" a child who is restless or provocative, has a low tolerance for frustration or a short attention span, relates aggressively to his teachers and classmates, daydreams, cannot read, lacks curiosity, or resists learning is misleading and irresponsible. This chapter will, hopefully, provide a better understanding of these mislabeled children and a basis for determining what may best help them.

The Theraplay method, with its emphasis on Structure, Challenge, Intrusion, and Nurture, is well suited to children indiscriminately labeled "learning disabled." Children who have been deprived of, or are unreceptive to, stimuli require a high intensity of stimulation (Intrusion). Children who have been overstimulated, and those who have inadequate defenses to stimuli, require Structure. In addition, if their early relationships were absent, hurting, or insufficient, then children may have mistrust, low self-esteem, and inadequate confidence in themselves as fun-giving and lovable persons. This degree of low self-esteem may lead, in turn, to a fear of intimacy, to poor individuation and differentiation, and to a poor sense of body boundaries. The resulting distorted image of the human figure shown in their drawings, as Viola Brody says (personal communication), may eventually lead to an inability to negotiate symbols and abstractions, described by Rogan (n.d., p. 1) as follows: "Letters and numbers play tricks on the LD child. They turn themselves around, switch places, and sometimes turn topsy-turvy. The letter *b* becomes *d*. Sometimes it masquerades as *p* or *q*. The word *dog* becomes *god,* and *was* would be *saw*. The number 78 could be added as 87. Or a sign spelling *felt* might read *left*." This failure to deal with symbols and abstractions characterizes many of the children referred to the specialist in learning disabilities or reading. Faulty early relationships may lead to other common concomitants of "learning disability," such as withdrawal or hyperactive acting out, for example, or low self-confidence; undervaluing of own ideas, own expressions, or own productions; short memory and attention span; and poor perceptual-motor coordination. It appears as though the absence of early appropriate stimulation interferes with clarifying and sorting symbols inside the head and with the later expressing of them in communication with the outside world.

Mike's account (written after he took a doctoral degree with a medical specialty) in Louise Clarke's (1974, pp. 129-130) *Can't Read, Can't Write, Can't Talk Too Good Either,* describes his own learning disability. In it, he specifically refers to his failure to sense the full impact of incoming stimuli: "I have thought the trouble might be . . . that the actual primary imprint as received by the central nervous system was weak after the visual image had been received by the eye, so that when it traveled down the nerves of the eye to the brain it somehow didn't register very strongly. So that when registrations to the brain were categorized and put in associational areas for retrieval, the primary image was not strong enough. The brain could not distinguish this input from other images and so put the image in a unique associational area. When the time came to retrieve it, it might not be located in this unique spot, and an associated image was retrieved instead."

Let us assume for a moment that, early in Mike's life, someone had come along and made sure that the input he received was crystal clear and double or triple normal strength. What might then have been his experience? It is the contention of Theraplay that some infants need a greater "strength" or clarity of stimulus input than do others (or that they need it to be in a more pleasurable context). The Theraplay form of remediation is designed to provide the missing experience, either early in life, through educating his parents, or later on, when his problem, after repeated failures, has finally been diagnosed. It stands to reason, of course, that the later the experience is provided, the more Intrusive or Structured the approach must be. Thus, for the understimulated the singing must be louder, the blowing must be harder, the tickles must be stronger, and the laughter more rollicking. For the overstimulated, the rules must be clearer, the goals more attainable, the expectations more delineated, and the consequences more explicit. For both over- and understimulated, Theraplay once again takes place in the context of delight, warmth, emotional investment, and spontaneous fun. If the Theraplay approaches are rejected, as they are likely to be, they must be all the more persistent so that their presence will be felt.

"He (the LD child) may become hyperactive or withdraw altogether. He may become an educational and social dropout" (Rogan, n.d., pp. 1-2). The hyperactive learning-disabled child (see the discussion of overactive children in Chapter Seven) who rejects the very cuddling and comforting he so badly needs must be helped to find pleasure in infantile rocking or perhaps in bottle sucking. The child who has reacted with passivity, withdrawal, or "tuning out" (see the discussion of withdrawn children in Chapter Seven), however, must be activated and mobilized with spontaneous "tricks" involving his whole body (for example, horsey-back rides, wrestling, jumping, or spinning). Because of its almost universal rejection by the LD children who need it the most, Theraplay is difficult to carry out and requires intensive supervision with much support for the therapist. Because of the novelty of the Theraplay approach and because it sometimes generates discomfort in observers, it is often difficult for therapists or learning disabilities specialists to explain to supervisors or parents why they have chosen to do Theraplay with a particular child rather than using one of the more traditional techniques (such as breaking up units of learning or visual-motor practice). The rationale for using Theraplay with "learning-disabled" children relates to the child's low level of self-confidence, his poor body image, poor visual-motor coordination, lack of trust in others, distractability, and short attention span. It is these areas to which Theraplay will be directed. It is often helpful for the therapist to stress to questioning observers that the child as a whole, not the discrete tasks he per-

forms, provides the arena for Theraplay and that he is "rewarded" not for what he does but for who he is. The focus in
Theraplay, furthermore, is on competence, not on "disability."

The following case histories illustrate how Theraplay has
been applied to school-age referrals with learning disabilities. To
dispel the notion that Theraplay is too undignified for any but
the youngest child, the first example will be a high school boy
seen in Theraplay with his father.

Case 1. A Disruptive Adolescent

John, sixteen, was first referred to the learning disabilities
department of a high-income high school. Although this school
served normal children, the special education teacher commented, "We are getting so many children with learning disability problems nowadays, we're swamped."[1] John was
obviously highly intelligent, yet, to quote his parents, he
"doesn't know his own strength," and he was both a poor and
uninterested reader. His teachers had restricted him to the back
of his schoolroom because of his disruptions. He sat there
throwing pencils at the teachers and tearing up his assignment
sheets. He was referred for Theraplay at the point where the
principal informed his parents that the staff had done all they
could for John. If he did not get help now, he would face exclusion. By this time, a pattern of vomiting after meals and a diagnosis of "incipient ulcer" were also becoming established.
John's father was a respected executive and a well-intentioned
parent. Over the years, he and his wife had tried in vain to teach
John to concentrate, cooperate, and read. His father reported
being defiantly rebuffed each time he attempted to help John
with his homework. As they knew he was intelligent, both parents could only assume his nonachieving was deliberate. During
the intake interview, John's father said sadly, "I can't take any
more of this. If it keeps on any longer, I know I'm going to get
ill from the worry of it. I'm fast reaching the decision that it's
either John or me."

Since their conflict seemed so much to center around
John and his father, it was decided to focus the treatment

around that relationship. Father and son were seen together for a diagnostic Marschak Interaction Method (MIM)—the structured series of tasks performed by parent and child in interaction with each other (see Chapter Five). Items selected for John and his father from the Adolescent Scale of the MIM included (1) "parent and child each draw a picture"; (2) "parent teaches child something he doesn't know"; (3) "parent and child study each other's palms and read each other's fortunes"; (4) "parent and child thumb wrestle"; and (5) "parent asks child, 'Tell me about when you're an adult.' "

Throughout their performance, the father's message to John was clear: (1) John should grow up at once; (2) he should become an outstanding business executive; (3) he (father) would tolerate no regression or error; (4) their relationship (and life itself) was a deadly serious business that allowed no room for play. John's response to his father's lengthy preachments and superior expectations was to "tune him out" or to spill or "mess up" what he was doing. Rarely was there eye contact between them. Although this sixteen-year-old boy nearly equaled his father in physical strength, he consistently and meekly lost the thumb-wrestling rounds.

It was decided to begin Theraplay. Sessions were to be geared toward (1) helping John see that it was safe to compete with his father (without fear of father's having a "heart attack" as a result); (2) adding a dimension of fun and frivolity, humor and surprise, to their relationship; (3) encouraging intimacy and trust between them; (4) raising John's self-esteem and raising father's respect for John; and (5) broadening the relationship beyond father's aspirations for the verbal, intellectual, and cognitive to include the physical.

Because of the father's out-of-town business trips, Theraplay was to begin on a schedule of half an hour every two or three weeks. With John's knowledge, his father first sat with an interpreting therapist behind the one-way window. While he observed his son in Theraplay, the father was encouraged to repeat some of the same activities with him at home and to consider what these activities might mean to John. The interpreting therapist pointed out to him, for example, that John seemed to back away from competing with his male therapist and asked him, "Why do you suppose John does that?" Or "Do you see how he really enjoys doing something silly like making hand-prints on the floor? Can you think of some 'silly' things the two of you could do together at home?" In the process, the father came to see that his own appearance of perfection, coupled with his high expectations of John—related still to his (the fa-ther's) having to "prove himself" to his own castrating father—put John in constant awe of him. He began to try out at home some of the therapist's techniques for reducing the gap between them.

John and his male therapist in the Theraplay room wres-tled, matched muscles, dressed each other up in silly hats, painted each other's faces, and drew around John's silhouette. Following John's first four sessions in Theraplay, his father joined him for the last half of each of the remaining four ses-sions. Whenever he did so, the therapist acted as umpire while father and son had wrestling matches and pillow fights, gently combed each other's hair, and, sitting down slowly back to back, competed for the largest area of floor space. Throughout, their interactions were carefully controlled yet were designed to be the most fun possible for both participants. When John was given theatrical makeup and instructed to "make your father look as young as you can," with deft strokes of the greasepaint John gave him cheerful red cheeks, a sprinkling of freckles, and a little boy's straw hat tied under his chin. As they surveyed his masterpiece in the mirror, both father and son giggled with de-light, and John appeared obviously relieved.

A few months after termination, John's father dictated his follow-up impressions of the Theraplay experience:

> Some two and a half years ago, we first became aware of a problem John had at school. The actions of John at the time consisted mainly of temper tantrums and violent reactions to instructions from teachers which resulted in throwing of books, breaking of pencils, and generally disrupting the class. Whenever he didn't like an instruction, couldn't do the work, or wasn't willing to listen, he would either disturb his neighbor or disturb the

class, or throw his books, break his pencils, or even walk out of the room and slam the door.

We have been engaged in Theraplay sessions, attending some eight sessions over a period of several months. Prior to the Theraplay sessions, John indicated that he hated school, that he couldn't wait until each day of school was finished, and that he was very reluctant to go to school in the mornings. Since the Theraplay sessions have begun, we have noticed a decided change in John's attitude not only toward school but toward other things as well. He no longer has a very bitter taste or distaste of school. He seems to be coping with his schoolwork much better and is very happy when he comes home from school and also seems to be anxious to get to school in the morning. This occurs almost every morning and is not an isolated case. He has been doing much better in this past term and is not afraid of his homework or his schoolwork. We have been advised by his various teachers that he has even contributed in class without being asked and has taken the initiative on many instances. I'm not positive that the reason for this is the Theraplay except prior to the Theraplay sessions there was no obvious improvement in John's attitude toward school or toward other factors which affected his daily life. I'm referring basically to his relationship with me.

Since the Theraplay sessions, however, which in my mind and in his are inane to say the least, he resents having to come down for them and doesn't like them and continually says he doesn't want to come, that he does it, I suppose to please me, there has been tremendous improvement. He's a much happier boy.

He is much more able to cope with his school surroundings and his environment and has been much better able to cope with the schoolwork. He doesn't seem to have the resentment toward school and toward school authority. We have not been advised of any untoward incidents by the school in the last several months. Even before that time, at the beginning of the Theraplay sessions, the incidents that occurred were few and far between and were of a very minor nature. He has continued to engage in horseplay with his peers at school, and the only times when he has been sent out of the room were when they were all engaged in some kind of horseplay that was initiated, not by him, but by other people and he just happened to be a bystander, and the school has pointed this out to us. They are quite pleased with the improvement in John's attitude and condition. I might point out that the school he goes to grades in two separate ways: One is in achievement, and the other is in attitude and effort. We have always had a problem with John's attitude and effort, it's always been very poor. His recent report cards have indicated that there has been a tremendous change in his attitude and effort and that the teachers have noticed it. This has improved very substantially since the advent of the Theraplay sessions. He's a much happier boy as I have previously said. He's doing much better in school, and we're looking forward to a productive academic career.

In the last years, John had indicated some stomach problems in that his stomach was always hurting him. On many occasions after eating, particularly dinner, he would throw up, and Dr. J. recommended that we see our family physician. He (family physician) thought that it might be the starting of an ulcer and recommended that we have John take the upper gastrointestinal series of tests, which we did. (The report was entirely negative.) Since the advent of the Theraplay sessions, John has exhibited little or no problems with his stomach nor the throwing up that we noticed previously.

The relationship that I have noticed between John and myself—there seems to be less of a strain between the two of us. I never noticed any strain on my part but the strain on his part with me was noticeable. He comes to me more frequently now with his problems, and he doesn't always try them out with his mother first before he discusses them with me. We have worked together side by side on various of his homework projects, and he has taken the initiative very substantially in the last few months. Previously, I did most of the work, and he just copied it, but now that role has certainly been reversed, and he seems to understand the work better. We have a much freer and easier relationship than we used to have, and I'm hoping that will continue to improve. He is much more talkative than he used to be, and he is making his feelings and his inner thoughts known much more frequently than he used to, particularly with me.

In summary, it would appear that the effectiveness of the Theraplay method of treatment for John was a function of the following:

For John:
1. Building his self-esteem
2. Developing a sense of trust
3. Relieving his anxiety that he would hurt his father if he confronted or competed with him
4. Helping him view himself as a lovable and "fun" person
5. Teaching him performance (perceptual motor) skills (always in a fun—not work—context)
6. Removing the pressure to achieve and showing him that it was legitimate sometimes to satisfy regressive needs
7. Helping him feel comfortable when calm
8. Acquainting him with his body boundaries

For John's father:
1. Showing him what a good time he and John can have together
2. Helping him take the pressure off John to succeed
3. Helping him see John as lovable
4. Building self-confidence in his role as father
5. Teaching him how to regress occasionally and take life less seriously himself
6. Helping him show patience with, respect for, and appreciation of, his son

One possible explanation for John's apparent improvement may be, as Theraplay critics often say, "He couldn't have been so badly off after all, else he wouldn't have gotten this much better." Another might be that the Theraplay experience eradicated whatever had disabled his learning. Somewhere in between is the possibility that, given clear-enough, pleasurable, high-impact input, opportunities for confidence in self, for trust of others, and for a happy and optimistic outlook, the effects of even the most profound damage can be alleviated to some degree. By the time a boy John's age and degree of disruptive behavior is referred for Theraplay, his self-esteem is, of course, badly shaken. In terms of his diagnosis of "learning disability" (and the relatively quick reversal thereof), it would seem that John's learning difficulties were less organically based than emotional. Yet who can say—perhaps psychological treatment affected this part of his soma, as it probably did his "incipient ulcer." It remains for many more years of mind-body research to answer questions such as these.

Case 2. A Hyperactive Five-Year-Old

Suspected of having minimal brain damage, Lester, age five, was referred for distractability, inability to complete tasks, profoundly disrupting his classroom, and hyperactivity. There was no question, from the school's point of view, that he deserved the "learning disability" label.

The pediatric neurology department of a local hospital had evaluated Lester as having possible minimal brain damage and had prescribed Ritalin. With his physician's consent, the medication was discontinued before the beginning of Theraplay. In his Theraplay evaluation, Lester was considered to be suffering from stimulus deprivation and from having had to renounce his infancy too early.

It was decided to provide Lester the following experiences in Theraplay: (1) first, all the infantilizing he required, together with (2) the feelings of being important and "special," followed, as he became ready for it, by (3) help in delaying gratification and (4) enjoying peer group cooperation, leading, (5) finally, to seeing himself as a competent student.

Early in his treatment, he was given a baby bottle. He initially resisted, then sucked with vigor. After this and other infantile activities (such as being bathed, being cooed to, being carried), he was gently encouraged to begin to practice delay (for example, deliberately going through the steps of setting the table before he ate or mixing the paint and cutting paper to the right size before he and his therapist made their toeprints). Finally, under the close supervision of his therapist, he was helped to participate in group activities and eventually even to share with his classmates.

Even though at no time is a learning or a cognitive task the focus of a treatment session, three years later Lester eagerly performed a writing assignment, played cooperatively with his friends, and obviously felt content and confident. As stated in the section on overactive children (see Chapter Seven), children like Lester hear a lot of "No," "Don't," and "You don't know how." In Theraplay, they hear "Oh, how well you (push, or throw)" and "How strong you are," and "Hey, let's see that muscle." Instead of "Don't," they hear "I'll have to hold you (or sit on you, or hold your hand) until you can manage." The messages they hear in Theraplay are never ignoring, impersonal, isolating, punitive, or "time out" messages. They are, instead, "I'll stay right here beside you till we ride this out together" or "I'll have to hold your hand till you can manage not to hurt with it." Thus the messages children such as Lester hear in Theraplay are personal and engaged. They communicate confidence that the children will manage. Once such children master their own impulses, Theraplay may expand into perceptual motor areas that deal with the world directly. Even these activities, however, are always in the context of surprise and fun. A child may be told by the therapist who has just hopped with his feet onto a card labeled "how," "Watch me. I'm going to hop onto this 'wow' word." The learning-disabled child, by this time in his treatment full of spunk and confidence, will laugh and "correct" his "retarded" therapist. "That's not 'wow,' that's 'how'!" The penalty the loser pays may be a tickle from the winner. Memory functions can be strengthened by allowing children in a group to ask each other three personal questions at the beginning of the session, which are to be recalled and answered at the end (see discussion of group Theraplay for children, in Chapter Four). The proper sequencing of letters to make words can be taught as follows: After a child has made his painting by walking wheelbarrow-fashion (with help, of course) on paper with finger paint on his hands, finger paint is put on his big toe, and he is encouraged to name and label his picture (with his toe) in words beneath it. There is not the flavor of a serious, repetitious "task" with right and wrong answers. There is no criticism for errors. There is just fun. Throughout, of course, the severity of the "damage" determines the upper limits of his intellectual potential, but Theraplay can at least hope to approach that potential. Although most children referred for Theraplay—except for some in Head Start—show no positive evidence of gross organicity, many are labeled at the point of referral as likely having "minimal brain damage."

Case 3. A Nine-Year-Old Underachiever

Charles, nine years old, was first referred to another agency for work to help him learn within the limits of his "minimal brain damage" (suspected by his private school on the basis of his poor reading and general underachievement). Both his parents were successful academicians who took intellectual achievement so seriously that they reported teaching and discussion had been their primary mode of communication with Charles ever since he was a baby. Since "he tends to get hurt," they seldom roughhoused. When he was angry, they sent him up to his room to contemplate his misbehavior. Both parents admitted to being uncomfortable with physical displays of affection ("He knows we love him without that") and with "silliness." The respect for privacy was uppermost in this family's life-style, and often this meant long periods of minimal interpersonal communication.

In treatment, Charles soon began testing limits. His father, particularly, needed help in learning to curtail Charles' outbursts, at first by actually sitting on top of the flailing boy. His mother needed help in learning how to tolerate, then enjoy, a nightly hair combing and tucking Charles into bed (rather than banishing him into the upstairs quarters all alone). The family as a unit began having "fun" and relaxing together both in the treatment sessions and outside, and the father, particularly, began to take great pride in his son "as a person." At this time, the school reported, "Charles is opening up like a budding flower."

Three years later, Charles was doing well at school and loved to read, play with friends, and share his father's hobby of remodeling their house.

Theraplay and IQ

Sometimes children are referred for Theraplay because of the high discrepancy in verbal and performance IQ's that accompanies some of the learning problems occasionally labeled "learning disability." Viola Brody (1971b) has demonstrated an increase in IQ in her sample of special education schoolchildren treated in Theraplay-like sessions in Florida, and Terrence Koller (1976) reports similar rises in the performance IQ scores of Indiana schoolchildren following Theraplay. Two of his examples follow.

Case 1: Shelly

Presenting Problem: Shelly, five years old, was first referred for help because of school difficulties. Her mother stated that "Shelly sometimes has great difficulty in accepting direction and/or corrective criticism from adults. She doesn't seem to understand our directions, and if we tell her to carry her scissors with the point down instead of up she corrects her behavior for a short while but then reverts back to her old habit." Her teacher said, "Shelly won't cooperate. She pushes other children out of line and always wants to be near me and hold my hand. When others get too close to me, she doesn't like it and pushes them away." This behavior was quite a surprise to the teacher because of the child's "sweet-looking appearance." She further stated that whenever Shelly misbehaved she took her aside and told her, "People don't like people who are always getting into trouble." The child responded to this with tears and promised to behave in the future but quickly returned to her old "trouble-making tricks." At the time of the referral, the teacher told the therapist, "I have thirty-one children in my class, and Shelly is the worst. She is very uncooperative and disrupts the class often. She always wants to hit or kick another child who is doing nothing to her." Although her academic work was quite good in general, her teacher said because she was so inconsistent she would like to have her tested by a "learning disability specialist." Since this meant waiting on a months-long waiting list, a psychological referral was made instead.

Treatment Plan: The Wechsler Intelligence Scale for Children (WISC) showed Shelly to be functioning in the bright-normal range with a full-scale IQ of 119. The difference between her verbal and performance scores was marked, however, with a verbal IQ of 128 and a performance IQ of 106. The Bender Visual-Motor Gestalt test revealed difficulties with making angles and perseveration on a number of the designs. Her drawings of people were very primitive, lacking a large number of common human body parts.

Because of Shelly's difficulty in following directions and her apparent need for attention, it was decided that she would enter Theraplay on a once-per-week basis for a period of eight weeks. Each session was to last for half an hour, with the parents joining in at the last session.[2] From the very first session, the child "tested" her therapist. She resisted all attempts at getting her to focus on herself as pretty or fun. She hid her nose when her therapist tried to touch it in a game. She pushed her therapist away, and when she was successful she made a run for the playroom door (only to be caught by her therapist and brought back to the activity at hand). By the third session, Shelly resisted all her therapist's attempts to initiate activities and spent the entire session crying and arching her back as her therapist tried to comfort her. Despite this seemingly distressing session, Shelly entered the room for the fourth session with a smile on her face and for the first time was willing to go along with her therapist's plan of playful, physical activities. It was all downhill from this point on. She began to love looking at herself in the mirror and not only played what her therapist suggested they play but also did so with vigor. She looked enthusiastically at her therapist, waiting to see what he would do next. Although now able to look to him for direction, Shelly was neither dependent nor passive. She was creative in her play and frequently surprised her therapist by designing new "twists" to each activity (thereby revealing her understanding of their true intent). While blowing bubbles with straws in a bucket of soapy water, for example, Shelly scooped up a handful of bubbles and placed them on her therapist's head in the shape of a crown. (Note: Coming late in the treatment course, this kind of initiative taking is usually seen as spontaneous, sharing, and creative. Were the same behavior to occur earlier, it likely would be viewed as controlling, manipulative, or taking charge; that is, born of reluctance to "give in.")

In an attempt to check out their seeming newfound talent at playing with Shelly, Session 8 included her parents. The therapist's job was easy; Shelly did most of the "work." It was quite apparent that she had become her parents' "therapist"—it was she who now helped them "feel better" about themselves

Outcome and Follow-Up: Even before the final session, both Shelly's parents and her teacher remarked on her improvement. Her mother said that there are "few signs of the hostility she used to show toward adults." Her teacher noted that Shelly's improvement began even before the end of Theraplay and that she now found her to be "a delightful child to have in the classroom."

Four months after the beginning of Theraplay, Shelly was retested. Her intelligence test scores and her drawings of people showed marked improvement. Her full-scale IQ moved from 119 to 128, placing her in the superior range of intellectual functioning. Her verbal score did not change from the first testing, remaining at 128. But her performance score rose significantly (from 106 to 124) (see Figure 1, WISC Record Form). Her "people" drawings became much less primitive and now looked like those of a bright, healthy five-year-old (compare Figures 2 and 3).[3] Although there were still signs of perseveration on the Bender-Gestalt, she showed much less difficulty both in executing the figures and in significantly reducing the degree of overwork.

Six months after termination, the therapist called both

Figure 1. Shelly's WISC Before and After Theraplay

Before Theraplay

	Year	Month	Day
Date tested	73	8	31
Date of birth	68	5	14
Age	5	3	17

	Scaled Score	IQ
Verbal scale	72*	128
Performance scale	54*	106
Full scale	126	119

*Prorated if necessary

	Raw Score	Scaled Score
Verbal Tests		
Information	9	18
Comprehension	11	20
Arithmetic	4	12
Similarities	4	11
Vocabulary	16	11
(Digit span)		
Sum of Verbal Tests		72
Performance Tests		
Picture completion	8	14
Picture arrangement	4	11
Block design	6	13
Object assembly	5	8
Coding	12	8
(Mazes)		
Sum of Performance Tests		54

After Theraplay

Verbal Tests	Raw Score	Scaled Score
Information	8	15
Comprehension	8	14
Arithmetic	5	14
Similarities	6	14
Vocabulary	23	15
(Digit span)		
Sum of Verbal Tests		72

Performance Tests	Raw Score	Scaled Score
Picture completion	7	12
Picture arrangement	18	17
Block design	10	15
Object assembly	13	12
Coding	22	11
(Mazes)		
Sum of Performance Tests		67

	Year	Month	Day
Date tested	73	12	28
Date of birth	68	5	14
Age	5	7	14

	Scaled Score	IQ
Verbal scale	72*	128
Performance scale	67*	124
Full scale	139	128

*Prorated if necessary

Figure 2. Shelly's Drawings Before Theraplay (August 31, 1973)

Person 1
female

Person 2
male

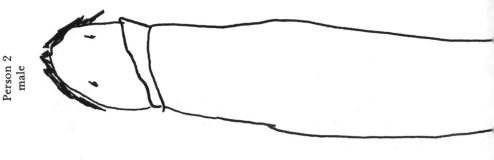

Figure 3. Shelly's Drawings After Theraplay (December 28, 1973)

Person 1
female

Person 2
male

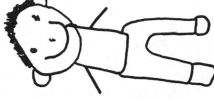

family and teacher, as part of a routine follow-up. Her mother said, "Shelly's overall personality is much easier to deal with. She has a sunny disposition. Rebellion creeps up at times, but it is well within the normal range. She is doing beautiful work in school—top of the class. She's putting forth effort to relate to others." Her teacher said, "Shelly has become a sweet, understanding little girl. She feels for other children and understands if they get hurt. She possesses a compassion that she certainly didn't have before. She still doesn't like it when other children push her, but she never pushes another child nowadays. Before, she used to be the first to start pushing. She's a changed child. I know that you helped her. After she began therapy, I occasionally told her what a good job she was doing, but otherwise I gave her no extra attention. I treated her just like everybody else. She's a smily, happy little girl." It might be interesting to note that although Shelly was never enrolled in tutoring for the "learning disability" that had led her teacher to consider an LD referral at the outset, these very "disabilities" did totally disappear after her eight weeks of Theraplay.

Case 2: Jill

Presenting Problem: Jill, eleven, came to the attention of the treatment center when, at the suggestion of her school, her mother called for an appointment. Jill worried the teacher because of her problems with reading, mathematics, and reversals in her writing. The teacher commented, "Jill is slow in making friends. She's an outsider and approaches others slowly. She's too quiet. She's a hard worker and hands assignments in on time but still she has academic problems." Recently she had become sick almost daily at school and is fearful about entering the building. The learning disability specialist diagnosed her as having a learning disability and promised, "We will try to get someone to tutor her as soon as possible. But, because she is new in the school system, there are others from last year ahead of Jill for these services." Jill's mother confirmed that the learning disability diagnosis was also made at her previous school and added that she thought Jill had a "low self-image," that "She won't try and thinks of herself as dumb," and that "I can't go anywhere without her lately, and she won't leave the house alone. There are times when I have to call the school to tell them that she's sick because she kicks and screams when I try to take her there."

Although Jill's problems intensified when she learned that the family might move again, she had been seen by a previous therapist for similar difficulties. While in therapy, she had seemed to do somewhat better but quickly regressed to her old behavior when tense. The previous therapist had done traditional "insight, talking therapy" mostly centered around the sandbox. She was seen at that time for approximately six months.

Treatment Plan: Because of the intake therapist's concern with Jill's depression and feelings of insecurity, it was decided that Theraplay would be an appropriate treatment method. Theraplay would be active, fun, and infantile and would help her get the feeling of her own strength without insisting that she be prematurely "grown up" or independent. It was agreed that Jill would be seen for eight half-hour sessions (later to be extended to fourteen because of the prolonged resistance—to be described).

The treatment began with her therapist encouraging Jill to arm wrestle, have pillow fights, and enjoy piggy-back rides. Jill resisted these activities, remaining aloof, and "looking down at" the therapist. She was minimally involved and became angry when not allowed to take charge. By Session 4, she was actively resisting, forcefully pushing the therapist away and refusing to do more than sit on the floor staring at the ceiling. Fortunately, the therapist had prepared her mother for this type of activity. When she called in a distressed voice to say that Jill did not want to come to therapy any more because she thought it was "too babyish," she was reminded that this was to be expected. She seemed relieved and promised to bring Jill to the next session. Jill's "testing" diminished, and she became increasingly more involved. She smiled more and seemed to enjoy even the most infantile activity. She began to wear clothes more appropriate for active play and now even asked to be given rides on her therapist's shoulders. Her therapist was especially aware of her increased eye contact and her "light-footed" trot to the Theraplay room at the beginning of each session.

Outcome: Jill's parents prided themselves on telling the therapist about Jill's increased desire to "go places on her own." Her fear of school, already diminishing during the initial resistive sessions, was no longer observable. Her teacher noted that she had stopped becoming sick in the classroom or on the playground.

Periodic intelligence testing showed increased scores from an initial full-scale IQ of 100 before the Theraplay experience to 106 at the beginning of Theraplay to 112 at termination. Although the school said It was unable to provide learning disability services to Jill, it arranged to test her at the end of Theraplay. The results of the Developmental Test of Visual-Motor Integration and selected subtests of the Illinois Test of Psycholinguistic Abilities showed her to have a slight developmental lag, but the tester stated he did "not consider this to be a serious impediment to learning." The following is a summary of the tester's impressions: "Jill is a reasonably well-adjusted young lady. Her visual-motor and fine motor skills are low, but she is compensating well for this disability. Her auditory tests remain low, as in the previous testing, and a hearing check is recommended. Specialized and individual help would no longer be a high priority for the young lady." This report was shown to Jill's teacher, who agreed fully with the findings.

As these case studies demonstrate, Theraplay provides a new approach to many children labeled "learning disabled," particularly when, in the absence of positive neurological evidence, this label is used to describe school behavior. The degree of possible organic involvement is, of course, important in setting the upper limit with regard to expected improvement. It also determines the degree of compensatory effort the child must make. Nonetheless, it is suggested that for the vast majority of children labeled "learning disabled," Theraplay could well be the treatment of choice. In its focus on abilities, not disabilities; in its effort to rectify poor self-image and poor perceptual-motor coordination; in its stimulus excitation as antidote to early stimulus deprivation; and in its optimistic message with regard to fun in interpersonal relationships, Theraplay can turn many children labeled "learning disabled" into enthusiastic learners.

The Speech Problem Child

"Speech Theraplay" is the name Phyllis Kupperman (1977) gives high-impact articulation therapy. Its basis, as with all Theraplay, lies within the early mother-infant relationship. Particularly significant to the baby's development of speech is his wish to participate with his mother in their verbally playful interactions. Thus it is her singing, babbling, making funny and surprising noises, chattering, clicking, clucking, and so on that he strives to imitate. And, as he does so, she, in pleasure, of course responds with even more. The actions between them are spontaneous, emotional, and fun. Even though she never uses even one exercise, one articulation drill, one command that he should perfect his enunciation or correct his errors, still, within this context of surprise, touching, pleasure, and being made to feel so special he learns to talk accurately and to articulate well. Speech Theraplay draws on these same principles. According to the description given by Kupperman, the articulation therapist using Theraplay methodology "begins with a standardized diagnostic procedure. The child's articulation patterns are analyzed, and *groups* of target phonemes are identified, using either the distinctive features or developmental approach. The child's attention is then focused on these target articulation patterns through exciting, spontaneous, intrusive, interactional play based on intensification of the normal parent-infant interactions" (p. 3). She goes on to suggest the following guidelines for speech therapists working with articulation problems using speech Theraplay.

1. Therapist and child are in close physical contact, and it is this relationship which is the important aspect of speech Theraplay.

2. Props or materials that would draw the child's attention away from the therapist are not used.
3. The therapist enhances the child's desire to communicate precisely by giving high-impact responses to the child's speech behavior.
4. The therapist uses target phonemes, words, and phrases in an intensely playful way but never demands direct responses from the child. Activities may include babbling, noise making, song singing, feeding, and endless variations on the things parents do with infants.
5. Activities may be exciting and stimulating or quiet and nurturing but always are fun and full of happy surprises.
6. The child is made to feel good about himself as a communicator, and "errors" are not pointed out.
7. The child is induced to become totally immersed in the speech play (1977, p. 4).

Kupperman goes on to give the following example of a speech Theraplay interaction:

"Therapist: 'Let's see if your toes make a funny noise (touching child's toes and saying a funny sound using one of the child's target phonemes, such as 'boo' or 'lalala' or 'meow'). It does make a funny noise. Let's try mine. (taking the child's hand to therapist's foot, therapist pauses a second to allow the child to make the sound or makes the sound him or herself): You made my toes go 'boo.' (Looking for sounds made by ears, fingers, tummies, and noses, the child soon is drawn into the irresistible play, finding new places to make sounds, and making sounds of his own)."

In a before and after measure (the Fisher-Longemann Test of Articulation), the average increase for the six children treated by Kupperman in twelve speech Theraplay sessions was 10.8 items, which represents a decrease of 29 percent in the number of sounds that have been poorly articulated.

The Language-Delayed Child

Referring to Noam Chomsky's description of the "language acquisition device" that must be activated within all chil-

dren to make them the "little linguists" they ultimately become, Sally Bligh (1977b), speech therapist of Elmhurst College,
raises the question "What will activate the child to figure out
(these) rules and regulations (of language)?" In her answer, she
turns to the Theraplay paradigm: "The baby [who] feels
secure, eager, excited about communicating, and sure that he
can make an impact on this world and who views his world as
an exciting, fun, loving, and secure place to be is in an ideal
situation to want to develop adequate communication skills."
She goes on to say, "Most of the children seen by speech therapists have had this process of reciprocal interaction between
parent and child interrupted by some factor . . . Language depends directly on the interaction. Without the interaction, there
is no communication, and without communication there is no
language. . . . Theraplay is designed to give the child those experiences which activate the communication system between
the child and the therapist" (1977b, p. 3).

In her paper, "Theraplay: Facilitating Communication in
Language Delayed Children," Bligh (1977b) describes seventeen
children "severely delayed in the acquisition of language" who
had twice-a-week half-hour Theraplay sessions at the Elmhurst
College Speech Clinic. She divides the children into the following three groups: those with no communicative speech, those
with limited speech, and those who have become talkative.
After four to eight months of primarily Nurturing Theraplay,
Group 1 (the group with no communicative speech) has made
no noticeable progress on the Vineland Social Maturity Scale
(VSMS), although therapists and parents report "small but significant changes in behavior . . . an increase in the child's awareness of his world and the people around him." Bligh (p. 8)
accounts for the limited change as follows, "During this time,
no change in the VSMS score appears because [in their Thera-
play] the children are reworking earlier issues—issues present
during the first twenty-four months of life—and they remain
nonverbal. This is reflected by their lack of verbal communication. They are still asking the first question, 'Who am I?' "

After the same exposure to Theraplay, Group 2 (the group
with limited speech) "presents quite a different picture," says
Bligh. "They [now] have a good idea as to who they are and

now are asking 'Who are you?' " Theraplay activities with this group, as she describes them, provide Intruding and Challenging activities in addition to the nurturing ones provided to Group 1. "The goal here is for the child to realize that he is big and strong and capable of making a significant impact on his world. As with a child of two years, the child begins to move from the vocal play and jargon to words. Progress on the Vineland in the four- to eight-month treatment period is an indication [that his] self-concept changes from a rather small two- or three-year-old to a much more important four-year-old" (1977a, p. 10).

"Parents and teachers report," says Bligh, "that [children in this group] are starting to initiate interaction with people" (p. 12).

Group 3 (those who have become talkative) "consists of four children who have completed their Theraplay treatment program" (p. 13). On admission, these children resembled those in the other two groups. The children in Group 3 began treatment at approximately three years of age. They were all non-verbal. They were in the program two to three years. At the point of termination, "all four children's social age became commensurate with their chronological age," as was true on their Peabody Picture Vocabulary Test and, for three of the four children, on the Houston Test of Language Development. Treatment of children in this group lasted for three years of weekly half-hour sessions (except during academic interim breaks)—not an inordinately long time in Theraplay for children this sick.

"Activities in the last sessions of Theraplay," writes Bligh, "often include other children," thus helping them to answer the final question,"who are we in this group?" (p. 14).

Follow-ups on these four children one year later show them all to have test scores commensurate with their chronological age and to be in regular kindergarten or first-grade classes.

Children with Other Handicaps

The early sections of this book describe the reciprocal nature of the early mother-infant relationship and how important the baby's babbling, cooing, and gurgling responses are for the mother's continued playful verbal mothering. They describe how important are his eye, facial, and overall body responses if she is to continue to maintain her high and varied state of activated eye, facial, and body movements. Now, just as a mother can be "turned off" if her baby fails to respond (Dundass, 1969), so also can a therapist be "turned off" if a child fails to respond to, or even more, to perceive, his Theraplay efforts. If the therapeutic perception and response is to one select modality only, the behavior of the unskilled therapist can appear strange and artificial indeed. A session of swings in the air, tummy ticklings, and peek-a-boo conducted without sound appears as mechanical as a session of noisy giggles, singsongs, and chatter in the absence of eye contact, grimaces, and body movement. Thus the therapist working with a deaf or blind or non-ambulatory child in need of Theraplay is as much challenged with respect to his competence and resourcefulness as is the mother who has given birth to a baby who cannot see or hear her or reach up to touch her. He (the therapist) has a multi-faceted task: He must overcome his own apprehension about dealing with a child who has an "unfamiliar" life-style, and he must understand that his difficulty in doing so may be a function of one or more of the following. First, the therapist may be aware that, incapacitated as this child standing or propped up before him is, he has, nonetheless, managed in some manner that can only be guessed at. During the long period before his and the child's first meeting, in other words, there has been an unshared life, a deep, dark secret. The therapist may, thus, momentarily feel that he (the therapist) is the one who has been excluded. Second, the therapist may fear the appearance of the deformity—the fear that this particular infirmity or one like it could yet happen to him—a revived childhood fear of mutilation. Third, he may feel impotent, may feel that the physical handicap is here to stay. (Many persons in the helping professions have sought out the field as part of an effort to be omnipotent.) Thus he responds with impatience and annoyance at being confronted both by his own unacceptable fears and incompetencies and by the imagined rejection in the child. Fourth, he may feel guilt and shame over his own annoyance.

"After all," he says to himself, "how can I feel annoyed when this person has it so much worse?" For example, with respect to the therapist's possible discomfort in relating to blind children in particular, Selma Fraiberg (1977, pp. 93-94) gives an account of her own experience in relating to blind and seeing children: "when I talked to (nonblind) Lennie long enough" (in contrast to her interactions with Toni, who was blind) "I got brief moments of visual fixation of my face and a meeting of eyes. If I could sustain his fixation long enough, I got a ghost of a smile. Later, I talked to (Toni) more frequently but always I had the sense of something missing, something that should be coming back to me from Toni. There was, of course, no visual fixation of my face."

Thus, for the therapist working with the physically handicapped child, perhaps even more than for the therapist working with any other group of children, it is necessary to be in touch with his underlying conflicts and anxieties and with his consequent reactions. For this reason, he, even more than other therapists, will need the regular availability of a perceptive supervisor. All of the foregoing, of course, applies to all kinds of professionals conducting all kinds of services for all kinds of handicapped persons. It applies as much to physicians, schoolteachers, and traditional physical, occupational, and speech therapists as it does to psychotherapists. Those professionals whose contact with the handicapped is distant, irregular, or administrative, however, have often arranged their lives so as to be minimally affected by the issues mentioned. Yet, just as often, these are the very people who should have insight into their own discomfort, for they must support staff and supervisors in their discomfort.

The more a professional's contact with a handicapped person is intimate, physically involved, and one-to-one over a relatively long period of time (like that of the mother herself), the more the relationship itself is designed to be the instrument that enhances growth; in other words, the more will the cautions mentioned apply. Thus, the nutritionist who monitors the diet, the schoolteacher who administers the cognitive regime, and the traditional speech therapist who focuses on the task of speaking all are dedicated to helping a handicapped person achieve his optimum, and all may do so within a one-to-one context, possibly even involving body contact. Ordinarily neither they, the physician who conducts the monthly checkup, nor the traditional occupational or physical therapist who teaches motor skills, however, are quite as engaged in the emotional development of handicapped persons as are psychotherapists. Again, neither traditional psychotherapists who sit behind a desk nor traditional play therapists who may sit alongside on the floor are in as intimate contact with their patients' direct (not symbolic) emotional communications as are mothers with their small infants (Finnie, 1975). To the degree that traditional (or, for that matter, behavior-modifying) psychotherapists are able to maintain a distance that a mother and baby cannot, to that degree they are safe from some, not all, of the hazards earlier referred to. (Their own histories with mutilation, real or fantasied, make it impossible to be totally "safe.") It would seem, therefore, that professionals doing Theraplay—approximating as it does the mother-infant relationship —are the most vulnerable of all. Their effectiveness depends on the extent to which they use not only their own personalities but also their own physical selves, in the parentinglike intimacy that promotes emotional growth. Only if they have acknowledged their resistance to this intimacy can their performance be truly beneficial. Beyond this necessary inner watchfulness— which, of course, also pertains to all other applications of Theraplay—Theraplay is different with different forms of handicap. It requires a different set of techniques and expectations to conduct a Theraplay session with a person who is blind and a person who is deaf. And techniques useful for both of these, in turn, may be quite impractical in working with a person who is nonambulatory or multiply handicapped. To assume otherwise would prove seriously disadvantageous to patients and frustrating to therapists. It goes without saying that, while a game of "wink" may be quite appropriate for a nonambulatory child, it would be without meaning for a child who is blind.

Because this book is largely concerned with intellectual and emotional disturbances, the following paragraphs cover

only children who clearly are perceptually or physically handicapped. (Autism, in this context, may be viewed as a combined
organic and emotional disability and is discussed elsewhere.)
The following discussion covers disorders from the least to the
most severe as these are generally thought of in terms of degree
of "normal" functioning. For purposes of organization, deaf
children will be considered first, blind children next, mobile
cerebral-palsied children next, and nonambulatory children last.

Theraplay with the Deaf

In addition to the necessary self-awareness just described,
ingenuity and unself-consciousness are required to behave playfully, intrusively, and "in charge" with a child who cannot hear
what his therapist is saying. A good therapist learns, just as a
mother learns early with her deaf baby, that, in addition to all
the therapist's compensatory games and ways of stimulating and
relating to him, a deaf child's not understanding speech need
not keep his therapist from speaking to him. It takes a skillful
therapist indeed to be free enough to keep up a happy chatter
while Challenging his young deaf charge to a seed-spitting match
or a pillow fight. It takes more skill yet to carry out some of the
Theraplay activities that are Nurturing, such as singing a lullaby. Yet if he does not make the accompanying normal sounds
that a normal adult would normally make, the therapist would
appear to the child as wooden, half-human, restrained.

James Thomas, in his Theraplay work with the children
referred to him by the Chicago Hearing Society, has developed
an approach for Theraplay therapists that is particularly well
suited to children who are deaf. Aware that the deaf child's
casual suspicion "Others are talking about me" could evolve too
readily into a paranoid conviction, the therapist must avoid activities and behavior that could reinforce such fears. Theraplay
with the deaf therefore should avoid surprises such as creeping
up from behind or back-to-back activities (such as walking backward into position for a water pistol duel, or standing, backs
touching, and then gradually lowering into sitting position for a
contest of who gets to occupy the largest area of pillow space).

The absence of sound should not preclude stimulation as a way of making a significant impact. The deaf child needs compensatory input, and the therapist must give it by exaggerating what the child *can* perceive. To quote James Thomas (personal communication), "If you're working with a hearing child, you can communicate with your tone of voice what a fabulous impact he is making on you. With a deaf child, you have to *act* it out instead. When I arm wrestle, for example, and lose at it, I put on an exaggerated form of defeat. I don't just allow him to plant my arm down on the table top, I literally let him bowl me over. That way I let him know I just marvel at the strength of such a little fellow knocking over a great big guy like me. If he were a hearing child, my tone of voice would tell him that." By the same token, according to Thomas, "facial expression tells it all."

Even more than therapists working with troubled children generally, therapists working with emotionally disturbed children who are deaf must be tuned in to how they (the therapists) are "coming across." They must be ever alert to potential mistrust. For this reason, the initial greeting, for instance, is not carried out in the bold, quick Intrusive way usually characteristic of Theraplay. Instead, if the child knows signing (Bornstein, 1975), the following, in sign language, may be the therapist's first communication, "My name is Jim Thomas. I am your friend. What is your name?"

If the child is not familiar with sign language, a clear, nonverbal, friendly—but not surprising—greeting is appropriate. The "teaching" of signing—in as joyful, gratifying, relaxed, and playful a manner as possible—will be the first priority.

A dialogue from a sample signed Theraplay session follows:

Therapist: Stand up. Now jump. Fine (applauding). Climb on my knee. Wonderful (applause). Now walk on my feet. I'll show you. Try again (putting arm down for arm wrestling).

Child: ("wins" round)

Therapist: Me best try hard (in mock determination). Maybe

	OK this time. [But] I'll show you.
Child:	("wins" round)
Therapist:	Try again (grimacing in "agony").
Child:	("wins" round)
Therapist:	Again.
Child:	("wins" round)
Therapist:	Again (as though to convey "I don't believe this happened"). Try again.
Child:	("wins")
Therapist:	Wonderful. Stop. We have to do something else now.

[At the end of the session, the therapist applauds, signs "We've finished," and, adding "I have to go now. I'll be back tomorrow," he gives the child a big hug and leaves.]

James Thomas describes his treatment of Frankie, a deaf child referred for help because of hyperactivity:

> I saw Frankie in his home. Grandmother, mother, and aunt presented him to me at the first session daring me to try my hand, as though to say "There he is. Now let's see what *you* can do." Throughout, these individuals were present and bewildered by my never echoing their refrain of "no," "stop that," "don't do that." Instead I caught his testing behavior and gave it back to him with fun and joyfulness. He tried and tried at first, but he never could get into trouble with me because I made everything into an OK fun thing.
>
> In the beginning, he didn't know what to anticipate, and communicating with signing was very difficult. But I showed him. He was very anxious at the beginning and tried to run from one side of the room to the other. I caught him firmly as he ran and swung him in the air for a merry-go-round. He laughed and tried to run again. When he did so, I caught him and flipped him. Then I jumped him. A few sessions later, after he had toned down, I showed him how to walk up my body as I stood up, starting at my knee and finally making it to shoulder

height. He was scared at first but then got more confidence and jumped to the floor with my holding him safely.

One day I put him upside down and put his hands on my shoes. I held him by the legs, and we walked around the room with him lifting up my feet and putting them down, clearly loving the feeling that it was *he* who was controlling *my* walking. After that, he was much more willing to work with me as a team—to be stiff when I needed him to be, to wait before jumping, and so on. He began looking forward to the sessions and began having more fun every time. Although at the beginning he was seldom calm and anyone watching thought he would never stop, at the end (fifteen sessions later) he often sat quietly for long periods. His mother and his grandmother describe him as a different individual.[4]

It is clear from the foregoing that a child's failure to hear the happy chatter of a Theraplay therapist need not preclude growth and self-confidence anymore than a small baby's inability to hear his mother's voice necessarily leads to stunted personality development.

Theraplay with the Blind

There is no more excellent reference for techniques similar to Theraplay for working with blind children than Selma Fraiberg's (1977) suggestions for mothers of babies blind from birth in her book *Insights From the Blind*. The insistent efforts she prescribes by means of which mothers can succeed in engaging their blind infants are tailor-made for Theraplay therapists working not only with blind children but also with all children, particularly autistic ones, who require insistent and playful intrusion. As the Theraplay guidelines define the poor therapist in Chapter Two (fleeting and diluted focus on the child), so also does Fraiberg define poor mothers of blind babies: "The mother was barely distinguished from other persons; her comings and goings were unnoticed" (p. 10).

Although at the Theraplay Institute we have as yet had no direct experience with blind children, for therapists interested in applying Theraplay-like methods to troubled or "frozen" blind children,[5] some of Fraiberg's work may be valuable here. Her particular sensitivity to the reasons underlying the autistic behavior often accompanying blindness in infancy is nowhere more apparent than in her description of Toni, a baby blind since birth: "When Toni could not touch her mother or hear her mother's voice, she was robbed of her mother and of a large measure of the sensory experience that linked her to the world outside of her body. In this insubstantial, impermanent world, her own body and body sensations became at times the only certainty, the only continuous source of sensory experience in the otherwise discontinuous experience of darkness" (Fraiberg, 1977, p. 21). Just as Des Lauriers, in the book *Your Child Is Asleep* (Des Lauriers and Carlson, 1969), sees the therapist as waking the autistic child, so also does Fraiberg. Her goals for intervention, however, are specifically tailored to *keeping* awake the child whose blindness might otherwise make him fall asleep. Her methods for keeping him awake are specifically geared to correcting his poor prehension and developing his gross motor development, language, and so on. "There [is] no formal program or 'curriculum.' . . . The program itself [is] highly individualized, allowing for much invention on the part of parents and baby and capitalizing on the assets of each family, each baby, in seeking adaptive solutions" (Fraiberg, 1977, p. 160).

Fraiberg elaborates on the importance of activities: "The tactile reciprocity between the blind baby and his human partners is, of course, only a component of a tactile-auditory-kinesthetic dialogue. The mother and other partners who hold the baby, rock him, feed him, caress him, and play motor games with him, are at the same time partners who talk, who sing, who create movement for the baby as they walk with him, shift postures, [and] offer him rhythmic experiences" (p. 118).

In her treatment of nine-year-old blind Peter, Fraiberg used both "useful interpretations" (for example, "You don't have to be afraid. I won't go away") and experiences that are perhaps more like Theraplay: for example, "[playing] peek-a-boo games and hiding games . . . [playing] hide and seek games with him and [teaching] him to find me through tracing my voice . . . [and teaching] him to find the cookie jar in the kitchen and get his own cookies" (Fraiberg, 1977, pp. 32-38). She also suggests encouraging "independent walking, simple climbing, swimming, playing ball . . . [encouraging] him to express his needs and wishes in words . . . [Don't be] too quick in anticipating his gestures, and tactfully postpone gratifications until he expresse[s] his wants in words," and "permitting and even encouraging the throwing [of objects]" (Fraiberg, 1977, p. 44). Other good activities are "[making] bean bags which have enough weight and [make] a sufficiently satisfactory noise on contact so that they [give] satisfaction, . . . [trying] to encourage tactile discrimination by bringing him various textiles and textures for him to handle . . . introduc[ing] him to a toy flute . . . [and] encourag[ing] this newly found interest [in sea shells] and collect[ing] shells for him" (Fraiberg, 1977, pp. 32-38).

Also consistent with the Theraplay format is Fraiberg's involvement with parents. "Since the blind child's learning must emanate from the experience with mother, insufficiencies in mothering or deficiencies in the mother-infant ties can cut off all possibilities for learning in this sphere" (1977, p. 4). Thus "the mother of a blind baby must find some ways of helping the baby find the route." Fraiberg's (1977, p. 9) way of "help[ing] the mother provide the essential nutriments for sensorimotor experience" is to make her the teacher ("The mother . . . carries the main burden of 'teaching' the blind infant"). She is helped to become the teacher through a "concurrent education and guidance program" that promotes the attachment of baby and mother. The education program consists of "interpreting [to the mother] the blind baby's experience," including "sharing [an] understanding of the developmental deviations and lags," and "sharing vital information and guidance."

"Guidance" obviously includes "giving comfort and support and hope to parents who were without hope and still stunned by grief," as well as "developing strategies" (for example, "to bring the hands together in order to promote midline organization").

The family Theraplay model described in Chapter Five has much in common with Fraiberg's intervention model. The dialogues behind the one-way window comprise "education" and "guidance" ("As you can see, Beth has to refuse to have her shoes put on as a way of 'saving face' . . . a way of remaining in control"; "Tonight in the bath be sure to speak to Ryan firmly and hold him tightly if he kicks you"). Theraplay is even more directly intervening when it guides mothers to cuddle their children in positions that maximize eye contact, for example, and Fraiberg surely does the same in teaching them games of patty-cake, and so on.

In summary, Fraiberg (1977, p. 223) writes, "Our interventions had positive effects in facilitating the blind baby's attachments to his mother, with close correspondence in milestones to those of sighted children. . . . Expanding the blind infant's tactile-auditory experience with persons and things was essential to the coordination of ear and hand and for attributing substantially to things and persons 'out there'—a crucial first step in naming. . . . The interventions in gross motor development facilitated locomotion in our group of blind children (and brought them closer to sighted-child ranges than to blind-child ranges). . . . These locomotor experiences, in turn, had effects upon language development."

In working with the blind, as in working with children with other handicaps, there are specific hazards—hazards emanating from the therapist's own needs for a response. Fraiberg (p. 97) notes: "The blind baby has a meager repertoire of behaviors which can initiate social exchange. . . . The absence of eye contact gives the negative sign of 'no interest.' " Theraplay therapists working with blind children must make certain that they do not respond to the seemingly unfriendly blind child with reciprocal rejection.

Theraplay for Children with Cerebral Palsy

My own direct experience with children who are diagnosed as cerebral palsied (CP) is even more limited than my experience with blind and deaf children. Yet the need for help with CP children is great, and Theraplay experience with them is growing. Such agencies as the Abraham Lincoln Center in Chicago and such individual therapists as Anthony Vitiello, in Michigan City, Indiana, and Margaret Nezezon, at the Esperanza school in Chicago, between them have contributed all the case material in the section to follow.

Cerebral palsy is defined by Nichtern (1974, p. 120) as a "disorder of the nervous system characterized by disturbances of motor function [which] may be accompanied by sensory disturbances, seizures, mental retardation, learning difficulties, or behavioral disorders." Huttenlocher (1975, p. 1423), in *Textbook of Pediatrics* (Beeson and McDermott, 1975), defines CP as "any nonprogressive central motor deficit dating to events in the prenatal or perinatal periods. It is one of the commonest crippling conditions of childhood; there are almost 300,000 affected children in the United States alone."

Attention to children with "CP" has traditionally been directed primarily to the mental retardation that was thought to accompany the condition. "It is only during the last two decades," to quote Jack Tizard (1970, p. 625), "that any serious thought has been given to the possibility that cerebral-palsied children are not all mentally defective."

Because Theraplay essentially recreates all the positive aspects of the mother-infant relationship, the following recommendations (including direct quotes), based on Nancie Finnie's (1975, pp. 17-18) primer for parents of cerebral-palsied infants, contain clear elements of Structure, Challenge, Intrusion, and Nurture and thus are made-to-order directives for Theraplay therapists working with cerebral-palsied children:

1. She talks of providing "physical contact . . . vocal stimulation, and total physical care in a relaxed, joyful way . . . transmitted through voice and physical handling."

2. Gradually he should be encouraged to do more and more observing, vocalizing, exploring, and manipulating, "learning to do things he couldn't previously do. . . from a basis of security resulting from [the therapist's] warm, tender, stimulating care, and moving gradually and steadily." He should be supported "in his efforts . . . toward self-confident achievement."

3. "The frequent and close imposition of the 'talking face' in front of the baby teaches him the vital skill of concentrating on one set of meaningful and associated stimuli, rather than vaguely scanning the world in general. He learns to filter out confusing and irrelevant sensations and to pay attention to one problem at a time."

4. The CP child should be played with in a way that is pleasurable—"mutual pleasure for [adult] and child. If the child is smiling and excited, he is playing and learning. Physical contact games (cuddling, tickling, stroking, rubbing noses, kissing); visual games (approach and retreat of adult's face, movements of mouth, tongue, and head, hiding and reappearing); and vocal games (singing, gentle talking, lip and tongue noises, blowing and puffing air) lead on to activities of a more structured type, such as 'clap hands' . . . and fathers' [kind of] play. ([Fathers] play differently and roughly even from the beginning)."

5. The CP child should be talked to—never handled silently. Rather than asking him to imitate single words—he should hear "the singsong rhythm of normal speech, and the flow of normal language."

6. Noises he makes should be imitated—"even a burp or a chuckle." If the [therapist] waits a little while and repeats the noise again, the CP child later on will listen for that response and smile when he hears it. "He is now playing with sounds! Still later he will make his noise in order to get you to copy, and then you are 'throwing sounds back and forwards like a ball, with enjoyment. You can then vary the sound and he will try to follow you . . . (you are teaching him to enjoy learning to control his speech organs to make the sounds he wants). If he tries to imitate your play or your voice, repeat the procedure and wait again, so that he knows it is his turn."

7. If the CP child is to be helped to complete tasks on his own, the therapist must carefully gauge how long to let him struggle and when it is appropriate to step in. "He must be shown the task, and then helped to go through the movements with his own hands or body. . . . After he begins to move with you . . . gradually withdraw your effort, particularly at the end of a sequence so that he completes the task by himself."

8. "The teaching period should be kept short. . . . The session must be fun for both of you. . . . Try to be positive—encourage and praise every effort rather than criticizing for clumsiness, messiness, or failure to complete."

9. Rather than risk a battle, the therapist should maintain his position. The CP child both resents pressure for conformity and enjoys upsetting grown-ups. *"Don't let him enjoy upsetting you* (and don't relent). In the long run, it is kinder to be firm."

10. The slow, handicapped child requires patience and *time.* Even though he may be unable to respond quickly, he still may be quite able to understand.

11. Even if improvement is very slow, the therapist should persevere, often looking for only very small signs of progress.

12. Therapists working with CP children should learn to concentrate on helping the child *now* rather than worrying about the future. "What is needed is a determination to help him develop to the maximum of his capabilities," not a preoccupation with whether he will ever approximate the normal.

13. "Handicapped children must develop socially appropriate behavior like everybody else." Therapists must be firm and consistent in requiring reasonable conformity.

14. The therapist must insistently make his presence felt. The CP child who receives "little attention, stimulation, or social contact will tend to occupy himself with body manipulation, especially if he has partial or complete loss of vision or hearing or in some cases is severely mentally handicapped."

15. The therapist should encourage interest in the environment through peek-a-boo games and the hiding and finding of objects (see also Fraiberg, 1977).

16. The therapist must initiate desirable activities rather than move in to terminate undesirable ones.

Modeled as it is on the wholesome mother-infant relationship, Theraplay for cerebral-palsied children is a relatively new application of the Theraplay technique. Its advantages and pitfalls when used for these kinds of children are only beginning to become clear now. The Theraplay goals of increased self-confidence, affirmed body boundaries, and improved coordination, however, make it an appropriate method of treatment for cerebral-palsied children. Since it is so decisive, directive, and cautiously Challenging, it cannot help but encourage the cerebral-palsied child to "do his best." Certain exceptions and certain modifications, nonetheless, must be made in the therapeutic strategy.

It must be borne in mind, for example, that the cerebral-palsied condition makes it difficult for these children to contain their excitement, to control their movements, and to make contact in appropriate ways. Particularly in group situations, they "act out all over the place," bite each other even if they are good friends, and bite their adult caretakers, bump heads, punch each other in the eyes and arms, and pull each other's hair. The hair pulling is particularly difficult because, having grasped, the cerebral-palsied child is unable to release his grip. Thus, in an effort to reduce excitement, time and tempo must be carefully monitored. Activities must be smoothly flowing, contain only few and small surprises, avoid quick shifts and movements, and proceed without upsets. Phrased in Theraplay terms, there must be more Nurturing and Structuring than Intruding, and Challenges must be ever-so-carefully issued. "Do not," writes Nancie Finnie (1975, p. 3), "be tempted to spur [the] child on to achievements that are beyond his capacity."

Cerebral-palsied children are limited not only to stereotyped movements, but also in their reactions and responses to being moved. The cerebral-palsied child cannot respond as the normal one does to being dressed, toileted, fed, or carried. Rather than moving in synchrony with the adult who does the caretaking, he can only cry and become stiff and frightened.

Regarding athetosis (mobile spasms), Yahr (1975, p. 643) writes, "More often than not, patients with cerebral palsy have marked alteration in muscle tone consisting of a combination of spasticity and rigidity. Typical athetosis possesses the following features in varying degrees: One or both sides of the body are involved. The movements involve the upper limbs to a greater extent than the lower and primarily in their distal segments. The muscles innervated by the cranial nerves are invariably involved so that facial grimacing, writhing movements of the tongue, and disturbances in articulation and swallowing are encountered. Abnormal postures of the limbs are assumed."

Two types of children with CP deserve special mention. Finnie (1975, p. 44) describes the athetoid CP child as follows: "[he] has difficulty in maintaining his weight against gravity and when standing either collapses or falls backwards. For this reason he has no standing balance and cannot shift his body weight sideways or forwards. If he is able to stand and if one of his legs is lifted, the other leg will bend and he will collapse."

Known by workers in the field as "floppy," this kind of child is unable to maintain body tonus. His involuntary movements and the constantly changing tone of his muscles make him easily lose his balance and fall over. Unless he is propped up against a wall, he will "flop" down; unless he wears braces, he will "crumble"; unless he is supported and held, he will collapse. Passivity, not activity, characterizes his day. Unable to carry out most activities, his tendency is to lie down rather than sit. Generally, he gives the picture of being poorly defined with respect to his body. Occasionally screaming or yelling, the sounds he makes are for the most part gutteral.

Characteristics of the spastic CP child are discussed by Finney (1975, p. 44): "The variations in standing of the spastic child are many ... standing on such a narrow base with the weight on the inner side of the foot means that balance and the shifting of the weight sideways or forwards is impossible. If you hold the child under his arms and 'walk him,' all he can do is to fall forwards from one leg to the other, his weight falling more and more onto his toes and his legs becoming stiffer and later crossing."

Jerky and uneven in movement, his very overactivity is sometimes his downfall. In the excitement that is both responsive to and generative of his high activity level, he may "lock" in position and remain thus frozen until someone comes along to "unlock" him. "He is stiff and becomes stiffer if not handled well as you move him" (Finnie, 1975, p. 5).

These two kinds of palsy obviously require different kinds of treatment, different durations of attention, different tempos, and different Theraplay activities. The Theraplay therapist must first observe the child to determine whether and to what degree he is spastic or "floppy." In either case, the skilled therapist knows that he "must handle a cerebral-palsied child slowly and give him a chance to make his own adjustment as he moves in on him, supporting him when and where necessary but waiting and giving him time . . . without allowing him to be passive" (Finnie, 1975, p. 50). Having determined what kind of palsy he is dealing with, he must plan his activities accordingly. He knows that if the child is spastic activities should be avoided that may intensify the spasticity, or the child may "freeze." He also knows, however, that this freezing is not catastrophic; it only takes time and soothing activity to release the tension and get the child "unlocked." If the child is "floppy," he is not so likely to encounter disorganized behavior but he will have to motivate, mobilize, energize, and activate. In order to keep the child attending, he should use a wall as back support and position himself squarely in front of the child. Furthermore, his activities must be particularly well defined. Therapists working with "floppy" cerebral-palsied children, unlike those working with children who are spastic, must remember that their work will take a long time and will bring few rewards.

Given these limitations, the following are Vitiello's suggestions for Theraplay therapists:

Theraplay for "floppy" cerebral-palsied children:
• Plan longer-lasting activities.
• Scream in imitation.
• Encourage lower- and higher-pitched screaming, to practice control.
• Even though as rudimentary a motion as patty-cake may take months to teach, it provides an important experience.

Theraplay for spastic cerebral-palsied children:
• If "locking" occurs, shift activity to fluid, down-and-out movement for relaxation.
• If spastic stance occurs, encourage child to "stay put" while you help him out. Discourage the "running around" he may wish to do instead.

- Avoid surprising, jerky, or too-quick activities—a spastic child, attempting to follow, may become "locked."
- Be careful in holding child. Carry him on side, straddling therapist's hip. A spastic child may lock his legs if carried from the front.
- Plan short, not long, activities—a spastic child may become "flooded" if worked with too much.
- Keep activities flowing evenly and smoothly.
- Emphasize soothing activities (such as lotion, powder, and bubbles), but remember the child may be hypersensitive to tactual stimulation.
- If the condition is not too severe, some Intrusive (silly) activities such as pulling a pretend "something" out of the child's ear may be possible.
- Predictions or announcements of activities to come are not necessary (see Chapter Two).
- Poking or playful jostling is unwise.

Vitiello gives the following account of the Theraplay activities he used in working with one spastic cerebral-palsied child: "A typical session would include first taking handprints or footprints, then measuring his or her size, crawling under me for 'tunnels' (difficult but not impossible; wheelbarrow usually is impossible). Then I would shift to something soothing like hiding candy or combing hair or blowing bubbles. (Timing is always important. These children act up if an activity continues too long.) After a soothing activity, I could switch to something active like arm wrestling (difficult, though, with a really spastic cerebral-palsied child), then back to quieting down, putting on shoes, and leaving" (personal communication).

And Margaret Nezezon of the Esperanza center describes her work with a more handicapped child yet:

Rose Marie is a twelve-year-old athetoid cerebral-palsied child. The level of development at which she "got stuck" was a very early level—her reflexes are limited to very early ones. Thus she has an asymmetrical type of neck reflex. Like a small baby, her head goes out and her hand goes with it. This reflex never got integrated, and it is generally thought she'll never get beyond that. During the first ten years of her life, Rose Marie lay on a carpet on the living room floor, her loving family having no awareness that there could be any alternative for her. All this while, of course, the chances of her reflexes being integrated have become more and more slight. She is so rigid and so hypertonic it would seem that nothing can be done with her.

Still, I tried to figure out what could be done, and I thought of heated massage oil; since then, I sit her on my lap, which is tricky in itself because I have to flex her knees up and cross her arms in front of her on her stomach. Her ATNR reflex [Asymmetric Tonic Neck Reflex] goes to the right, so I turn her so I can support her with my knees and my arm. Then she turns to the left, and I also have to hold her lap.

Recently we've started doing imitation. First I blew in her face over and over, trying to get her to copy me. After half an hour, she was able to get all her muscles working at last, and she blew in my face. I threw my head back and acted as though there were a great west wind. I pulled an "Ernestine." [Ernestine Thomas is a Theraplay Institute field supervisor.] She reacted as though she thought this was really something. It was the first time I'd ever gotten a response out of her which was more than an undifferentiated holler.

I decided to generalize that to the people on her ward where she spends most of her time. Workers on wards tend not to understand these residents—they tend not to realize that "there's someone in there." I spent time with each child worker teaching her to fall over backward. It wasn't long before Rose Marie was blowing every one of them down.

The whole thing has given her a sense of personal power. She had never before been able to manipulate her environment.

One week Rose Marie had the flu, so she missed her Theraplay session. As I came up to her floor the following week and she spotted me down the hall, she screamed at me angrily. I came close and put my face next to hers. She blew with such force and "knocked me down" so hard that I know she just wanted to punch me in the face.

Two months later Rose Marie was observed by Koller, who noted: "What I saw was impressive. The quality of the interaction indicated that not only was this child able to 'blow' on command but that this blowing was done in a manner which indicated that Rose Marie (who had apparently related to no one) did now recognize her worker and enjoyed engaging in this game. She laughed, lost her limp posture, and made intense eye contact with her new friend. I was then told that this child could now communicate her preferences for food at meal time. By placing a small flag by items on a plate, she could blow the flag indicating her preference. The staff is so enthusiastic that they are exploring the possibility of buying an electric board which when correctly blown at can be used to communicate with others."

Only if his family can be involved, however, can help for the cerebral-palsied child be truly effective. For, as Mowatt (1970, p. 425) describes a group of mothers at a cerebral palsy center in Seattle: "Many a mother seemed ambivalent with regard to her child, particularly about his growth toward independence, and tended to be overinvolved, hovering, and protective." Like the mothers of the retarded children seen by Cummings (1966, pp. 595-608), the mothers of cerebral-palsied children showed, in Mowatt's (1970, p. 425) words, "a high level of preoccupation with the child as well as possessiveness and depressive feelings . . . . the parents responded resentfully; resentment led to guilt feelings; guilt kept the mothers overinvolved; thus the vicious cycle kept going, with turmoil and friction constant in many of the homes." Nancie Finnie (1975, p. 17) also reminds parents of cerebral-palsied children that "Regrets, recriminations, worry, sentimental sympathy, or painful longing for miracles, are not helpful. Effort is needed (instead), not an excessive preoccupation with the child to the exclusion of your happiness and that of the family."

Anthony Vitiello incorporates the parents—and sometimes the siblings as well—into Theraplay sessions with the cerebral-palsied child. In so doing, in engaging the family in the active "effort," there is no place for condescending pity or recriminatory guilt. Indeed, within the Theraplay session itself a new and healthier balance of forces may obtain within the family. Brothers and sisters may be freed of their burdens, for example, as they are told, "Holding Jim steady is Mom's job, Jane, not yours" or "So you moved a mite too fast, Jack; you haven't really hurt her, see? All you got to do is wait a bit and she'll be quite OK." But mostly, with the take-charge confidence mentioned before, the Theraplay therapist encourages, "Come on, Dad, he's not going to break if you play a little" or "Come on, Mom, you can help him to help himself—like this, see? He doesn't *have* to be helpless, you know. . . . Come on, surer than that, surer than that . . . don't let him talk you out of it now, come on . . . " As it gains in momentum, a healthier family climate follows. As Nancie Finnie (1975, p. 17) warns, "It may give a mother a satisfaction to feel the child is totally dependent on her, and will always be so, but this is really a poor substitute for the joy of helping one's child to learn, to struggle, and to overcome his handicap." She further warns, "Beware the tendency to say 'He's only a baby'—or 'It's time enough for that later,' or 'He can't understand.' It may well be that these remarks stem from a wish to deny the handicaps, with a consequent tendency to 'infantilize' the child so that he is thought of as a baby (and treated as one) in order to explain his helplessness. . . . To keep the child totally and uniformly helpless in order to deny his disabilities . . . is to deny the child his right to develop maximal independence. For optimal development of the child, you must be gradually changing your relationship with him. . . . One day he is going to have to live without you, and even if he is grievously handicapped, he will be better prepared for the parting if he at least . . . needs and enjoys the company of others [while] still emotionally attached to [you]." It is exactly this change in relationship that family Theraplay aims to achieve for the cerebral-palsied child. Only through the Theraplay kinds of experiences of encouragement in "letting go"—within a playful setting—can many parents begin the difficult process of encouraging independence. And, as the process gains momentum, a healthier family climate often follows. Challenge is very often the name of the game.

Theraplay with the Nonambulatory

Theraplay with children who are congenitally immo-
bilized is perhaps the most difficult of all forms of Theraplay.
These children respond the least and are often the slowest to
benefit. Their emotional growth comes in the least perceptible
increments of all. Therapists working with these kinds of children either should be working concurrently with other patients
who have more potential, or they should be certain that gratifications are there for them in their outside life. Understandably,
neither group will, or can, be as motivated for patient progress
as are therapists working with children of high potential.

Theraplay goals for these children who are nonverbal,
whose bodies do not move, whose mouths drool, and whose
faces are expressionless may reach no further than the hope that
one day their eyes will sparkle as they see their therapists approach or, even further, that a smile may cross their lips or their
drooling diminish somewhat. The means for bringing this about
will be the Theraplay therapist's repertoire of warm, playful
clowning and surprises combined with techniques to make each
patient feel special, important, attractive, and, most of all, as
capable of making some impact on his or her therapist. Thus a
nonambulatory child who remains isolated and not-interacted-
with for most of his everyday life can hardly fail to be im-
pressed by the following cheerful greeting given in a lively, surprising, and intensely personal way: "Well, if it isn't Ellen, my
friend with those beautiful big brown eyes and that gorgeous
soft hair (feeling it)! And look what I see! I did! I saw it! I saw
a little bit of a smile peeking out right there! Oh! there it went
again! And I caught it and put it in my pocket and look! Here it
is! Look how it makes me smile! Here it comes back to you,
Ellen, right behind your ear! What do you mean, behind your
ear? Why, that's no place for a smile (searching for it). Why, it's
right here on your lips where it belongs. Hey, you fooled me!
You fooled me, you know that? You're a tricky kid! I think
that's why I like you. You're always thinking up new tricks
like . . . oh! I saw you blink there! How did you do that? Like

this? (clowning) No? Like this?" and so on. Provided on a regular basis, even these interactions, "silly" and simple as they may seem, should begin to bring about some change, even if only a small change, for the better. The most incapacitated child will feel the warmth, the sparkle, the optimism, and the engagement. Given the therapist's drive to involve, no "turnoff" can last forever. The preceding monologue describes one example of a therapeutic interaction with a child who is severely handicapped. The severity of the handicap delimits the range of interactions possible. Limited to being made up in front of a mirror, having his cheeks blown on, having peek-a-boo played with a blanket, or dabs of cold cream passed from the tip of the therapist's nose to the top of the patient's forehead, and a few other activities, a child like this one cannot be involved in running, jumping, hiding, or in games of vigorous competition. The more mobile the child, in other words, and the more he approaches physical normalcy, the broader the range of Theraplay experiences he can be given.

The message has been the same throughout this section on Theraplay for children with handicaps. Whether the emotionally troubled handicapped child is deaf, blind, cerebral palsied, or totally nonambulatory, the analogy between the relationship of the ideal mother with her handicapped infant and the Theraplay therapist with his patient applies: Growth-promoting harmony, regardless of the obstacles, should be the goal for both.

Notes

1. James S. Miller's (1978, p. 220) comment with regard to the literature on hyperkinesis may well be relevant to studies on learning disabilities: "Studies showing 'overactivity,' 'hyperactivity,' 'restlessness,' 'disruptiveness,' and so on in 30 percent to 50 percent of elementary school pupils are ignored."

2. The family Theraplay model of parents joining in from the fifth session on is not always rigidly adhered to. In some cases, the child needs time to consolidate his or her gains, and sometimes parents make such good use of the observation

sessions that their participation is more effective if put off until the end.

3. Viola Brody (1966) first demonstrated the change in human figure drawings of patients treated by the Des Lauriers method. She found that facial features, particularly eyes, appeared and came into focus and that overall body movement increased in the drawings of individuals who evidenced change on other diagnostic instruments (for example, the TAT, or Thematic Apperception Test).

4. His mother, in fact, was so proud of Frankie's newfound cooperativeness that she willingly agreed to bring him to a class for demonstrating Theraplay with the deaf.

5. "Some blind babies may never find the adaptive routes and remain frozen in the state of body centeredness, passivity, immobility and ultimately, nondifferentiation" (Fraiberg, 1977, p. 22).

9

Autistic Children

The growing body of literature on the causes, diagnosis, and treatment of autistic children probably less reflects an increasing number of these children than it reflects an increasing interest in this particular population as well as a rising to the challenge of trying to understand the unexplainable manner in which environmental influence and biological predisposition combine in this disease. Although the autistic child is a relatively rare phenomenon, occurring in less than 1 percent of the general population, it is an important one nevertheless—not just because of the heartache such a child brings to his parents but because here, perhaps at last, we can find the key for unlocking such basic riddles of human behavior as, for example, the relative importance of biology and environment in the prevention, cause, and treatment of emotional disease. Increasingly, the *normal* mother-child dyad is viewed as a reverberating circuit, "neither partner being a *tabula rasa* at any point" (Schaffer, 1977, p. 53). The behavior of each partner both influences and reacts to the behavior of the other—the mothers' expressions of positive emotion correlate with their children's expressions of

300

happiness, and both change over time. Among the most significant determinants of the quality of the mother-infant relationship is the extent and nature of the eye-to-eye contact between them; "The appeal of the mother's eyes to the child (and of his eyes to her) is facilitated by their stimulus richness. In comparison with other areas of the body surface, the eye has a remarkable array of interesting qualities" (Robson, 1967, p. 14). In normal families, this transaction is a given; we will now focus on conditions wherein the positive flow from one to the other is "spoiled" or interrupted. Such conditions produce not "competence" but its opposite—in extreme form, the pairing of "an initially malfunctioning infant . . . with an unresponsive mother." This relationship, according to Ainsworth and Bell (1974, p. 98), makes for "the poorest prognosis for the development of infant competence." Anthony sees just this breakdown when insensitivity and unresponsiveness in the mother combine with a constitutionally thick barrier in the child. This combination, precluding as it does the development of a healthy "ego barrier," terminates, according to Anthony (1958, pp. 211-223), in autism. Or, as stated by Des Lauriers and Carlson (1969, p. 74), "[Autism] is consequent to an inborn functional neurophysiologic imbalance [which results in] an absence in the autistic infant of any real capacity to send out signals or cues to which the parents could appropriately respond."

Observing the autistic child, particularly through the concentrated focus provided by the one-way window, is like observing the occupant of a well-insulated bubble. The inexperienced observer is likely to see a child who is beautiful to look at, often appears to be goal directed in his activity, is clever in his behavior, and seems to be motorically skillful. As he works some complicated jigsaw puzzle, reads aloud from an adult-sized book, repeats a television commercial jingle, or sits and rocks in serious contemplation, the moderately severe autistic child only appears to possess a talent for sober absorption. Yet we are talking about an initial observation only, for an inexperienced observer can be fooled by these children. A quick, casual observation may result in the judgment that the autistic child, as would be true of any other child, is content to be busily engaged in a project of his own choosing. Any impression he may give of detachment or preoccupation is dispelled by his physical beauty. "Such an attractive child," the novice reasons, "must surely elicit universal affection." More detailed, thoughtful analysis, however, shows that the autistic child repels, not attracts, affection. Even on a short ride on a train or in an elevator, the autistic child attracts with his appearance, then coolly repels, the attentions of strangers around him. Initially charmed adults approach him eagerly, only to pull back as their eyes meet his empty gaze. Were the observer to remain on the scene a few moments longer, he or she would note a discrepancy: The autistic child's clear, wide-open eyes, which had appeared to be so interested and so alert, are alert in initial appearance only. As Des Lauriers has described them, these children are, indeed, "asleep" (Des Lauriers and Carlson, 1969). The autistic child's apparently goal-directed activity unfortunately has a singlemindedness of purpose. Even more than the obsessive child (Adams, 1973) or than "children with circumscribed interest patterns" (Robinson and Vitale, 1954, pp. 755-766), the autistic child allows no interference whatsoever. Clancy and McBride (1969, p. 237) describe him thus:

> As the child grows, he improves his skills in manipulative behavior to communicate a preference for being left alone. In particular, he develops and extends a capacity for "cut-off" behavior (Chance, 1962, pp. 71-89). "Cut-off" is nonverbal and refers to any act or posture which occurs in a social situation for the express purpose of limiting social input.
>
> The autistic child uses many cut-off devices—for example, he acts as if deaf; he avoids direct eye contact; he engages in rhythmic repetitive activities such as spinning or tapping objects, and these absorb his attention totally. Such behaviors powerfully maintain his social isolation. . . . The family soon learns not to attempt to intrude on the child's isolation, unless it be on his own terms. The alternative may be a temper tantrum. These relationships do become stable and resistant to change. In particular, the child violently rejects any deviation in the

nature of his contacts, so [powerfully reinforcing] the existing set of conditions. Equally powerful intrusion is necessary to alter any part of his routines, and since this is extremely disruptive (temper tantrums), it is seldom achieved in a stable family.

Unless his behavior is blatantly "peculiar," his cleverness will be striking. Far from being retarded, he appears in the first moment of observation to be ingenious at negotiating himself into the right place at the right time or even clever at unlocking doors that bar his path or at crossing tricky passageways. Far from being intellectually slow, he may perform mathematics, master musical complexities, speak—if he does speak—in language far beyond his years. Yet, this very cleverness, when looked at in depth, soon shows itself for what it really is: a rigid, ritualized exercise quite devoid of meaning from our point of view—a personal set of purposeless motions conducted in the privacy of his insulated bubble. As for his motoric skills some-times awkward, yet often smoothly functioning—the highly refined movements of his fingers as he plays piano, draws pictures,[1] or picks lint off the carpets, or of his feet as he twirls around on tiptoe—these skills, it soon becomes apparent, are the skills of a machine. Nothing about them resembles the activities of a wholesome, happy, human child. Even the apparently high degree of interpersonal involvement of some autistic children may be only deceptively that. The autistic child may leave his bubble, approach another person, and lead him or her by the hand for water. He may at other times even appear to give a hug. Looked at more closely, however, the act of leaving the bubble and the approach itself has an "unreal" quality, its unreality being in no way more conspicuous than in the almost universal absence of eye contact. What we see is one machine approaching another, not a little child valuing a relationship. Rather than the water at the sink representing the good aspects of an enjoyable togetherness, the water itself is the goal; the human hand accompanying him there is just a tool. ("Clearly [my] hands are to lift him ... my leg is a surface to lean against ... I feel nonexistent"—Meltzer, 1975, p. 38). As for the hug—which, the observer may note with pleasure, the child gives to his mother and which is for most children the shared, physical affirmation of loving and joyful feelings—for the few autistic children even capable of doing it, the hug is an act that serves another purpose. In contrast to the meaning of hugging for Emily—a normal child, who has told her mother, "I love to hug you like this, Mom, but there's one trouble; when I do, I can't look at you"—hugging for the autistic child provides a safe refuge out of eye-contact range. In addition, hugging may provide access to the shock of hair that is soothing to finger, stimulating to twirl, squeaky to pull on, and stringy to suck. In autistic children, hugging, infrequent as it is, is noteworthy for one important reason: An autistic child's hug, whether of his mother or the caretaker (who, through presentation of an M&M may reward him for his hug), appears to untrained observers (often including his mother) to be only a warm, happy, and a thoroughly interacting piece of "normal" behavior in an otherwise highly abnormal child. As such, it is understandable that a hug should make a mother feel relief and should tempt a diagnostician to rule out his "autistic" diagnosis.

Most writers on autistic children agree on how these children look and act. Underlying causes, as these relate to treatment, however, are explained differently by different authors. Rimland (1964), for example, attributes autism to impairment in the reticular formation; Kanner (1943, pp. 217-240), to the "ice box" personality of the mother. Treatment methods proposed, of course, vary with the theory. Thus Rimland, who sees autism as a biochemical malfunction, if not a structural defect, treats autistic children with chemotherapy and "training." Meltzer, in contrast, viewing autism as intrapsychic discord and early failure in object relationships, treats autistic children with Kleinian (Klein, 1932) psychoanalysis: "The core of the method is a systematic and uncompromising investigation of the transference" (Meltzer, 1975, p. 4). Charles Maclean (1978) describes as follows the "treatment" of two "wolf children"—similar in behavior to autistic patients: " 'It is only possible if you can create a liking in them for the change so desired. To create a liking, you must make them understand that you are their well wisher and that you love them sincerely . . . their understanding turns them from aversion to friendliness' " (p. 123). "The period of massage was lengthened and repeated morning and evening. With a gentle, sure touch, Mrs. Singh worked over every inch of her (Kamala's) body, from under her eyebrows to the soles of her feet. . . . While she was giving the massage, she would talk to her all the time, reassuring her with endearments 'expressed in the most loving terms possible' " (p. 137).

Clancy and McBride suggest that both the approaches of Bettelheim (1967) and of Lovaas (1977) are too circumscribed: Bettelheim for attributing the child's autism to the mother's behavior and attitudes (for example, rejecting and depriving) and Lovaas for treating the child alone. Clancy and McBride (1969, p. 242) themselves treat autism through intrusion and operant conditioning of family systems.

In an article entitled "Infantile Autism and the Holding Relationship," A. B. John and B. A. Allen (1969, pp. 69-70) describe the following experiment in adult holding of autistic children:

> The purpose of this study was to observe and record how some autistic children respond when they are held, carried, and supported in a number of different ways. Two holding positions were of particular interest. The first was holding-for-restraint, and in this position the experimenter placed the child on his lap and restricted his movements by holding the child's hands and ankles. The purpose was to oppose or counteract any gross movements of the child by slightly tactile pressure. For instance, if the child began to move his hands in a manneristic fashion, the grip on his hands was increased to prevent such movements. The second position was holding-for-pleasure. This was different from holding-for-restraint and consisted of cradling the child in the arms, gently rocking him from side to side, tickling, and later swinging by the wrist and ankle. Speech was not used as much as pleasurable utterances and the echoing and extension of noises made by the child. . . . Each session lasts two hours, and for the first ninety minutes holding-for-restraint is used, while the last half hour is taken up with holding-for-pleasure and in providing and encouraging the child to play as he wishes.

The authors conclude, "Improved eye contact and relaxation in human contact tends to follow and to lead to pleasurable interpersonal interaction and to attachment of a kind that had not previously existed. Some exploratory behavior also developed."

Nurturing approaches generally characterize the treatment method of Mira Rothenberg (1978) in her book *Children with Emerald Eyes.* Alan Ward (1977, p. 121), in his book *Childhood Autism and Structural Therapy,* describes the following (primarily Intrusive) guidelines in his approach to autistic children:

1. The therapist is trained to identify the stereotypic behavior of the child and to interrupt it. . . .
2. The anxiety and anger created by the interruption of the stereotypic behavior is used to focus the attention of the child upon part of the therapist as a meaningful part object or object. Analytically-oriented interpretations accompany the use of structural therapy. . . .
3. Development of a recognition relationship with the child is followed by presentation of a number of novel and patterned activities which draw the child's attention to his own body. . . .
4. The development of body ego is stimulated by the use of physical, gamelike interactions that make the child more aware of his own body and of his differences from the similarities to his therapist.
5. As behavioral ego functioning decreases and body ego becomes more predominant, more conventional play therapy techniques are included in the treatment.

Des Lauriers describes his therapy as follows: "The 'therapist' must establish himself as the most important intruding factor in the life of [the child]. . . . It is a matter of *presence*: a forceful, insistent, intruding presence of the therapist to the patient, so that the [patient] cannot escape this presence. All the energies of the therapist must be geared to establishing, maintaining, or encouraging and developing 'contact' between the patient and himself. . . [including] physical, sensual, intellectual, affective, emotional, conative, and motoric contact between the patient and the therapist" (1962, p. 63).

The essential elements of Theraplay (Structuring, Challenging, Intrusion, and Nurturing), alone or in combinations of two or three, characterize most of the aforementioned therapeutic strategies. Mollie Dundass, for example, Nurtures; Clancy and McBride Intrude, Structure, and Challenge. Even Meltzer Intrudes, Phyllis Booth suggests (personal communication). Booth says:

> Kleinians claim they maintain their analytic position—that is, they continue to stand to one side (metaphorically) and analyze or interpret what is going on. Yet even then they become, in their quiet way, a force or person to be reckoned with, to be taken into account rather than to be used by the child for his own purposes, like the rest of the environment (as simply part of the safe and familiar furniture of the child's world or as another mechanism for carrying out the child's omnipotent wishes). To the extent that they fail at this, Kleinian therapists fade into the meaningless background of the child's self-contained world.
>
> In contrast to Theraplay therapists, behavior modification therapists make an impact and demand a change and thus do part of what is necessary, but they often fail to add the element of enticement or fun which the child needs to make him *want* to continue being in this newly expanded world.
>
> And they feed the autistic child's inherent rigidity rather than working toward the spontaneity which is the really crucial problem.
>
> Theraplay tries to provide maximum impact in combination with fun and spontaneity.
>
> When everything goes smoothly according to what the child is used to, no new impact is made on him. And we must make an impact, or we cannot move him out of his cocoon into our world.
>
> We do not wait for the child to bounce off us, but we move in and bounce off him. We do not let ourselves become part of his magically controlled world. We set the

limits—"I want you to stay here with me. I want you to
have fun with me. I will insist when necessary. This is safe
and fun, and I want you to enjoy it."

It is probably the degree to which Theraplay therapists
do not "wait for the child to bounce off us" that most distin-
guishes Theraplay from most other therapies and certainly from
most other dynamically oriented therapies. The best definition
of all comes from Austin Des Lauriers: "Theraplay . . . emphasizes the central factor of high affective impact in all stimulating
contacts or communication with the autistic child; this is done
through play, games, and fun. In this relaxed atmosphere, no
special effort is made at teaching the child anything; there are
no specific special education methods or tools utilized. What
the child learns first is that it is good to be human with another
human being, that it is fun to be a member of the human race,
and that grown-up human beings are worth having around to
make life pleasant" (1978, p. 317). Because of the debt we owe
him and because of his great success in working with autistic
children, the contribution of Des Lauriers to Theraplay merits
extended discussion at this point.

The reader, by this time, must be aware that Des Lauriers
is the inspiration for and the spiritual father of Theraplay. While
Des Lauriers might not want to claim this responsibility fully,
neither he nor any of us who have worked with him fail to see
that his ideas are at the core of this therapy. As Des Lauriers has
stated them, the goals of treatment are to help the child come
emotionally alive. Theraplay, as here described, thus shares not
only Des Lauriers' treatment goal but also most of the ways in
which this change is brought about. It shares the fun and spontaneity, the vigor and healthy partnership. It shares the confidence that if the world is filled with pleasure the happiness will
follow. And although Des Lauriers may not appear to "plan"
his sessions, it is obvious from observing him that a sensitive
diagnosis and carefully honed format do underlie his therapeutic style. However, the kinds of activities that are uniquely
Des Lauriers' and that work so well with autistic children are
modified to some extent at the Theraplay Institute. They have

been modified of necessity, and, in the process, these modifications particularly have been found extremely effective with autistic children.

Therapeutic systems, like other human enterprises, are shaped by individual personalities, historic realities, and external exigencies. Theraplay as described here is a form of treatment originally designed to be effective not only with autistic children, but with children of widely divergent pathologies who must be treated in a short span of time by therapists from varied backgrounds and treated not only in clinical settings but in homes and schools as well. It was to meet the broad and challenging needs of this client population that the concepts and formulations of the Theraplay Institute were developed. The list of do's and don'ts (see Chapter Two) was first assembled for a course in Theraplay at Northeastern Illinois University. Perhaps at first glance the do's and don't's appear like cookbook formulas. In fact, they grew out of many therapists' experiences with several hundred children, and they grew out of the need to simplify, which, while often unfortunately sacrificing descriptions about (although not, of course, the use of) nuance, flexibility, flair, and personal style, does nonetheless provide a usable, barebones framework. It is these do's and don't's, furthermore, that Theraplay therapists (and parents) have found so helpful since 1974, when these "rules" were first compiled. By and large, the guidelines reflect Des Lauriers, especially to the extent that they promote the physical, the fun, the focused, and the personal. Yet there are some differences from Des Lauriers' approach, and these need explaining.

Guideline 14, for example, states, "The therapist uses himself as the primary playroom object—books, dolls, puzzles, and checkerboards do not belong in the Theraplay room." This "rule" is stated this way because the temptation to use "props" seems universal. Once made available, the books, dolls, or puzzles seem to take on a therapeutic life of their own and, whereas the Theraplay principle states there should be only human interaction, there now is a third, nonhuman party, the "toy," which can come between and can impede the relationship. Asked "Why did you use those stacking blocks?" for example, the beginning therapist will likely confess, "Because it made *me* more comfortable." Des Lauriers, however, uses toys more freely and with great therapeutic effect—for example, " 'let me see you hit Bobo [inflated toy clown] over there.' Adam looked Bobo over, then flailed away" (1962, p. 115).

Guideline 17 states, "The Theraplay therapist . . . does not play 'Let's pretend you and I are somebody or something else' games. Those serve only to provide both therapist and child an escape from the here-and-now." The rationale for this "no fantasy" rule is similar to the one for "no toys" already stated. Therapists who fall far short of Des Lauriers' expertise can interpret license to fantasy as license to escape (from the immediate, the urgent, the intense, and the personal). All too often, beginning therapists cannot resist the temptation to suggest "Let's pretend we're in a jungle," "Let's play we're both spacemen," and so on. The scene having been set, the relieved psychotherapist takes off with the willing child and together they follow a script that has nothing whatever to do with the here-and-now setting; nothing to do with mutually enjoying their real-life engagement. Again, Des Lauriers' play of war games, while clearly effective, is quite different and has a different quality—the kind of quality few beginners could hope to match.

Guideline 20 states, "The Theraplay therapist is not so concerned with protecting the child's equilibrium as he is with coaxing him to try alternatives—even though this may at first be reacted to as though it were uncomfortable."

It is in the area of psychologically forcing, intruding, or pushing that Des Lauriers himself differs perhaps most radically from many of his fellow child therapists. He sometimes quipped that some therapists take notes while the patients go nuts. Yet Theraplay as described herein sometimes seems to go further still. Theraplay therapists working in half-hour sessions, having the school year's ending as a deadline, and seeing children only once or twice a week must work even more intensively than therapists in traditional settings. Finding prolonged caution, patient observation, and "waiting until the child is ready" not practicable, these therapists have to engage quickly and must actively begin to Structure, Challenge, Intrude, and Nurture. These exigencies lead to an ordering of priorities sometimes unlike that of Des Lauriers. Whereas Des Lauriers can Intrude and Challenge in small increments, extending the child's reach slowly, gently, and subtly, the Theraplay therapist under the pressure of Head Start realities, for example, has to move deliberately, rapidly, and with conviction. Harsh, punitive, and crass as this approach may sound, its Nurturing and Structuring are anything but insensitive. Its Intruding and Challenging are boisterous, engaging, and upbeat but not cruel or sadistic. Yet, rather than prolonged coddling and protecting (except in rare cases, of course), the Theraplay therapist is deterred neither by the child's initial pained look nor by his expressions of wishing to be elsewhere. It remains for succeeding sessions and the child's clear joy at reunion with his therapist to prove how meaningful, in fact, the initial sessions were. (It is only in the delicate task of mirroring the autistic child's noises and expressions, furthermore, that insistent Intrusion at first appears genuinely uncomfortable.)

Guideline 3 states, "No activity is so repetitiously carried out as to be predictable." Again, whereas Des Lauriers, in his finely tuned response to children, can sense when repetition is appropriate and will allow or encourage it in the interest of learning or mastery, the beginning therapist may be dulled by repeated activity, and the child may be lulled into total withdrawal. The round "Row, Row, Row Your Boat" is a favorite of beginners, but (to caricature a bit) before child, therapist, or supervisor is aware of it, all three are virtually lulled to sleep by the song's repetition.

Guideline 4 states, "He does not allow the child to 'call the shots.' " Again, in his interactions with troubled children, Des Lauriers clearly is "in charge." However, he tolerates vast variations, and in the interest of encouraging initiative he may allow the child to "call the shots." Not so the beginning Theraplay therapist. Given the freedom to decide who is in charge, he will more often than not turn to the child for ideas, for approval, and for permission. If none of these is forthcoming, he may plead, bargain, compromise, and eventually, in his impotence, feel resentment and despair—hardly, one would say, a health-promoting stance for any therapist. In summary, while the ideas, inspiration, training, and valued friendship of Des Lauriers have formed the foundation on which Theraplay is built, the edifice is in some respects not one he would have designed, although he generously gives it his unqualified approval.

Our work with autistic children has forced the recognition that the person behind the mask, the baby inside the bubble—not the outer symptomatology—will determine what should be done to help the autistic child. He can be left inside, of course. His privacy can be "respected," his decision to exclude himself left up to him. "When he is ready to join us," we could say, "we'll welcome him. In the meantime," we could add, "we have no right to foist our will or norms on him." For fear we may upset him and drive him yet further away, we could continue to speak to him gently and carefully. If he is musical, or mathematical, or verbal, we might rejoice and, always hoping to encourage his music, his math, or his words, we might surround him with concertos, formulas, or books. Like Bettelheim (1967), we could treat the autistic child permissively and acceptingly, giving in to his demands, allowing him to lead the way. Gradually, as Bettelheim does, we could replace with a "good" parent the mother who presumably was his nemesis.

We can also, however, take a more active stance in helping him out of his bubble. We can, for example, as in the behavior modification model, focus our efforts on eliciting behavior from him that is more appropriate to children in a civilized society. The behavior itself then can be seen as all-important, and we can reward its discrete units—regardless of whether or not they have "meaning." We can, while we are at it, even define as "behavior worthy of reinforcement" those arbitrary motions, such as hugging, that combined together spell "relationship."

Or we can approach the autistic child through Theraplay. We can plan sessions specifically tailored to entice him to join us at the level he was—no matter how early—when he first "tuned out" the world. If, for example, he tuned out at the level of a newborn, we may stroke his eyelids, blow on his earlobe, cuddle, kiss, and sing to him. If he tuned out at a four-month-old level, we may encourage his studying his mother's face or his reaching out to touch her cheeks. We may lay him down horizontally and lean our face down close to his. We may take his fingers and patiently help him to explore the contours of our lips (and to babble as he does so). We may let him feel the inside of our mouth, as little babies like to do, and help him attend while we "mirror" him. In all these ways, we may feel free to insist that he join us in a relationship that we know ultimately will give him pleasure—not because his "civilized behavior" is the condition for our involvement, but because we know that what we have to offer would be enjoyable to any normal healthy infant. The concepts of "pleasure" and "enjoy" are critical for Theraplay. Although they certainly are not *always* present, these principles reinstate in the autistic child-parent dyad the spontaneous warmth and expressive pleasure of a normal mother with her normal infant that differentiate Theraplay from other similar but more "hard headed" treatment styles, such as Clancy and McBride's (1969) intrusion and operant conditioning treatment of family systems.

Theraplay with autistic children, using Intrusion to the extent it does, basically follows the models of Des Lauriers and Carlson (1969) and Fraiberg (1977). It extends Intrusion even further, sometimes going so far as to deliberately oppose some of the patient's new desires. "Otherwise the child may never develop beyond the point of seeing the therapist as a gratifying, playful, enjoyable object whose only role is to supply his oral demands" (Ward, 1977, p. 122). With respect to Nurturing, however, Theraplay follows the aforementioned models less closely than it does that of the Marlborough Day Hospital's unit for autistic children in London. Even here, however, there is a difference: the caretakers give only as much physical contact as the child will take. Theraplay gives this contact whether or not the child accepts it. Dundass (1969, p. 77), describes the work at the Marlborough Day Hospital's autistic children's center: "A number of voluntary workers attend for one or more sessions a week. They become the 'auntie' or 'uncle' of one particular child. They concentrate on this child in an approximation of the way a happy mother does on her baby. A relationship is slowly formed. The child is helped to regress to as young an age as possible, and the auntie gives him as much physical contact as he will accept, and the needful early experience such as cuddling and bottle feeding, with as pleasant concomitant feelings as possible."[1]

Yet the autistic child needs more than Intrusion or Nurturing alone. And because treatment must overcome the profound degree of disturbance, the early onset, the consequently faulty mother-child bonding and, more than likely, the biological origins, Theraplay with the autistic child takes considerably longer, overall, than does Theraplay with other kinds of emotionally disturbed children. The eight-session family Theraplay model described in Chapter Five does not apply to family Theraplay with autistic children. Rather, the sessions—still half an hour long, once or twice a week, on an outpatient basis—may go on anywhere from six months to three years. The degree of success even then is variable. All autistic children in Theraplay improve. Some gain increased language, higher test scores, greater interpersonal functioning, and even placement in a normal schoolroom (see Bligh, in *The Language-Delayed Child*, 1977a, chap. 8).

Others, while they become happier and relate more easily and while they are less fearful and ritualistic, are nonetheless still "slow" children. Still others reach an early plateau. The goals for each child vary with the degree of involvement possible on the part of the parents, along with other factors, including the hypothesized thickness of insulation of the "bubble." The more permeable the bubble, the younger the child, and the more willing for intensive involvement are his parents, the greater will be his chances for recovery.

Whereas the hyperactive child is on the go and requires constant limits (Structuring); the withdrawn child, having "dropped out" requires constant boosting (Intruding); the immature child requires Challenging; and the obsessive child requires Nurturing and Intruding, the autistic child often requires all these and more. Theraplay with autistic children demands more of therapists and parents than does Theraplay with any other group of children. As will soon be seen, Theraplay with autistic children demands of their parents and of the therapists the utmost in dedication, energy, imagination, self-esteem, optimism, resilience, caring, perspective, and insight. Theraplay with autistic children often requires indescribable cheer and superhuman perseverance even in the face of frequent total "turnoffs." Because autistic children are uncaring and unresponsive, the adults working with them must have a relatively low need for others' emotional responsiveness and for external admiration. An adult who demands constant affirmation from others would be likely to become enraged by the autistic child's indifference. Along with the cheer and perseverance, the job requires a high level of investment and a tolerance for regression. An adult who is frightened by his own wish to regress might encounter difficulty bottle feeding a six-year-old autistic child. "Quite frequently [the world of the psychotic child] is the world of the very young infant set in the twilight of consciousness. . . . The degree to which we can understand him will depend on our preparedness to enter into a unilateral and unrewarding relationship. The psychotic child is separated from us by the extent to which we ourselves, the investigators, are alienated from our childhood and from our potential or latent psychosis" (Anthony, 1958, p. 212). Just as mothers of normal infants can be seen to open their own mouths while feeding their babies, for example, so the good Theraplay therapist can sometimes be seen to be equally in tune with the autistic child. Yet even more is required than perseverance, cheer, energy, low self-centeredness, and a tolerance for regression. Matter-of-fact confidence, high self-regard, and firmness are required. The child must feel the therapist's "Thereness"—with a capital T. As stated in Chapter Two, he must feel the therapist as so much *there*, making such a strong impact, that he knows there is no escaping him, no blotting him out, no forgetting what he looks like, feels like, tastes like, smells like (Meltzer, 1975, p. 15), sounds like, and so on. Never must the adult come across as merely a shadow, a spirit, a fleeting vagueness.

Although in their persevering, stimulating, loving, and guiding ways the parents of Raun in *Son-Rise* (Kaufman, 1975) provided their son with many of the experiences we have listed, even they, with their remarkable dedication, still did not show all the required behaviors, attitudes, and kinds of relating recommended for parents of children in Theraplay. Although the Theraplay-using parents would also have kept up a steady stream of stimulation (albeit more directed to humans than to objects and tasks) and although they too might have kept Raun in his bathroom as a confining place in which they could be intimately together, the Theraplay parents, unlike Raun's parents, would never permit him to "turn them off" or "tune them out." Much as he might resist their Intrusion or appear pained by their insistence, they would insist and would Intrude. This is not to say they would be cruel, for they would remind themselves that they are asking of their autistic child no more and no less than a normal child would enjoy. They would do this because, as Clancy and McBride (1969, p. 242) have so aptly put it, "Permissiveness is actually harmful to the autistic child. In the autistic process, as we see it, the child actively shapes the family's behavior so that he achieves isolation. This is most clearly seen in his use of cut-off and the family's acceptance of it. The temper tantrum is clearly used to demand relationships on the child's terms. This is the reverse of normal socialization, which requires leadership and control by the parents, not the child. Accordingly, we reject permissiveness and would argue for forceful demands by parents, to intrude and to reinforce negatively both cut-off behavior and temper tantrums." In this sense, the parents of Ann in *For the Love of Ann* (Copeland, 1973), with their campaign of constant Intruding, Challenging, and Structuring, most closely approximated Theraplay—their recourse to drilling and slapping notwithstanding.

Autistic Bryan was five years old when he began treatment at the Theraplay Institute. Bryan's parents, like Raun's and Ann's, were intent on helping their autistic child. Bryan's dramatic progress could hardly have come about without their enthusiastic spirit. During the first half of each weekly half-hour session, they observed Bryan being played with by his therapists, and while they watched they asked questions of the interpreting therapist, discussed the happenings of the past week, and conjured up activities for the week ahead. During the second half of each session, both mother and father joined Bryan, as intent as his therapists on engaging Bryan in eye contact and on participating in the tummy printing, toe lathering, leapfrogging, the attempts to bottle feed, and so on. They were exceptionally open to criticisms, suggestions, and new ideas. When his mother permitted, and even enjoyed, Bryan's hugging her, for example, she was shown that unfortunately he only used the hugging to bury himself inside her hair. She was encouraged to find other satisfying acts to do with him instead (like guiding his hands to touch her cheeks). His parents' main contributions to his improving condition, however, came about not at the weekly sessions, but as a consequence of their time with him at home. For Bryan, home had become one big Theraplay room. When his mother was not romping, rolling, or gently feeding or powdering him, his older sister was. And every evening first father alone and then father with the whole family Intruded on and Nurtured Bryan in ways that were cheerful and imaginative, irresistible, and fun—ways that always had the aim of attaining eye contact. It was not too long, in fact, before they reported Bryan wandering in from the sidelines on his own and placing himself in the midst of all the noisy, tumbling, family joy. This letter, written after his family's move to another city tells a recent story:

> You wouldn't believe Bryan. He has been fantastic. He didn't find the move at all upsetting. If anything, he has progressed instead of regressed. We arrived at the new house on Sunday to look around and do a little cleaning. He ran all around looking at everything. Monday we arrived just ahead of the moving van. He was so excited to see all the furniture. He had a great time getting into everyone's way. That night when I was getting him ready for bed I was thinking. "OK, this is it. He is sure to throw a fit when I put him to bed in his new room. After all, autistic children are supposed to be upset by a major change." Everything went beautifully.
>
> The first day of school at the university he climbed off the bus and said, "Hi, teacher." The gal couldn't be-

lieve her ears because she had been told that he didn't use much language.

His teacher is working on the possibility of getting Bryan into a kindergarten class next year, with his own aide. If he continues to progress as he is now, she feels he will be ready. It is so fantastic. At school, he is using some sentences and words to express his feelings. We haven't seen it at home but they are keeping a list at school. Things like "I don't want to do that." "Take this off me." "Untie my shoe." Needless to say, Jim, Barbra, and I are so thrilled. We owe so much thanks to all of you who worked so hard with us to help Bryan on his way. We hope things continue to progress. We are still doing Theraplay with him most evenings. If you ever need an endorsement for Theraplay, *just call us.*

Autistic children share certain behaviors (such as ritualizing, perseverating, isolating, preoccupation with power, and rigid guardedness) with obsessive children. Theraplay with the autistic child therefore in many ways resembles Theraplay with the obsessive child, although the latter is far less disturbed. While probably stemming from quite different origins, the behavior of the two groups often differs more in degree than in kind. Obsessive children are tenacious in their rituals, pitiful in their tenseness, hesitant in relating, and single-minded in their determination to "run the show." The treatment methods for the two groups will be alike to the degree that these kinds of behavior are similar. Treatment of children in the autistic group will require more intensity according to the severity of their behavior. The Theraplay treatment of obsessive and autistic children shares these guidelines:

1. The therapist, not the child, must be in charge.
2. The therapist attends as little as possible to the verbal, the intellectual, the cognitive, or the fantasized (Des Lauriers, 1967, pp. 194-201).
3. Wherever possible, the therapy consists of regressive, indulging, Nurturing activities.
4. At every opportunity to do so, the therapist surprises, In-

trudes, and varies the child's predictable routine. The child is provided no opportunities for ritual within the session (although it is extremely important, as it is with all therapies based on trust and the reducing of anxiety, that the session itself be consistently scheduled as to time and place).

In addition, autistic children require these treatment strategies:

1. Whenever possible, the therapist sings, not speaks, communications. Centers such as that for "autistic-like" children at the University of Minnesota have found that autistic children tune out normal talking tones but tune in to singing. (It remains for future research to demonstrate whether this is because the autistic child responds to a wider range of sounds than does the normal child; because speech is more difficult for him to sort out, being more complex than music; because he suffers a deficiency in the left brain hemisphere; or because of other factors.)

2. The therapist never lets go of the child. Just as with overactive children, the therapist working with the autistic child also keeps in constant physical contact. Observing these children through a one-way window, it is striking to see how quickly, on loss of physical contact, they "fade out" and "disappear." Thus, even when the therapist quickly goes to find a Kleenex or briefly turns to check for shoes at the end of the session, it is important that he keep the autistic child "in tow."

3. At every opportunity, the therapist engages the autistic child in eye-to-eye contact. This is perhaps the most difficult therapeutic task with these children, for they are masters at escaping such engagement. Often they look physically pained when their eyes have been "caught" even momentarily.

4. At the point where the child clearly and insistently wishes to communicate and where he appears obviously frustrated that he is unable to send messages in words, then the Theraplay therapist introduces *signed English* as an opportunity —not a drill—into the Theraplay session. "*Signed English* is an educational tool meant to be used while you speak and thereby help you communicate with deaf children. It is a way of pre-

senting meaning by gesture or sign along with speech" (Bornstein, 1975, p. viii). In line with the joyfulness in relating that is
the treatment's core, the sign for *hug* makes a good beginning.
To make this sign, "Cross arms on chest as if hugging something" (Bornstein, 1975, p. 125). The therapist, talking engag-
ingly all the while, having so crossed the child's arms, gives the
child a happy hug. As he does so, he repeats "hug" (for example, "Chelsea give Vicki 'hug.' " (Vicki Darrow is Chelsea's
signing therapist who joins in the last ten minutes of her weekly
Theraplay session for enjoyable "lessons" in signing.) Later,
crossing his own arms, he pulls the child close so that he (the
child) hugs the therapist. This sign, *hug,* may constitute the
only sign for many sessions. It never becomes a heavy task; it
never loses the Theraplay spirit of noisy fun and intimacy. The
word itself and the pleasure of saying it make language and
communication appear tempting indeed. The sign for *more* may
follow, or the sign for some favorite food.

    5. No chapter on autism would be complete without a
section on mirroring. Mirroring is, for these children, perhaps
the most Intrusive Theraplay of all. Although mirroring autistic
children is a relatively recent addition to the Theraplay repertoire, the results have been so encouraging that they already
warrant its inclusion. In mirroring, the adult deliberately places
himself in direct visual range and adopts the child's frame of
mind. In that stance, he behaves just as the child does. If the
child groans and grimaces, the adult does this also. If he squeals
with delight, so does the adult. Never once abandoning eye contact, the adult mirrors the pitch, volume, and rhythm of the
child's voice and the frowns, smiles, looks of surprise, despair,
sadness, and so on, on his face. The adult, who is well versed in
mirroring and paces his responses so that they come almost
simultaneously with the child's, acts in such a high degree of
synchrony that the picture is one of empathic responding, indeed. The Intrusiveness of this activity is often so great that it
startles the autistic child, who, having scarcely uttered the
sound or grimaced the grimace, finds his behavior "doubling
back" on him.[2] The instant startle that crosses the face of the
mirrored autistic child is generally followed by an all-out effort
to escape. He begins to protest, to try to look away; he at-

tempts to wriggle free of the restraining, mirroring stimulus. The adult does not permit him autonomy but rather holds him very tight, continuing all the while to "catch" his eyes and mirror his moods. In all our hours of mirroring so far, we have found the period of vigorous protest (often including screaming and efforts to bite) eventually diminishing, to be replaced in turn by increasing moments of mutual cooing, humming, singing, and giggling. Ideally it is the therapist who first engages the autistic child in the pursuit that leads to mirroring, and it is therefore the therapist, not the parents themselves, who is first subjected to the child's full rage. Only after they have had every opportunity to learn as observers are they encouraged to take their turns as participants. And then only with warm staff support, including protection from kicking feet, scratching fingernails, or biting teeth; a comforting arm around a shoulder or a cool washcloth on the forehead; and eager words of praise and encouragement. After two or three controlled periods of mirroring, parents are usually ready to introduce mirroring into the home. At first, a few brief mirroring moments may be all that is possible in the course of a week. Eventually parents find their impact so powerful and their child's response so gratifying that they begin to enjoy extending the periods. By the time parent and child are "speaking" softly to one another, giggling noisily, or smilingly gazing into one another's eyes, progress is well along the way.

Case Studies

Tim, age eight, was seen in Theraplay for thirty-nine half-hour sessions in a community mental health center. Tim was an extremely attractive boy with smooth, white skin and large, beautiful, brown eyes, the picture of esthetic symmetry. He was referred for treatment by his pediatrician because, at three and a half years of age, signs of autistic behavior were "apparent." The following intake notes appear in his case file:

Mother has been aware and concerned and has had Tim tested and taught at many places. The conclusion has been that he is autistic.

Tim's mother reports he was a pleasant child. Mother was upset at the time of her own pregnancy. Birth was normal ... Tim was "slightly jaundiced for a couple of days after birth."

He was breast fed, sat at six months, crawled at seven months, and walked at fourteen months. He was toilet trained at three and three-fourths years through being rewarded with Cracker Jacks. Behavior problems include nail biting, hair pulling, a rapid rubbing of his hands together, the rapid shaking of one hand in the air, the tapping of one foot, and the repetition of high-pitched squealing sounds.

During early childhood, Tim occupied himself for long periods by playing with mechanical things such as record players, small appliances, and light switches. He had no playmates, always occupying himself alone. He learned to read on his own, but mother is concerned that he "cannot draw or cut." He "grabs his penis all the time," she complains. Mother says she never insisted that he dress, and she feels now that she should have been more firm.

Mental Status:

Approximate intelligence: borderline (on part test—although he has been untestable)
Judgment: fair
Orientation: fair
Attention span: short, easily distracted
Eye contact: short
General activity level: active
Verbal responsiveness: quick, although not always appropriate
Significant behaviors observed during evaluation: Interested in clock on desk. He continually watched it and occasionally called out the time. He rubbed his hands briskly and strongly on his pants. He occasionally rocked. His smiling seemed inappropriate. He tended to wander mentally and physically.
Impression of Tim: Seems involved in a world of his own. Delusions or hallucinations questionable. Affect inappropriate. He is cautious and moderately withdrawn. Autistic tendencies.

Needs to be more assertively handled. (Mother is uncertain as to her role.) Masturbates openly and frequently. (mother's report)

Previous psychiatric evaluation: "Severely emotionally disturbed—autistic."

The following progress notes describe Tim's half-hour Theraplay sessions (T. Koller is his therapist):

Session 1 (6/4). Repeated many sentences therapist said. Often stared into the air.

Session 2 (6/11). Came into Theraplay room. Headed directly for mirror and sat down. Lots of daydreaming. Appeared to have difficulty concentrating on therapist. Wanted to direct the activity.

Session 3 (6/13). Session went well. He was very playful but easily distracted. Some bizarre actions such as jumping up and down, rapid flapping of hands, mouth open, shrieking, [while] inhaling and exhaling.

Session 4 (6/25). Looked better today. Wanted therapist to let him go. Relatively enjoyed playing horseback ride. Liked to be swung and picked up. Engaged in a game of "try to find my hand" and did some teasing.

Session 5 (7/2). Very negative today. Almost went into tears at times. Rocked. Flapped hands. He became quite angry near the end, and the ending seemed abrupt.

Session 6 (7/9). Liked to look in mirror, be swung, and be sung to. Gave many directions to therapist (for example, screamed "Swing me! Swing me! Swing me!"). Got quite angry when therapist joked and teased. Wanted to run away and run in circles. Complained of headaches when his "orders" weren't followed.

Session 7 (7/23). Active today. Follows directions well. Asked about therapist—when he goes to work in the morning and when he leaves in the evening. Asked if therapist did similar things when *he* was younger. Some flapping of hands yet. Played hide and seek with head under the pillows.

Session 8 (7/30). Critical of therapist's games and methods. Wanted to direct activity. Mother reported that he has been telling her more of what has been bothering him. She also said he now tells her not to bother him.

Session 9 (8/6). Prepared patient for mother's participation in the therapy sessions. He resisted this terribly, but we will begin to include her starting next week. (Mother has been prepared for his rejection of her.)

Session 10 (8/20). First session with mother. Patient screamed and yelled. (Secretaries and others in building found it necessary to close their doors for this and subsequent sessions.) He wanted us to follow his commands; for example, "Now swing me" and "Now let me jump." He told mother to get out of room. He said he wouldn't love us any more. He hit at mother, kicked, screamed. Mother hung onto him. She tended to want him to tell her his problems (for example, "What's bothering you?").

Session 11 (8/29). Screaming. But was playful for about fifteen minutes of session. Began directing action. Told mother "I won't love you any more." Told both of us to let him go. Told us we were holding him too tight, choking him, and so on. We finally restrained him, but with less difficulty this time than last.

Session 12 (9/5). Slightly more attentive today. Enjoyed being swung. Seems to go out of contact if the activity is too smooth, too easygoing. Again said, "I wish I was in here alone." Kicking, crying, tears.

Session 13 (9/10). Some screaming again today. Likes to shut out mother and therapist by being very active and loud. Quite verbal. Engaged in a pillow fight.

Session 14 (9/17). Mother did more of the activity today. Spun him around in circles; bounced him. Played wheelbarrow, quieted him, made him go through tunnel of pillows, over pillows, carried him over shoulders, and played peek-a-boo through legs. At end of session, he became tantrumlike and insisted he be swung. Mother directed him out of this effectively.

Session 15 (9/24). Still resistant. Still insists on directing play. Enjoys much of play but uses "swinging" as a power ploy. Cried, screamed, almost epilepticlike jerking. Mother did well, was creative throughout.

Session 16 (10/1). Stated, "Leave me alone. You're disturbing my life." Fewer tantrums today with more quieting down. Strength is needed by the adult to calm down his tantrums. Mother came up with idea of soothingly blowing over his fingers—like candles—when boy throws tantrum.

Session 17 (10/8). Verbalizes he won't come back. Periodic bizarre screaming. Quiet in general, though. More appropriate affect today. Mother took over.

Session 18 (10/15). Paper play planned for this session. Ran through large pieces of paper, "punched" through them with his body. Less crying and screaming. Seemed to enjoy activity more. Mother said he has recently verbalized that he does not want to come to the center—has been doing this for last two sessions.

(10/22). Therapist canceled because of illness.

Session 19 (10/29). Little "testing" today. No screaming. Playful. Said, "I have to do what adults say." Mother mentioned good reports from school.

Session 20 (11/5). More relaxed today. More willing to participate. When he asked to be swung, he went into a stare ("spaced out"). This was pointed out to mother as evidence for why she should avoid repetitious activity ("See what happens?"), and she was shown how to change the activity.

Session 21 (11/12). Action primarily with mother today. Some weepiness and crying, screaming. Willing to jump. More relaxed at being handled in spontaneous ways.

Session 22 (11/19). Demanding. Tried to take control of the session. Screaming. Demanded own way.

Session 23 (11/26). Very negative today. Would not cooperate in taking test (House Tree Person). Wanted to take total control again.

Session 24 (12/3). Cooperative and playful today. Used pronouns. Interacted well. Still some hand flapping.

Session 25 (12/10). Somewhat less active today. Cooperative, playful. Agreed to initiate a pillow fight.

Session 26 (12/17). Much more cooperative today. Agreed to initiate some activity on his own. Doing better in school.

Session 27 (12/31). Open but quiet. Mother was passive about initiating games. Sometimes mother still reverts to "follower" not "leader" role (typical of many mothers of autistic children).

(1/7). Rescheduled.

(1/14). Rescheduled by therapist.

Session 28 (1/21). Enjoys spitting on command and screaming in different tones. Not so much taking control as usual. Still careful. Easily "lost" if activity level not high.

Session 29 (2/11). More eye contact. Tears and yelling. Therapist talked to mother about getting father more involved. (She became quite angry and upset with this.) Father will call for an appointment.

Session 30 (2/18). Mother came without son. (She said she feared her own feelings of not wanting to come.)

Session 31 (2/25). Made up each other's faces today. Tim painted mother. Therapist had *her* give the directions.

Session 32 (3/6). Tim very much in control today. Mother was depressed looking and seemed uninvolved. She will speak to therapist next week about termination. (Ultimatum given to mother if she does not bring father in.)

Session 33 (3/11). Session went well, and he had more face contact. Was able to follow through with tasks. Treatment plan outlined for mother as follows:

• Two more *weekly* visits after this
• Two visits *every other week*
• Two *one-month* follow-ups

Session 34 (3/18). Playful and verbally abusive but concentrating. Got angry but did something with anger (instead of flapping and flailing, he did something directed).

Session 35 (3/25). Talked with mother. Tim is doing well in school, and his teacher feels he should be in a regular classroom.

Session 36 (4/8). Mother and son doing well. Mother taking more control with good eye contact. Tim looks alert.

Session 37 (4/22). Some twiddling still. Much more focused behavior. Still "floating away." Cooperative.

Session 38 (5/20). Tim was negative.

Session 39 (6/24). Final visit. Some inappropriate speech. Socialization much improved. Plays in after-school play group. Promoted to second grade.

The therapist, fearing that the strains at home resulting from the parents' divorce might lead to regression, maintained contact with both the school and the mother after termination. As with Bryan, however, despite the upsets in Tim's life, there was no evidence of regression either at home or at school. Reports from the school and the mother indicated that Tim maintained his gains and continued to improve.

School Report (11/13).

Reading: "Tim reads very well orally. He has difficulty reading independently."

Arithmetic: "Tim knows many number facts from memory."

Writing: "Tim has improved in this area but he still needs extensive work in hand coordination."

Personal Development and Conduct: "Tim has made steady progress since the beginning of school. The first few weeks he did nothing but sit. I would start him on his work, and as soon as I left he would quit working. He still does this to an extent. He is working far below first-grade level in much of his work—simply because he does not do it. We need to give him more responsibility at school and at home to show him that he can do things alone."

Three-Year Follow-Up: Tim, age eleven

Therapist: How has Tim been doing since the last time you were in with him?

Mother: Just fine, I wish you could see him. He has a much better self-image, more self-confidence. He's growing like a weed and eats so well. This may seem piddling, but eating was such a problem for him before.

He's so much more outgoing, doing better in school. He's able to express negative feelings—that's wonderful. He had all these feelings before but they were like deep, dark demons which were never expressed. He's strong enough to say things now.

He still has some immature behavior—teasing and calling other kids names—but still, that is progress.

He's somewhat of a recluse on the playground but not the isolate he used to be. He's in Cub Scouts and regularly goes to meetings. Last summer he joined a baseball team and played baseball on the playground every day. He also played pee-wee basketball. His physical coordination is better, I think because he loosened up.

Two days ago, he visited a friend of mine in another city. He rode the train alone where my friend met him. He really enjoyed the experience.

He's closer to his brothers but still teases them; at least now he plays games with them, though—card games.

He has hardly any nervous twitches any more.

Therapist: What about the hand flapping and clapping?

Mother: That's what I call nervous twitches. None of that except for a residual here and there. He has calmed down so much.

Recently he brought home a D in math. Remember, that's why he was held back in second grade when he brought this grade home. I got mad and threw a fit. I can now get mad at him, like I would with his brothers. Since that time, he has been bringing home weekly reports from the teacher which show that he has improved.

Also at the Christmas program this year Tim sang all the songs, projecting like a ham. More friends are necessary, but I think they will come.

Theraplay helped Tim, but even more it helped me.

Therapist: It sounds as though you're really invested in him and spend a lot of time and effort on him.

Mother: I always did, but I needed direction. I really wasn't sure that I was doing the right thing. I'm sure when you brought me into the sessions you were teaching me at the same time. Before that, I was always afraid of hurting him.

Five-Year Follow-Up: Tim, age thirteen

Mother: I am so pleased with him. It's not just me—my [new] husband agrees; he works well with him. He's still in Scouts and takes swimming lessons. He's eating well now. He eats everything—he even eats liver. He lifts weights. He does his jobs around the house. I'm more secure about his future than I've ever been before. He's not the same person you used to know.

Because autistic children, even more than other children referred for help, are intent on maintaining a distance, they, more than others, use both ritual and pseudoindependence to fight off closeness whenever possible to do so and to avoid eye contact at all cost. When fighting it off does not keep closeness away, the autistic child's panic appears extreme. Since Theraplay therapists are so persevering and boisterous in their Intrusions and so intimately cuddling when they are Nurturing, the responses of a child who is autistic reveal in almost exaggerated caricature the feelings and behaviors typical of other children in Theraplay.

Unlike other children (such as the overactive or obsessive child, who is ever up to new tricks) however, autistic ones demonstrate their entire repertoire in just a single session. Thus, as we observe Ernestine Thomas (who is not his therapist) demonstrating Theraplay with Larry, we see a typical sample of his behavior with his regular therapist.

Larry began Theraplay nine months earlier, at three and a half years old, having been referred as nonverbal and autistic. Mrs. Thomas and Larry had never seen each other before this

meeting. Both his parents sat among the audience in the back of
the room. His regular therapist was not present.

Larry:	(screams as he sees Mrs. Thomas approach—out of the corner of his eye, of course, for he consistently avoids direct eye confrontation with her)
Mrs. Thomas:	What you mean screaming at me like *that* for?
Larry:	(screaming harder)
Mrs. Thomas:	You know what I'm going to do? I'm going to fly you *up* in the air like this . . .
Larry:	(through his screaming) No! No! No up! No up! No up!
Mrs. Thomas:	(beginning to raise him in the air with a gentle swoop, her hands and arms firmly supporting his body)
Larry:	(screaming yet louder) Noooooooo!
Mrs. Thomas:	And *down* . . .

[At this point, mother arose from her chair and announced to
Mrs. Thomas that Larry suffers from vestibular disorders and
should not be treated in this manner.] [3]

Larry:	(continuing to scream) No down! No! No! No down . . . !!
Mrs. Thomas:	No down this way? Then how about I put you down this way?
Larry:	No! No down! I scared! No down! No down!
Mrs. Thomas:	Oh! I see! You want to be sideways like this.
Larry:	(screams louder than ever)
Mrs. Thomas:	(singing a little song as she works with him) Ah da de dum,/ Look at that thumb,/ Ah da de dum . . .
Larry:	No! No! No sing! No sing! (His voice is adamant, demanding.)
Mrs. Thomas:	OK! Then I'll hum . . . hum, hum, hum, hum . . .
Larry:	No! No! No hum! No! (tyrannical screaming)
Mrs. Thomas:	Oh look! A belly button I found!

Larry:	No!
Mrs. Thomas:	And I can blow on it! This way . . . and this way! And like this! (making funny sounds)
Larry:	(violently screaming again)
Mrs. Thomas:	*Fussy! Fus-sy!*
Larry:	(begins to quiet down now, although he re— sumes the screaming each time he discovers himself enjoying Mrs. Thomas' attentions)

The session continued in this vein. Mrs. Thomas got close to him, enchanted him, provided him with new experiences, and ignored the screaming, which she knew to be not genuine terror but manipulation. That Mrs. Thomas had not "hurt" him was evidenced by his parents' report the following day: "Last night Larry had one of his best nights ever."

This short demonstration points up once again the importance of sensitive assessment—initial as well as ongoing—in doing Theraplay with troubled children. The way in which Mrs. Thomas paid initial attention to the genuineness and "fraudulence" of his screams, to his body tonus, and to the alternations in his responses to her as a person, together with her awareness of anxiety or lack thereof, all determined her decision to keep the action going. (Jay Haley, 1973, pp. 212-213, writing of the tyranny of the autistic child, says: "Even when dealing with severely disturbed children, such as an autistic child, [Milton] Erickson does not approach them as children who need love as much as children who have more power than they can tolerate. He feels that a child's insecurity can come from an uncertainty about what limits are set upon him, and the therapeutic approach is to enforce limits.")

The dynamics of the mother who needs to perceive a situation as more pathological than it really is is a topic for discussion elsewhere. In this particular case, Larry's ongoing Theraplay had helped him to the point where he not only began to speak but also did so in a vocabulary far beyond his years.

Having described one individual Theraplay session with one autistic child, let us now turn our attention to the overall treatment course as it generally evolves with autistic children in

Theraplay. Over a period of several sessions, the following is often observed: At the outset, appearing oblivious to his therapist's presence, the child stops at nothing to remain within his "bubble." He seizes every opportunity to reinstate an aloof, self-occupied, and physically separate posture. Even though the child appears uncomfortable, perhaps even frightened, and more intent than ever on reestablishing his old routine, the therapist moves in, insistent on making his presence felt. The therapist continues to pursue him, never allowing him to find refuge inside his "bubble." The child looks away, moves away, arches his back, moans, or screams. Undeterred by these maneuvers, the therapist continues intruding—now moving to catch his patient's eyes, now swinging him around, now mirroring him, now lifting him high and higher, now laying him down supine and straddling him. All the time, he "forces" the eye contact—always gaining it, not as a discrete bit of behavior that in itself deserves a reward but within the context of some other action (for example, peek-a-boo or wiping of eyebrows) and within the pleasurable aspects of the relationship itself. The bodily position of therapist looking down on the horizontal child lends itself beautifully to establishing eye contact within an ambience that is natural, caretaking, personal, and intimate—resembling as it so closely does after all, the highly engaging position of the mother as she is diapering her infant, or washing him, or playing little games with him at bedtime. It is in this position, for example, that she coos down at him, peeks out from behind a diaper at him, blows on his nose or tummy, and so on. The therapist can use this position just as the mother does, for suddenly popping into view from between his two legs (as suggested by Norma Resnick), for "teaching" him language by joyfully playing with his lips or by making cupping sounds on the therapist's cheeks with the child's two big toes. Many as are the objections of the autistic child, this position of lying on his back face up seems to be one which he protests the least. Yet, just because the predictable is so counterproductive for these children, this particular interaction, positive as it is, must not become routine, or he will tune it out as he does all other routines. Holding the prone child above the supine therapist is just one variation.

Over the weeks of treatment, as activities are introduced, embellished, and insisted on, apprehension gives way to rage. A series of sessions begins in which the protesting becomes less frightened than it is angry, the screams less ones of terror than of outrage. Along with this change, a new phenomenon can often be seen to emerge: In place of the anxious averting of eyes and avoidance of eye contact, the enraged autistic child begins directly and visually to confront his "enemy," the intrusive therapist. For moments at a time, he begins to look at him fiercely—yet intently. In the process, he begins to appear more "alive." He may, along with the looking, lash out at his therapist physically—but the lashing out is purposeful, even integrated, and distinctly directed to a human being who must, to him, feel bothersome at best. In the process of enraged lashing out or thrashing about, he feels his therapist firmly contain him physically and matter-of-factly taking charge. He will feel him holding him, protecting him, securing him in a position that allows maximum eye contact with a minimum of threat either to child or adult. Although differing from Zaslow (1967) in the total therapeutic strategy (that is, less Structure, overall, and more Nurture), Theraplay shares with Zaslow the effort to approximate the mother-infant holding position, and to bring about cooperation, relaxation, and meaningful human contact through reducing the rage and taking charge of the child's bodily actions. In the histories of children we have been seeing, this period of rage evokes for the first time the picture of a human child feeling appropriately angry toward a frustrating human adult. The picture, at first, may last but a minute. In the sense that a normal child would find the therapist's actions merely amusing, the reaction of violent rage is altogether out of proportion to the incident that has produced it (for example, a party hat placed on the head, lotion rubbed into hands, or a left shoe put on a right foot).

Once this phase of direct confrontation—with or without angry screaming—is well underway, another phase sometimes makes its appearance: the phase of sobbing. Having engaged in a direct confrontation (possibly accompanied by enraged screaming) with his therapist, who holds firmly—but never cruelly—to his position, the child may relax a bit. The therapist uses this opportunity to begin the final phase, the long process of instituting mother-infant competence (Ainsworth and Bell, 1974). During this phase, first the therapist and then the mother herself will hold, rock, and perhaps sing a lullaby to her new "baby," all the while attempting to obtain the "long, visual engagement" observed by Rheingold (1961, pp. 143-171) in the early weeks of life. Quite unexpectedly, the child may begin to moan, to weep, and eventually even to sob. The sobbing, when it happens, is intense and deep, like something from a distant past—and it can be profoundly moving. Both the change in the child's behavior and the moving impact this makes on the adults is illustrated by the following case of a seven-year-old autistic girl.

Betty was referred by her neurologist for help because of autistic behavior with what was thought to have a neurological base. In her behavior, she was isolated, ritualistic, fearful, and noncommunicating. She flopped her hands and panicked when thwarted or even when presented with ordinary experiences of living (such as new foods, hair on her clothing, music boxes). She never manifested eye contact. In Theraplay, she whined at being lifted or spun and froze when being tickled or when having her toes covered with finger paint. She refused fluids and candy—allowing these, as many autistic children do, to dribble out from between her lips when they were placed inside her mouth—and she went limp in games of pushing or pulling or handstands. The therapists (Phyllis Booth and Charles West) persevered in their efforts and so did her parents. In weekly half-hour Theraplay sessions, the therapists presented activities that most normal children love but that Betty always avoided. She resisted, for example, the game of wheelbarrow, which is sometimes used by the therapists to add excitement on the long trip down the corridor to the Theraplay room. First she refused and collapsed altogether, then, moaning, over the next few sessions she passively propped herself on her elbows; then, whining, she allowed her forearms to carry her weight and finally, weeks later, still grumbling, she supported herself first on the backs of her hands and then, at last in normal fashion, using the heels of her hands and her fingers. The therapists ignored her moans, her efforts to wriggle right side up, and her falling flaccid to the floor. They also ignored the whining with which she greeted each new activity. Very gradually the whines changed to outbursts and with them to an angry screaming. She screamed when Play-Doh earrings were put on her ears, roller skates on her feet, powder on her tummy. She screamed hardest and loudest of all when little pretzel rings were placed on her fingers. The therapists found it very difficult to "hang in there." Frequently they were tempted to back off, to change the activity, or even to console her. They found it hardest of all to meet her confrontations head on—not to apologize, not to assure her that she would feel better. Rather, they were able to insist, "Betty, I know this makes you angry, but this (food or game or sweater) is what we are going to do (or eat or play or wear) now." Betty seemed intent on "winning" in her refusal to cooperate, intent that she should "run the show." As her therapists held their ground in the bitter battle that followed, the observers in the observation room squirmed uneasily. So did her parents. The interpreting therapist (who sat with the parents during the first half of each session prior to their joining in during the last half) placed her hands on their shoulders and repeatedly reassured them that Betty was not, in any reality sense, being hurt. She urged them to be patient and explained to them the purpose of the therapist's insistence. She called their attention to the increased frequency with which Betty was "coming into focus." The interpreting therapist asked them to note that "This is the most eye contact we have ever seen her make," to notice how "She looks so real now," and so on. Indeed, for fleeting moments, she was beginning to look directly at her therapists' eyes.

A few weeks later, as always at the ending of the session, Betty's therapists and her parents were gathered on the mats for a quiet time with Betty. They were singing a soft lullaby while her mother cradled her in her arms, and her father stroked her hair. Both of them looked intently down at her as they sang:

"Bye bye baby bunting
Daddy's gone a-hunting
To buy a little rabbit skin
To wrap his little Betty in. . . ."

Betty was gazing deeply into the eyes of her mother. Suddenly tears rolled down Betty's cheeks, and as the singing continued— "Bye bye baby bunting bye"—she began to sob, audibly, deeply, and without stopping. The therapists quietly directed the parents to stay with her and to continue cuddling and holding her, while they gently told Betty they understood that she was feeling very sad right now. They did not introduce cheer, they did not distract her. Nor did they encourage her to "talk about it." Although Betty's sadness permeated the room (and affected the observers in the observation room as well), they assured her neither that "there's nothing to cry about" nor that she "will be feeling better soon." They allowed her to continue in her grief as long as she needed to, saying nothing more than an occasional soft, "It feels *so* sad." When Betty finally quieted down, both parents carried her out of the room as they would a sleeping infant.

In the following weeks, Betty's direct confrontations diminished. The sobbing, however, stayed on. After another two sessions of sobbing, her mother phoned to tell us: "A strange thing happened in the grocery store today. I was standing in the checkout line. Suddenly, out of the clear blue sky, Betty said 'Bye bye baby.' I thought perhaps she was talking about the song we sing in our sessions, and I asked her, 'You want me to sing that song to you?' She nodded. So I put aside the shopping cart, and I sat down on the floor, right there by the checkout line. (Usually I'm a bit self-conscious when I shop, but today I didn't care what anybody thought.) I just sat there on the floor, and I held Betty in my lap, and I sang 'Bye bye baby bunting,' and you know what? She began to cry again, quietly at first and then that deep, deep sobbing . . . " The mother phoned again a few days later to report a similar episode "only this time," she added, "I found myself starting to cry, too. Is that all right?" she asked the interpreting therapist. In subsequent sessions, the crying gradually diminished. Betty began to use language instead, and her mother told an anecdote in which Betty one day stomped into her room announcing, "I angry," and a week later she admonished her mother, "I angry. You never listen." Within three more months, she used full sentences replete with descriptions of other people's feelings. Her dentist reported "She has become a totally new child" in these three months, and her neurologist told Betty's parents, "We had thought before that she had very doubtful potential. Now we would say her potential is unlimited."

Betty's clearly delineated development characterizes the healing process in many—although, of course, not all—autistic children in Theraplay. Not all children go through these phases of course, nor do all those who experience them do so in the same sequence. Yet we have seen the pattern frequently enough that no chapter on Theraplay for autism would be complete without cues to recognizing and suggestions for handling such occurrences. The inclusion of fun, cheer, empathy, and Nurturing, in addition to the Intrusiveness described by others, would seem to make Theraplay more "natural" and less formalized than are perhaps strictly Intrusive treatment regimes.

In summary, with its emphasis on empathy, intense eye contact (including mirroring), Intrusion, and Nurturing, Theraplay with autistic children, perhaps more than with any other patient group, closely resembles the "competent" mother-infant dyad. Since it is postulated that this very experience was lacking early in the lives of these children, it would seem appropriate that, at least at the point of referral, the child and parent be offered the chance to "do it over" and grow up "right." Furthermore, if they "accept" the offer, we know that many more good things follow, not the least important of which is the wish to communicate. As so skillfully demonstrated by Sally Bligh (1977a and 1977b), it is from this wish, not from speech and language drilling, that meaningful, effective, verbal exchanges evolve.

Notes

1. For a collection of unusual artwork produced by a preschool autistic girl see Selfe, Lorna, 1977.

2. Adams (1978), describing his use with adult addicts of a technique similar to mirroring, has this to say about the patient's experience: "The dual impact of having his own words come back to him after having 'passed through' the analyst gives the patient a heightened sense of his own realness and validity of his feelings" (p. 40).

3. According to Brown (in Rutter and Schopler, 1978, p. 473), "Specific remediation of these [vestibular] difficulties through sensory-motor integration techniques appears to be a promising avenue for furthering optimal outcomes."

10

Adolescents

Typically, adolescents are referred for help because of poor peer relations, poor relationships with authority figures, poor school performance, antisocial behavior, emotional unpredictability, or disengagement. As can be readily imagined, the Theraplay therapist working with adolescents typically meets greater resistance than does the therapist working with younger children and thus requires greater perseverance, self-confidence, imagination, and sense of humor. Although the general approach is the same, there are the following differences:

1. *Physical size.* The adolescent's greater height, weight, and strength call for activities in which the therapist's control generally does not depend on his being able to "take hold" physically. Rather, the therapist's tone of voice, certainty of movements, and commanding attitude must carry the message that the patient does not "run the show."

2. *Sexual development.* The adolescent's heightened sexual awareness preclude many of the Theraplay activities appropriate to younger children. No longer can the therapist rub baby powder on tummies; blow on belly buttons, on ears, or on eye-

339

lids; or hold the patient on his lap while singing lullabys. No longer can there be cross-sex leg wrestling or, with some exceptions, tickling. Yet Theraplay activities can be chosen that are still fun and physical, raising self-esteem and enhancing growth. In tailor-making treatment programs for adolescents, as for any other group, it is important to draw on activities that Structure, Challenge, Intrude, and Nurture.

Structuring activities with adolescents include making life-size body tracings, hand- and footprints, hand and foot plaster impressions, and aluminum-foil nose, ear, or kneecap molds. They include demonstrations of the fact that head-to-foot length is equal in span to arm spread, and they can delineate where to and not to aim the orange seeds, the water pistol, or the basketball. Challenging activities for the adolescent differ little from those for younger children except that the competition is stiffer. Thumb, arm, or leg wrestling becomes a more strenuous exercise (for both therapist and patient), and contests such as musical chairs require more precision. Intruding activities are perhaps the most difficult to carry out, simply because it is harder to surprise a seventeen-year-old than a five-year-old. Nonetheless, unexpected tickles, finding valued objects under shirts, disappearing acts, "Boo!" and "I got you!," and sleight-of-hand tricks, and so on all serve well the purpose of Intruding. Hair combing, nail polishing, M&M (or orange slice) feeding, cider sipping (through two straws), lotioning, powdering, and trying on flattering hats are all acceptable forms of Nurturing. Nurturing and Challenging are probably the two easiest styles of Theraplay for teen-agers. In apple bobbing, as in the game of "Whose bite is going to be the one to knock the pretzel off my finger?"—Nurturing and Challenging are combined.

Although some children at every level are affected by the therapist's sex, at adolescence and beyond it becomes of crucial importance. Just as a seductive eight-year-old boy or a sexually stimulated six-year-old girl should not be assigned opposite-sex therapists, most adolescents should be worked with only by therapists of their own sex. Again, there are occasionally cases where life experience or sex role confusion may preclude a male treating a male or a female treating a female. For the most part, however, if it is impossible to recruit two therapists, one of each sex, then it is advisable for the therapist to be of the same sex as his or her adolescent client.

3. *Intellectual development.* Adolescents may well feel more self-conscious, be more defensive, and act more challenging. To the accusation, "This is dumb," the therapist can answer, "I know. But I read about it in my psychology book, so we got to do it." Both patient and therapist can thus share in common a humorous way of "saving face." The adolescent's protest often seems to be a necessary precondition first of his acceptance and then of his enjoyment. It is as though he needs to go on record as having renounced such childish carryings-on before he can settle down to participating in them.

Adolescents tend not to follow the overall treatment course of the younger child. There is generally no opportunity for the relationship to evolve slowly in intensity from warm (albeit lukewarm) acceptance through negative rejection to active participation. Rather, the adolescent's "negative phase" starts early in his therapy, and it has a strength and conviction that is likely to persuade an off-guard therapist to let up. Once the therapist gets caught in "discussing" the treatment rationale and in "listening" to the patient's resistance against it, much ground has been lost. From then on, in a vein of heavy seriousness, admitted concern with issues of "respect" and "understanding," and implied therapist and patient equivalence, the therapy can be interrupted at any point while the client calls for a restatement of the contract or for an explanation of "How's this particular activity going to do me any good?" Only when treatment can proceed without this kind of shifting in and out of playfulness can it be smooth, enjoyable, and free.

The adolescents described in the following pages were selected to show therapeutic styles with a wide range of typical referrals. The clients varied both in degree of resistance they offered their therapists and in kind of presenting pathology. On the scale of resistance to Theraplay, June was a neurotic, minimally resistant girl; Ken, a more resistant boy, diagnosed as "adolescent reaction"; Ralph, an extremely resistant aggressive personality; Carl, a schizophrenic; and Paul, fifteen years old, an

autistic who, consistent with his autistic label, resisted vigorously but did so entirely through muteness, ritual avoidance,
and an overall stubborn determination to stay behind his
"wall." A short segment of Theraplay with Dan and his mother
demonstrates the modified application of this technique to a resistant acting-out child in the presence of a parent. John's case,
in Chapter Eight, demonstrates Theraplay with adolescents in
direct interaction with their parents.

The Neurotic Adolescent

June was referred because of her poor relationships with
peers and her underachieving at school. A tall, attractive, fourteen-year-old girl with coal-black hair and bright blue eyes, June
was clearly of superior intelligence. The way in which she used
her intellect, in fact, pointed to Theraplay as the treatment of
choice. Through her verbal fluency, catchy phrases, apparent
ease with psychological concepts, and ready logic, she managed
to maintain control of her "talking" therapy sessions and of the
therapeutic relationship at all times, thus maintaining the only
kind of balance with which she felt comfortable and which
allowed her to perpetuate a rigidly defensive posture. Had she
been permitted to continuously resist another's indulging attentions, she probably would never have been able to form affec-
tively meaningful relationships. Given her unvarying need to
"call the shots," her openness to new experiences and to new
learning would always have been limited. It was not unusual in
her therapy for her to quote poetry in support of her "feelings"
and to formulate—accurately—both her own dynamics and the
dynamics of her parents. Despite her poise, however, she gave
the impression that she would appear not as the young adult
sophisticate, but as an awkward little girl, were she ever to find
herself in a situation not of her own making. Aware that a
frightened little child cowered inside this worldly woman, in the
twenty-fifth session her therapist replaced "talking" therapy
with Theraplay.

The following material is excerpted from the record of
the first Theraplay session.

Notes on Therapist's Dialogue and Actions	Dialogue and Actions		*Notes on Patient's Dialogue and Actions*
	Therapist	*June*	
	Theraplay Session 1 (It is winter)		
No questions are asked here. No "How are you?" or "Would it be OK if I took your coat?"	Hi, June. Here, let me take your coat.	(Enters the room animatedly describing an incident with a woman on the bus and explaining that she was late because the bus had broken down) I tell you the lady wore a plunging neckline. It came right about down to here —I swear to God. Bridget Bardot!	June, characteristically, is (1) "running the show," (2) keeping her references to events *outside* the session, (3) focusing on adult sexuality (not inappropriate for a girl of fourteen, yet inappropriate for June, whose developmental level is essentially that of a much younger child.)
No attention is paid to the story of the woman on the bus, no interpretation made of June's own emerging sexual drives. No introductory remarks are offered with	Oh my. How cold your hands are! Let me rub them for you.		

Notes on Therapist's Dialogue and Actions	Dialogue and Actions		Notes on Patient's Dialogue and Actions
	Therapist	*June*	

Notes on Therapist's Dialogue and Actions	Dialogue and Actions Therapist June	Notes on Patient's Dialogue and Actions
regard to the change in format. (Indeed, to explain the new treatment style would make it impossible for it to be spontaneous and "fun.")		
1. "Your cheeks . . . " calls attention to a part of June's body. 2. " . . . so pink" describes her to herself, helping her to identify her physical self. 3. " . . . so pretty" gives positive value to her. 4. Therapist takes charge in a direct, firm, physical, and caring way.	And your cheeks.[1] They're so pink![2] They make you look so pretty![3] (Taking her hand and guiding her across the room)[4] Let's look in the mirror. Ohh! Just look how beautiful you look with those pink cheeks!	
	(Looks at herself, obviously pleased. A	Children such as June are often reluc-

Notes on Therapist's Dialogue and Actions	Dialogue and Actions *Therapist*	*June*	*Notes on Patient's Dialogue and Actions*
		flicker of a smile crosses her lips.)	tant to admit enjoying the session or to feeling engaged with their therapists.
1. " . . . walk all the way"—The therapist "takes off" on June's stimulus yet not in any way that she (June) could have anticipated or manipulated. 2. Therapist shows empathy for June's sore feet. 3. " . . . let's take off these shoes" —no questions asked, the therapist "runs the show." 4. Children, beginning as toddlers, often cathect their shoes almost as much as they do their feet.	Did you say you had to walk all the way over here?[1] Boy! Your feet must be worn out![2] Here, let's take off these shoes and look at them.[3] Those are fine shoes, yes indeed![4] They're absolutely made for all that walking around in school you do.[5]	(Trying to reclaim her shoes.) They're OK.[1] I was going to tell you about my friend Tina. Do you know that just before English she . . .[2]	1. June is more comfortable on her own terms. A momentary power struggle ensues over the ownership of her shoes, first a physical struggle, then a verbal one ("They're OK"). 2. Then she turns her efforts to directing the session in a style that is typically hers

Notes on Therapist's Dialogue and Actions	Dialogue and Actions Therapist	June	Notes on Patient's Dialogue and Actions
5. Therapist shows an empathic understanding of June's day. Her parents, incidentally, do not. They attend to June's school achievements only.			(that is, with introduced content).
1. Therapist takes off June's socks in a manner that is warm but matter-of-fact. 2. "... just look at those calluses ..." Therapist has attended to a hurt body part with concern. 3. "... you sure do do a lot of walking ..." Therapist shows compassion, has clearly put herself in June's place,	(Takes off socks).[1] Oh yes! Just take a look at those calluses.[2] You sure do a lot of walking on these feet, I can see that, all right.[3] I think if we ... oh, let's see how well you can hop on the other foot if I carry this one (holds one of June's feet, giving her ample time and room for hopping).[4]		

Notes on Therapist's Dialogue and Actions	Dialogue and Actions Therapist	June	*Notes on Patient's Dialogue and Actions*
demonstrates both active engagement and the investment of energy that goes with caring. 4. Therapist forces (Intruding) June to be dependent on her (Nurturing) yet makes her do a difficult hop (Challenging) while organizing (Structuring) an activity that catches June off guard (Intruding).			
		I can't do that.[1] I'm out of condition.[2] Besides, my feet smell.[3]	1. Immediately somewhat panicked "I can't do that." 2. Backs this up with what would appear to be a legitimate excuse. 3. A warning as to how unpleasant her

Notes on Therapist's Dialogue and Actions	Dialogue and Actions		Notes on Patient's Dialogue and Actions
	Therapist	June	
			"real self" may turn out to be if it were discovered.
	Here we go.	Where are we going?	June still needs to predict what will happen rather than allowing herself to enter into the spontaneity.
Therapist does not surrender control.	It's a surprise. You'll see . . . (They arrive at the sink.)		
1. The caretaking of a mother for her infant.	Now, some nice warm water to warm your cold foot up a bit (allowing water from faucet to run over foot while sink is filling).[1]	(peers down, interested)[1]	1. In spite of herself, June is intrigued.
2. Concern for a hurt. Theraplay therapists always attend to injuries, no matter how trivial. 3.	Oh, dear, what do I see?[2] This toenail. It needs some special care.[3] Let's soap it up a bit first.[4]	Oh. That one's OK.[2] Been like that for a long time.[3]	2. She says again "leave me alone." 3. She backs up with rational

Notes on Therapist's Dialogue and Actions	Dialogue and Actions Therapist	June	Notes on Patient's Dialogue and Actions
Identification of an injured body part. 4. Nurturing			adult behavior her wish to leave the scene.
1. Again, the therapist understands June's pain ful life. 2. Nurturing	And here's the callus from all the walking.[1] Soap on it too.[2]	I read that's bad for them.	The power struggle continues. Outside authorities are introduced in the effort.
Nurturing	Now we'll pat it dry.	I can do that.	Her reluctance to accept caretaking only attests to the intensity of the underlying need for it.
More indulgence. Nurturing.	And now some nice-smelling cream.	(attempts to reclaim foot)	The struggle turns physical again.
1. Therapist indicates that in spite of all June's protests the caretaking will continue.	I'll hold it till it's all soaked in.[1]		
2. In response to June's view of herself as disgusting	(puts foot up next to therapist's cheek)[2] Oh, that feels	What are we doing anyway?	Again, the need to remain "in charge."

Notes on Therapist's Dialogue and Actions	Dialogue and Actions		Notes on Patient's Dialogue and Actions
	Therapist	June	
("It smells"), therapist indicates her (June's) physical appeal and then confirms it verbally. 3. Note: There are no references to achievement. Positive comments refer only to properties intrinsic to June (for example, "so nice and soft").	so nice and soft.[3]		

It is clear from the foregoing that

1. The therapist "ran the show." The therapist was in charge at all times and "called all the shots." Although what June did, wore, brought, or said may have provided the springboard, her therapist generally did not respond to it in the manner June intended. The therapist never asked, "OK if we . . . ?" "Would you like to . . . ?" "What would you like to do today?" or "OK?"

2. The therapist made no demands on June to talk, to produce, to perform, or even to discuss what was worrying her.

3. Just like a mother with her small baby, the therapist kept up a constant, running commentary—a commentary that, requiring no response, conveyed only attention and caring.

4. The therapist's conversation was intensely focused on

June—her body, her appearance, her life-style, and her state of health and well-being.

5. The therapist focused on the positive qualities intrinsic to June as a separate person. Her therapist did not focus on June's achievements or on her accomplishments—even though June's accomplishments may sometimes in themselves have enhanced the therapist's own self-esteem.

6. The therapist established body contact at every opportunity.

7. The therapist did not attend to June's efforts to entertain or to direct the conversation.

8. Except for responses conveying empathy (for example, "Oh, my! How cold your hands are!"), the therapist made upbeat comments only.

9. The therapist moved spontaneously into new activities. She neither announced nor introduced what she and June were about to do.

In the sessions that followed, June and her therapist engaged in a variety of activities together. They walked to a local clothing shop and tried hats on June in the millinery department; they drew silhouettes of each other's faces; they made foot paintings with June's feet and put nail polish on her toenails; they jumped the rocks barefoot at the lakefront and they buried each other in the sand at the beach. In one session, they sewed a skirt for June from the material they had selected together the week before, and often her therapist spoon fed June ice cream or applesauce or pudding. By and large, the activities were perfectly appropriate for a normal younger child, and once she could allow them they were obviously appropriate for pseudosophisticated June.

As June herself said during the appointment she made to see her therapist twelve years later (to introduce her fiancé), "I remember every detail of every active thing you and I ever did together. I remember the first time you washed my toes—how startled I was. Nobody had ever done that for me before. And how you oiled my elbows and fed me bananas. And the day we tried on hats. You know, it's funny, I don't remember anything at all about the time when I was coming to see you and we just talked."

The Adolescent with Adjustment Problems

Not all adolescents, however, are as cooperative as June was in accepting Theraplay. A sample of a session between Terrence Koller and his fifteen-year-old patient, Ken, follows. Ken, whose parents were recently divorced, was referred for defiant behavior toward his mother.

Notes on Therapist's Dialogue and Actions	Dialogue and Actions		Notes on Patient's Dialogue and Actions
	Therapist	Patient: Ken	
	Session 1		
No elaborate introduction.	Hi, Ken! I'm Terry. Let's go down stairs.		
Therapist does not ask for permission nor announce what they are about to do. Instead, there is immediate physical contact and positive body image reference.	Boy! Those look like big muscles you have there (checking his arms).	(Pulls away)	This is a quite appropriate reaction of a teen-age boy toward a stranger who behaves so presumptuously.
1. This paradoxical Theraplay is designed to turn Ken's	Bet you can't knock me down.[1] I'm really strong.[2]	Silly (mumbling)	Ken is still "saving face."

Notes on Therapist's Dialogue and Actions	Dialogue and Actions *Therapist*	*Patient: Ken*	*Notes on Patient's Dialogue and Actions*
negativism into coopera- tion. 2. An assertive self- statement, the therapist offers his own self- confidence for identifi- cation.		(Goes through the motions only)	He is still master of his own destiny. Not an inap- propriate stance once it becomes truly his own, ra- ther than based as it now is, on the defiance born of anxiety.
1. Paradoxical Theraplay 2. The Chal- lenge grows.	I told you you couldn't do it[1] 'cause I'm so strong.[2]		
		(Begins to push in earnest.)	He can no longer resist the Chal- lenge. In addi- tion, his ther- apist is begin- ning to look like a fun- filled, appeal- ing person.
Therapist praises Ken for the person he is, for his assets. It is clear that his therapist, un- like his moth- er, has no stake in Ken's cooperative- ness, nor need to be loved by him.	Oh, you are strong.		

Notes on Therapist's Dialogue and Actions	Dialogue and Actions Therapist Patient: Ken	Notes on Patient's Dialogue and Actions
	(They tussle vigorously. They alternate "winning.")	The vigorous tussling will help to impress on Ken who this adult is and how involved with him, as a fun-loving person, he has become.
1. Identification and description of body parts in ways that are positive yet not related to performance. 2. Announcement of ongoing activity rather than seeking permission to initiate it. 3. A joint Challenge, Intrusion, and a cooperative venture related to making Ken aware of body parts. 4. Again, no question is asked. There is nothing tentative,	Those are big hands.[1] Here, let's put some paint on them[2] and see how different we can make your fingers.[3] (Grabs Ken's hand[4] and carefully covers it with many colors).[5]	

Notes on Therapist's Dialogue and Actions	Dialogue and Actions Therapist	Patient: Ken	Notes on Patient's Dialogue and Actions
apologetic, or approval seeking. The assumption communicated is "What we are going to do is fun, you're going to enjoy it, and I know what's best for you." 5. Playfulness, beauty, and caring are all expressed through this activity.		This is dumb. (studying the process interestedly)	Although he continues to "save face," he is clearly beginning to enjoy himself.
1. Therapist expresses enchantment and excitement like a mother discovering a new characteristic of her baby. 2. Therapist is "in charge" of an activity that he is certain is fun as well as novel and surprising.	Wow! That is beautiful.[1] (Takes the painted hand and "walks" it up the paper-covered wall.)[2]	God, this is so dumb![1] What you doing all this for anyway?[2]	1. Same as above. 2. He shifts again to the man-to-man dialogue that is obviously his more familiar style,

Notes on			*Notes on*
Therapist's			*Patient's*
Dialogue and	Dialogue and Actions		*Dialogue and*
Actions	*Therapist*	*Patient: Ken*	*Actions*
			allowing him to keep control.
With humor and lightness, rather than with a heavy focus on Ken's pathology, his therapist conveys that he takes neither himself nor the "problem" that seriously. He introduces hope and pleasure into a relationship that is nonetheless intense and focused on the patient.	Oh, I got to do this. They taught it to me in Psych 205 at college.		
1. More variations in making Ken aware of his body boundaries in a way that is positive, yet intensely interpersonal and	(Later, pressing Ken's foot into wet plaster of paris[1]) This one I learned in Human Behavior 709.[2]	(Laughs,[1] then looks at	1. Finally Ken lets down his

Notes on Therapist's Dialogue and Actions	Dialogue and Actions Therapist	Patient: Ken	Notes on Patient's Dialogue and Actions
Nurturing. 2. Having established a common bond —reference back to the earlier "Psych 205," Ken and his therapist reaffirm their "membership in the club."		his therapist with good eye contact[2])	defensive vigilance. 2. He allows himself to interact with his therapist for the first time.

The points made earlier in regard to June also apply to this case. Ken's therapist also "called the shots," also made no demands for task performance, also kept up a running commentary intensely focused on Ken's inherent, positive qualities. He also used every opportunity for body contact and did not allow himself to be distracted by Ken's efforts to entertain or to direct the conversation. He moved spontaneously from one activity to the next, and, except for expressions of empathy when these were called for, he made upbeat comments only. Ken's therapist was a little less Nurturing and a little more Challenging than June's. There was less occasion for commiserating and empathy, more for the focus on Ken's strength and power. There was more light humor in Ken's treatment, and there were more surprises. As a result of these variations in method (as well as differences in the four personalities involved in the two cases), Ken's course of therapy was stormier. (He missed appointments, for example, and, unsolicited, he attempted to include members of his peer group in the sessions.) Yet he progressed well in the eight sessions and, his mother reported, was easier and more pleasant to communicate with at home.

The Schizophrenic Adolescent

Although Carl at twenty-one was technically beyond adolescence, his treatment sessions with Terrence Koller were
basically no different from what they would have been had Carl
been two or three years younger. He was a tall, slender, pasty-
faced youth with a "spaced-out" look, hesitant in both speech
and movement. He had lived in a variety of institutions (currently, a weekday arrangement) and was referred for Theraplay
by a member of a distant university's faculty. He had been diagnosed schizophrenic both at that clinic and at others. In addition to a pronounced thought disorder, he was obsessed with a
passion for "tall women" and a fear of choking.

A series of eight weekly half-hour Theraplay sessions was
planned for Carl, following which there was to be a case review.
Only the first three sessions are presented here, as illustrative of
Theraplay with schizophrenic adolescents.

Session 1

Carl:	What do you think of tetanus shots? My mother won't allow me to have a tetanus shot.
Therapist:	Why do you need a tetanus shot?
Carl:	Because of my foot.
Therapist:	Let's see your foot. (approaching Carl's foot)
Carl:	No.
Therapist:	Did you hurt your foot?
Carl:	Yeah.
Therapist:	You step on something?
Carl:	Yeah. A nail. It hurts.
Therapist:	Let me see your foot. (reaching out for Carl's foot)
Carl:	No.
Therapist:	I need to look at it. (touching Carl's foot)
Carl:	No.
Therapist:	Here, let's take off your shoe. (beginning to re-move Carl's shoe)
Carl:	You don't want to do that.
Therapist:	I really do want to.
Carl:	Are you sure you want to see my foot?

Therapist:	Yeah. (takes shoe off halfway, as though "teasing for permission")
Carl:	I can't believe you actually took my shoe off! I can't believe it!
Therapist:	(looks at foot)
Carl:	(stares at own foot)
Therapist:	(rubs foot; puts oil on foot)

[Later in session]

Carl:	I'm going to choke one day. I just know I am.
Therapist:	No. You're not going to choke.
Carl:	They do the Heimlich if you choke.
Therapist:	Yeah. It goes like this. (demonstrates gently) Now you do it to me.
Carl:	(does so very apprehensively)
Therapist:	Now I'll do it to you. Wow! Listen to those funny noises we can make your stomach make.
Carl:	(looks down at his stomach, fascinated)

[Session ends with therapist cheerfully putting Carl's shoes back on.]

Session 2

[Therapist has prepared and covered three coffee cans with brightly colored paper and decorated them with ribbons. The first contains M&M's, the second Oreo cookies, and the third animal crackers. (The introduction of these cans of food may seem a violation of the injunction against props, and the later discussion about elephants may appear to contradict the warnings about using fantasy. However, a skilled and experienced therapist should always be free to ignore or bend rules if it is therapeutic to do so. As noted in Chapter Two, the Do's and Don't's are guidelines only.)]

| Carl: | (comes into room and chooses to sit in the most distant chair) |
| Therapist: | (selects a "patient" chair, rather than his own "therapist" chair, and moves it close to, and facing, Carl) |

Carl: (remains where he is—startled but not objecting)
Therapist: I have some things here today that will help us
                 practice so you won't need to be so afraid of chok-
                 ing.
Carl: (looks at the therapist suspiciously)
Therapist: But first I have to find out if you're ticklish.
                 (tickles him) And I have to find out where you're
                 the *most* ticklish.
Carl: (reacts only mildly to ticklish spots)
Therapist: (takes out boxes) I brought you some practice
                 food for your choking.
Carl: (looks incredulous) You made all those boxes?
                 And put in all those cookies and everything? For
                 me?
Therapist: (removes first cookie and aims for Carl's mouth
                 with it)
Carl: (resists adamantly)
Therapist: (tries again, this time making airplane noises)
Carl: (tries to stop him)
Therapist: (insistent)
Carl: (tries to grab cookie to feed himself)
Therapist: No. *I've* got to do it. Otherwise it's not real prac-
                 tice. (searching in animal cracker container) Now,
                 where's that lamb? Oh, here we are. Here it *comes*.
                 (aiming lamb cracker into Carl's mouth)
Carl: (reluctantly permits therapist to feed him)
Therapist: OK. Now, let's try a really difficult one. Let's try
                 you with this great big elephant. (In fact, animal
                 crackers are all the same size.)
Carl: (Chews sloppily, cracker crumbs all over mouth,
                 clothing, and floor)
Therapist: Boy! If you can chew that elephant, we'll *know*
                 you can make it!
Carl: You know, right now I don't have a fear of chok-
                 ing any more. Do you think that's just in here? I
                 mean, do you know if it'll carry over to other
                 places? Like if I go to a restaurant? Will I still have
                 to be afraid there?

Therapist: Of course it'll carry over. An elephant is an elephant. If you can chew an elephant, especially if you can chew it even if I tickle you (tickles him), then you can chew anything.

Carl: You think so?

Therapist: Yeah. Here, let's check your foot again. Let's see how it's coming along. (begins to take off Carl's shoes and socks)

Carl: (resists)

Therapist: (persists in taking off Carl's shoes and socks) That looks OK today. (puts oil on foot and rubs it) Now . . . for next week I want you to bring a chicken sandwich.

Carl: That would spoil my lunch.

Therapist: What's more important? A spoiled lunch or no more problem with choking?

Carl: I like to eat at McDonald's.

Therapist: No. You bring a chicken sandwich. Have your mother make it.

[As Carl leaves with his mother, he is heard to say, "Mom, when I come in next week I have to bring a chicken sandwich."]

Session 3

[Mother has phoned to say she feels more hope than she has ever felt before. She also says, "I took your advice and drew around his hands on paper. You're right. He really doesn't know what he's like. I've begun to notice him too, how grubby he is, so now I've started to comb his hair and I bought him some pants that don't look so baggy, and I said to him, 'We can't have you going out looking like that.' Mother says he has become more willing to spend weekends at home.]

Carl: (comes in looking nicer than at previous session, carrying a bag that contains a giant chicken sandwich)

Therapist: (brings own lunch. Sets up small table to look like restaurant. Both sit down at table.) Now, let's look at your sandwich and see if we can find some different-size pieces. Ah! One tiny one, one middle-size one, one great big one. (begins to feed them to him one by one)

Carl: I don't think I'm going to choke after all. (He is still a sloppy eater, and at one point he bites the inside of his mouth.)

Therapist: (checks inside Carl's cheek for bleeding. Holds tissue to it.)

Carl: I'm a schlemiel. You know what that is?

Therapist: Yeah. It's like Inspector Clousseau (knowing Carl likes films). You know, the Pink Panther?

Carl: Yeah. Are you Jewish?

Therapist: No.

Carl: Then how do you know?

Therapist: I have friends. You have Jewish bread there.

Carl: Yeah. Jewish rye. How do you know? You must be Jewish.

Therapist: No. (takes bread and feeds it to him) You've got to save room in there to eat more elephants today. Why don't you put that apple away for later?

Carl: Oh, oh yeah. (between the bites he's being fed) I like about you that you're action. All the other people I've been to, they're all talk. But you, you're action.

[Following this session, the custodian of his weekday living quarters reports Carl no longer seems preoccupied with "tall women."]

Critics of Theraplay may say that any therapy that is so frivolous and so avoiding of the "deeper issues," any therapy that appears to be "teasing," "demeaning," and "disrespectful" could only hurt a patient who is already as disturbed as Carl was. It may be said that what Carl really needed was a compassionate, nonimpinging presence. Or that what he really needed was someone to help him understand why he became the way he is and to explore with him the underlying meanings of his communications. His therapist, in other words, should have dealt with him through the symbolism of his symptoms—the longing for women over six feet tall for example, or his fear of choking. It may be a point of worry that he was led to believe (almost teleologically) that one animal cracker was larger than another just because the animal it represents is larger than another animal. Or that he was teased into believing "If you can chew that elephant, we'll know you've made it" (or, "if you can chew an elephant, then you can chew anything"). It may be of concern that the Heimlich technique, in the mind of the young man a life-and-death matter, was dismissed so lightly and relegated to "tickles" and funny noises in his stomach. It may seem disrespectful to have removed his shoes and socks and particularly to do so against his will. And it may seem downright rude to have paid no attention to Carl's communication about the neglectful mother who forbade him to have the tetanus shot.

Writing of therapy with schizophrenic adolescents, Des Lauriers (1967, pp. 197-199) says:

> the therapist's concern will be directed, relentlessly and without diversion, to one simple goal: restoration in the child of the conditions of reality experience and object relationships. This means to create for the child the basic conditions of ego development and ego functioning. . . the child should be made very acutely aware that the therapist is there with him . . . the therapist must arouse . . . the interest of the patient in the therapist . . . the therapist [must] make his presence known physically to the patient. . . . The patient's behavior must reflect an alert attention and interest in what is happening to him when the therapist is there. . . . Thus a sort of communication is established which is physical, concretistic, immediate, and full of sensory stimulations . . . . Tactile contacts are most useful if they are not contrived, mechanical, or unwarranted; they must demonstrate the spontaneous and honest attentiveness of the therapist to the child and be used at times to control, restrain, or comfort him; and at other times, to stimulate pain or pleasure in various parts of his body. . . . The therapist . . . need not feel he must now discuss with the patient the underlying motives, aggressive or libidinal, which make [him] so fearful of tactile sensations. . . .

A mother, in reaching for her little boy's hand to comfort him or just for fun, does not stop to ask herself whether she's being seductive and will cause all manner of anxiety in her child. Only a sick mother would let such fantastic notions interfere with her attentive activity toward her boy. On the other hand, if her child had burnt his arm and was suffering in pain, she would not, except with great care and delicacy, touch his arm or try to move it. She would just try to make this child comfortable. A therapist also needs this much amount of good sense, delicacy, and sensitivity.

From here on, however, Theraplay and Des Lauriers would appear to diverge somewhat. For, although the good Theraplay therapist certainly is "delicate," "careful," and "sensitive" and would urge parents to be the same, the degree of care, delicacy, and sensitivity seen as being needed by psychotic children would seem to be not the same from the two viewpoints. (Nor has the experience of Theraplay therapists to date, working both with hospitalized and with ambulatory schizophrenic adolescents, given any evidence that they (the therapists) should do it otherwise. Whereas Des Lauriers advocates sometimes not touching at all for a while ("Once the therapist realizes this [that the child may not want to be touched], he can wait and make himself "touchable"), the Theraplay therapist, with respect to touching rather than "waiting," does move right in. He may move in slowly and gently or quickly and definitely but in any case the patient's reluctance does not deter the therapist from touching. Thus, Terrence Koller, Carl's therapist, said, "Let me see your foot" and, even though Carl protested, he went on to again say, "Let me see your foot" and then responded to Carl's repeated "No" with "I need to look at it," and so forth, all the time moving closer to the injured foot. Had this therapist withheld physical contact on the grounds that it might have "frightened" Carl or "panicked" him, it might have been a long while before Carl would have gotten to experience the pleasurable interchange that followed.

There is a further apparent divergence, this one concerning initiation. Whereas it is a Theraplay principle that the therapist, in approaching the patient, initiates both the contact and the activity, Des Lauriers (1967, p. 199), writing of his sixteen-year-old patient Terry, says, "physical contacts were not enjoyable unless she made them herself, first. Once the therapist realizes this, he *can wait, and make himself "touchable"* (our italics). Thus, heeding Des Lauriers' overt advice, Koller might have sat in the room with his patient, making himself "touchable" but not initiating the touching. Certainly, in time, Carl would have approached his therapist on his own. But would Carl really have been that much more helped for having been permitted to take the initiative? In fact, Des Lauriers probably is more intrusive, more initiating, and considerably more likely to be the one to first do the "touching" than this particular article of his suggests. Although perhaps not readily apparent to readers of both, the disparity between Des Lauriers' actual working style and that of therapists trained in Theraplay probably is a disparity more in appearance than in fact.

The Aggressive Adolescent

"What can Theraplay do for adolescents whose illness takes the form of explosive acting out?" This is a question frequently asked by psychiatric, probation, residential care, and education personnel. The answer, "Theraplay can indeed often be of help," must be carefully elaborated. Only the most self-aware, professionally competent, and personally adequate therapists should even attempt to do Theraplay with a belligerent, frightened adolescent who has lost control. The case of preschool Sam, described in the chapter on overactive children (Chapter Seven), sets the principle: "Mrs. T. intervenes to make him right the chairs, and in the process she holds him. He struggles to free himself, shouting obscenities as she half-carries, half-drags him off to a chair in a secluded corner of the classroom. There she seats herself, places the struggling Sammy in her lap, and begins to rock and sing a lullaby."

Note that Mrs. T.'s degree of struggle and Sam's experience of feeling safe about "giving in" were necessary prerequisites for meaningful progress. The bigger and stronger the child, of course, the more difficult the struggle. And herein lies the reason for ensuring an emotionally healthy therapist. A "struggle" with a physically resistant teen-ager, unlike one with a resistant preschool child, sometimes calls not only for strength to (more than) match his strength but also for self-protective measures. If the experience is provided in the context of calm, confidence, and growth-enhancing messages, the patient can feel reassured, cared for, guided, and protected. Carried out in the spirit of derision, threat, and sadism, however, the experience can only be devastating. Thus it is that in Theraplay with aggressive adolescents it matters more *who* does it than *what* is being done. These cautionary notes are necessarily repetitious and elaborate. Patients such as the young man whose case is presented next can only be effectively treated with Theraplay provided his two therapists share a level of comfort that allows them to give each other open feedback. This assures a system of checks and balances where, even when physical means are used that might easily lend themselves to "getting even" with a threatening, belligerent, hurting patient, therapist behavior never damages the patient's self-esteem. If cruelty is even a slight possibility, Theraplay with aggressive adolescents is contraindicated. If the treatment is likely to consist only of curtailing activities, then Theraplay is also to be discouraged. In order to be effective, Theraplay must move beyond the inhibition of old, destructive behavior to the creation of new, pleasurable experiences.

Major confrontations played a large part in the early stages of Theraplay with Ralph, an adolescent in the partial hospitalization adult program of a psychiatric ward. Ralph had set fire to the unit's wastebaskets and had terrorized other patients with his wild shouts and brandishing of billiard cues. At the point he was referred for Theraplay, Ralph had failed to respond to all other treatment forms and was about to be evicted from the program altogether. For obvious reasons, two male therapists (rather than a single therapist or a cross-sex or female team), N. Gilbert and J. Samelson, were assigned to work with him during first once-weekly and then twice-weekly half-hour Theraplay sessions.

Notes on Therapists' Dialogue and Actions	Dialogue and Actions		Notes on Patient's Dialogue and Actions
	Therapists A and B	Patient: Ralph	
	Session 1		

Notes on Therapists' Dialogue and Actions	Therapists A and B	Patient: Ralph	Notes on Patient's Dialogue and Actions
1. No questions are asked, no permission is requested. 2. Like a parent leading a child out of danger to safety, Therapist A firmly, but not punitively, indicates he knows what is best for Ralph and intends to help him do it.	Therapist A: Ralph, today you're coming with Norm and me[1] (guiding him firmly by one arm).[2]		
3. See Therapist A. Ralph's defiant refusals have not influenced the therapists to back down.	Therapist B: (Guiding the other arm) Right in here, Ralph.[3]	I'm not going with nobody![1] I already told you.[2] I do what I damn well please around here.[3]	1. Ralph feels threatened at the outset and announces his intention as though to command. 2. He expresses his expectations that people should obey him (as, of course,

Notes on Therapist's Dialogue and Actions	Dialogue and Actions		Notes on Patient's Dialogue and Actions
	Therapists A and B	Patient: Ralph	

Notes on Therapist's Dialogue and Actions	Dialogue and Actions (Therapists A and B)	Patient: Ralph	Notes on Patient's Dialogue and Actions
The suggestion is given, the stage is set. There is no extensive exclamation and no checking, "Would that be OK with you?"	Therapist A: Let's sit down right here.		they always have). 3. He reiterates who he is and what his rules are.
Therapist B has "hooked into" Ralph's facade of toughness. He has made it impossible for Ralph to refuse the Challenge and still maintain his tough facade. (This is done only in the interest of bringing about the opportunity for a positive, highly engaged experience. Never is the goal one of causing an-	Therapist B: I want to see how tough you can arm wrestle.	(looks surprised)	He is not used to being rewarded for his strength. Ordinarily it is his very aggressiveness that leads to rejection.
		I'm not wrestling nobody,[1] I'm getting out of here.[2]	1. He recovers himself just as he is about to "give in" to another's invitation to him. 2. "Getting out of here" is a familiar solution to

Notes on Therapist's Dialogue and Actions	Dialogue and Actions Therapists A and B	Patient: Ralph	Notes on Patient's Dialogue and Actions
other to "lose face.")			Ralph. He is quite used to running away when he feels himself "trapped."
The directions are clear, the action is swift, and body contact is accomplished before Ralph can rally his resisting forces. All this, however, is done as "good, clean fun." Nowhere is there a "put-down."	Therapist A: Here, you grab Norm's arm with yours like this.		
1. The ease with which therapist initiates physical contact must convey to Ralph that he is worth getting close to. 2. Challenge but not threat.	Therapist B: (encircling Ralph's arm with his own)[1] OK. I bet I'm going to beat you![2]		
Therapist A expresses his confidence and his wish.	Therapist A: Come on, Ralph, come on. I know you can do it.	(enters into contest strain-	Ralph has agreed to be-

Notes on Therapist's Dialogue and Actions	Dialogue and Actions Therapists A and B	Patient: Ralph	Notes on Patient's Dialogue and Actions
Therapist B praises Ralph again in the very area that has been Ralph's downfall, his physical aggressiveness. This is both surprising and positively valuing of him.	Therapist B: Boy! Ralph, if I'd a known you were this strong . . .	ing with all his might)	come engaged.
1. Therapist A's cheering lends suspense to the engagement. 2. Probably this is one of the very few times in his life that Ralph has ever felt anyone cheering for him. 3. Nor has he often been the winner. For this moment at least, he should feel he has an ally and a fan.	Therapist A: It's a tie! It's a tie! . . . No, it's not . . . oh, this is close![1] . . . Come on, Ralph! Show him, Ralph![2] Ah! The winner! The winner, in this corner is . . . Ralph . . .[3]	(struggles hard to push therapist over)	His negativism has been channeled, while at the same time he remains physically engaged with another person in a way that is safe and fun.
1. Therapist B praises and	Therapist B: Good work,		

Notes on Therapist's Dialogue and Actions	Dialogue and Actions Therapists A and B	Patient: Ralph	Notes on Patient's Dialogue and Actions
thus reassures Ralph. 2. He lets Ralph know that he can have impact on another person in a way that is playful rather than dangerous. 3. When working in teams like this, therapists often organize the next activity aloud.	Ralph![1] Oh! am I beat![2] Jeff, how about cooling the contestants off?[3]		
An example to Ralph of cheerfully cooperative team work.	Therapist A: (Bringing the damp cloth) Here comes the wet towel now.	(Rejects any effort to "cool" him off.)	It is probably the very fleeing from his infantile wishes for Nurturing that has made Ralph behave as he has.
	(Therapist A alternately fans Ralph and Therapist B with a wet towel.)		
Therapist chatters cheerfully. Clearly he expects no answer.	Therapist B: Those breezes feel so nice and cooling, don't they Ralph?		

Notes on Therapist's Dialogue and Actions	Dialogue and Actions Therapists A and B	Patient: Ralph	Notes on Patient's Dialogue and Actions
		Mhm . . .[1] No they don't.[2]	(1) He is caught off guard for a moment . . .
	Therapist B: (Arm around Ralph's shoulder) You look cooler to me already . . . and handsome . . .	(turns to bite) You get your filthy hands off me.[3] (A smile flickers fleetingly across Ralph's lips.[4])	(2) Then recovers his oppositional and (3) negativistic stance (4) again, he is momentarily disarmed . . .

The Theraplay principles illustrated in the sessions with June and Ken, described earlier, of course apply to Ralph as well. Yet it can be seen that the stronger is the resistance against participation, the more will the therapist's (or therapists') work be restricted to basic confrontations and the settling of power struggles. Thus, whereas with June it was unnecessary to do much more than ignore her efforts to control and with Ken these efforts had to be attended to but could nevertheless be handled with humor, with Ralph it was impossible to focus on anything but his unrelenting struggle for power. The more effective the therapy, the greater is the ratio of therapist-initiated activities to those in which the therapist counteracts patient-initiated activities. Except for a wrestling match, Ralph, during his first session, of necessity received little in the way of therapist-initiated treatment. Thus the range of experiences provided him was unfortunately limited. There were few surprises (Intrusions), few opportunities for spontaneity, for fun, or for Structure. There was only minimal Nurturing and not really the range of Challenge his therapists knew he would enjoy. Over the succeeding sessions, however, he allowed himself to participate in a far greater number of experiences (hair combing, foot painting, aluminum-foil casting of knees and elbows, and so on), and at times even allowed himself to enjoy and obviously to look forward to the weekly sessions. After thirty twice-weekly half-hour sessions, he sought out Therapist B for conversation and pool games and had social telephone contacts with him when he had to miss his sessions. At last report, Ralph had returned to school and was doing well. His drawings, collected immediately before and several months after the treatment period, convey his increasing openness, joie de vivre, and willingness to relate (compare Figures 4 and 5).

Depending upon the make up of their own character, therapists working with aggressive adolescents may find it all-too-tempting to respond with sadism or masochism. Beginning therapists should watch carefully, for example, any tendency to administer too-painful hammer lock holds on the one hand; any tendency to incur broken eyeglasses or torn shirtsleeves, on the other. Should this happen to one therapist, it is important that both therapists become aware of it, discuss it between sessions, and plan a strategy in which opportunities for brutality or victimization cannot again present themselves. It is far more therapeutically effective for a vulnerable therapist to initiate the role of straight man, than for his co-therapist to repeatedly have to bail him out. The earlier in the treatment these roles can be assigned, the more smoothly will the sessions run. Some very good teams may combine one motorically active, physically strong leader with a "supportive cast" partner who is "maternal," soft-spoken, and helpful. Optimum team work depends upon agreement as to who will play which role as well as "what will we do if . . . it doesn't work?" Suggestions for session planning have already been discussed in Chapter 2. Issues of therapists' psychological vulnerability will be taken up in more detail later (Chapter 12). It is in doing Theraplay with aggressive adolescents that both become particularly crucial.

The Autistic Adolescent

Although overcoming their resistance plays a large part in the treatment of the three adolescents just described, the resistance itself serves as only an external layer of their personalities and behavior. Once dealt with and rendered unnecessary, resistance is no longer an issue, and the therapeutic relationship, using the mother-infant model, can proceed to create and

Figure 4. Drawing by Ralph, an Aggressive Adolescent, Before Theraplay

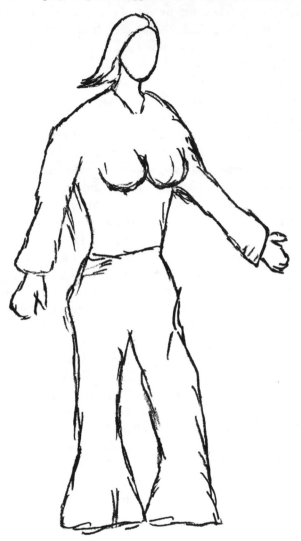

Figure 5. Drawing by Ralph After Theraplay

strengthen a basically healthy personality. The autistic adolescent, however, presents a somewhat different picture of resistance and reconstitution. For him, it appears, resistance is the name of his entire game. As though there were no inner core, he tenaciously resists the session, adamantly keeping his therapist out of his conscious awareness. Children like Ralph keep their therapists at bay by cruel and vigorous means and with full acknowledgment that their therapists are making an impact ("Just wait till I get free! I'm going to kill you both")—in other words, by acts of commission. The autistic child wages the same war, but he does so by acts of omission. He appears so sealed off from his therapist and so immune to the therapist's efforts to relate that he seems to be protecting an inner emptiness, not a personality with the capacity to relate. He seems to be protesting against an impersonal nuisance—a gnat or a puff of wind, for example—rather than trying to deal with the warm, caring intrusion of a human being. Because their resistance is so far-reaching and because what lies underneath is so empty, with these adolescents Theraplay often looks, in its boisterous intensity, like a caricature.

Eighteen-year-old Paul was referred for Theraplay by the teachers of his special school. His diagnosis: autism. In spite of his being six feet tall, his solid build, his generally appropriate dress, and his reported language skills ("He uses words, but not for communicating"), Paul looked like a very frightened much younger child.

Notes on Therapist's Dialogue and Actions	Dialogue and Actions Therapist	Patient: Paul	Notes on Patient's Dialogue and Actions
Therapists working with autistic children take the position of a mother who expects no response from	(guides Paul into therapy room by means of his arm around Paul's waist) Come on, Paul, we're		

Notes on Therapist's Dialogue and Actions	Dialogue and Actions		Notes on Patient's Dialogue and Actions
	Therapist	*Patient: Paul*	
her infant and thus all the effort goes in only one direction: from therapist to patient.	going to go right in here. OK. Here we are, and let's close the door.		
		(allows himself to be propelled as though he were a metal post)	There is no evidence as yet that Paul is aware of his therapist.
		(He could be described as "standing at attention"[1] except that he shifts constantly from foot to foot and that his hand never stops picking at his hair and clothing.[2])	1. Standing at attention is Paul's method for keeping out intruders and for keeping his world unvarying.
1. Therapist gives positive attention and labels body part. 2. Elaborated description of body part. 3. Caretaking gesture and body contact.	Paul, that's a neat haircut you have there![1] It got kind of mussed coming down.[2] Here, let me comb it.[3]		2. His increasing agitation attests to the fact that he is beginning to experience something in the situation.
		(Looking like a frightened animal, he leaps away as soon as he sees the comb approaching.)	He is becoming more aware of the therapist's Intrusion.
1. Therapist describes sit-	Tell you what we're going to		

Notes on Therapist's Dialogue and Actions	Dialogue and Actions *Therapist*	*Patient: Paul*	*Notes on Patient's Dialogue and Actions*
ting activity as though he were describing a body function. He is not asking permission or even delaying the activity. He is also chattering. 2. Therapist clearly initiates and takes the lead through body contact and decisiveness.	do. We're going to sit right down here[1] (pushing him so that he lands in a sitting position)[2] . . .		
		(He becomes more rigid.)	He can no longer tune out what is happening to him, although he tries hard.
Granted this response is more appropriate for a toddler or a nursery school child, his therapist is not deterred by what is or is not "age appropriate."	and take off your shoes (does so). Ah! Cowboy boots. What great boots you have.		
		(Now gets extremely agitated. Both hands are	It is obvious, from Paul's discomfort that he is hav-

	Dialogue and Actions	
Notes on Therapist's Dialogue and Actions	*Therapist*	*Patient: Paul*	*Notes on Patient's Dialogue and Actions*
		picking—one at the fabric of his trousers, the other at his hair.)	ing increasing difficulty "tuning out."
Therapist is not concerned whether Paul understands this tease or Intrusion (surprise). Were Paul to be diagnosed schizophrenic instead of autistic, therapist would avoid Intruding (surprising) and would rather Structure instead. (The schizophrenic's inner world already is too filled with "tricks" and illogic.)	And let's take the socks off too. We'll pull it right off. Look at those toes (counting): one, two, three, four, five toes on that foot. Let's see how many you got on this one (counting): ten, nine, eight, seven, six on that foot. Looks like you got eleven toes today.		
1. Therapist moves in very closely—face to face—in an effort to promote eye contact. 2. He	Here we go, let's just see how you look (peering at Paul's face close up).[1] Let's see . . .		

Notes on Therapist's Dialogue and Actions	Dialogue and Actions		*Notes on Patient's Dialogue and Actions*
	Therapist	*Patient: Paul*	

Notes on Therapist's Dialogue and Actions

labels Paul's body parts not as a somber classroom lesson, but all in the context of fun. 3. Therapist encourages body contact and the kind of pull and push and strain that is designed to make Paul feel the tension and relaxation of his own muscles in action. 4. In the most intrusive move so far, therapist tickles Paul. Rigidly walled-off patients appear to find the tickling at one and the same time very painful and yet very integrating. (When interviewed toward the end of her

Therapist

yeah, you brought your freckles along . . . your beard . . . and your moustache.[2] And those arms (testing them) Oh! Those muscles! Let's see this one. Oh! Strong, strong arms you got[3] and all that nice brown hair and brown shirt you brought to go with it. And oh . . . (tickling)[4] just the tiniest little tickle. Just the tiniest.[5]

Notes on Therapist's Dialogue and Actions	Dialogue and Actions		*Notes on Patient's Dialogue and Actions*
	Therapist	*Patient: Paul*	

Theraplay treatment, a young woman diagnosed catatonic had this to say "When they touch me, it's like electric wires burning my skin. The sessions are the highlight of my week though. I wouldn't miss them for anything." On a few occasions, this same young woman had been known to make a drive 300 miles round trip for her twice-weekly fifteen-minute sessions.)

5. "Just the tiniest little tickle. Just the tiniest." Even the most fleeting of responses is at-

Notes on Therapist's Dialogue and Actions	Dialogue and Actions Therapist	Patient: Paul	Notes on Patient's Dialogue and Actions
tended to in severely disturbed (or profoundly handicapped) individuals. Even the "tiniest" reaction is considered a response. In an otherwise nonresponsive patient, such a reaction is seen as a significant breakthrough.		(Squirms in response to tickling.)	Paul has begun to react to an impinging stimulus. This behavior heralds the first signs that he is relinquishing his posture of impermeability.

Again, as in the cases previously presented, the therapist was Intrusive, playful, intensely personal, and physical. With autistic adolescents, the approach is essentially the same as with others—it is particularly similar to Theraplay with the obsessive—but for autistic adolescents the intensity must be many times magnified. Even a momentary distraction on the part of the therapist can result in dramatic "dropping out" by the autistic adolescent. Recapturing him may require redoubled effort. It is for this reason—the autistic adolescent's too-ready dropping out—that activities with these individuals must be so fast-moving and so unpredictable (see Chapter Nine).

For financial reasons, his weekly visits were terminated with the tenth session. He returns for quarterly "checkups" now, and by all reports has maintained his gains. He is said to have become more friendly and outgoing, not only being chosen by other boys for tennis matches but also occasionally initiating

activities with his parents and his sibs. His eye contact is markedly improved, and there is far more, although still not much,
use of language. His peculiar mannerisms (for example, the
repetitive touching of the crease in his pants and the twisting of
his hair) have diminished, although they have not disappeared.
Just before terminating, his mother was pleased to report that
he had begun telling her about his schoolwork and that he no
longer pulls away when she touches him. How far Paul's development will take him is hard to say. There is no doubt that he
will continue to grow now that he has "found the way." It is
probable that Paul will never be "normal" in the sense of being
a fully functioning, wholly autonomous person. However, his
parents are considerably more optimistic about his future since
his therapy and have hopes that he will become self-supporting;
we can only hope that their optimism is well-grounded.

The Situational Acting-Out Adolescent

Occasionally the "fun" part of Theraplay with adolescents consists of Intrusion and Structure that is verbal as well as
physical. This combination seems most helpful when the patient's inappropriate behavior, rather than being characterologi-
cal, is in response to a particular change in his life situation.
Theraplay, then—and treatment itself, for that matter—is more a
process of providing perspective, a fresh outlook, and fresh solutions than of the usual kinds of Structuring, Challenging, Intruding, or Nurturing, although elements of the last three may
well be represented. Occasionally a second (or even a third)
individual is involved in the way an adolescent adjusts—or fails
to adjust—to the new situation. Since both are affected, both
together must work out solutions; for this, therapy is sometimes
necessary. Family therapy or problem-focused discussion and
"sharing of feelings" is one way of improving communication
between family members—another is Theraplay that helps a
family set down guidelines in a more light-hearted atmosphere.

Dan, fifteen, was referred for help after he had "earned"
thirty notices to report to the principal's office for thirty different offenses in the first half of his freshman year in high school.

Except for two A's, his grades were all failing ones. He had
begun stealing, and his mother had become unable to control
him. Her fearfulness of Dan brought her into the treatment sessions with him.

The following part of his first Theraplay session, conducted by Terrence Koller, serves to demonstrate what Koller
calls "part Theraplay." All three (Dan, mother, and therapist)
were sitting in chairs in Koller's office:

Therapist	Dan	Mother
		He's been just awful lately. I don't know what to do. He gets into trouble and fails at school . . .
(addressing mother) What happens when he starts acting like you describe?		
		Nothing.
	She can't do nothing, and (to therapist) *you* can't do nothing neither!!	
Yes, I can (moves over to Dan's chair and demonstrates, sitting down on top of him in chair)		
		He's going to end up in boy's school. I just know it.
(sitting back down in own chair) No, he's not.		
	How do *you* know? *You* can't make me!	
Yes, I can.		
	OK. Show me how *you* think you're	

Therapist	Dan	Mother
	goin' to *make* me.	
(laughing) I'll sit on you on my chair. That's how.		
	You couldn't do that and do your work too.	
Yes, I can, 'cause then you'll shake hands with the patients while I sit on top of you and write out their appointment slips.		
	(laughs)	

In the foregoing, there is no wrestling, no tickling, and no nose—or toes—painting. However, in its silliness, lightness, and humor, and also in its firmness and refusal to deal with complex relationships or causes of the pathological behavior, this session indeed is Theraplay. After only a few more sessions, the acting-out disappeared, and, after announcing that he had decided to become a psychologist, Dan asked Koller for reference books.

Because Theraplay is based so extensively on the therapist's being "in charge" and because adolescents try so especially hard to tip this balance Theraplay is particularly challenging when conducted with adolescents. It requires a broader repertoire, a greater sense of humor, and more imagination and spontaneity than does Theraplay with younger children. Exclusively "talking" therapy expects adolescents to relate to their therapists as adult-to-adult—verbally, cognitively, and with reference to past and future. Theraplay therapy is directed to those not-yet-grown-up parts that have presumably remained unfulfilled. Since therapy with adolescents may sometimes be a combination of the two—talking and Theraplay—particularly sensitive diagnostic skill and pronounced therapeutic talent are obvious prerequisites. Therapists can often find considerable gratification in conducting well thought out and well directed, yet spontaneous and fun filled Theraplay with adolescents.

11

Adults

Theraplay with adults? It hardly seems possible, for, in our society of macho aspirations and taboos on touching, where everybody's neighbor "does his own thing," the very idea of one adult Nurturing and Intruding (perhaps less so, Challenging and Structuring) with respect to another seems ludicrous at best; at worst, rude and presumptuous. Yet, perhaps by virtue of the prevalence of these very values, adults in our society, just as much as their offspring, often require physical help. Furthermore, many adults' areas of need and weakness often correspond to children's. Theraplay for adults, both alone and in groups, offers Structuring, Challenge, Intrusion, and Nurturing. Because the rules that govern appropriate adult conduct apply as much to the therapist as to the patient, it is often even more difficult for the therapist to give it than for the patient to receive it. Nonetheless, Theraplay for adults is often indicated.

Theraplay with Psychotherapy Patients

Based on the premise that many adult patients referred for psychological help were deficient in early mother-child attachment-fostering and autonomy-enhancing experiences, the Theraplay therapist, even when working with these older subjects, still relates as though he were providing pleasurable parenting to a small infant.

Like the wholesome mother-infant interaction, Theraplay is

1. Structuring, defining, organizing, and limiting
2. Challenging, teasing, and sometimes a little frustrating
3. Intruding, exciting, stimulating, and surprising
4. Nurturing, indulging, reassuring, approving, and caring

The Theraplay method, being such fun, so lively, and so direct, caring, and physical, tends to be short-term and impactful. Since emotionally disturbed adults often resist such intimacy, however, the treatment may be difficult at the outset, and the inexperienced Theraplay therapist may find himself backing off. Theraplay is often found to be effective with adult patients who are referred for inappropriate or flat affect, for problems of relating, for passivity, or for obsessive or bizarre thought processes. Occasionally individual adults are referred because they feel inundated by reality problems of overwhelming proportions (for example, Phyllis Booth's case, later in this chapter).

Instead of the dollhouses and chessboards often used in traditional child therapy, or the chair or couch used for adults, the Theraplay treatment room has gym mats on the floors, mirrors on the walls, large pillows for sitting, and small pillows for throwing. The Theraplay therapist working with adults may use baby powder, skin lotion, theatrical makeup, a scale for weighing, Band-Aids for attending to minor sores, seeds for spitting, a doughnut to take turns eating in little bites, and bubbles for blowing onto each other's noses. More than any other "prop," however, is the therapist himself. Verbalizations of the therapist, even when working with an adult, are like the chatter of a mother to her small baby. Difficult as it may be to imagine it, Theraplay activities may include cuddling, peek-a-boo, piggyback rides, or feeding applesauce.[1] Just as a mother does not "interview" her infant, so the Theraplay therapist also takes no case history, interprets no dreams, reflects no feelings, nor asks for fantasies. Unlike the flexible, ever-available mother, of course, the Theraplay therapist is present for only a thirty-minute session, scheduled only once or twice a week.

The cases to be presented next will illustrate several different kinds of Theraplay referral. The first two adult referrals are specifically referred for Theraplay. In other words, it was felt in both cases that straight Theraplay is the treatment of choice. The third case to be presented is illustrative of Theraplay as a follow-up to traditional therapy. The fourth is Theraplay as preparation for "talking" therapy. And, finally, there is Theraplay in conjunction with more traditional methods.

Referral for Theraplay: A Psychotic Woman

A psychotic mother of four, thirty-three years old, white, married, high school graduate, was referred for Theraplay after she had been twice hospitalized for psychotic depressions. She signed herself out of the first hospital against medical advice and was discharged from the second "unimproved." At the time of referral, she had been living with her mother, apart from her husband and four children. For the past months, she was reported to have been sitting, staring at, but not watching the television.

Little was known of her childhood except that she had had to be bandaged and hospitalized for a skin condition when she was six months old. Her mother, a taxi stand owner, was described by patient's husband as a compulsive gambler.

On referral from another city, and at her husband's insistence, it was agreed to accept Mrs. S. for a trial course of Theraplay. She reluctantly agreed to be brought down for her Theraplay sessions, providing, as we found out later, that she need come just once a week. Initially, in her dress and behavior she looked like a woman in her sixties. She was mute and stony-faced. During the first session, she never turned to face her therapist; she avoided eye contact and remained rigidly wooden. Her therapist, Elizabeth Dwyer, tried to keep the sessions fast-moving and cheerful. Given such resistance, this was a difficult job indeed, particularly for a therapist in training.

Theraplay activities typically correspond to the four kinds of mothering listed previously. The following examples are taken from Mrs. S.'s therapy.

1. *Nurturing.* Her therapist's nurturing, indulging responses included saying, "What a good voice you have . . . what a pretty voice," "You have a nice forehead," "You're a good hider," "You look like a queen," "You're tired," and "You like these in your hair."

2. *Structuring.* Typical structuring instructions were "Now you make one for me," "Blow it off my nose," and "I'll teach it to you."

3. *Intruding.* Intrusive Theraplay activities included unexpected tickling, surprise appearance of therapist from behind a screen, sudden leapfrogs.

4. *Challenging.* Teasing and even frustrating her patient a little, Ms. Dwyer invited her to aim soft pillows at her in peek-a-boo and to undertake the job of rearranging her therapist's hairdo. Arm wrestling and eventually the tricky singing of rounds while tapping body parts comprised some of the challenging interactions between them. "Now you've got to find the crumbs on me" completed the challenging samples.

Following are twelve of the Theraplay principles (listed in Chapter Two) that most benefit Mrs. S.

1. The therapist is in charge of the session at all times.
2. The therapist uses every opportunity for making physical contact.
3. The therapist attempts to keep the session cheerful, optimistic, wholesome, and health oriented.
4. The therapist keeps his sessions spontaneous, flexible, and full of happy surprises.
5. The therapist uses himself as the primary playroom object.
6. The Theraplay session contains minimal—but some—frustration, challenge, discomfort.
7. The therapist conducts his sessions without regard to whether the patient "likes" him.
8. The therapist focuses on the here and now and on the future.

9. The therapist's focus on the patient is intensive, exclusive, and often intrusive.
10. The therapist uses every opportunity to help the patient to differentiate himself as unique, special, separate, and outstanding.
11. The therapist initiates, rather than reacts to, the patient's behavior.
12. The therapist is responsive to nonmanipulative cues given by the patient.

(Other guiding principles are not as appropriate in the treatment of this particular individual. They have to do with the therapist's responses to the patient's moods, outbursts, efforts to take control, and physical hurts.)

Following is a segment of one of Mrs. S.'s Theraplay sessions. Numbers to the left of each interaction refer to the Theraplay principles therein applied. It is typical of Theraplay, as of other kinds of treatment, that several principles may apply at any one time.

The following interchange occurred during a session in which Mrs. S. was beginning to verbalize her negativism.

1, 2, 3, 6, 7, 8, 9, 11   Therapist: (perching a doughnut on the tip of patient's finger, then holding it out to her) Here, Rusty, you take a little bite, and then I'll take a bite. We'll see who gets the last bite before it falls off.

Patient: (chewing gum with grim stubbornness) I don't want to eat the doughnut.

1, 3, 4, 7, 8, 10, 11, 12   Therapist: (acting as though she does not hear the refusal, takes a bite herself and then hands a bite to Patient)

Patient: (eats bite)

1, 2, 3, 4, 5, 6, 7, 8, 9, 10, 11   Therapist: (hiding the crumbs that have fallen on her own body) Now you've got to find the crumbs on me.

Patient: (looks at therapist astounded, then begins to search for crumbs)

These Theraplay interchanges, of course, are only examples of the many, varied activities engaged in by a lively, imaginative, optimistic, yet sensitive therapist during each of the several fast-moving half-hour sessions. The most remarkable breakthroughs occurred when Mrs. S. was offered the opportunity to "get back at" her therapist. It was strikingly clear to the observers watching through the one-way screen that Mrs. S. seemed to "come alive" during pillow fights, water pistol duels, leg or arm wrestlings, and the chance to wash her therapist's feet in unexpectedly icy water. During these activities, Mrs. S's face brightened, her muscle tone sharpened, her voice became assertive, and her language was direct. Sometimes, before she caught herself doing so, she almost burst out laughing.

Activities that seemed to make her wander, lose interest, withdraw, or look confused were ones that are repetitious (such as singing "Row, Row, Row Your Boat") or predictable (as when her therapist first announced an activity: "Let's sing some songs" or "We're going to finger paint"). Consistently, Ms. Dwyer "lost" her patient whenever she (Ms. Dwyer) made self-denigrating statements that, rather than being real-life and fun (such as "I goofed"), were fantasy or pretend (such as "I'll be your slave") when she cooled her off with a paper fan.

Mrs. S. also lost interest whenever activities were out of eye-contact range (for example, when combing the back of her therapist's hair or when her therapist was applying polish to Mrs. S.'s nails). Additionally, she lost interest just as soon as she found herself in a situation where she was autonomous. And, finally, she reverted to preoccupied "absence" whenever there was an opportunity to merge with her therapist (as when they rocked in unison, played imitation games, or when her therapist made statements about their mutual similarity).

As Mrs. S. gradually came out from behind her wall, became responsive to her therapist, initiated games and ideas, and began to show interest in her therapist as a person, her therapist predictably found the sessions fun and a time to look forward to. By June 7, Mrs. S. knew that in three more weeks her therapist would be leaving for the summer. Having developed curi-

osity by that time, she expressed interest in Ms. Dwyer's explicit plans. She was promised regularly scheduled phone calls
from halfway across the continent, and she agreed to be there
to receive them. In the meantime, her interest in the world had
become more generalized and now included a desire to understand the lives of her mother and sister. Both reported their surprise, first when she began actively to watch their comings and
goings, then when she voiced open interest, and finally when
she expressed compassion. Her children, whom she had excluded from her world for nearly four years, now came to visit
her frequently. Although she still lived apart from them, she
was reported to be helping them with their homework, insisting
on their taking showers, and volunteering to mend their socks.
By the time of the session just prior to her therapist's departure,
Mrs. S. was an eager and chatty participant in the "goodbye
party." As they separated, they agreed again on the time of the
scheduled phone calls. Her therapist set their next meeting for
August 31, and Mrs. S. wished her a good summer.

The therapist noted, regarding phone calls, in early July:
"I call, as planned, every Monday night. Sometimes the line is
tied up on her end *all* night. Then it may take me two days to
get through to her. Mrs. S. answers the phone herself. Her con-
versations are brief but she seems cheerful. I tell her what I've
been doing, but I can't get her to tell me what she does. She seems
to enjoy the postcards I send her."

Mid July. "She starts talking about their weather and asks
me questions about my work."

Last week in July. "She immediately tells me I'd have to
call at a later date because she won't be home. They are going
away on vacation—their first in years—to Ohio. She seems en-
thused. She surprises me by asking specifically about my work
with the newspaper (which I have mentioned in a postcard)."

August 30. I haven't been able to reach her for days. She
had told me that she couldn't meet me August 31 (as planned
in June). Her reasons were vague—yet she held fast to her decision. She couldn't meet me until later the next week."

At summer's end, although Mrs. S. claimed to be reluctant to resume Theraplay sessions, she did willingly accompany

her therapist on trips through the city on the therapist's bicycle-built-for-two. She was also agreeable to going with her on walks through small downtown arts and crafts shops, where she initiated interested interactions with the artists.

After this, sessions once again took place in the Theraplay room. In mid November, Mrs. S. announced that she was finished and that she would not be coming back. Except for a few more telephone calls, there was no further interaction until the following February, when Ms. Dwyer received a Valentine:

> I could search all over, high and low
> and never find anyone nicer to know

(Therapist responded to card with a telephone call.) In early spring, Mrs. S. issued an invitation for her therapist to join her for a play at a local theater, where Mrs. S. once ushered.

Early in her treatment, during a particularly negative phase, Mrs. S. had shut herself overnight in her closet. Her husband, fearing suicide, called to ask for help. She refused to emerge even when her therapist arrived. On another occasion, in an attempt to persuade her to increase the frequency of her sessions, her therapist went to Mrs. S.'s house for what she hoped would be an on-site Theraplay session. Mrs. S. reacted to her therapist by remaining mute and unmoving in her rocking chair. Now, four months following their last formal session, Mrs. S. invited her therapist to see her house and "meet the kids." (After four years of separation, she had resumed living with her husband and children in his, or their, apartment.) In early May (six months after termination), she called to invite her therapist to a clubwomen's garden party.

Referral for Theraplay:
A Young Man Diagnosed as Chronic Schizophrenic

In the hope that he might become more engaged with people and less given to wandering aimlessly in the neighborhood around his halfway house, Blake, age twenty-nine, was referred from a distant city for Theraplay. Although he had

always attained high scores on intelligence and achievement
tests, his verbal responses were slow, he paced, became restless
and forgetful, and had poor nutritional habits. He was diagnosed schizophrenic, paranoid type 2953. He had been seen in
outpatient psychiatric treatment for ten years prior to referral
for Theraplay, having made unsuccessful efforts both to continue college work and to maintain a job. "He has been dependent upon his parents for financial support and in all likelihood
will remain so for the foreseeable future," said the letter from
his former therapist. In 1975 he was put on Thorazine. He has
been on Stelazine and Cogentin since 1977. His mother nego-
tiated the referral for Theraplay and made arrangements for him
to live with relatives. It was agreed to schedule one "trial" session
and then to evaluate whether a course of Theraplay would be
helpful for Blake. Prior to this session, his mother telephoned to
caution his therapist, Charles West, "You had better not try to
take off his shoes or anything . . . and don't use any lotion . . . he'd think activities like that would be dumb. You
know, he really is very intelligent."

Mr. West proceeded with the first session in true Theraplay style, without heeding either the warning of Blake's
mother or Blake's own query, "Do you use the Bettelheim approach here?" The trial session included the following activities,
one after another, in fairly rapid succession:

- Analyzing Blake's and therapist's physical characteristics
- Pillow sit (The two contestants stand back-to-back. Between
  them is a stack of large floor pillows. They compete to be the
  first to sit down on the largest area of pillow space. After
  each round, one more pillow is removed from the stack.)
- Taking off each other's shoes and socks
- Powdering feet
- Making powder footprints
- Comparing horizontal arm stretch with head-to-toe length
- Arm wrestling
- Pulling each other up to standing
- Tug of war
- Wind hockey (blowing dried peas across smooth surface)

- Tunneling (through mountain of pillows to meet in center)
- Sharing watermelon chunks
- Seed-spitting contest

Throughout, Blake was intently absorbed in the activities. Throughout, he remained engaged with Charles West. At the end of this trial session, Mr. West told him that if he planned to return at another time he (Blake) would have to let him (West) know and then return to his home town for his clothing. Blake's response: "No. I don't even have to go back home. I could just stay here."

In subsequent sessions, there was decreasing evidence of hallucination and increasing eye contact. Mr. West continued to ignore his occasional "technical" questions (for example, "Isn't there a Freud Institute in this city?"). In the meantime, we were told by his relatives that each evening following one of the twice-weekly half-hour sessions he demonstrated in detail to them every one of the day's Theraplay activities (for example, "and today, when I laid on the floor I could lift my leg *this* high"; "I beat Chuck at high jump today. Look how I did it."

After six weeks of treatment, he went in search of a job, and during the holidays he was said to have made some efforts to relate to (unfamiliar) women. The following conversation, with the aunt who initially referred him, took place after his thirteenth session: "He seems to be doing very, very well. A remarkable change. He's talking, relating, doing very, very good. He even looks different physically. He gained twenty pounds—weight he lost by pacing before. The mother is somewhat reluctant to say the change is due to Theraplay, but I think we made a good referral."

In the short period of twenty-seven half-hour Theraplay sessions, Blake's psychological tests already show some changes. While during the second testing he shows some evidence of rigidity, constriction, and aloofness, he shows less of the ego-centric, bizarre, loose and motor-driven state demonstrated on the first testing. The tentative nature of his controls shows that he could still profit from treatment. However, the decided improvements give us some reason for optimism that he is both ready and able to be helped to achieve a stable, constructive, self-respecting state of health. Overall, he has become less distractible, less driven, and less impulsive. He has developed a more casual, light-hearted view of himself, and a greater understanding of, and empathy toward, others.

His reduced distraction and impulsiveness are manifested in his slightly improved digit span and object assembly subtest scores. Although these are only two and three point increases and thus no more statistically significant than are the increases in verbal IQ from 108 to 114 and in performance IQ from 94 to 98, they do point in the direction of improvement when viewed against the backdrop of other changes in his protocol. His Rorschach leads to similar conclusions and indeed suggests almost a "backlash" tightening up. His productivity, for example, drops from an R of 32 to 18. His F+ percentage climbs from 62 to 90. Affective ratio drops from 44 percent to 33 percent. Shift from self-centeredness to empathy is attested to not only by a trend from 3 CF and 2 FC to 0 CF and 5 FC but also by the shift in his sentence completion from "Brothers and sisters . . . are an act of God" to "Brothers and sisters . . . help each other."

As for the reduction in his impulsivity, both his sentence completions and his Rorschach tell the story. (Increased ability to delay is illustrated by the following shifts in sentence endings: "The part of my body most easily hurt . . . is my genitals" changes to "The part of my body most easily hurt . . . is my head." "A man's man is a guy who . . . loves men" becomes "A man's man is a guy who . . . is honest and kind." "I would rather do without . . . greed" becomes "I would rather do without . . . being stubborn.") In Rorschach content, his categories now comprise one response (nature) beyond the basic humans and animals—quite a striking change from his "Mantrom," "Mothra," "Trion," "breast," "vagina," "uterus," "butterfly with a penis," "face on fire" and "man . . . impaled on a penis." Not only have sexual and anal content virtually disappeared but his Sentence Completion Test shows increasing calm, restraint, mellowness, and reflection replacing driven action: for example, "When I'm put under pressure I . . . try my best to relieve it" changes to "When I'm put under pressure I . . . try to remain calm," "If I'm alone, I . . . drive" changes to "If I'm alone, I . . . think to myself," "At night I . . . masturbate" becomes "At night I . . . meditate."

The sentences further suggest a newfound perspective (also perhaps reflected in the three point increase in his WAIS similarities subtest score) and light-hearted, casual view of himself and his world: for example, "I will do anything to . . . be infinite" becomes "I will do anything to . . . laugh at myself," "A person who always smiles is a . . . person with lockjaw" becomes "A person who always smiles is . . . giddy," "Being younger would . . . sicken me" now is "Being younger . . . would be nice."

The sentence "When they laughed at me I . . . jumped to my death" now becomes "When they laughed at mc I . . . walked away" and reflects his recently improved life view and self-image as does the following recent Thematic Apperception Test (TAT) story:

Blake's TAT Story
Prior to Theraplay
Card 14 (11" - 110"):
It's a picture of a man, standing, at an opening of a building—probably up in his room. (Pause) And he's looking out at the skyline, the sky itself. I should suppose that the outcome would be for him to eventually walk away from the window. Although taken in a different sense he could be a suicidal person and he could be just worrying or contemplating a jump. So in those circumstances the outcome would be for him to jump—but there's no real indication of that. I would just say it's sim-

Blake's TAT Story
After Twenty-Seven
Theraplay Sessions
Card 14 (9" - 64"): This is a picture of a man staring out a window in an otherwise totally dark room. Uhm, he seems to be looking up—probably looking at the stars and the sky. He probably came up there to look at them. He'll probably leave—he'll probably leave after he looks at the stars. It seems to be left rather open.

Blake's TAT Story
After Twenty-Seven
Theraplay Sessions

Blake's TAT Story
Prior to Theraplay

ply a picture of a man looking
out.

The increased integration, certainty of boundaries, light-heartedness, differentiation, and reality awareness are perhaps nowhere more clearly demonstrated than in his two sets of drawings (see Figures 6 and 7).

A note from his mother just prior to the testing said simply, "He looks fantastic!" Following his return home at the end of his thirty-third, and trial termination, session she writes: ". . . Blake is doing very well—he is starting a six month training course at the local vocational school soon. He made these arrangements himself. He knows that whenever he decides he wants to go back to Theraplay he may go and is planning on flying to Chicago on his first vacation to see Chuck . . . I am extremely grateful for all you have done for Blake. . ."

Ultimately we expect that Blake will continue in treatment —indeed he will probably have several more months of Theraplay. His progress so far is noteworthy, however, if only to reassure us that we are on the right track.

The foregoing cases illustrate patient-therapist interaction consisting of Theraplay activities throughout the treatment period. The contract, in a sense, is for Theraplay from the outset. More commonly, in the treatment of adults, Theraplay is combined with other, more traditional treatment forms—if not concurrently with them, then prior to, or following them. Then, in contrast to pure Theraplay referral, the transition offers a unique challenge to the therapist. The following cases represent each of the three circumstances: Theraplay following traditional work, Theraplay prior to traditional work, and Theraplay carried on concurrently with traditional work.

Theraplay Following Traditional Therapy: A Woman Contemplating Divorce

Mrs. R., thirty years old, a boutique owner, was seen by Phyllis Booth in once-a-week traditional psychotherapy. Poise and competence had always characterized this slender, blonde model. Now the stress of a daughter with ulcerative colitis and an alcoholic husband who demanded much and gave little rendered ineffective her lifelong coping mechanisms. Rage and grief accompanied her recognition that, if she were to survive psychologically, she would have to make some major life changes. In "talking psychotherapy," she responded rapidly to Mrs. Booth's initially supportive treatment and found herself more able to handle the real-life crises that confronted her. Her therapy, however, led her to want to focus increasingly on herself. At the same time, she experienced the long week between sessions as extremely frustrating. Her appointment times, therefore, were increased to twice a week. Shortly after this increase, her unhappiness seemed no longer to be alleviated by "talking."

One day, two months after the onset of therapy, Mrs. Booth, greeting her in the waiting room, suggested, "Let's play today" and said, in answer to Mrs. R.'s bewildered look, "I sense you're feeling so bad, and I just want to make you feel better." Mrs. Booth took hold of Mrs. R.'s hand and guided her playfully to the Theraplay room.

In fact, Mrs. Booth reports, she had held her hand "right from the beginning": "She was crying, and I reached out to her. She was telling me that she felt so alone and empty. It was very important to her that I was holding her hand, she said, because she'd never let anyone know how bad she felt. For me not to draw away, she told me, was extremely important . . . . There were two or three other times when she just cried and held my hand very tight."

In one earlier session, Mrs. R. told Mrs. Booth that whenever it was *she* who was not feeling well her husband would make extra heavy demands on her rather than offer her food and a chance to lie down. Mrs. Booth subsequently offered hot chocolate and ice cream cones; "She always accepts."

Initial Theraplay sessions consisted mostly of active play (for example, taking Giant Steps, high jumping, hopping, leapfrog, Follow the Leader, marking papered wall with painted toes, and ducking under-over-and-around the circle of each other's hands), always interspersed with "getting her to relax."

Nurturing activities, as she seemed increasingly able to

Male   Female

Figure 6. Blake's Drawings Prior to First Session of Theraplay

Figure 7. Blake's Drawings After Twenty-Seven Theraplay Sessions

Male

Female

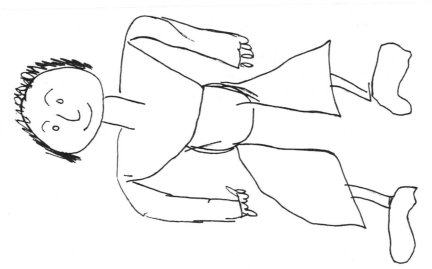

tolerate and need these, came to include the therapist's removing Mrs. R.'s boots and placing her cold feet in warm water and gently rubbing them. "Sometimes she seemed to need a hug. I reached over and held her close to me. Some sessions I simply held her and she cried."

She began to feel angry with the therapist, who sometimes did not understand her just right and whose absences she resented. She could not remember ever having experienced rage or ever having displayed angry behavior. Now, with the early appearance of it toward her therapist, Mrs. Booth introduced appropriate activities into their Theraplay sessions. They began to have pillow fights, water pistol duels, "snowball" fights, tug of wars, arm wrestling, pillow pushing, and so on. At the same time, Mrs. Booth continued to comb her hair, polish her toenails, and place Band-Aids on her minor cuts and bruises.

A typical session proceeded as follows: "We tried to run back and forth across the room seeing how many hats we could put on one another's heads. Next, I had her push her hand through an outstretched newspaper I was holding. She did that with a great deal of force. (It reminded me again of the intensity of her anger.) We had a lot of shattered newspapers then and wadded them up into "snowballs" that we each threw at the other—each of us hiding behind a barricade of pillows. She tried to crawl around the barricade and to sneak throws at me when I wasn't looking. We took small, soft plastic cylinders and "shot" them at each other in a series of attacks. I had her lie down comfortably, then challenged her to kick pillows and other objects off her raised feet. After all that activity, I had her sit, and I put her feet in the tub of warm water. I rubbed them in the water, then dried them, patted powder on them, and put her socks back on. We usually ended with ice cream dixie cups or graham crackers with honey. When the honey dripped through the little holes, we made a game of licking it off each other." Sometimes Mrs. Booth "cooked" the dish for Mrs. R., with Mrs. R. licking the spoon and pan.

After sixteen sessions of Theraplay, Mrs. R. felt ready to embark on the very difficult life changes she knew she would have to make. She also began to prepare for the termination of

her therapy. Mrs. Booth reports, "Although she had a tremendous amount of stuff to get through, life has really opened up.
She sleeps well now and takes good care of herself. She feels
that where she was 'dead' before, she can now at last feel 'alive.'
She got so she could tell me how angry she was with me for the
impending termination and yet how much she felt I'd opened
things up for her." Mrs. Booth adds, "Her progress, of course,
had to do not just with Theraplay ... the crucial episode, in
fact, probably came at the beginning, when I was able to hold
her hand and be there when she cried."

Theraplay Prior to Traditional Therapy: A Tongue-Tied Professional Male

Attempts at "talking therapy" produced only muteness, a
frozen face, and the awareness in the therapist (Ann Jernberg)
that this twenty-six-year-old lawyer would soon "drop out" of
treatment. Thus it was that Theraplay seemed appropriate as
preparation for the traditional therapy that Mr. B. had sought in
order to overcome his "social awkwardness." The transition to
the new format was introduced as follows:

Therapist: You know, you look as though you've lost some
            weight.
Patient: (does not respond)
Therapist: Stand up.
Patient: (does so ... without realizing he has changed his
            posture)
Therapist: Oh yes. I can see your belt is a bit loose on you.
Patient: (looks interested)
Therapist: Now turn around.
Patient: (turns)
Therapist: Oh yes. In the back, too, your belt's sagging a
            little.
Patient: (remains standing)
Therapist: I wonder about your ankles ... Sit down and let
            me take a look.
Patient: (sits)

Therapist: (removing shoes and socks) My, those are cold feet! We're going to have to do something about that. Come on, come with me . . . and take your shoes along.

Patient: (follows therapist down the corridor to the Theraplay room)

Therapist: (seats Mr. B. on pillows; chatters while filling tub with water)

Patient: (sits observing attentively)

Therapist: OK, now. Let's have your foot (reaching for it). Oh . . . it really is cold . . . I'll have to rub it really hard. And that callus . . . you sure must do a lot of walking around. Now to dry it off (doing so). Oh . . . much better . . . we'll rub some lotion into that callus. There we go. (same treatment with other foot) Oh . . . that's much softer . . . and now some powder so your socks'll go on nice and easy . . . there!

Patient: (listens, watches, touches each foot often during the process as though to confirm therapist's observations)

Therapist: Now your feet are all set, but how about the rest of you? You look as though you could brighten up your shirt a bit. Tell you what, we'll find you some nice, bright material (gets red tissue paper) and fold it this way, and press out the creases thus, and put it around your neck like so, and look . . . (pulling him by hand over to mirror) . . . a perfect bow tie. Voilà!

Patient: (studies reflection in mirror and grins)

[At the end of the session, he announces he would like to keep his "bow tie" on rather than remove it. Shy as he is, he says he would like to wear it on his grocery-shopping trip.]

Theraplay was continued over the next few sessions and included weighing "light" and "heavy" on scale, relay races with hats piled high, or hopping with peanuts curled inside toes, seed spitting, timed balancing acts with book on head and ping-pong ball on spoon, and always tender caretaking of wounds, no matter how minor. On his birthday, the session included a "party" with party hats and a lit candle inside a watermelon slice. Within about three weeks, Mr. B. was participating fully and cheerfully. He was told, "Next time, let's go back to trying to help you with some of those dating and socializing problems that brought you in." He agreed that he felt ready. The following week, traditional therapy was resumed. Communication was now open; he related freely and verbally. Without any preconceived plan not to do so, neither his therapist nor he ever alluded to the Theraplay sessions. He soon showed his capacity for insight, his motivation for change, and his awareness of the meanings of his transference feelings. He brought in dreams and early memories. The frequency of his therapy was increased. In another year, he was happily involved with a female coworker and had made some constructive life decisions necessitating his move to another city—possibly together with her. Subsequent letters told of his continuing adjustment to his new life.

Theraplay Concurrent with Traditional Therapy: A "Hen-Pecked" Older Man

Therapist Anthony Vitiello began Theraplay with Mr. Tate when it was apparent that the worried ruminations of this presently "disabled" fifty-six-year-old blue-collar worker during his sessions were getting him nowhere. To the contrary, as he talked on and on, he reached an ever-rising pitch of anxious excitement. Finally, Mr. Vitiello determined to engage him in Theraplay concurrent with his therapy. A segment of the initial Theraplay session follows:

Therapist: "We've got a special treat, Mr. Tate (indicating corridor to Theraplay room). Right in here. Right in here, Mr. Tate. We've got a special treat today. Put your cigarette away. Put that cigarette away. You're not going to smoke that today. That's no good for your lungs (taps patient's chest). Put that away. OK. We just want to make sure everything's

in shape here. OK. How you got your fingers
today? Looks good. Up here, too (examining
wrists). Looks good. OK. Everything looks good
today. OK. I'm glad everything's going really well
here. Good. Elbow's well-oiled. How's this one? Oh
this one's dynamite, too! OK! Come over here, Mr.
Tate. Have a seat. Come over here and have a seat.
Oh you sit up there. OK. Listen. Let's see your
toes here. Wow! You got them all. Dynamite! OK!
Oh real good! You got them all over here, too?
OK! They work real well? Very good. OK. Oh
really good. You got 'em over here, too. OK. They
work real well?

Patient: Yeah. I got a corn on that one though.
Therapist: Oh. You got a corn on that one? Let me see. Here,
let me lotion it. OK. Now you stay right there,
OK? I want to make . . . put your old hand right
down here. Put your old hand . . . oh, OK . . . this
is where our hands meet . . . OK (draws around patient's hand). OK, let's see. Pick that up. Got it!
Put your other hand on this paper. Put it over here.
OK. Oh boy! such good strong hands. Such good
strong hands. OK. There you go. OK. we can do
mine and we can compare mine to yours. Take a
pencil. Do mine right here. Oh boy. Good strong
fingers. Good fingers. Do my left hand. Right here
. . . Boy! . . . Wow! Let's do the other one.

Patient: That's the same one we just did.
Therapist: Oh dynamite! OK . . . Let's put your name . . . OK
. . . good. That's real good. Let's see. We'll put that
over here, I know just where we'll keep it.

During the sessions, as they powdered each other's elbows,
washed each other's fingers, painted each other's noses and
cheeks, and so on, Mr. Tate discussed with decreasing anxiety
the relationship with a domineering and critical wife. He began
to gain confidence in the sessions and often asked with surprise,
"Really? I'm that good (or talented or strong or handsome)?"

and commented, "You know, no one's ever told me that before." As he said this, he spoke of the "put-downs" he felt coming from his wife. Eventually, as they "played" together, Mr. Tate formulated a plan for gaining "the upper hand" in his marriage. He was going to take over from her the management of their small rental business and would encourage his wife to work in their vegetable garden. When he had proven himself as a landlord, he said, he would resume his work at the mills.

This case illustrates not only the use of Theraplay in conjunction with "talking" therapy but also the way in which Theraplay can be used to discharge the tension, dissipate the low self-esteem, and focus attention in patients where anxiety, poor self-image, and distractibility hamper the development of the therapeutic relationship. For such individuals, "talking" becomes less threatening if it is not the primary focus, and the inclusion of other activities serves to "take the pressure off." For others, the experiencing of such pleasure, warmth, or attention may lead to the recall of painful childhood relationships, the experiencing of present sadness, or the development of valuable insights, all while being fed grapes, blowing bubbles, or having their nails manicured.

Ways in Which Theraplay with Adults Differs from Theraplay with Children

It is as a function of two distinct variables that Theraplay with children differs from Theraplay with adults. First there is the difference between adults and children in competence, defensiveness, and therapist-patient similarity (with respect to age, goals, education, life experience, and so on). Second, there is the therapist's own uneasiness, identification, defensiveness, self-consciousness, and so on, all brought into focus by doing "silly," physical, infantile activities with another adult who has the potential to demean, ridicule, reject, or expose the therapist's weaknesses.

Thus, in working with adults it is essential for the therapist both to know himself and to plan for all eventualities. It is apparent from the foregoing case illustrations that therapists doing adult Theraplay are confident, flexible, undefensive, and comfortable with physical intimacy. It is also apparent that they plan their sessions carefully and tailor them particularly to the individual patient's specific needs. Theraplay therapists working with adults should have developed prior competence doing Theraplay with children and should have access to ongoing evaluation or supervision if at all possible.

If these guidelines are followed, Theraplay with adults can be highly gratifying. The words of a catatonic adult (diagnosis by Alan Rosenwald; patient seen by therapists Anthony Vitiello, Janet Waxmonsky and later Vitiello and Marja Booker) in her mid-treatment interview are words that would challenge any therapist to succeed: "When they [the therapists] touch me, it's like electric wires burning my skin. The sessions are the highlight of my week though. I wouldn't miss them for anything."

Theraplay with Parents

Parent group Theraplay (see discussion later in this book) is helpful to parents whose relationship with their children is beset with problems that arise from the parents' failure to experience it through his (the child's) eyes. Yet there are some mothers and fathers for whom even group role playing—involving and absorbing as it is—is still not sufficient. And there are other adults (regardless of whether they are parents at all) whose childhoods were so devoid of self-enhancing experiences that they do not have in their personalities the strength, resourcefulness, and conviction necessary either for their own autonomy or for encouraging their children toward emotional growth. Individuals whose problems are usually too vague and unfocused to bring them into traditional psychotherapy are often quite willing to sign up for Theraplay, saying, "If it'll help me become a better parent (or more adequate teacher, and so on)" or, simply, "I want to learn how to play." Unlike out-and-out conflicted neurotics, these people appear uncommitted, chameleonlike—more like actors on a stage than like genuine human beings experiencing genuine human feelings. If they are students, they often do not know what field to pursue. If they are housewives, their days lack direction. Their relationships with others seem programmed, superficial, and often desperately needful. The question of one young mother, "Was it all right to feel sad?" is one example of the uncertainty these individuals often have about "who they really are." Helpful as group Theraplay may be for these people, the group experiences seem to serve primarily as a "script" to follow. And follow it they do . . . to the letter. The leader, serving as an undisputed role model, is imitated in voice and gesture. Temporarily, these individuals may appear to get better. Yet, presented with a novel situation or with an unexpected turn in their relationships, they are unable to adapt. Although the deficit is obviously too pervasive to be so easily remedied and although a referral for more intensive psychotherapy often follows, individual parent Theraplay with just one therapist (usually of the same sex) may provide beginning help. For many, it may provide the first awareness that change through help is possible, without which awareness they only give lip-service acceptance to psychotherapy.

The playfulness and joy of individual parent Theraplay make it possible for the parent to be treated as though he or she is still a small child. As with children in Theraplay, although less formally, an assessment is made of the developmental level at which the deprivation occurred. What was often clearly missing in adults requiring Theraplay was the sense of being special, just as the little boys or girls they were. Often, for example, love was conditional on good behavior and sometimes on being someone they were not (for example, natural instead of adopted, firstborn son instead of the later-born daughter, cheery instead of tearful, verbal instead of athletic). Generally the deprivation dates back to a very early period. The emptiness created then sets the direction the treatment now takes. Specific manifestations of these early deficits show up most clearly in the performance of these individuals as parents in interaction with children during the diagnostic phase (for example, in the display of undue neediness, the lack of capacity for empathy, the abdication of responsibility, and so on) and in their behavior during the course of family Theraplay itself (for example, in the inability to share, to set consistent limits, to understand where their child "is coming from"). (See discussions of Marschak Interaction Method and of Family Theraplay, in Chapter Five.) In treating the individual adult, just as with the individual child, the intake interview helps the therapist(s) formulate a plan that is carefully tailored to his or her individual needs (be they for Structure, Challenge, Intrusion, or Nurture). Also, just as with children, the assumption must be communicated that "This is going to be fun (or feel good), whether you're chronologically six or sixty." Recognizing that, for the treatment to be effective, adult and therapist must first come to know each other well during the earlier diagnostic phase (see discussion of Family Diagnostic Phase, Chapter Five), the following segments depict typical therapist-adult interactions in later individual parent Theraplay.

Always on the go, Mrs. Green led an active life as charming hostess for her husband's colleagues and as a successful career person in her own right. It was seen during the early phase of treatment that Mrs. Green required Nurturing.

Therapist (Phyllis Booth):	Come right in here, Nancy, and sit down. Today you're going to be special.
Mother:	(sitting, with some hesitation)
Therapist:	Right down here on these soft pillows and let me make you comfortable. (begins by placing pillows all around her)
Mother:	(sitting upright) Oh now, Phyllis, you don't need to go to all that trouble.
Therapist:	Yes I do. I want to make sure you're really relaxed and comfortable. (begins to take off Mrs. Green's boots)
Mother:	(resisting her efforts) I can do that myself.
Therapist:	(continues, playfully but forcefully,

	to remove boots) You look warm. Here, let me cool you off. (begins fanning her with pillow)
Mother:	No, no, let me cool *you* off instead.
Therapist:	And look at how chapped your hands are. . . . We're going to put some nice creamy lotion on them . . .
Mother:	(begins to relax noticeably)
Therapist:	. . . and make them so soft.
Mother:	(Tears can be seen first glistening on, then rolling down, her cheeks.) I haven't cried since I was little, but I'm crying . . . and I don't even know why . . . except . . . I . . . think I like this.
Therapist:	Here (getting tissue), let me dry those tears for you.

Her reaction was not atypical. Individual parent (or adult) Theraplay, in its offer of total caring and unhampered empathy, often evokes sadness—perhaps, as with the children, a sadness reminiscent of an earlier longing.

Mrs. Rudolph was an effortfully cheerful, highly conscientious person who, in spite of her success in the antiques business, appeared more like a china doll than like a deeply responsive human being. The therapist felt, during the getting-acquainted period, that Intrusion and Challenge, in a Nurturing context, would make her "come alive." In view of her already overly rigid life-style it was felt that Structuring would not be good. The following segment is taken from her third session in individual parent Theraplay.

Therapist:	(feeding Mrs. R. an orange slice)
Mother:	(reaches for slice)
Therapist:	No, I'm going to feed you. There. Now let's save the seeds . . .
Mother:	Whatever for?

Therapist: Surprise.
Mother: Can I guess?
Therapist: Nope! Surprise! (continues to feed her) Now. Here
             are *your* seeds and here are *mine*. Put one in your
             mouth . . .
Mother: (does so, laughing)
Therapist: And I'll put one in mine . . . Now, let's see who can
             spit the farthest. On your mark! Get set! Go!
Mother: (laughing) You've got to be kidding!
(Both spit vigorously.)
Therapist: Boy, what a good spitter you are! Look at that!
             You beat me by . . . let's see . . . that must be a
             good three inches.

[After several more rounds of spitting orange seeds, therapist
begins to dress Mrs. R. in fancy dress-up hats.]

Mother: (still giggling) You know, I'm beginning to realize
             something. I think I know now what was missing
             from the relationship I had with my mother when I
             was a very little girl. You know what was missing?
             It never was any fun . . . (slowly) we never played
             together. (reminiscing) She never made me feel she
             enjoyed me.

[Note: All these insights come without any talking on the part
of the therapist and with no overt encouragement of memories
or insight.]

Two episodes from individual parent Theraplay sessions
with Mr. Mack will illustrate one other form these sessions
sometimes take. Mr. Mack, a disorganized jack-of-many-trades,
found steady work performance and firmness in his dealings
with others just about impossible. Structuring experiences were
what he appeared to need. Charles West is the therapist.

Session 1

Therapist: I know, Mr. Mack—OK if I call you Bill?—that you
             said you have trouble getting Louis to put his bike

away by dinner time. Let's see how you get him to do that. I'm Louis. Here (showing large pillow) is my bike. (moving quickly around room "steering" pillow, humming to himself) It's dinner time. What you want me to do?

Father: Put your bike away.

Therapist: Well, tell me that.

Father: Son, we'll be having dinner soon . . . would you like to put your bike away?

Therapist: (goes on "riding" his "bike," whistling cheerfully)

Father: Son? Put your bike away? Please?

Therapist: (still circling room, unheeding)

Father: OK, son? Put your bike away so we can have dinner? OK?

Therapist: (whistling louder, moving about more anxiously) OK. Let's stop a minute. How are you feeling?

Father: Very frustrated. But that's just how it goes. Maybe by now I would have gone in and consulted with my wife.

Therapist: OK. Now I'm going to be the Dad, and you're going to be Louis. Go on, wander about, be "at loose ends."

Father: (drifts chaotically about the room, picking up objects and dropping them, glancing at the mirror, appearing to be totally without direction)

Therapist: (varying the form rather than having the session deal exclusively with one example) Louis, I want you to put three of those little bean bags on me. The first one on my left foot . . .

Father: (does so)

Therapist: . . . the second into my right hand . . .

Father: (obeys)

Therapist: . . . and the last one on top of my head.

Father: (does that)

Therapist: Now I want you to bring me the lotion bottle.

Father: (brings bottle)

Therapist: OK, sit down.

Father: (sits)

Therapist:	And hold out your left arm.
Father:	(extends arm)
Therapist:	Now let me roll up your sleeve so I can put some lotion dots on it. OK. Now let's take that one big right toe and write your name in the dots.
Father:	(cooperates)
Therapist:	Beautiful! OK. I'm going to pull you up and help you to stand straight and strong.
Father:	(allows self to be raised from floor and "straightened up")
Therapist:	There we are!
Father:	I see what you mean. It feels much better when the parent takes charge.

Session 2

Therapist:	I'm Louis again. This time you're going to make sure you let me know that you mean it when you want something from me.
Father:	I mean it, son. Get the bike away.
Therapist:	(listens but then hastens on, singing) There's so much noise over here, from the squeaky wheels and the dogs barking and all, I can't hear you.
Father:	(moving closer to "Louis") Son! Get that bike put away now!
Therapist:	That's better, Bill, but it's still not enough to stop me because I know I can say, "Aw, Dad. I will. But I just got to do two more rides around, OK?"
Father:	OK.
Therapist:	Look, Bill. *Is* it OK with you? Or do you need me in *right now* for dinner?
Father:	I need you in right now.
Therapist:	Well? What are you going to do about it?
Father:	I don't know *what* to do. I never know what to do about that problem.
Therapist:	OK! Let's change roles again for a minute. You be Louis.
Father:	OK. (gets on "bike" and "rides" around room)

Therapist:	Louis, I'll count to three. If you're not off your bike by then I'll have to put the bike in myself and then carry you in for dinner.
Father:	(continues "testing" the therapist—riding and whistling)
Therapist:	One . . . two . . . three.
Father:	(still "testing")
Therapist:	All right, Louis, that's it. (approaching him) Off the bike.
Father:	(alights from "bike" but begins moving away from therapist)
Therapist:	I'll just have to hold onto your hand while we put this bike away . . . here. (holds on tightly to his hand) There we go. Now I'm going to have to carry you into the house . . . like this. (symbolically carries him)

These initial efforts gave Mr. M. the Structuring experiences that would help him become more directed himself and firmer and more limit setting in dealing with others. Later on there might be further, more traditional explorations as to his apprehensiveness about doing so. But for now Mr. M. had the gratifying experience, at least in certain circumscribed situations, of behaving with more predictability and order. This gratification in experiencing change is, for many, the prerequisite for utilizing psychotherapy later.

Mothers and fathers such as Mrs. Green, Mrs. Rudolph, and Mr. Mack all seem to need, and eventually to welcome, the experience of being nurtured, played with, and cared for in an intensely personal, take-charge way. For people like these, beginning to feel enough "reality" about themselves leads to their initiating the process of genuinely relating to others. This greater capacity for a better approach to others is most apparent in their relationships with their children (beyond their now engaging in more playful, physical, and structuring activities with them) and can be recognized by the more "genuine" quality of voice when talking with and by eye contact when looking at significant others. Again, this is not to say that, sooner or later, intensive, long-term psychotherapy may not be indicated. Indeed, psychotherapy is generally recommended. To set in motion (1) the wish to pursue further treatment and (2) the enjoyment of more empathic and mutually rewarding relationships in the meantime, however, individual parent Theraplay frequently is the initial method of choice.

Group Theraplay for Parents

As has been suggested in other sections of this book, the most ideal forms of Theraplay involve maximum parental participation. The family Theraplay format, described in Chapter Five, certainly approaches this ideal. Most parents readily "catch on" to Theraplay principles as they observe their child's weekly sessions followed later on in the program by weekly participation in those sessions themselves. It is always surprising to see how easily parents are able to change their behavior. They are, furthermore, pleased to see the impact of their changed behavior and are gratified by the results in their children. These results in turn lead to yet more willingness for change. Occasionally, however, it is necessary to go to yet further efforts to gain parental commitment. Some parents compartmentalize, keeping separate what they know to be true from what they feel. Some parents may "know" intellectually that their children could benefit, for example, from an opportunity to relax and indulge infantile longings. But when asked to feed them bottles, give them back rubs, or sing them lullabies, these same parents feel repulsed, become withholding, and revert to discussions of activities appropriate to age. Empathy is virtually impossible for these people until they can actually come to experience how it must feel to be their own problem child. Because this experience often is best provided for them by having others play the way they act as parents, parent group Theraplay can be most beneficial. Four or five couples convene weekly with one or two therapists for a series of six or eight evening meetings. Each set of parents is invited to tell their most vexing childrearing problem of the week. The problems first attended to are those which are common to two or more pairs. Thus, one week, for example, the Smiths, the Joneses, and the Blacks may all report having had trouble controlling their children's temper outbursts. One of the therapists may begin, "Mr. Black, describe exactly what happened with Johnny. Tell us where he was, what happened, what you did about it, and so on." Mr. Black then contributes his version of the event. "Johnny was eating his breakfast cereal, sitting at the kitchen table. He peeled his banana, looked at me, and tossed his peel to the floor." Mrs. Black is asked, "Is that what happened?" and she is given the opportunity to modify and elaborate. "Now, Mr. Smith," the therapist continues, "see if you can be Johnny. Do exactly what Mr. Black has just described Johnny as doing." Mr. Smith proceeds defiantly to throw a "banana peel" to the floor. The therapist turns back to Johnny's father. "Now, Mr. Black, show us how you reacted when Johnny did that." Johnny's father demonstrates how he asked Johnny to pick up the "banana peel," how he discussed, reasoned, pleaded, and argued with his son. Mr. Smith, meanwhile, is instructed, "If what your 'Dad' does makes you feel better, then improve in your behavior; if it doesn't, then keep on or act even worse." Finally, Mr. Black himself is cast as Johnny, and others in the group are asked to demonstrate how they typically handle this kind of problem in their homes. Following each effort, "Johnny" is asked to "tell how that felt"— including what he was saying to himself about each particular "parent" during the playing out of the scene, what he felt like doing about it, and what element was missing in what they did. Eventually, one of the therapists takes over as Johnny's parent, demonstrating the Theraplay principle of "taking charge," decisiveness without sadism, staying right there with the child rather than banishing him, and so on. "Johnny" is asked to tell his reactions to this last approach. More often than not, parents who are cool, rational, and permissive in their approach and tentative in their manner express surprise. "Why, I'd always thought to be treated with such control would feel frightening and demeaning. But, you know, when Mr. Koller (Terrence Koller, the therapist) sat on me to keep me from kicking him I felt, for the first time, really calm and cared for." Parents who tend to handle problem children with arbitrary punishment will come to listen, understand, and empathize. These, of course, are just some examples of the myriad problems parents present. The scenes to be reenacted may depict parent-child confrontations in the grocery store, over the dinner menu, around leaving for school, and so on. When possible, individuals are matched so as to include in one group parents who share one kind of child-rearing attitude (such as permissive) and in another group parents who share another (such as punitive). The direction the therapists take will, of course, differ with eeach group. Playing the role of a child subjected to constructive and destructive treatment and having the opportunity for discussion afterward provide a fresh view for these kinds of parents. Some parents may have feelings like those expressed by one mother: "Why didn't someone try to understand *me* like that when I was little?"

Note

1. The author, working with a middle-aged woman suffering from anorexia nervosa, first used regression and Nurturing in 1956, giving her as much physical contact as possible and feeding her jars of baby food (Margolis and Jernberg, 1960).

12

Selecting
and Training
Theraplay
Therapists

Selecting a Competent Therapist

Given the exacting and complex requirements for doing Theraplay, how is the competent Theraplay therapist selected? Traditionally, a candidate applying for a job as psychotherapist in a mental health facility is asked to appear in person for interviews with existing staff members. The focus of these interviews varies with the psychological approach of the organization.

Some interviews only use straight questions and answers dealing
with the candidate's academic background, work experience,
and future work-related goals. Others, still within the traditional
interview, draw out the candidate and include areas related to
work by inference only. These interviews may include such
questions as: "What are your favorite books?" "Why did you
choose this field?" "What kinds of things upset you?" There is
no clear-cut research to demonstrate that readers of Russian
novels make good therapists or that one chooses a mental health
occupation for reasons other than "to meet one's own needs."
Yet we have come to know, almost by instinct, that good mental health practitioners are aware of their own unconscious
processes, have had experience with human nature in all its
ramifications (including in novels), and have empathy with
others while yet being in touch with their own motivations. We
know that a modicum of emotional tension is a necessity but
that too much of it limits the energy that must be available for
investment in the healing process. Depending on the character
of our own institution, we tend to select therapists who are
dedicated, earnest, introspective, well read, and intellectually
curious or (to exaggerate the two extremes) those who are outgoing, cheerful, friendly, and optimistic. The selection may be
more a matter of preferring to surround ourselves with our own
kind (or with the kind we need, or wish we were) than a matter
of selecting therapists truly suited for helping.

Only after the new therapist—to do Theraplay or any
other kind of therapy—comes "on board" do we, unfortunately
all too often, ask the question, "Whatever in the world made us
think he'd do good therapy?" Only then does the unnecessarily
long and expensive process of remedial training begin. The
candidate with the charming manners and the glowing creden-
tials may be, when he does therapy, manipulative and wooden.
The one who exuded compassion and warmth may appear diffuse and abdicating of his professional role. The therapist who
in his interview was profound and introspective may convey
gloom and hopelessness in his therapy. The one who was all
light and cheer may show intolerance for conflict, for negative
transference, or for sad feelings—"improvement" in his patients

may be a function of the degree to which they feign change or use denial. (Faced with a patient who has experienced a trauma, this therapist may find it virtually impossible to cope in a therapeutic way.)

How can we really know, except by inferring on the basis of what we have been told of his past performance, what we should expect of the candidate psychotherapist in the future? Will we know, from evidence about his past plus his interview behavior, how he typically behaves in his first session as helper to a troubled child? Do we know with anything approaching certainty whether he will convey support, interest, and optimism with regard to change, or whether he will present himself as uncaring, preoccupied, and pessimistic? Do we know whether he will accept or abdicate the "expert" role? Do we know how his defensiveness and openness fluctuate within one session or how a child might feel being in a room with him?

These are all difficult questions to answer. They are made all the more difficult in those cases in which the only available data (for example, course credits) have virtually nothing to do with performance on the job (for example, intense, interpersonal, therapeutic interaction). They are only slightly easier to answer when some one characteristic of the evaluation situation fits closely with some one feature of the actual working situation (for example, the tolerance for stress is assessed by "stress interviews" in the evaluation procedure of some clinics, psychoanalytic institutes, and training institutions).

It follows from this discussion that, the greater the congruence between evaluation procedure and actual Theraplay working circumstances, the greater should be the confidence in the prediction of effective Theraplay job performance. Ideally, the evaluation would be based on observations of Theraplay performance within the context of a real-life working situation.

Just such a method for predicting Theraplay job effectiveness on the basis of observing a candidate's style within a real-life Theraplay work situation has been developed in two unrelated mental health facilities. This predictive method, by virtue of its initial intensity, saves a great deal of subsequent staff supervision and training time. The functions of the two mental health facilities are different, as are the populations served, the kind of treatment provided, the job definitions, and the locale. Center 1, the Theraplay Institute, is located in a metropolitan area, serves large numbers of middle-class and urban poor children—primarily of preschool age—and hires, for treatment purposes, a large part-time paraprofessional staff. In contrast, both rural and small-town residents comprise the clientele of the other agency, a community mental health center (Center 2). It hires, for treatment purposes, full-time psychiatric social workers and clinical psychologists. Center 1 serves school-referred children and their families in short-term, noninsight, reparenting, school-based Theraplay. Center 2, in addition to providing traditional adult and child psychotherapy, also provides Theraplay for children. The method to be described has been used in the evaluation of approximately 150 job applicants to these two centers.

Screening of applicants to Center 2 is conducted as follows: First, résumés are analyzed, and persons clearly lacking relevant background and so on are easily eliminated. Traditional candidate-employer interviews follow, and then those applicants still "in the running" are evaluated thus: A "normal" child is presented to the candidate with the instruction, "Pretend this is your first therapy session with a child who's been referred for help." The candidate is given no further direction, except that he is told that members of the center staff will be observing.

The following encounter illustrates observed candidate-child interactions. Jamie, a normal five-year-old, was introduced to the therapist-applicant with the instruction, "Pretend he's a client here at the center." The applicant, Miss X, took him into the playroom while staff members observed their interaction through the one-way window. Applicant X sat on a chair four feet away from the child, who was turned so that his back was toward the adult. He looked glum. There was silence. At last Applicant X asked, "Well what would you like to do?"

He did not answer. Applicant appeared to be tightly controlling her affect. She said, "Would you like to play a game?"

No answer. Still remaining in their respective positions, he on the floor, she in her chair, she asked in a tense, high-pitched voice, "What game would you like to play?" The scowl on her face betrayed the anger his unresponsiveness was generating in her. Her "sweet" voice reflected the strain she was under, probably both because she did not know what to do with her anger and because the observation itself put her in a bind. In any case, the observers had only to ask themselves two questions: (1) Can someone this tense and hostile with children, even granting the reality stress, possibly be a good child therapist? (2) Would I want this person to treat a child of mine?

The same child was introduced to another would-be staff member, Applicant Y, who was carrying a bottle of bubbles in one hand, a doll in the other. "Let's blow bubbles," she said. The child seized on the bubble suggestion, and together they began to blow bubbles. Although she chattered (for example, "I haven't blown bubbles in a long time . . . I don't know how to do it"), there was little interchange between them, as both therapist and child were focused on the bubbles. Child remained solemn throughout. It could be seen that although this applicant had poise, warmth, and the capacity for eye contact her style of therapy was going to be long-term and "indirect."

Applicant Z, however, was active, engaging, fun, and physical. Z and child entered the therapy room and sat down together, Z positioning himself to face the child. Immediately Z said, with cheerful warmth, "Boy, you look good today! Let me see, what color are those eyes?"

The child began to smile shyly, and after a few more positive, personal, interacting observations on Z's part, he became clearly enthusiastic. Not long thereafter, he was talking and sharing with his new-found friend.

On the other side of the viewing room, the staff responded to the intensely empathic interchange. They found it difficult not to feel the growth-enhancing quality of this particular applicant.

In child programs, as for adults, treatment styles vary from one institution to another. Yet it is easily apparent which applicant is suited to do Theraplay and which applicant is not. The method described, of course, does consume staff time. Yet during those few times of the year when there are staff openings at Center 2 for individuals who will be trained in Theraplay, the time expenditure is more than compensated for by obtaining the most skilled and appropriate candidates.

Suppose, however, a center has many openings at one time, for which a large number of individuals apply? This very situation occurs once a year at Center 1. By late winter, children have been diagnosed, dispositions made, and the number of referrals for psychotherapy has mushroomed. This center may find itself overnight with as many as 100 to 200 children on its waiting list. Openings for up to fifteen therapists are advertised. During peaks of unemployment particularly (but always to some extent), telephones ring often. Applicants are given an initial telephone screening to determine experience, reliability, and motivation. They are then mailed a formal application blank (the Worthington Personal History), which serves both as a résumé and as a projective evaluation instrument.

After screening of the completed forms, the applicants are scheduled for a group selection session. Sessions are arranged in groups of twenty to twenty-five. The procedure is as follows: Candidates sit on the floor along the walls of a large room that is bare except for carpeting or gym mats. They are asked to count off by twos and then are told, "All Number 1's will be children, all Number 2's will be the adults trying to help them. Number 1's, this time you're going to be children who are withdrawn, quiet, perhaps nonverbal, timid, shy. You know the picture. Number 2's, each of you is going to do your best to help the child assigned to you. Your job is to try to make that child feel better." In sequence, then, each adult-child pair comes to the center of the room and, as the others watch, the "adult" works to help the "child." Each is allowed enough time, so that he feels satisfied he has done his best. The "child" is instructed, "If it begins to feel as though you would be becoming more comfortable, act accordingly. If it seems as though it would be making you feel worse, then you should indicate that, too. Try to be tuned in to how your 'therapist's' behavior would be feeling to you if you were that shy, unhappy, withdrawn child."

Within such a large group, there tends to be marked variability in technique, perseverance, imagination, resourcefulness, energy level, tolerance for frustration, and so on.

Following this first assignment, the Number 2's are next asked to be withdrawn children and the 1's to be adults—not necessarily within the same partnership—and the same procedure is followed.

Next there is a renumbering. The new number 1's are instructed, "Now we want each of you to be a child who is hyperactive, aggressive, acting out. Again, we ask you to respond as such a child would to whatever is being done with you. If it feels good and relaxing, let us know by the way you act. If it makes you more uncomfortable yet, then react accordingly." The procedure is the same. Everyone is given a turn to be both overactive, angry child and helping adult.

A break follows while staff members confer. As the group reconvenes, members are offered the opportunity to discuss their reactions to the procedure. Then it is lunch time; only those considered to be good prospects are asked to return after lunch. They, together with the most promising of all the other groups of applicants (observed concurrently in the same fashion in other rooms), are invited to participate in one more group selection session. The procedure is essentially the same, except that experienced staff members now play the role of the child. Their accounts of how the treatment "felt" determine the final verdict on each applicant. If there is still a doubt or if there are more eligible candidates than openings, interaction with a normal child may be arranged and observed through the one-way mirror in the manner previously described (see Center 2).

This method for screening and selection of applicants to be Theraplay therapists is probably unique in that it allows observation of the candidate in direct interaction with a simulated child patient. On the basis of such observations, judgments made regarding an applicant's talent for the job are more likely to accurately predict than those inferred from data less directly related to performance of therapy (such as résumés and interviews with other staff).

So far, in the use of this method, it should be said we

cannot be certain how many "false negatives" there may have been; that is, people may have been eliminated who would have turned out to be good therapists. But certainly there have been no "false positives"; that is, no one about whose skills the staff was uniformly enthusiastic (on the basis of either the group or individual evaluation) has proved to be other than an effective Theraplay therapist.

Even though this method does require initial extra staff investment and even though an institution only gradually becomes truly proficient at conducting and making predictions from such an approach, nonetheless it has been our experience that the later results, including the reduced need for supervision and training, thoroughly justify the effort.

Training the Therapist

Although there is a good deal of overlap and although different trainees require different direction and emphases, the overall presentation, teaching style, and format are the same for all. The amount and kind of additional Theraplay exposure depends on the personality attributes and past experiences of each candidate. Since Theraplay so closely parallels the early mother-infant relationship, each trainee must be thoroughly familiar with early childhood phenomena and must learn to discriminate between different patterns of parent-child communication.

It is important that trainees recollect and understand the impact of Theraplay-like and non-Theraplay-like approaches in the interactions they themselves had with significant adults during the time of their childhoods. It is expected that as part of this training candidates will come to experience for themselves how the child would feel and behave if given Theraplay-like and non-Theraplay-like treatment.

Theraplay is a method that is intensely personal and demanding of conflict-free involvement on the part of the therapist. As explained in more detail in the next section, it is important that trainees be as thoroughly in tune as possible with their own intrapsychic responses, for they have to cope with a multitude of "negative phases" and to experience the struggle of multiple terminations. This may mean making significant efforts toward personal change—often including undergoing their own psychotherapy.

The Do's and Don't's Therapist Rating Scale, developed by Terrence Koller, has proven to be an effective method for supervision. When trained to be reliable observers, peers can rate one another's performance on this rating scale. Videotaped sessions provide ideal material for observer training.

The Scoreboard (Item V) serves as a shorthand method for keeping track of the therapist's "taking charge" behavior. Each participant's attempts to "run the show" are recorded and tallied like a ping-pong game. The inexperienced Theraplay therapist's protocol is likely to look like this:

Therapist	Child
II	TTTT TTTT TTTT

The experienced Theraplay therapist's session will be recorded as follows:

Therapist	Child
TTTT TTTT TTTT	II

Once more, it goes without saying that simple, arbitrary dictatorship does not make for good Theraplay. "Taking charge" is necessary, but it is not sufficient. The quality with which the shots are called is crucial (Items I-IV). There may be some few times, in fact, when "taking charge" is not even necessary.

The teaching of Theraplay takes place through a combination of didactic, practical, and experiential approaches. Throughout, trainees are helped to understand healthy parent-infant interactions. They are encouraged to test out the effectiveness of a variety of other therapeutic approaches. And they are expected to be able to explain the Theraplay rationale. Observers' assessments of Theraplay activities are often helpful in rating Theraplay talent. The activities rating scales assess quantity of activities per session, appeal of activities, and variety of activities.

The Theraplay Institute
Do's and Don't's Therapist Rating Scale

I. The Therapist's Personality
   The therapist
   1. Is confident, certain, has
      leadership qualities   1 2 3 4 5 6 7 8 9 10
   2. Is appealing, delightful   1 2 3 4 5 6 7 8 9 10
   3. Is responsive, empathic,
      in tune with others   1 2 3 4 5 6 7 8 9 10
   4. Is cheerful, optimistic,
      wholesome, and health
      oriented   1 2 3 4 5 6 7 8 9 10
   5. Is spontaneous, flexible,
      and full of happy sur-
      prises   1 2 3 4 5 6 7 8 9 10
                                                      Total_____

II. Therapy Behavior
    The therapist
    1. Is in charge of the session
       at all times (see Score-
       board, Item V)   1 2 3 4 5 6 7 8 9 10
    2. Uses every opportunity
       to make physical con-
       tact with the child   1 2 3 4 5 6 7 8 9 10
    3. Insists on eye contact   1 2 3 4 5 6 7 8 9 10
    4. Focuses on the child in
       an intensive and exclu-
       sive manner   1 2 3 4 5 6 7 8 9 10
    5. Initiates (rather than ne-
       gates or counters) the
       child's behavior   1 2 3 4 5 6 7 8 9 10
    6. Focuses on the present,
       future, and the here   1 2 3 4 5 6 7 8 9 10
    7. Focuses on the child as
       he/she is   1 2 3 4 5 6 7 8 9 10
    8. Is responsive to cues
       given by the child (for
       example, incorporates
       the child's body move-
       ments into his or her
       repertoire)   1 2 3 4 5 6 7 8 9 10

9. Uses every opportunity
to differentiate himself   1 2 3 4 5 6 7 8 9 10
10. Uses every opportunity
to make the child feel
unique and special   1 2 3 4 5 6 7 8 9 10
11. Helps the child "label"
his feelings   1 2 3 4 5 6 7 8 9 10

Total_____

III. The Session

The Theraplay session

1. Has the therapist as pri-
mary playroom object   1 2 3 4 5 6 7 8 9 10
2. Clearly defines times,
places, and persons   1 2 3 4 5 6 7 8 9 10
3. Has many different seg-
ments, each having a
beginning, a middle,
and an ending   1 2 3 4 5 6 7 8 9 10
4. Contains optimum
quantity of activities
(Activities are as many
in number as the situa-
tion calls for and the
time can accommodate)   1 2 3 4 5 6 7 8 9 10
5. Contains optimum vari-
ety of activities (Activities are varied, surpris-
ing, unpredictable)   1 2 3 4 5 6 7 8 9 10
6. Contains optimum ap-
peal (Activities are irresistible, delightful,
highly interesting)   1 2 3 4 5 6 7 8 9 10
7. Contains minimal, but
some, frustration,
Challenge, and discom-
fort   1 2 3 4 5 6 7 8 9 10
8. Offers Nurturing op-
portunities   1 2 3 4 5 6 7 8 9 10
9. Structures (body boundaries, play space, rules,
expectations, and so
on)   1 2 3 4 5 6 7 8 9 10

10. Intrudes into the child's
personal world   1 2 3 4 5 6 7 8 9 10

                                            Total____

IV. Contingencies
    1. Temper tantrums:
       The therapist makes his
       insistent presence felt
       throughout the dura-
       tion of a child's temper
       tantrum.   1 2 3 4 5 6 7 8 9 10
    2. Rejection of therapist:
       The therapist conducts
       the session without re-
       gard to whether the
       child "likes" him.   1 2 3 4 5 6 7 8 9 10
    3. Excessive anxiety:
       The therapist curtails
       and prevents excessive
       anxiety or motoric
       hyperactivity.   1 2 3 4 5 6 7 8 9 10
    4. Accidents:
       The therapist attends to
       physical hurts.   1 2 3 4 5 6 7 8 9 10
    5. Calling the shots:
       The therapist does not
       permit the child to call
       the shots (see Score-
       board, Item V).   1 2 3 4 5 6 7 8 9 10

                                            Total____

V. Who "calls the shots"?
   (Place marks in appropriate   Scoreboard
   column as session moves   _____
   along; for example,   Therapist   Child

        Therapist   Child
          ꒒꒒꒒   ‖)

The scoreboard is a work-
sheet for Items II-1 and
IV-5.

What Goes on in the Therapist's Head

The Hazards of Countertransference Acting-Out

In doing Theraplay, more than in doing traditional psychotherapy, there are all too many opportunities for, and too few safeguards against, unwitting acting out. As in any therapy, therapists doing Theraplay must be ever vigilant against the temptation to satisfy their own needs first; that is, to act out in the countertransference. This is not to say that countertransference phenomena do not occur. Racker's (1968, p. 132) requirements for psychoanalysts must apply equally to Theraplay therapists: The therapist must not be so objective that he experiences neither anger nor anxiety, nor must he be so vulnerable that he "drowns" in these experiences. In any case, the therapist should "normally experience these situations with only a part of his being, leaving another part free to take note of them in a way suitable for the treatment" (p. 141). In any therapy with children, perhaps even more than in therapy with adults, there is the strong and omnipresent temptation to re-enact one's own childhood. In Theraplay especially, the physical contact, the intimate interaction, and the regressive focus all serve as too-available invitations. The direct and intensely personal nature of Theraplay, as well as the emphasis on body contact, body boundaries, and body experiences all invite many forms of countertransference acting-out. There is the invitation to do to the child what was done to the therapist as a child, for example, or to do to the child what the therapist feared or wished would have been done. The rapidity with which activities are carried out and the amount of physical, mental, and emotional involvement leave little opportunity for on-the-spot self-exploration. Thus, for example, while cuddling and bottle feeding a child may stimulate one's own oral longings or tickling or spinning may stimulate one's sadism, there is no time to inquire of oneself about the sources of one's own anxiety. Yet a Theraplay therapist, perhaps more than any other therapist, must make it part of the ongoing therapeutic enterprise to investigate himself. Although this is difficult to learn, the therapist, while conducting a session of Theraplay, must have a ready set of self-directed questions inside his head, an awareness of the likelihood that countertherapeutic tendencies are being activated, and a quick resolve to take the matter up in more detail with himself later on. The questions he must ask himself include (1) "Why am I doing this particular activity?" (2) "Why am I reacting this particular way?" and (3) "Am I or am I not 'using' the child?"

1. "Why am I doing this particular activity?" is shorthand for "In whose interest am I doing this particular activity?" The certain answer to this question must be "I'm doing it because this child requires it for his or her improved mental health." If this is not the certain answer, then the implied one very likely is "I am doing it for my own neurotic needs," and so the activity should be promptly discontinued. If, for example, the reason for organizing a pillow fight is clearly that the child needs to experience competition in a nonthreatening situation, then it is appropriate to continue. If the therapist's own competitive striving is the determining factor in the choice of a pillow fight, there is no justification for continuing the activity.

2. "Why am I reacting this particular way?" can be elaborated thus: "What about the child, the activity, or the interaction between us is making me have this reaction? If what I am doing is objectively appropriate for the child's needs, why am I *feeling* guilty, angry, anxious, or abandoned? If the activity I have chosen to do is appropriate, why am I *behaving* in an overprotective, overcompetitive, neglectful, or clinging way?"

The answers to the question "Why am I reacting (or why am I behaving) in this or that inappropriate way?" will be as varied as there is variety in human personality. For some, the answer may lie in the fact that the therapist identifies the child with some important figure (for example, a younger sibling) in the therapist's own childhood (or perhaps the therapist him- or herself.) For others, the answer may lie in the unconscious recollection of an early life experience touched off by the activity as such. Peek-a-boo, for a simplified example, may rearouse an infantile memory of a game with, or the disappearance of, the therapist's mother. Tickling may recreate the activity and image of the therapist's feared and hated uncle.

3. "Am I or am I not 'using' the child?" expands to "Am I using the child to reenact, act out, or attempt to resolve my own conflicts? Am I using his or her improved health or success and mastery for my own omnipotent needs, for example? Is my exhibitionism being fed by the public recognition of this child's accomplishments? Does the intimacy with this opposite-sex child satisfy a buried wish for possession of my opposite-sex parent? Is my prolonging the treatment and forestalling termination a function of my chronic anxiety over separation?" These examples are only a sparse sampling of the many possible ways and likely tendencies a therapist may have to "use" the child. The following represent more specific guidelines for dealing with countertransference acting out. Although there may be other areas requiring alertness, the Theraplay therapist must be particularly aware of (1) anger, (2) dependency, (3) sex, and (4) competition.

1. *Anger.* Anger may be a natural reaction to someone hurting one physically (kicking, biting, scratching, hitting, and so on) or lowering one's self-esteem (remarking about one's areas of vulnerability, causing another to criticize one, and so on). It is also a natural reaction to being rejected.[1] Thus it is no wonder that a therapist's raw response to indignity, insult, physical pain, or abandonment should be one of anger. Indeed, one's talent for doing good therapy must be in question when one denies having any but benign feelings toward the patient who has just bitten one's forearm or spit in one's face. Of almost as much concern are therapists whose initial flare-up of reactive anger leaves them so shaken that they cannot deal with it, understand it, or move beyond it. The best therapists experience their anger, understand its origins, then use it to help the patient reintegrate. The therapist should especially examine anger that is not a universal reaction to a particular stimulus (for example, anger in response to a child sucking on a bottle).

2. *Dependency.* Dependent longings may be a natural reaction to illness, separation, another's orality, another's nurturing. Thus it should be no surprise to find that a therapist's

passive, regressive, or dependent longings have been stimulated by a patient's termination of treatment, or curling up for cuddling, or offering to guide or feed the therapist. Again, denial is often suspect. More suspect still are dependent longings stirred for no apparent reason.

3. *Sex.* Sexual arousal may be a natural reaction to prolonged intimacy, seductive behavior, erogenous body contact, or verbalized sexual provocations or preoccupations. Again, both the denial of obvious sexual impulses and their presence in response to apparently nonstimulating behavior are suspect. It behooves therapists to acknowledge the presence of their eroticized responses, then quickly neutralize them and move on, changing the activity if need be.

4. *Competition.* Competitive strivings may be a natural reaction to another person's ambition, success, or put-downs, or to another person's not winning. Competitive reactions when there have been no stimuli to arouse them are as needful of self-examination as is repeated failure to rise to the challenge.

Among other nontherapeutic or countertherapeutic therapist responses such as projection, exhibitionism, merging, overidentification, sadism, and masochism, two kinds of guilt are of particular interest. First there is guilt over intruding into another's life space or "playing God," which makes it extremely difficult for some therapists to do effective Theraplay. Underlying their difficulty may well be the fear of arousing their own infantile feelings of omnipotence or of the anger assertiveness may imply to them. Second, there is guilt over "enjoying." Because Theraplay can be such fun, instead of dreary hard work, some therapists find themselves very uneasy. They may refuse pay, or they may turn the sessions into effortful burdens.

A particular developmental phase (for example, oral, anal, or genital) may arouse untoward anxiety in some therapists because it is related to conflict areas in their own development. These therapists find it difficult to treat a child who is fixated at, develops to, or is regressed toward a particular psychosexual stage. One therapist may find it virtually impossible to bottle feed, for example; another, to finger paint; and a third, to engage in same-sex competition. Depending on whether the therapist's own primary level of conflict occurred during the oral, anal, or oedipal phase of development, a patient having difficulty with a corresponding area is likely to generate anxiety in the unskilled therapist. By the same token, therapists still in the throes of their own struggle over merging and differentiation may find it hard indeed to deal with an autistic child who "melts into" the body of the therapist.

Avoiding Countertransference Acting-Out

The following can be helpful in avoiding countertransference acting-out: (1) preplanning sessions, (2) supervisor or peer observation, (3) supervisory discussions, (4) role playing, and (5) personal psychotherapy.

1. For the therapist who is not yet "onto him- or herself" and for one who has had minimal Theraplay experience, preplanning is crucial. Preplanning should include not only a blueprint of Theraplay activities for the session ahead but also, equally important, a preparation of "what if's" (for example, What if he bursts the balloon before he throws it? What if she spits the orange seeds at me rather than into the target? What if he refuses the bottle?). No amount of preplanning, of course, will account for all eventualities.

2. Supervisor or peer observation allows for the objective collecting of evidence of countertransference acting-out. Ideally, observation is conducted through a one-way window or by means of videotape. If necessary, though, observers can view the session from within the therapy room itself.

3. Supervisory discussions with a regular supervisor allow the therapist to become aware of his or her tendency to act out in countertransference. With the help of a perceptive, nonthreatening senior therapist, the origins of a particular episode can be traced, and new solutions explored.

4. Supervised role playing of particularly troublesome patient-therapist interactions allows for co-worker scrutiny of the countertransference. At the moment of inappropriate action, the demonstration is halted while the therapist and his or her coworkers explore the reasons for "doing what he or she did." Reconstruction and attempts at a better solution follow—still within the role-playing framework.

5. Personal psychotherapy can, of course, increase therapist awareness and understanding. A therapist who plans to do effective Theraplay should heed John Rosen (1953, pp. 9-10):

> The therapist's own psyche must be in order. His instinctual drives of love, hate, and aggression must have come into such a balance that, as he relates himself to the patient, the patient will thrive. . . . Holding us to our task is a loving instinct intensely stimulated by the knowledge that either we are right and win in the face of these odds or we are responsible for (the consequences). . . . As in all human relationships, the more time you spend with an individual, the less of a stranger he is and the more he means to you consciously and unconsciously. . . . Once the initial investment of interest, effort, and time is made, the agreeable or disagreeable qualities of the patient are not the factors that sustain the therapist in his devotion. . . . One of the motivating forces that compel you to do for a patient in some way has to do with the force that motivates you to do for yourself.

Note

1. Campbell (1978) cites the study conducted on a pediatric ward where it was noticed that the variable that differentiated those children who had many visitors from those who had few was the amount of eye contact the child offered. "The least popular children would initially look at the visitor briefly, then immediately look down or away" (p. 40). The children's avoidance of eye contact obviously made visitors feel too rejected (and thus too hurt or annoyed) to want to relate to them. Writing of the subjective experience of interacting with blind children, Fraiberg says, "The blind eyes that do not engage our eyes, that do not regard our faces, have an effect upon the observer that is never completely overcome. When the eyes do not meet ours in acknowledgment of our presence it feels curiously like a rebuff" (1977, p. 96).

13

Future Directions

Up until now, children of preschool and primary age have constituted the bulk of individuals receiving Theraplay, and this book has primarily focused on experiences with these age groups. Yet there are other troubled populations where Theraplay would seem to be of benefit—among them, the very, very young and the very old.

Work with babies is at its beginning. Observations of infants in the first weeks of life indicate how important engagement and empathy are (Klaus and Kennel, 1976). Only gradually are these observations being translated into prescriptions for action. We have even further to go in educating those who initially have an impact on the mother-newborn dyad. Ideally, the pediatrician (if not obstetrician), nurse, and others in the newborn nursery will soon become "neonatal specialists" and will know how to recognize and intervene in high-risk relationships where there is evidence of poor bonding and attachment. (Robertson [1979] observes that the mother "bonds" to the infant and the infant "attaches" to the mother.) When very early intervention becomes a recognized form of treatment,

437

some Theraplay techniques are likely to apply. The most applicable technique will be the specialist's taking charge and Intruding, for he will virtually have to force the new mother to look at, hold, talk to, and mirror her baby. Terrence Koller describes his work with a mother and her sixteen-week-old infant, referred for help because of poor bonding:

> [Session 1] Joey's mother's characterization of her relationship with her infant as "We're not close" was borne out in their joint performance on the first administration of the Marschak Interaction Method (MIM). [See Chapter Five.] He screamed ceaselessly, while she remained at a loss to understand the origin of his trouble. (It is noteworthy that the group of observers in the observation room experienced such anxiety as they watched this scene that many of them had to leave the room.) Even when I knew what was bothering Joey, his mother was unable to ascertain the problem or to comfort him.
>
> Her greatest difficulties came when she was required to mirror him. I began to coach her: "Lie on your stomach next to him. Now do just what he does. See? He's sticking out his tongue. You stick yours out too." She could not even raise her arm when he raised his. We discussed her difficulty with mirroring. She determined to try again, and, at last, with my support, she attempted the tongue-sticking-out activity. As she caught on and Joey responded, she actually came to enjoy this. At the end of the session, I encouraged her to continue the mirroring at home and set up an appointment for her next visit.
>
> [Session 2, three weeks later] Right from the beginning of this visit I could tell that things were different. Mother cooed and gurgled in perfect synchrony with her baby, doing it just the way her baby did. Spontaneously and fully, she mirrored his feelings and activities. She took great pride in her performance, and she seemed to be attending more to her own appearance as well. She reported that she felt much closer to her son. As for Joey, he looked markedly more mature, more alert, more smiling. He was beginning to initiate and no longer cried. Mother and baby looked at each other often.

> [Session 3, one month later] Progress is continu-
> ing. Mother and child are more engaged than ever. She
> says she finds herself going out of her way to find time
> just to be with her child.

The importance and naturalness of mirroring with infants
is self-evident. However, it can be just as essential with disturbed older children as a therapeutic tool. As seen in the following description of a session with four-year-old Scott and his
mother, Theraplay with autistic children resembles the natural
behavior of mother-infant pairs.

Scott had been positioned by the therapist so that he was
lying face up in the crook of his mother's arm, the therapist
having pulled the mother's long hair out of their line of vision
and fastened it in a pony tail. The mother was now helped to
look directly down into Scott's face. Scott whimpered and
looked away. The therapist showed the mother how to retrieve
his gaze—by actually turning his head sometimes, by moving her
own at other times, and always by "chasing his eyes." Then she
was taught to mirror his whimper.

Because Scott had been such a disappointment to her for
so long, the process was difficult and took time. New mothers
who fail to attach to their newborns are often disappointed,
and, in addition to being given permission to discuss their disappointments (as Scott's mother was), they must be carefully
guided to establish the bonding. If all new mothers who show
an absence of bonding were provided these sessions on a regular
and frequent basis, there should be a marked reduction in the
incidence of child neglect and abuse—as demonstrated in the
studies of Peter Dawson (1978) at the University of Colorado
Medical Center—as well as a drop in the number of children referred for therapy.

Chapter One detailed the "how to" of treating abused
and molested children. Given the apparent growth of this problem, and in a preventive vein, it would seem wise to add at least
the Nurturing aspect of Theraplay to existing programs. No
amount of talking, reenacting, and desensitizing can ever replace
the stroking, the cuddling, the feeding with which mothers
soothe and comfort anxious babies. Child abuse tells the abused

child that he is a bad person inside a bad body. Theraplay conveys the opposite. Programs such as those at the Illinois Childrens' Home and Aid Society, Utica's House of the Good Shepherd, and the Elizabeth Mitchell Center in Little Rock all provide Theraplay to build the esteem of children suffering abuse. Hopefully, many similar agencies will soon follow suit.

Programs for children from the newly born to age three are proliferating under funding for handicapped and at-risk children. Project BEAM (Billerica Early Assistance Model) in Massachusetts, in an effort to cut down the risk to potentially damaged children, teaches Theraplay to parents. BEAM's model could be offered fruitfully nationwide.

At the other end of the developmental continuum is another group with the potential to benefit from Theraplay. If sensory-deprivationlike experiences account for childhood autism, as Des Lauriers has postulated, then other individuals in our society, deprived of other sensory input, should be disturbed as well. For example, aged individuals living out their days virtually without sight of or sound from anyone should suffer low self-esteem, poor sense of impact, disorientation, mistrust, and so on. It was Morris Stein (personal communication) who observed: "Old folks, too, need Theraplay. They need to have their ears tickled with exciting sounds and their eyes stimulated by animated and personally engaging faces."

The similarity of need is striking, and we all know the impact Intrusion and Challenge can have. Yet, again, there may be concerns that Theraplay with old people would be presumptuous, arrogant, or disrespectful. Consider the following notes of C. West's regular "sessions" with Mrs. A., a woman of seventy-nine, living alone in unhygienic circumstances in a crumbling, isolated farmhouse:

> At the time I began to work with her in March, Grandma showed signs of depression and anxiety. She often talked to herself and seemed confused. She was hard of hearing and seemed overwhelmed by most modern conveniences. She refused, initially, to do almost everything I suggested to keep her busy. Her sense of time and its passage seemed hazy and often inaccurate;

she forgot, often, what day it was. Grandma seldom, if ever, bathed and seemed almost always to have some sort of sore (a scratch, a blister, or a bruise) on her arms, legs, or face. She normally slept until seven or eight in the morning, took two or three long naps during the day, and went to bed around five in the afternoon.

She had been so dependent on her husband for making all the decisions affecting her life and giving her most of the emotional input she received that it was a stunning blow, not only emotionally, but to her ability to function, when he died.

I bought her a new hairbrush and encouraged her to use it, telling her how nice her hair was it's very long and silky when she brushes it. Whenever I would see an open sore, I would wash it for her and put antiseptic on it and remind her to take her medicine. She really wanted company and attention.

While there was little of the vigorously physical sort of attention we usually associate with Theraplay, the principles were very much the same. I worked hard at satisfying her needs for attention and telling her how valuable she was. It seemed difficult for her to imagine, at first, but she gradually began to act as if she were beginning to believe it. She began to pay more attention to how she looked; she developed a few friendships among the neighbors and seemed to take on a new role of increased responsibility. Sometimes in the summer I would arrive to find that she had walked down the road to visit a neighbor, and she was often working on a homemade gift for someone she knew. She even had a small garden of her own! By late autumn, she seemed to have plenty of people to keep her happy most of the time, and she was staying awake more. (She had told me one day that the reason she slept so much was that there just wasn't anything to do.)

Impressions: Although I felt, when I first began working with Grandma, that she was senile and that most of the difficulty had come about as a result of unhappy experiences and a recent lack of attention, in retrospect it seems much more probable that this wasn't entirely the case. Rather than negative stimulation, it seems more likely to have been a case of *no* stimulation. There was certainly an element of depression caused by the loss or absence of loved ones, but many of the things I did with her and many of her experiences during this time were [all the more meaningful because they provided stimulation] . . . The feelings they stirred were *new* feelings, *new* impressions of her own worth, and *new* skills she was developing. It is fairly common for us to work with a nine- or ten- or eleven-year-old who has the [needs] of a much younger child—but to find many of these same [needs] in a reasonably intelligent woman in her late seventies is a difficult concept indeed.

Presumptuous? Disrespectful? Age does not erase the value of healthy self-esteem. It does not erase the need to feel important and special, lovable, talented, and handsome. Yet in our present society there are few ways for the elderly, in particular, to fulfill or allow others to fulfill these needs. Theraplay may be one answer. Not the kind of Theraplay in which the therapist picks up an aging man and gives him a piggy-back ride, of course, or plays peek-a-boo with an older woman, but a Theraplay that draws on the myriad ways we all use to make someone feel beautiful—such as hair styling, skin lotioning, or pedicuring. There are ways of evoking the optimum in effort and performance, such as thumb-wrestling, bean-blowing, apple-bobbing, or song- and dance-composing contests. There are ways to introduce surprise and other ways to bring order into an older person's life. And there are all manner of ways to nourish. In conducting Theraplay with the socially isolated geriatric person, there is as much room for Structuring, Challenging, Intruding, or Nurturing as with younger people.

Because Theraplay is so engaging, and thus so "enlivening," it would seem that (individual or group) Theraplay, not performances by visiting choir groups, would be the most health-promoting (or health-maintaining) way to enhance the quality of life of older persons. Gay Gaer-Luce's (1976) sensitive and creative group experiences for the elderly (SAGE)— unfortunately still on a relatively small scale—do strive to meet the need.

Having identified two major avenues that Theraplay may one day take, we can also point to a third that has been tested occasionally: conducting Theraplay to benefit the "therapist." As Chapter Twelve so explicitly cautioned, there are grave dangers in unskilled Theraplay; thus, such a format must be carefully explained. The model of patient-as-therapist treating another patient can be safely followed only if a third individual —a highly competent therapist—is present at each session and supervises at all times. Given this arrangement, a schizoid older adolescent, for example, can be markedly "brought out" through playful physical interaction with an unhappy preschooler. It is encouraging to examine the "before" and "after" drawings made by adolescent and adult patients assigned to do Theraplay under the watchful eye of a staff therapist: along with improved health for the child, drawings by adolescent or adult patients suggest increased self-esteem, engagement, and energy level. In addition, the few therapists who have been referring their adult and adolescent patients to us for the experience of doing Theraplay report being pleased with the effect.

A related format, although preventive rather than therapeutic, is the plan we have used in some high school "education for parenthood" programs. Small groups of adolescents are assigned a semester of working in a setting with preschool youngsters. They are taught Theraplay techniques, and their training is conducted along the same lines as is training for Theraplay therapists (see Chapter Twelve).

Theraplay could make yet one more contribution in the future. Although to many it may seem the farthest out, an ever-increasing group of others will say that it is self-evident—Theraplay for cancer patients, always, of course, in conjunction with medical procedures. We have attempted it so far with only one patient; yet the clinical regression of seven-year-old Luke's disease (neuroblastoma), in the course of his Theraplay with Deanne Starbird, certainly warrants trying it with other patients.

Both as treatment and as primary prevention, then, the idea of therapy to benefit the patient-therapist (as well as the child) could profitably be expanded in the years to come.

It remains for others to discover further applications, and most certainly it remains for future researchers to study, both extensively and intensively, the conditions under which and the populations for whom Theraplay is most effective. Group outcome studies such as those by Bligh (1977a and 1977b ; Bligh and others, 1979) and Brody (1971a) and Brody, Fenderson, and Stephenson (1976) have already been cited. In-depth studies will help explain the why's. In the meantime, the Theraplay method will continue to grow, embodying all the variations that the variety of individuals practicing it will contribute. This variety, more than any other, is the reason why Theraplay promises to become an ever richer, more fun-filled, and more effective treatment method.

References

Adams, J. W. *Psychoanalysis of Drug Dependence* New York: Grune & Stratton, 1978.

Adams, P. L. *Obsessive Children: A Sociopsychiatric Study.* New York: Brunner/Mazel, 1973.

Ainsworth, M., and Bell, S. "Mother-Infant Interaction and the Development of Competence." In K. Connolly and J. Bruner (Eds.), *The Growth of Competence.* New York: Academic Press, 1974.

Allport, G. W. *The Individual and His Religion.* New York: Macmillan, 1956.

Anthony, E. J. "Experimental Approach to the Psychopathology of Childhood." *British Journal of Medical Psychology,* 1958, *31,* 211-223.

Axline, V. *Play Therapy.* New York: Ballantine, 1969. (Originally published 1947.)

Bandura, A. *Principles of Behavior Modification.* New York: Holt, Rinehart and Winston, 1969.

Bax, M., and MacKeith, R. *Minimal Cerebral Dysfunction.* London: Heinemann, 1963.

Beeson, P., and McDermott, W. (Eds.). *Textbook of Medicine.* Philadelphia: Saunders, 1975.

Benedek, T. "Motherhood and Nurturing." In E. J. Anthony and T. Benedek (Eds.), *Parenthood: Its Psychology and Psychopathology.* Boston: Little, Brown, 1970.

Bennett, S. "Infant-Caretaker Interactions." *Journal of the American Academy of Child Psychiatry,* 1971, *10* (2), 321-335.

Bergman, P., and Escalona, S. "Unusual Sensitivities in Very Young Children." In A. Freud (Ed.), *The Psychoanalytic Study of the Child.* Vols. 3 and 4. New York: International Universities Press, 1949.

Bettelheim, B. *The Empty Fortress.* New York: Free Press, 1967.

Bligh, S. B. "Theraplay: Opening the Door for Withdrawn and Autistic Children." Paper presented to Illinois Speech and Hearing Association, Chicago, April 1977a.

Bligh, S. B. "Theraplay: Facilitating Communication in Language-Delayed Children." In J. Andrews and M. Burns (Eds.), *Selected Papers in Language and Phonology,* Vol. 2: *Language Remediation.* Evanston, Ill.: Institute for Continuing Education, 1977b.

Bligh, S. B., and others. "Activating Communication Skills in Autistic Children: Five Case Studies." Unpublished paper, 1979, available from author, Speech Clinic, Elmhurst College.

Bornstein, H., and others. *The Signed English Dictionary.* Washington, D.C.: Gallaudet College Press, 1975.

Bowlby, J. *Attachment and Loss.* Vol. 1: *Attachment.* New York: Basic Books, 1969.

Brazelton, T. B. *Infants and Mothers: Differences in Development.* New York: Dell, 1969.

Brazelton, T. B. *Doctor and Child.* New York: Delacorte Press/ Seymour Lawrence, 1970.

Brazelton, T. B. "Stages of Early Affect Development: The First Four Months." Presentation to the Chicago Psychoanalytic Association, April 1978.

Brody, V. "Changes in Test Behavior of Children Treated by a Structured Approach to Therapy." Paper presented to the Research Seminar, Psychosomatic and Psychiatric Institute, Michael Reese Hospital, Chicago, 1966.

Brody, V. "Treatment of a Prepubertal, Twin Girl with Psychogenic Megacolon." *American Journal of Orthopsychiatry,* 1963, *33* (3), 569-573.

Brody, V. *Don't Hold Me, I Won't Run Away.* 16 mm film, 1971a, available from author, 519 Playa Seville Ct., Treasure Island, Fla. 33706.

Brody, V. *The Play Is the Thing.* 16 mm film, 1971b, available from author.

Brody, V. "Developmental Play: A Relationship-Focused Program for Children." *Journal of Child Welfare,* 1978, *57* (9), 591-599.

Brody, V., Fenderson, C., and Stephenson, S. *Sourcebook for Finding Your Way to Helping Young Children Through Developmental Play.* State of Florida, Department of State, 1976, distributed by Pupil Personnel Services Demonstration Project, All Children's Hospital, 801 6th St., St. Petersburg, Fla. 33701.

Brooks, V., and Hochberg, J. "A Psychophysical Study of Cuteness." *Perceptual and Motor Skills,* 1960, *11,* 205.

Broussard, E., and Hartner, M. "Maternal Perception of the Neonate as Related to Development." *Child Psychology in Human Development,* 1970, *1* (1), 16-25.

Brown, J. "Long-Term Follow-Up of 100 'Atypical' Children of Normal Intelligence." In M. Rutter and E. Schopler (Eds.), *Autism.* New York: Plenum, 1978.

Buehler, C. *From Birth to Maturity.* London: Routledge & Kegan Paul, 1960.

Bugental, D., and Love, L. "Nonassertive Expression of Parental Approval and Disapproval and Its Relationship to Child Disturbance." *Child Development,* 1975, *46,* 3.

Campbell, R. *How to Really Love Your Child.* Wheaton, Ill.: Victor Books, 1978.

Cantwell, D. P. "Clinical Picture, Epidemiology and Classification of the Hyperactive Child." In D. P. Cantwell (Ed.), *The Hyperactive Child: Diagnosis, Management, Current Research.* Holliswood, N.Y.: Spectrum, 1975.

Chance, M. R. S. "An Interpretation of Some Agonistic Postures: The Role of 'Cut-Off' Acts and Postures." *Symposium of the Zoological Society of London,* 1962, *8,* 71-89.

"Charisma, Friendliness Helpful in Folk Psychotherapy." *Brain/ Mind Bulletin,* 1979, *4* (15), 1.

Chess, S., and Thomas, A. "Differences in Outcome with Early Intervention in Children with Behavior Disorders." In M. Roff (Ed.), *Life History Research in Psychopathology.* Vol. 2. Minneapolis: University of Minnesota, 1972.

Clancy, H., and McBride, G. "The Autistic Process and Its Treatment." *Journal of Child Psychology and Psychiatry,* 1969, *10,* 233-244.

Clarke, L. *Can't Read, Can't Write, Can't Talk Too Good Either.* New York: Penguin, 1974.

Clarke-Stewart, K. A. "Interactions Between Mothers and Their Children: Characteristics and Consequences." In *Monographs of the Society for Research in Child Development.* Vol. 38, Nos. 6-7, Serial No. 153. Chicago: University of Chicago, 1973.

Clarke-Stewart, K. A. *Child Care in the Family.* New York: Academic Press, 1977.

Condon, W. Presentation to the Theraplay Institute, Chicago, February, 1974.

Copeland, J. *For the Love of Ann.* London: Arrow Books, 1973.

Cummings, G. T., Bayley, H. C., and Rie, H. E. "The Effects of the Child's Deficiency on the Mother: A Study of Mothers of Mentally Retarded, Chronically Ill, and Neurotic Children." *American Journal of Orthopsychiatry,* 1966, *36,* 595-608.

Dawson, P. Illustrated presentation to the Quality of Life Conference on Child Abuse, sponsored by the Office of the Mayor, Chicago, October 31, 1978.

Des Lauriers, A. *The Experience of Reality in Childhood Schizophrenia.* New York: International Universities Press, 1962.

Des Lauriers, A. "The Schizophrenic Child." *Archives of General Psychiatry,* 1967, *16,* 194-201.

Des Lauriers, A. "Play, Symbols, and the Development of Language." In M. Rutter and E. Schopler (Eds.), *Autism.* New York: Plenum, 1978.

Des Lauriers, A., and Carlson, C. F. *Your Child Is Asleep: Early Infantile Autism.* Homewood, Ill.: Dorsey, 1969.

Dreikurs, R. *Fundamentals of Adlerian Psychology.* Chicago: Alfred Adler Institute, 1950.

Dundass, M. "Physical Contact and the One-to-One Relationship with Autistic Children." Paper presented at annual conference of the British Psychological Society, Edinburgh, March 1969.

Ekstein, R. *Children of Time and Space, of Action and Impulse.* New York: Appleton-Century-Crofts, 1966.

Evans, S., Reinhart, J., and Succop, P. "A Study of Forty Five Children and Their Families." *Journal of the American Academy of Child Psychiatry,* 1972, *11,* 440-454.

Fenichel, O. "Early Stages of Ego Development." In O. Fenichel, *Collected Papers.* Vol. 2. New York: Norton, 1954. (Originally published 1937.)

Ferenczi, S. "The Phenomena of Hysterical Materialization." In J. Rickman (Ed.), *Further Contributions to the Theory and Technique of Psychoanalysis.* London: Hogarth Press, 1926.

Finnie, N. *Handling the Young Cerebral-Palsied Child at Home.* New York: Dutton, 1975.

Fraiberg, S. *Insights from the Blind.* New York: Basic Books, 1977.

Frankl, V. E. *Man's Search for Meaning: An Introduction to Logotherapy.* New York: Washington Square Press, 1963.

Freedman, D. Presentation to the Group for the Study of Attachment and Bonding, Chicago, April 1978.

Freud, S. *Beyond the Pleasure Principle.* London: Hogarth, 1922.

Fries, M. E. "Psychosomatic Relationships Between Mother and Infant." *Psychosomatic Medicine,* 1944, *6,* 159-162.

Gaer-Luce, G. "A New Program for the Aged (SAGE)." Illustrated talk presented at the Conference on Holistic Medicine, Detroit, Mich., September 1976.

Gardner, B. T., and Wallach, L. "Shape of Figures Identified as a Baby's Head." *Perceptual and Motor Skills,* 1965, *20,* 135-142.

Greenberg, M., and Morris, N. "Engrossment: The Newborn's

Impact Upon the Father." *American Journal of Orthopsychiatry,* 1974, *44,* 520-531.

Haley, J. *Uncommon Therapy: The Psychiatric Techniques of Milton H. Erickson, M.D.* New York: Norton, 1973.

Haley, J. *Problem-Solving Therapy: New Strategies for Effective Family Therapy.* San Francisco: Jossey-Bass, 1976.

Harlow, H. F., Harlow, M. K., and Hansen, E. W. "The Maternal Affectional System in Rhesus Monkeys." In H. L. Rheingold (Ed.), *Maternal Behavior in Mammals.* New York: Wiley, 1963.

Hess, R., and Handel, G. *Family Worlds: A Psychosocial Approach to Family Life.* Chicago: University of Chicago Press, 1959.

Hurst, T. W. "Orientation to Theraplay." Paper presented to Chicago Committee on Urban Opportunity, March 1970.

Hurst, T. W. Presentation to Quality of Life Conference, American Medical Association, Chicago, April 1974.

Huttenlocher, P. R. "The Nervous System." In P. Beeson and W. McDermott (Eds.), *Textbook of Medicine.* Philadelphia: Saunders, 1975.

Jackson, D. D. "Action for Mental Illness—What Kind?" *Stanford Medical Bulletin,* 1962, *20,* 78.

Jensen, R. "Why Do Parents Apply for Help at a Child Guidance Clinic?" In A. J. Solnit and S. A. Provence (Eds.), *Modern Perspectives in Child Development.* New York: International Universities Press, 1963.

Jernberg, A. "Psychosomatic Similarities in Adoptive Mothers and Their Infants." *Human Development Bulletin,* paper presented at 9th annual symposium, Chicago, March 1, 1958.

Jernberg, A. "Theraplay Technique." In C. E. Schaefer (Ed.), *Therapeutic Use of Child's Play.* New York: Aronson, 1976.

Jernberg, A. "Lessons in Mirroring." Videotape by the Theraplay Institute, 333 N. Michigan Ave., Chicago 60601, 1979.

Jernberg, A., and Des Lauriers, A. "Some Contributions of Three Pre-School Children to Behavior Changes in Their Mothers." Paper presented to the Research Seminar, Psychosomatic and Psychiatric Institute, Michael Reese Hospital, Chicago, June 1962.

Jernberg, A., Hurst, T., and Lyman, C. *Here I Am.* 16 mm film, 1969, available from the Theraplay Institute, 333 N. Michigan Ave., Chicago 60601.

Jernberg, A., Hurst, T., and Lyman, C. *There He Goes.* 16 mm film, 1975, available from the Theraplay Institute.

John, A. B., and Allen, B. A. "Infantile Autism and the Holding Relationship." Paper presented at the London Conference of the British Psychological Society, December 1969.

Jones, E., and Berglas, S. "Control of Attributions About the Self Through Self-Handicapping Strategies: The Appeal of Alcohol and the Role of Underachievement." *Personality and Social Psychology Bulletin,* April 1978, 4 (2), 204.

Kalverboer, F. *A Neurobehavioral Study in Pre-School Children.* London: Heinemann, 1975.

Kanner, L. "Autistic Disturbances of Affective Content." *Nervous Child,* 1943, 2, 217-240.

Kaplan, L. J. *Oneness and Separation: From Infant to Individual.* New York: Simon & Schuster, 1978.

Kaufman, B. *Son-Rise.* New York: Harper & Row, 1975.

Klaus, M. H., and others. "Human Maternal Behaviors at the First Contact with Her Young." *Pediatrics,* 1970, 46, 187-192.

Klaus, M., and Kennel, J. *Maternal-Infant Bonding.* St. Louis: Mosby, 1976.

Klein, M. *The Psychoanalysis of Children.* London: Hogarth Press, 1932.

Kohut, H. *The Analysis of Self.* New York: International Universities Press, 1971.

Kohut, H. *The Restoration of the Self.* New York: International Universities Press, 1977.

Koller, T. "Changes in Children's Intelligence Test Scores Following Theraplay." Paper presented at workshop for Comprehensive Mental Health Center, Laforte County, Ill., April 1976.

Kris, E. "Notes on the Development and on Some Current Problems of Psychoanalytic Child Psychology." *The Psychoanalytic Study of the Child,* 1950, 5, 24-46.

Kupperman, P. "Speech Theraplay: High Impact Articulation

Therapy." Paper presented at the American Speech and Hearing Association, Chicago, November 1977.

Lamb, M. *The Role of the Father in Child Development.* New York: Wiley, 1976.

Laybourne, P., and Churchill, S. "Symptom Discouragement in Treating Hysterical Reactions of Childhood." *International Journal of Child Psychotherapy,* 1972, *1* (3), 121.

LeBoyer, C. *Calcutta.* Film presented at Birth Without Violence Conference, Milwaukee, Wis., April 1978.

Lewis, M., and Lee-Painter, S. "An Interactional Approach to the Mother-Infant Dyad." In M. Lewis and L. A. Rosenblum (Eds.), *The Effect of the Infant on Its Caregiver.* New York: Wiley, 1974. Pp. 21-48.

Lovaas, O. I. *The Autistic Child: Language Development Through Behavior Modification.* New York: Irvington Press, 1977.

Maclean, C. *The Wolf Children.* New York: Hill and Wang, 1978.

Malmquist, C. P. "Depressions in Childhood and Adolescence." *New England Journal of Medicine,* 1971, *284,* 955.

Margolis, P., and Jernberg, A. "Anaclitic Therapy in a Case of Extreme Anorexia." *British Journal of Medical Psychology,* 1960, *33,* 291-300.

Marschak, M. "A Method for Evaluating Child-Parent Interaction Under Controlled Conditions." *Journal of Genetic Psychology,* 1960, *97,* 3-22.

Marschak, M. *Nursery School Child/Mother Interaction.* Film, 1967, available from New York University Film Library, 26 Washington Place, New York City 10003.

Marschak, M. *Two Climates of Israel.* Film, 1975, available from New York University Film Library.

Marschak, M. *Parent-Child Interaction and Youth Rebellion.* New York: Gardner Press, 1979.

Massie, H. "Blind Ratings of Mother-Infant Interaction in Home Movies of Prepsychotic and Normal Infants." *American Journal of Psychiatry,* 1978, *11,* 1371-1374.

Mead, M. *Four Families.* 16 mm film, 1959, distributed by McGraw-Hill Films, New York, and the National Film Board of Canada.

Meltzer, D., and others. *Explorations in Autism: A Psychoanalytical Study*. Aberdeen, Scotland: Aberdeen University Press, 1975.

Middlemore, M. *The Nursing Couple*. London: Hamilton, 1941.

Miller, J. S. "Hyperactive Children: A Ten-Year Study." *Pediatrics for the Clinician*, 1978, *61* (2), 217-223.

Minuchin, S. "Family Therapy." Paper presented to Center for Family Studies, the Family Institute of Chicago, April 13 and 14, 1978.

Minuchin, S. *Families and Family Therapy*. Cambridge, Mass.: Harvard University Press, 1978.

Moreno, J. L. *Psychodrama*. New York: Beacon House, 1946.

Moses, K. "Elusive Grief." Workshop given at Illinois Masonic Hospital, Chicago, December 1978.

Mowatt, M. H. "Group Therapy Approach to Emotional Conflicts of the Mentally Retarded and Their Parents." In F. J. Menolascino (Ed.), *Psychiatric Approaches to Mental Retardation*. New York: Basic Books, 1970.

Nichtern, S. *Helping the Retarded Child*. New York: Grosset & Dunlap, 1974.

Parke, R. "Father-Infant Interaction." In M. H. Klaus, T. Leger, and M. A. Trause (Eds.), *Maternal Attachment and Mothering Disorders: A Round Table*. Sausalito, Calif.: Johnson and Johnson, 1974.

Pederson, E., Faucher, T. A., and Eaton, W. W. "A New Perspective on the Effects of First-Grade Teachers on Children's Subsequent Adult Status." *Harvard Educational Review*, February 1978, *48* (1), 1-31.

Perls, F., Hefferlein, R. F., and Goodman, P. *Gestalt Therapy*. New York: Julian Press, 1958.

Prescott, J. Cited in E. Hoover, "Affection As an Inoculation Against Aggression." *Human Behavior*, January 1976, pp. 10-11.

Racker, H. *Transference and Countertransference*. New York: International Universities Press, 1968.

Rappaport, H., and Dent, P. L. "An Analysis of Contemporary East African Folk Psychotherapy." *British Journal of Medical Psychology*, 1979, *52*, 49-54.

Rheingold, H. L. "The Effect of Environmental Stimulation

Upon Social and Exploratory Behavior in the Human Infant." In B. M. Foss (Ed.), *Determinants of Infant Behavior.* Vol. 1. London: Methuen, 1961.

Richards, M. P. M. "The Development of Psychological Communication in the First Year of Life." In K. Connolly and J. Bruner (Eds.), *The Growth of Competence.* New York: Academic Press, 1974.

Rimland, B. *Infantile Autism.* Englewood Cliffs, N.J.: Prentice-Hall, 1964.

Ritvo, E. R., and others. *Autism: Diagnosis, Current Research and Management.* New York: Spectrum, 1976.

Robertiello, R. C. *Hold Them Very Close, Then Let Them Go.* New York: Dial Press, 1975.

Robertson, J. "Mother-Infant Interaction from Birth to Twelve Months: Two Case Studies." In B. M. Foss (Ed.), *Determinants of Infant Behaviour.* Vol. 3. London: Methuen, 1965.

Robertson, J. "Attachment and Bonding." Paper presented to Erikson Institute, Chicago, April 1979.

Robinson, J. F., and Vitale, L. J. "Children with Circumscribed Interest Patterns." *American Journal of Orthopsychiatry,* 1954, *24,* 755-766.

Robson, K. S. "The Role of Eye-to-Eye Contact in Maternal-Infant Attachment." *Journal of Child Psychology and Psychiatry,* 1967, *8,* 13-25.

Rogan, L. "The Cove School." Catalogue of the Cove School, Evanston, Ill., n.d.

Rosen, J. *Direct Analysis.* New York: Grune & Stratton, 1953.

Rosen, M. "Origin of Mind: The Secret Brain; Learning Before Birth." *Harper's,* April 1978, pp. 46-47.

Rothenberg, M. *Children with Emerald Eyes.* New York: Pocketbooks, 1978.

Rubin, P. "Theraplay in the Public Schools: Opening the Door to Communication." Paper presented at the Illinois Speech and Hearing Association Convention, Chicago, April 1978.

Rutter, R., Graham, P., and Yule, W. *A Neuropsychiatric Study in Childhood.* London: Heinemann, 1970.

Sameroff, A. J. "Early Influences on Development: Fact or Fancy?" *Merrill Palmer Quarterly,* 1975, *21,* 267-294.

Sander, L. "Issues in Early Mother-Child Interaction." In E. Rexford, L. Sander, and T. Shapiro, *Infant Psychiatry.* New Haven, Conn.: Yale University Press, 1976.

Schaffer, H. R. *The Growth of Sociability.* Harmondsworth, Middlesex, England: Penguin, 1971.

Schaffer, R. *Mothering.* Cambridge, Mass.: Harvard University Press, 1977.

Scott, T., Mappes, L., and Comstock, C. "Treatment Approach Based on the Theraplay Model: Application to Children in Residential Treatment." Paper presented to the 5th annual spring conference of the New York State Council of Volun tary Child Care Agencies, Syracuse, June 1979.

Selfe, L. *Nadia: A Case of Extraordinary Drawing Ability in an Autistic Child.* New York: Academic Press, 1977.

Shapiro, D. *Neurotic Styles.* New York: Basic Books, 1965.

Sontag, L. W. "Implications of Fetal Behavior and Environment for Adult Personalities." *Annals of the New York Academy of Science,* 1966, *134,* 782-786.

Spitz, R. A. "The Effect of Personality Disturbances in the Mother on the Well-Being of Her Infant." In J. E. Anthony and T. Benedek (Eds.), *Parenthood.* Boston: Little, Brown, 1970.

Stayton, D., Hogan, R., and Ainsworth, M. "Infant Obedience and Maternal Behavior." *Child Development,* 1971, *42,* 1060-1061.

Stein, M. Comments while presenting film *Here I Am* on "Sunrise Semester," New York University television, July 1976.

Stern, D. N. "A Microanalysis of Mother-Infant Interaction." In E. Rexford, L. Sander, and T. Shapiro (Eds.), *Infant Psychiatry.* New Haven, Conn.: Yale University Press, 1976.

Stringer, L. *The Sense of Self, A Guide to How We Mature.* Philadelphia: Temple, 1971.

Sundby, H., and Kreyberg, P. *Prognosis in Child Psychiatry.* Baltimore: Williams and Wilkins, 1969.

Thomas, A., Chess, S., and Birch, H. "The Origin of Personality." *Scientific American,* 1970, *223,* 102-109.

Tinbergen, N. "Ethology and Stress Diseases." *Science,* 1974, *185,* 20-27.

Tizard, J. "Mental Retardation and Child Psychiatry." In F. J. Menolascino (Ed.), *Psychiatric Approaches to Mental Retardation*. New York: Basic Books, 1970.

Tronick, E., and others. "The Infant's Response to Entrapment Between Contradictory Messages in Face-to-Face Interaction." *Journal of American Academy of Child Psychiatry*, 1978, *17* (1), 1-13.

Walsh, F. "Concurrent Grandparent Death and the Birth of Schizophrenic Offspring." Paper presented to Group for the Study of Attachment and Bonding, Chicago, May 1978.

Ward, A. J. "Early Infantile Autism: An Etiological Hypothesis." Paper presented at meeting of American Association of Psychiatric Clinics for Children, Boston, November 1969.

Ward, A. J. *Childhood Autism and Structural Therapy*. Chicago: Hall, 1977.

Wickler, W. *The Sexual Code*. New York: Doubleday, 1972.

Wilson, P. "Review of *Here I Am*." *Hospital and Community Psychiatry*, 1973, *24*, 347-348.

Winnicott, D. W. *Mother and Child*. New York: Basic Books, 1957.

Yahr, M. D. "Athetosis." In V. C. Vaughan and J. McKay (Eds.), *Textbook of Pediatrics*. Philadelphia: Saunders, 1975.

Zaslow, R. W. "A Psychogenic Theory of the Etiology of and Implications for Treatment." Paper presented at the meeting of the California State Psychological Association, San Diego, January 1967.

Index

A., Mrs., as case of elderly client, 440-442
Abraham Lincoln Center, 287
Abused child: and Theraplay, 439-440; Theraplay contraindicated for, 29-32
Acceptance phase, tentative, of session, 38-39
Acting-out: by adolescents, 383-385; by therapists, 431-436
Adams, J. W., 338, 445
Adams, P. L., 24, 25, 302, 445
Adolescents: acting-out by, 383-385; with adjustment problems, 352-357; aggressive, 365-373; autistic, 373, 376-383; learning disabled, case of, 254-260; neurotic, 342-352; schizophrenic, 358-365; Theraplay for, 339-385
Adoptions, and Theraplay, 219-220
Adults: cases of, 388-407, 410-415; as parents, 408-418; as psychotherapy patients, 386-408; as psychotic, 388-393; schizophrenic, 393-398, 400-401; Theraplay with, 386-418. *See also* Parents

Age, and Theraplay style, 21-22
Aggression, among adolescents, 365-373. *See also* Overactive, aggressive child
Ainsworth, M., 10, 301, 334, 445, 455
Allen, B. A., 305-306, 451
Allport, G. W., 81, 445
Anger, during session, 64-65, 75, 85
Ann, as case of autism, 316
Announcement, of termination, 41-42
Anthony, E. J., 11, 301, 315, 445
Anxiety, prevented by therapist, 59
Appeal, of therapist, 49
Arousal, in therapist-child relationship, 18
Autism: among adolescents, 373, 376-383; blindness related to, 283-284; cases of, 315-318, 321-337; causes of, 301, 304-307; treatment of, 304-307, 308-315, 318-321, 331-334
Autistic children: behavior of, 301-304, 331-334; differentiation for, 53; and off-balance posi-

457